Faith, Scholarship, and Culture in the 21st Century

ALICE RAMOS and
MARIE I. GEORGE,
Editors

Introduction by ROBERT ROYAL

AMERICAN MARITAIN ASSOCIATION
Distributed by The Catholic University of America Press
Washington, D.C. 20064

Library of Congress Cataloguing-in-Publication Data

Faith, scholarship, and culture in the 21st century / edited by Alice Ramos
and Marie I. George with an introduction by Robert Royal
   p. cm. -- (American Maritain Association publications)
Papers presented at a meeting held in Oct. 2000.
Includes bibliographical references and index.
   ISBN 0-9669226-5-4 (pbk. : alk. paper)
   1. Faith and reason--Christianity--Congresses. 2. Religion and
science--Congresses. 3. Church and college--Congresses. 4. Sociology,
Christian (Catholic)--Congresses. 5. Catholic Church--
Doctrines--Congresses. I. Ramos, Alice. II. George, Marie I.
III. Series.
   BT50 .F35 2002
   261.5—dc21   2001008375

Manufactured in the
United States of America

Distributed by The Catholic University of America Press
Washington, D.C. 20064

Contents

Editor's Note

In October of the year 2000 the American Maritain Association held its annual meeting at the University of Notre Dame to discuss the theme that appears as the title of this volume. The conference brought together young and mature scholars from the United States and from abroad to discuss a topic of importance for the academy and for our world in the new millennium. While some intellectuals at the end of the nineteenth century argued that scientific progress would eventually cause the demise of religion, it is evident that this has not been the case and that contemporary science is in fact not necessarily inimical to a religious worldview. So, a fruitful dialogue between science and religion has become a reality. But there is also a more fundamental question that arises, which is not simply the relationship of the sciences or of other disciplines to religion, but rather whether our faith can and should have an impact on our teaching and research as scholars.

My basic premise in organizing the 2000 AMA conference was to hold that the Christian faith provides us with definite cognitive advantages and that to leave one's faith at the entrance of the campus, thus separating faith from reason, leads to a schizophrenic view of the Christian's intellectual life. The Maritain conference thus provided intellectuals who are also religious believers—not all of whom were Christian—with the opportunity of discussing the real influence of their faith on their scholarship. In consonance with the thought of Pope John Paul II, it is my contention that a faith which imbues research and teaching will effect a transformation not only in the intellectuals themselves, but also in their students and eventually in society; hence, a faith that is fully received, thought out and lived, will penetrate culture; and there is no doubt that present-day culture stands in need of transformation. In fact, the encyclical *Fides et Ratio* attributes the secularization of the West in great part to the separation of faith from culture. Maritain himself, more than fifty years ago, recognized that modern and contemporary culture had severed its ties with the sacred and in so doing had turned its back on humanity.

The essays that appear in this volume were thus selected from among the many papers presented at the 2000 Maritain conference; they have been arranged in four parts. Those in the first part deal with different modes of intellectual inquiry, from the classical and medieval to the modernist and postmodernist conceptions of inquiry. In order to understand the metaphysical and ethical questions that confront the human person, the authors have sought wisdom in the works of Thomas Aquinas and in Pope John Paul II's Christocentric conception of intellectual inquiry. The essays of the second part are concerned with education and with the need for good moral dispositions, faith, and prayer to enlighten reason. In the third part of the volume, faith's impact on science, bioethics, and time is evident in the authors' reflections. And in the fourth and final part, society and culture are viewed from different philosophical and theological perspectives.

Finally, I wish to express my gratitude to the former president of the American Maritain Association, Curtis Hancock, and to Peter Redpath and Anthony O. Simon, for their encouragement and support of my initial idea for the AMA conference of the year 2000; without their vote of confidence the conference would not have taken place nor would this volume of essays have become a reality. I am particularly indebted to the Homeland Foundation for a grant that has made possible the publication of this volume in a timely fashion. A special thanks goes to the co-editor, my colleague Marie George, for her efficient help in editing and formatting the essays; her computer skills and her keen sense of appropriate linguistic usage have proved invaluable in bringing the editing process to a speedy completion. I would also like to thank all the contributors for their essays, which show that the light of faith does indeed provide the scholar with cognitive advantages in his pursuit of truth. I am very grateful to Robert Royal, founder of the Faith and Reason Institute in Washington, D.C., for his willingness to write the introduction to this volume. He clearly points out that despite the lack of coherence and truth in our culture, human beings today—as in every epoch—have a profound need for meaning and transcendence—a need which Catholic thought at its best can help to satisfy.

A final word about the cover—Rembrandt's *Philosopher in Meditation*. It portrays well what the essays in this volume convey: that the light of reason and the light of faith can work harmoniously together in the journey and ascent to the truth.

Introduction

Robert Royal

One of the great ironies of the late twentieth and early twenty-first centuries is that an age positively awash in information ranging from the smallest subatomic particles to distant galaxies, structured by technological gadgetry produced by the most exacting scientific knowledge, and blessed by instant global communication, has a hard time believing that anything is true. In science, perhaps, we still value the notion of objective knowledge and the unbiased observer, though several postmodern currents have put even that form of truth into doubt.[1] But in all fields that touch upon the essential human things, we have either no truth or too many "truths," a skepticism that we can know anything at all, or a bewildering jumble of competing and conflicting arguments, which appear to admit no finally valid claims to truth.

While this predicament is hardly new—Plato and Aristotle spend a great deal of time sifting through the truths, falsehoods, and partial insights of their predecessors and contemporaries in search of a consistent way of thought— widespread acceptance of the hopelessness of trying to resolve problems and reconcile apparent contradictions may have reached something of a high (or low) water mark in the past one hundred years. And as is abundantly clear from the many seemingly insoluble questions that have arisen in our politics and social relations, our current crisis is not merely of interest to philosophers, or political theorists, or abstract thinkers of other kinds. It is the very atmosphere that we all, willing or not, now breathe. Incoherence seems to have become the very form of our culture.

It was largely in response to earlier manifestations of these circumstances

---

[1] For a good account of this emerging problem, see Paul R. Gross, Norman Leavitt, and Martin W. Lewis, eds., *The Flight from Science and Reason* (New York: Academy of Sciences, 1997).

1

that Jacques Maritain and his wife Raïssa dedicated themselves to renewing philosophy. For them, this was not a purely intellectual task. Early in their married life they made a mutual suicide pact. If they could not find their way out of confusion into a worthy and noble form of life, they preferred not to live. In a way they were repeating a basic philosophical impulse common to all ages and places. A reflective being like the human person can never be entirely content with mere animal and social existence. Our very natures demand and reach out for something that we cannot name at the outset and that transcends the various earthly things that we may try to substitute for it. This is one explanation for the passionate—and disastrous—commitment of many people to murderous ideologies in the century just past: Communism, Fascism, Nazism, nationalism, scientism, and other ersatz religions. Collective ideals, like other substitutes for the transcendent, may give us a sense of meaning and purpose in the short run. In the long run, they reveal themselves as a dangerous delusion.

Jacques Maritain was born into a liberal Protestant family and found himself in a world that placed great faith in science. He quickly perceived, however, that science itself could provide no answers to his most burning questions. Many people then and now blame science for our predicament. But as Mariano Artigas demonstrates in an incisive essay in the present volume, the very expectation that science has anything to say about non-scientific questions is not science's fault. Rather, the view that science can be made to affirm or deny truths that do not fall within science as currently understood is a *philosophical* error—committed by scientists and non-scientists alike. Science needs to be contextualized through other modes of thought, particularly by people concerned with religion: "Dialogue between science and religion requires a common partner that can be neither science nor religion. Philosophy is a good partner, probably the only real candidate."

This point has often been made. Many of us are dissatisfied with the low materialist science combined with skepticism that marks the West today. But how can philosophy perform this task? To begin with, it must identify certain presuppositions that often go unnoticed in a scientific culture. Take order in nature. Artigas remarks: "Empirical science studies natural patterns, which means order. The concept of order is so general that it can be considered a quasi transcendental." He adds that other notions such as organization, directionality, synergy, and complexity—to say nothing of the ethical questions that do not fit into value-free inquiry—offer other material for philosophical analysis. The very fact that human beings are able to make mute nature speak in intelligible terms suggests that human beings occupy a position that is both part of nature and that transcends mere nature.

True philosophy, then, by its very nature is a form of rationality that includes the human person in its irreducible transcendence. But this realization must lead us into much broader speculations on the nature of the intellectual life today. In his contribution to the present volume, Ralph McInerny rightly points out that the Maritains recognized this truth in the very way they chose to live out the intellectual vocation. In addition to Jacques' formal teaching, the Maritains hosted in their own home a diverse group of professional philosophers and people from all walks of life, and differing faiths, who passionately wished to engage the entire range of philosophical questions raised by the modern world. Philosophy done this way was not merely cerebral; it involved an understanding that the pursuit of wisdom demands the commitment of one's whole life.

The Thomist revival, in which they both played a major part, is often dismissed as a sectarian Catholic position, at best of intellectual interest in certain respects, but more probably just one more failed attempt at total explanation. But this is to misconceive the very nature of the kind of thought they developed and their model of philosophizing, rooted in Aristotle and Saint Thomas Aquinas. As T. S. Eliot once observed, Aristotle has no method other than to be "very intelligent," and later students of the great Greek did him a disservice by turning his work into "Aristotelianism," just as some followers of Aquinas mistakenly turned the later thinker into a "Thomist." The great value of both is that, in McInerny's words, they "seek sustenance anywhere and everywhere." That universality is what a Catholic philosophy at its best must pursue. Or as John Paul II observed in the encyclical *Faith and Reason*, the Implicit Philosophy that begins in the universal acknowledgment of certain principles and starting points is not merely one kind of philosophy, it is philosophy itself, rightly understood.

As a Frenchman, Maritain was particularly sensitive to the fact that many of the problems we currently face stem from a doctrinaire Cartesianism that, in its various permutations since Descartes, makes it impossible for us ever to get outside of our own minds. As useful as Descartes's thought may have been during a period of epistemological crisis, it became in the hands of other philosophers less a foundation for all valid thinking than a philosophical strait jacket that limits philosophy, which used to think it could range over the whole of the universe. For many subsequent thinkers, philosophy could only move within the kinds of rational propositions still permissible after the sure connection with the external world had been broken. Only the most reverent attention to reality at this point would allow us to break free of philosophy's self-imposed limits. Few professional philosophers are willing to make this effort or even to accept the principle as vital for real philosophy itself.

Descartes himself had to sidestep this problem. In a telling passage from the *Discourse on the Method*, he says:

> I have first tried to discover generally the principles or first causes of everything that is or that can be in the world, without considering anything that might accomplish this end but God Himself who has created the world, or deriving them from any source excepting from certain germs of truths which are naturally existent in our souls. After that I considered which might be deduced from these causes, and it seems to me that in this way I discovered the heavens, the stars, and earth, and even on the earth, water, air, fire, the minerals and some other things. . . .(Part VI)

Later thinkers, of course, would dispute even this move, but it gave Descartes a way to talk about things outside of the bare assertion of the *Cogito*.

Charles Péguy, one of Maritain's early mentors who admired, as did Maritain, the way that Henri Bergson had made it possible again to recover "the sense of the absolute," responded to this drily:

> Well, I say: what does it matter. We know quite well that [Descartes] did not discover the heavens. Rather, they were found all by themselves. Creation needs its Creator, to be. To become, to be born, to be made. It had no need of man, neither to be, nor even to be known. The heavens were found all by themselves. And they have never been lost. And they do not have need of us to be perpetually rediscovered in their orbits.[2]

This good sense cuts off at its root the notion that everything, including nature, is or should be derived from the workings of the human mind. Detected, perhaps. Assigned in various modes to the human sciences. But the things themselves are there whether any man comes to know them or not.

In a brilliant analysis in the present volume, Gavin T. Colvert outlines the ways in which some forms of postmodernism, notably that of Richard Rorty, have performed the double task of breaking with the narrow Enlightenment rationality that descended from Descartes, but at the cost of the broader kind of philosophy that posits truth. For Rorty and many others in his wake, philosophical systems previously discarded, such as medieval philosophy, may be re-admitted to a respectable status because, with the break-up of Enlightenment rationalism, all philosophical systems may now be seen to be socially constructed and finally unjustifiable. So the faith-reason, theology-

---

[2] Charles Péguy, *Note Conjointe sur M. Descartes et la philosophie cartésienne, Œuvres en Prose, 1909–1914* (Paris: Bibliothèque de la Pléiade, 1957), pp. 1301–02. This work was left unpublished when Péguy died in 1914, but was probably written during that year.

philosophy dialogue that marked medieval philosophy and its modern off-shoots is no less—or more—legitimate than other systems that posit some form of absolute truth in God or nature.

For Rorty, however, all such external authority is unfounded. We remain solely within the constructs of the mind and society. In the course of explicating various solutions and alternatives to these problems, Colvert wisely notes: "Perhaps the medievals, who lived in a less sanitized cultural space than ourselves, and who understood very well the reality of suffering and death, were better placed to see the mind-independent structure of reality." The Christian philosophy of the Middle Ages, unlike its modern and post-modern counterparts, did not place as much emphasis on the self, and invited the thinker to openness towards self-transcendence in both God and nature. Whatever philosophical problems transcendence entails, it is clearly a more expansive and inclusive kind of philosophy than the dominant form.

It is no accident that Rorty and other prominent postmodernists propose a philosophical system despite their own principles. For them, philosophy is a kind of therapy that should purge us of impulses towards seeking any outside authority in God or nature. But since this leaves very little in the way of public principle, Rorty, a committed American-style democrat, proposes that the only authority worthy of philosophical deference is "a consensus of our fellow humans." Of course, this begs the question of how we can know that others exist when we cannot find any reliable principle in nature or elsewhere. Democratic pragmatism becomes a kind of transcendence all its own, but locates its standards in mere consensus or majoritarianism.

Curiously, this position partially reflects an old Catholic notion of the community as an important factor in the pursuit of truth. For Christians, the Bible and the traditions that have evolved from the sacred text offer important clues to the philosopher carrying out his own proper task. Philosophy alone, of course, cannot substitute for revelation or theology. But it can, within its own domain, reflect on material offered to it from those domains and the living communities they have inspired. Historically, that engagement produced some remarkable work that preserved communities from setting themselves up as their own absolute arbiters of the whole of reality. That openness to transcendence had a salutary effect on the communities themselves. One reason for the evident crisis in the developed democracies today is precisely their reliance on the kind of insubstantial appeal to the community that Rorty advocates. Far different is the view of former dissident, now Czech president Václav Havel, a profound thinker who experienced several unfortunate aspects of undemocratic reality: "If democracy is not only to survive but to expand successfully and resolve . . . conflicts of cultures, then, in my opinion, it must rediscover and renew its own transcendental origins."[3]

How can people who value both liberty and the transcendent pursue this quest? Modern notions of scholarship and the intellectual life have been of little help, in fact have contributed towards creating the predicament Havel deplores. In his contribution to the present volume, John Goyette identifies a bifurcation that has been hidden behind even Catholic academic practices for some time. Saint Augustine represents one model: secular learning for the sake of theology. This approach obviously has its advantages and drawbacks. The greatest advantage is that we can never be under the illusion, under such a scheme, that our learning has some kind of ultimate value in itself. The world is not measured by man; the world provides standards of reality for us. But at least in our own time, such principles often seem to stand in the way of quite proper development of disciplines along their own fruitful paths, or at least that is the claim that is often made by critics. The problem seems to be that first principles, which are the beginning and end of other activities, are often made to usurp the intermediate conceptions that each discipline must discover.

Augustine himself saw little value in studying literature and science, for example. Many other Christian thinkers have pointed out that, while things that lead to salvation and human flourishing should be given priority, we should not conceive of these categories too narrowly. St. Thomas Aquinas advocated study of the Creation because errors about creatures sometimes lead to errors about the Creator. Many of the great early modern scientists, notably Galileo and Newton, were believers who thought that their work helped to understand God's Creation rather than merely what erroneous thinkers had thought about the Creation. Confusion over this point has often made it appear that Christianity opposed the use of our God-given talents to understand the world. Aquinas had already struck the right balance: He warned of a common deformation in the intellectual vocation: "it is through creatures that man's aversion from God is occasioned" (*Summa Theologiae* II, q. 9, a. 4). But nonetheless observed: "Right judgments about creatures belong properly to knowledge."

So there is a danger in studying Creation, but the same danger that we run in any study. The remedy for this is not to proscribe such study but to seek to inscribe it in our spiritual concerns. In dealing with some dangerous ideas of late antiquity, an age that had not yet been reshaped by Christianity, Augustine

[3] Václav Havel, "The Spiritual Roots of Democracy," speech given in Prague, Czechoslovakia, 1991.

may have been right to be careful about secular learning. In our time, Christians need to engage all knowledge, not in an attempt to reduce it to the mere slave of Christian thought, but to appreciate what may be gained from it.

Goyette points to Newman as proposing another Christian ideal of learning. Before the postmodern revolution exploded the very idea that there could be disinterested knowledge, many of us, believers and non-believers alike, thought learning was to be pursued for its own sake. Several distinguished Christian writers such as John Henry Newman and C. S. Lewis[4] have supported this view. Indeed in *The Idea of a University*, Newman provided as good a defense of the idea as we are ever likely to have. But for those of us who have seen the results of this allegedly disinterested pursuit, many doubts arise that lead us into a consideration of the foundations and very nature of rationality. And it may be that Newman's ideal, which could count on a fair amount of consensus outside the university, today needs to be supplemented.

To begin with, in religious terms, is it really possible to pursue something for its own sake? Is not this to set up an idol among the very real achievements of the intellect? Of course, it all depends what we mean by the term learning for its own sake. If we mean that humane learning, articulated as it must be into various disciplines, must adhere to practices congruent with the given subject, and that such learning will ultimately be of some sort of use if rightly carried out, the answer is certainly yes. All the real modern achievements have true value for human life and may indirectly lead to a better appreciation of faith.

The problem is that if we take learning for its own sake to mean that the intellect's achievements can have some absolute value in themselves, the term is patently false. Humane learning cannot provide the principles for its own validation any more than Descartes's reason could discover the world. Within a framework of moderate realism, perhaps, the notion of disinterested learning may have some validity. But Newman, Goyette reminds us, is forced to the concession that, though it does not necessarily have to be this way: "Knowledge, viewed as knowledge, exerts a subtle influence in throwing us back on ourselves, and making us our own centre, and our own minds the measure of all things." Even worse, it develops in us a spirit of arrogance about our own achievements (a spirit not unknown on both secular and religious campuses).

Newman's solution was St. Philip Neri's. We need, outside the academic confines, another movement—towards holiness. Newman was quite aware

---

[4] For Lewis's view, see "Learning in Wartime," in *The Weight of Glory and Other Addresses* (New York: Macmillan, 1980), pp. 20–32.

that, internal to the university, the study of theology was important, if only so that the university could live up to its own ideal of examining all knowledge. But as the history of secular and religious universities since his day has demonstrated, the mere presence of theology is not an automatic remedy. It is not only that the physical and biological sciences essentially established an independent kingdom for themselves (a problem that is rather easily dealt with by proper philosophical and theological formation). More worrisome, the disciplines that exist on the margins between science and the humanities—especially psychology, sociology, history, economics, and political science—tend to take the materialist assumptions of science as iron rules for the disciplines, rather than to include the ampler vistas on human things afforded by Christianity and other religious traditions.

What is the solution to this impasse? The very best thinking on these matters—much of which is reflected in these essays—will have little impact if it is not embodied in institutions. Individual teachers and learners, of course, must do the best they can until such time as better notions of the intellectual endeavor emerge. But that will take time and no little labor. In his contribution to the present collection, Frederick Erb III delineates some possible options for our moment. Catholic and other religious institutions, which still have intellectual resources that state and secular universities lack, need to think deeply again about the way they carry out their dual mission. This rethinking must do more than affirm a vague commitment to Christian scholarship. The enormous growth of higher education since World War II put pressure on religious institutions to imitate their non-religious counterparts. This had positive and negative effects. Faculties at religious institutions became more "professional," as professionalism is currently understood. But they also became less religious than they once had been. In those colleges and universities, we need a much more energetic attempt to reconcile the gains of the recent past with an older understanding of the institutional mission.

One important and much neglected opportunity is the growing movement to establish Catholic Studies Programs at secular institutions. This may seem impossible in an America that has come to understand the separation of church and state as requiring the banishing of religion from state-supported education. But European universities seem to have had much less difficulty in accommodating Catholic and Protestant teaching within pluralistic frameworks. As Erb points out, over eighty-five percent of Catholic students today study at non-Catholic institutions. Either those millions of young people must be simply abandoned or we must find ways to have some degree of teaching about Catholicism present at secular institutions. Catholic Studies Programs come in many forms and not a few have serious pitfalls. But Erb is certainly right that, at their best, they offer a promising approach to bringing Catholic thought to large numbers who will receive higher instruction in Catholic matters in no other way.

Rabbi Leon Klenicki puts a difficult question to this whole enterprise. Can the kind of intellectual work within Christian faith offered by many of the contributors to this volume accommodate or engage in truly respectful dialogue with members of other faiths, Judaism in particular? There is no single or easy answer to this question. Certainly, the great medieval philosophers drew a great deal on Jewish and Islamic sources. But medieval culture generally excluded or marginalized Jews and Muslims. The whole troubled history of Jews in what was once called Christendom cannot be overlooked by people who want to be faithful to the whole of the truth. Christian-Jewish dialogue has been more fruitful in our time than in any previous age, but does that give us reason to believe that the fear of Jews and other non-Christians can be easily managed?

A great deal hinges on how we conceive of that dialogue. Klenicki criticizes the Vatican's recent document *Dominus Iesus* and Maritain himself for their belief that Christianity has superseded its Jewish origins. He would prefer a recognition on the part of Christians that Judaism remains a valid and continuing path to salvation. In strictly logical terms, this may be impossible. Both Maritain and the Vatican are simply, in a sense, stating a truism. Catholics of course are convinced that theirs is the true religion willed by God, just as Jews, Muslims, Hindus, and Buddhists are about their own faiths. Without that recognition, we would fall into the very common and erroneous view that somehow all faiths are equally valid despite their differences with one another. Whether these inevitable commitments are the equivalent of the historic "teaching of contempt" for Jews cannot be decided in advance. We have to see how individuals and whole groups relate to one another in real terms, despite their deepest commitments.

But such objections usefully remind us that the intellectual life carried on from the standpoint of faith will, in modern pluralist societies, need to be especially vigilant not to fall into close minded blindness of its own. A culture infused with Christianity owes all people's consciences the deepest respect. As difficult as it may be, all institutions of higher learning need to be open to the light that may be available from all sources to remain true to the kind of philosophy Maritain himself saw as the ideal. In the Jewish case—and to a large degree in Islam—there are profound convergences in views about Creation, the nature of the human person, God's providential action in history, and the ultimate end of human life. Such broad agreements cannot resolve all the very real differences between different faiths. But they should not be underestimated as foundations for a respectful dialogue that is united in the belief that all human beings are made in the divine image and consequently are engaged in the perennial task of knowing—and living—truth.

PART I

FAITH AND REASON

Fides et Ratio: A "Radical" Vision of Intellectual Inquiry

Alfred J. Freddoso

Commentators on Pope John Paul II's encyclical *Fides et Ratio*[1] have not failed to notice the incongruity that envelops the Pope's defense of the powers of reason against contemporary forms of skepticism. As Nicholas Wolterstorff has put it: "How surprising and ironic that roughly two centuries after Voltaire and his cohorts mocked the church as the bastion of irrationality, the church, in the person of the pope, should be the one to put in a good word for reason."[2] In fact, given that professional philosophers of all stripes have largely abandoned the classical search for a comprehensive and systematic wisdom that provides firm answers to the deepest and most pressing human questions, Pope John Paul II's call for us philosophers to recover our "sapiential" vocation is not just ironic, but downright mortifying.

Still, the Pope's optimism should not obscure the fact that his defense of reason proceeds on his own terms and from within his own faith-filled perspective, and that it stands in marked contrast to those rationalistic tendencies, characteristic of some recent Catholic reflection on faith and reason, which have helped skew the course of Catholic intellectual life in general and Catholic higher education in particular. My aim in this paper is to argue, first, that John Paul II propounds a conception of intellectual inquiry that is very different from currently dominant conceptions in the West, and yet, second, that despite the radical and countercultural nature of this conception

---

[1] I am following the Latin text of the encyclical, and in some cases I have departed from the official English translation, which does not always pay as much attention as one might wish to subtleties.

[2] Nicholas Wolterstorff, "Faith and Reason: Philosophers respond to Pope John Paul II's encyclical letter, *Fides et Ratio*," *Books & Culture* 5 (July/August 1999), pp. 28–29.

of intellectual inquiry, it is philosophically just as plausible as its competitors and, in addition, much more hopeful.

In the first part of the paper I will briefly explicate John Paul II's assertion that reason can fully realize its own intrinsic ends only by means of intellectual inquiry conceived of Christocentrically. In doing so, I will highlight the continuity of his view with Plato's portrait of intellectual inquiry and of the philosophical life. In the second part, I will contrast the Pope's conception of intellectual inquiry with its most influential modernist and postmodernist competitors. In the end I will urge that, among the currently available alternatives in Western intellectual life, it is the Catholic intellectual tradition, guided by the teaching authority of the Church, which provides the best hope for overcoming the most intransigent intellectual problems that confront technologically advanced contemporary cultures, among which are: 1) the fragmentation of the intellectual disciplines, with an attendant neglect of the classical aspiration to achieve an integrated vision of the disciplines themselves and hence of the human person, and 2) a crisis of confidence within the specifically humanistic disciplines that has engendered a general cultural pessimism about the power of human reason to understand "the mystery of personal existence"[3]—a pessimism that poses a threat especially to the young.[4]

A CHRISTOCENTRIC CONCEPTION OF INTELLECTUAL INQUIRY

It is important to pay close attention to the structure of *Fides et Ratio*. The brief Introduction, in which John Paul identifies the search for wisdom as a universal phenomenon with the implicit search for Jesus Christ as the Way, the Truth, and the Life, is followed immediately by discussions of divine revelation (chapter 1) and of faith in that revelation as both a source of cognition and an affective prerequisite for the attainment of genuine wisdom (chapter 2).

This structure is significant and perhaps surprising. One might have expected the Pope to begin with a discussion of reason and so to proceed "from below," that is, from that which, on a classical Catholic view, reason can in principle see on its own without revelation and which would render it receptive to the transcendent and the supernatural. To be sure, John Paul II insists

---

[3] *Fides et Ratio*, no. 12.

[4] See ibid., no. 6. Here, as in so many other writings and speeches—not to mention actions, such as the convening of World Youth Days—Pope John Paul II appeals to young people to accept the challenge of the Gospel with a seriousness that runs counter to the general practice of their elders, especially in first world countries.

at various junctures that when reason operates correctly, it does indeed find itself open to the transcendent even in the absence of divine revelation.[5] But the unmistakable intent of chapters 1 and 2 is to underscore the claim that reason can operate with full adequacy only within the framework of an "act of entrusting oneself to God" which "engages the whole person" and in which "the intellect and the will display their spiritual nature."[6] This act of faith in God's gratuitous self-revelation, which John Paul II characterizes as the highest realization of human freedom, enables the subject's intellectual perception to attain a depth which would otherwise be lacking and which is necessary for attaining what we might call "sapiential certitude," that is, certitude about the nature of the world and of the human person as expressed in a rigorous and comprehensive manner.[7]

In both its cognitive and its affective dimensions, this is a strikingly bold and radical vision of intellectual inquiry. With regard to the cognitive dimension, the Pope is claiming that no matter how impressive particular human claims to knowledge might be, they will collectively fail to constitute genuine wisdom if not informed by faith. For without the light of faith the sum of human knowledge can approach neither the comprehensiveness nor depth of insight required for wisdom:

> Faith sharpens the inner eye, opening the mind to discover in the flux of events the workings of Providence. The words of the Book of Proverbs are very significant in this regard: "The human mind plans its course, but the Lord directs its steps" (16:9). That is, illumined by the light of reason, human beings know how to discover the way, but they can follow it to its end, quickly and unhindered, only if with a rightly tuned spirit they introduce the perspective of faith into their inquiry. Therefore, reason and faith cannot be separated without diminishing the capacity of men and women to understand themselves, the world, and God in a coherent way.[8]

And he reinforces the cognitive necessity of faith in Christ by citing one of his favorite passages from Vatican II's *Pastoral Constitution on the Church in the Modern World*:

> As the Constitution *Gaudium et Spes* puts it, "only in the mystery of the incarnate Word does the mystery of man take on light." Seen in any other terms, the mystery of personal existence remains an insoluble riddle. Where might the human being seek the answer to dramatic questions such

[5] See *Fides et Ratio*, nos. 23, 41, 60, 70, 81, 83 and 84.
[6] Ibid., no. 13.
[7] In *Fides et Ratio*, no. 4, the Holy Father singles out a rigorous mode of thought and systematicity (or completeness) as characteristic of speculative philosophy.
[8] Ibid., no. 16 (my translation).

as pain, the suffering of the innocent and death, if not in the light stream-
ing from the mystery of Christ's Passion, Death and Resurrection?[9]

In the Introduction to the encyclical, John Paul had explicitly coupled the
search for wisdom with the human quest for self-knowledge, in keeping with
the ancient dictum, "Know thyself." Every scientific and humanistic discipline contributes to this quest, since each counts some aspect of the human
person among its objects of study. But here we are told that we can understand ourselves fully and solve "the mystery of personal existence" only by
the light of "the mystery of the incarnate Word." Vestiges of this far-reaching
sentiment can still be found even nowadays in the mission statements of
Catholic universities, if not often in their day-to-day practice.[10] What it implies for philosophy is that the mysteries of the Christian Faith must appear
as first principles in any successful attempt to articulate the full truth about
God, the world, and ourselves. What is more, even though these mysteries are
not naturally evident to us and cannot be acknowledged as true except by
faith, without them we find ourselves in peril not only with respect to our supernatural end but also with respect to widely shared communal ends. For instance, John Paul explicitly ties the absence of the cognitive dimension of
faith to the "technocratic logic" that dominates formerly Christian cultures in
which economic and technological innovations now take place in what we
might aptly call a "sapiential vacuum," with no systematic advertence to the
transcendent metaphysical and moral questions that such innovations should
occasion.[11]

In treating the affective dimension of faith, the Pope begins by invoking
the attitude toward intellectual inquiry expressed in the Wisdom literature of
Sacred Scripture:

> The Chosen People understood that, if reason were to be fully true to it-
> self, then it must respect certain basic rules. The first of these is that reason
> must realize that human knowledge is a journey which allows no rest; the
> second stems from the awareness that such a path is not for the proud who
> think that everything is the fruit of personal conquest; a third rule is
> grounded in the "fear of God" whose transcendent sovereignty and provi-
> dent love in the governance of the world reason must recognize.[12]

[9] Ibid., no. 12.

[10] For example, the University of Notre Dame's mission statement, as revised as
late as 1995, still contains the following lines: "A Catholic university draws its basic
inspiration from Jesus Christ as the source of wisdom and from the conviction that in
him all things can be brought to their completion. As a Catholic university, Notre
Dame wishes to contribute to this educational mission."

[11] *Fides et Ratio*, no. 15.

[12] Ibid., no. 18.

Rectitude of affection—characterized here by humility, fear of the Lord, and a sense of urgency about attaining wisdom—is essential for seeing important truths clearly. Moreover, it is evident from the context that John Paul II means to affirm this not only for moral truths but also for important metaphysical truths—especially those having to do with God and the nature of the human person—which, when held with confidence, establish a framework in which subjects come to see self-transcending life-commitments as plausible paths to human fulfillment. However, it is precisely here that our moral defects tend both to blind us and to render us fearful:

> The natural limitation of reason and inconstancy of heart often obscure and distort a person's inquiry. . . . It is even possible for a person to avoid the truth as soon as he begins to glimpse it, because he is afraid of its demands. Yet even when he flees from it, the truth still has an impact on his existence. For he can never prop up his own life with doubt, uncertainty or deceit; such an existence would be infested with fear and anxiety. This is why the human being can be defined as *the one who seeks after truth*."[13]

In making these claims, Pope John Paul II is self-consciously appropriating within a Christian setting the ideal set forth in Plato's *Republic*, where Socrates emphasizes repeatedly that moral uprightness, which makes one fit for self-transcending and self-sacrificing friendship within a just community, is a necessary condition for leading the philosophical life and, other things being equal, the chief mark that distinguishes the philosopher from the sophist. As the encyclical puts it:

> One should remember, too, that reason needs to be sustained in its inquiry by trusting dialogue and authentic friendship. A climate of suspicion and distrust, which sometimes beset speculative inquiry, is oblivious to the teaching of the ancient philosophers, who held that friendship is one of the most fitting contexts for doing philosophy correctly.[14]

As we will see below, the claim that intellectual inquiry ideally takes place within a community of self-transcending friendship founded upon a robust conception of the common good is foreign in the end to both modernist and postmodernist conceptions of inquiry. But according to the classical conception of intellectual inquiry that John Paul is invoking here, the pursuit of wisdom will prosper only insofar as rigorous intellectual training and practice are embedded within a well-ordered program of moral and spiritual education consonant with the attainment of complete wisdom. In short, on this view

---

[13] Ibid., no. 28 (my translation).
[14] Ibid., no. 33 (my translation).

ideal intellectual inquiry presupposes a way of life that depends on and fosters rectitude of affection, where such rectitude is deemed essential for one's having certitude with respect to all the pertinent first principles.

Furthermore, as Socrates insists in the *Republic*, this moral uprightness is best inculcated and preserved in intellectual inquirers by a morally upright community. From the Pope's perspective the relevant community is in the first instance the *ecclesia*, the Church herself, and the affective rectitude induced by faith consists essentially in the friendship of charity with the Holy Trinity, which all the faithful, including intellectual inquirers, receive gratuitously through the merits of Jesus Christ and which reconstitutes on a new plane their friendship with one another. Further, because of its particular core beliefs, this community is outward-looking and hence naturally enters into conversation with the political, social, and cultural bodies that all human beings, including members of the Church, find themselves a part of. In this sense, intellectual inquiry as Pope John Paul II envisions it is always open to the stranger. This explains why it was fitting for the Pope to include a brief treatment of the Church's relationship to differing cultures within an encyclical on faith and reason.[15]

The communal setting of intellectual inquiry is absolutely crucial to the Pope's account. For even though inquiry is seen as perfecting the individual inquirers themselves, its most important function is to serve the broader community that gives rise to and sustains it. Inquirers are obliged to return to the cave from the sunlight—or, as St. Thomas puts it, "just as it is greater to illuminate than merely to shine, so too it is greater to give to others what one has contemplated than merely to contemplate."[16] So the ideal life of inquiry is essentially social in both its origins and its aims. In particular, as a servant of the broader community, intellectual inquiry is responsible to the first principles on which that community is founded. One of its main functions is to clarify those first principles and to deepen the community's understanding of the warrant for them and of their superiority to possible competitors.[17]

[15] See ibid., nos. 70–72.

[16] *Summa Theologiae* II-II, q. 188, a. 6.

[17] I am underplaying here the self-critical function of inquiry in order to emphasize that even this function is perspectival and not free-floating. Such self-criticism is made from a point of view and must hence take the form of criticizing theories and practices by appeal to prior principles which those theories and practices are seen to violate. To reject the prior principles themselves is in effect to "excommunicate" oneself from the community within which one began inquiry. Even though this might under certain specifiable conditions be a reasonable course of action, it itself involves an implicit appeal to a new set of first principles and hence presupposes the possibility of a community built around the new principles. The idea that inquiry can be entirely "free," i.e., free of any commitment at all to prior principles, is a fiction of the modernist imagination.

Finally, this conception of the nature of intellectual inquiry places no *a priori* restrictions on possible sources of cognition, but ostensibly invites inquirers to draw upon all the cognitive resources available to them—including both faith and reason—in constructing a complete and coherent set of answers to the deepest human questions.[18]

This is the context within which Pope John Paul II repeatedly acknowledges—and, indeed, insists upon—the autonomy of intellectual inquiry, a notion that can be misunderstood in much the same way that the autonomy of the human person can be.[19] I can only skim the surface here, but it is important to articulate at least the most general principles governing the autonomy of inquiry and the authority exercised with respect to inquiry by the community, especially where the relevant community is the Church.

Philosophical inquiry developed historically outside of Christian revelation with its own formal and material standards of success. It is this extra-ecclesial situation that the Pope calls the first of the three "stances" of philosophy.[20] In the *Summa Theologiae* St. Thomas self-consciously adopted Aristotle's formal conceptions of philosophical methodology and of the goal of philosophical inquiry in fashioning his own systematic presentation of Christian wisdom ("third stance of philosophy"), whereas in the *Summa Contra Gentiles* he engaged well-disposed classical and medieval non-Christian philosophers by trying to show that given just their own material assumptions it is possible to establish a large proper subset of Christian metaphysical and moral doctrines, the so-called "preambles of the faith" ("second stance of philosophy"). Thus, intellectual inquiry as a general phenomenon has a certain independence from Christian faith (though not, on this conception, from affective commitments *in toto*), and reason serves in its own right as a source of cognition. As such, reason plays an important regulative role in the articulation and defense of the mysteries of the faith and in the investigation of those revealed truths it is able to establish even in the absence of revelation. To put it most simply, because of God's veracity and hatred of falsehood, what is "contrary to reason" cannot be a part of any valid articulation of

[18] Where, after all, did Socrates get the belief in personal immortality that he puts to the test in the *Phaedo*? As is clear from the "judgment myths" found in the *Phaedo*, *Republic*, and *Gorgias*, they came from his inherited religion. Moreover, he seems content to treat this belief as innocent until proven guilty. That is, he is anxious to refute the objections of Simmias and Cebes, even though he acknowledges that his own positive arguments for the belief are inconclusive. In this sense, his investigation of the thesis of personal immortality is analogous to the Christian's investigation of the mysteries of the faith.

[19] See *Fides et Ratio*, nos. 16, 45, 48, 49, 67, 75, 77, 79, 85, and 106.

[20] See ibid., nos. 75–77.

Christian wisdom.[21] So intellectual inquiry has formal and material resources distinct from the Christian faith, and this gives it a measure of self-rule.

However, this general understanding of the autonomy of inquiry is fully consonant with the claim that inquiry is responsible to the community that gives rise to it and sustains it, and that the community, in pursuing the common good, legitimately exercises a normative role in inquiry beyond that which is exercised over inquirers by other inquirers. For just as genuine personal autonomy can be corrupted by weakness or willfulness into a moral blindness that obscures one's vision of genuine goods, both private and common, so too the autonomy of reason can be corrupted by moral weakness or willfulness into an intellectual myopia that both blinds one to important truths and skews one's vision of the common good to which inquiry is meant to contribute. What is more, there is no reason to think that the exercise of the purely intellectual skills necessary for inquiry renders one immune to this sort of corruption. Indeed, intellectuals often accuse one another of having fallen into it, and the "technocratic logic" I alluded to earlier is partly a result of the community's failure—or perhaps inability or even reluctance, in the case of pluralistic liberal democracies—to bring authoritative metaphysical and moral guidance systematically to bear on scientific and technological research. So just as moral autonomy, rightly understood, does not entail the illegitimacy of all claims to moral authority outside of individual subjects or groups of subjects, so too intellectual autonomy, rightly understood, does not entail the illegitimacy of all claims to intellectual authority outside individual inquirers or groups of inquirers.

Needless to say, opponents of John Paul II's account of inquiry will be quick to point out that the specter of possible injustice and oppression looms large here, especially when the community in question is a full-scale state with inescapable coercive power. This is one reason why the model of the *Republic* strikes many of us moderns as so perilous, despite the safeguards built into the education of the guardians. From a Christian perspective, the primary difficulty with the *Republic* is that the effects of original sin cannot be wholly rooted out in this life by any environment or process of education. The Church, though, is an institution which 1) has voluntary membership, 2) is not, at least in the contemporary world, closely allied with inescapable coercive political power, and 3) has even loftier moral ideals for individuals than does the *Republic*. To be sure, these factors have not always in the past guaranteed, and do not now guarantee, that communal leaders will have either

[21] See St. Thomas, *Summa Contra Gentiles* I, chaps. 7 and 8.

good intentions or good judgment in their dealings with inquirers. But they do provide standards of criticism that can legitimately be appealed to by inquirers. Further, the exercise of authority over inquiry by the community at large is part and parcel of a social conception of intellectual inquiry that will have been internalized by the inquirers in their education, and so they will be at least antecedently predisposed to see this authority as a helpful guide rather than a threat.

As regards the material character of the exercise of this authority, John Paul II explains in chapter 5 of *Fides et Ratio* that interventions on the part of the communal teaching authority of the Church are usually negative, warning against tendencies that might lead inquirers outside the bounds of orthodoxy. But inquiry is largely underdetermined by orthodoxy and so a large area for freedom of thought and individual discretion is left open. On the other hand, some such interventions are positive, urging, for instance, that certain lines of inquiry which have heretofore been neglected should be investigated. But in such cases the warrant for the intervention must always be some pressing intellectual or pastoral challenge to the common good of the community.[22]

I have sketched the general parameters of the Christocentric account of intellectual inquiry which Pope John Paul II proposes in *Fides et Ratio* and which he sees as a Christian successor to the classical philosophical traditions. I am under no illusion that this account will seem attractive to large numbers of contemporary intellectuals—just the opposite, and that is why I call it countercultural. But the encyclical in effect lays down a challenge to contemporary philosophers and scientists to formulate a plausible and satisfying alternative. This can be a healthy exercise, given that intellectual inquirers are not often called upon to think very hard or very deeply about the nature of inquiry itself. But it can also be a revealing exercise, since the contemporary alternatives turn out to have deficiencies that even their own advocates should be able to recognize.

COMPETING CONCEPTIONS OF
INTELLECTUAL INQUIRY

The nature of intellectual inquiry has been a disputed topic ever since Plato painted his portrait of the philosopher and of the philosophical life in dialogues such as the *Gorgias*, the *Phaedo*, the *Phaedrus*, the *Symposium*, the *Apology*, and the *Republic*. (Remember that in Plato's time the natural and human sciences had not yet branched off from philosophy, and so what Plato

[22] A faint—and far more dangerous—analogue of this second role is played in universities nowadays by governmental and corporate subsidies for scientific research.

was in effect proposing was an account of intellectual inquiry in general and of the life of intellectual inquiry.) And, in fact, the modern academy has its own pictures of intellectual inquiry and of the intellectual life—pictures that look very different from Plato's and very different indeed from what Pope John Paul II has in mind in *Fides et Ratio*. I now turn to them.

There are at least three important competing conceptions to consider: enlightenment or modernist rationalism, pragmatism, and Nietzschean anti-rationalism. My treatment of these conceptions in the present paper is broad-stroked and to that extent deficient. Still, it will be sufficient to highlight the deep differences that divide Pope John Paul II from the vast majority of contemporary intellectuals.

The Enlightenment Rationalist (or Modernist) Conception of Inquiry

According to the rationalist account of intellectual inquiry, an ideal inquirer, *qua* inquirer, is a wholly autonomous individual with no indefeasible intellectual allegiance to any political, cultural, or religious community and hence with no intellectual loyalty to any historical tradition of inquiry. As Kant puts it:

> Enlightenment is man's emergence from his self-incurred immaturity. Immaturity is the inability to use one's own understanding without the guidance of another. This immaturity is self-incurred if its cause is not lack of understanding, but lack of resolution and courage to use it without the guidance of another. The motto of enlightenment is therefore: *Sapere aude!* Have courage to use your own understanding![23]

At least in the context of inquiry, affective ties are deemed impediments to seeing the truth clearly and objectively—where truth is conceived of in realist fashion as distinct from consensus, though accessible to all methodologically competent inquirers. On this account, it is precisely because ideal intellectual inquiry proceeds from principles evident to "pure" or "cool" reason alone that it must be free from any explicit or implicit exercise of intellectual authority on the part of non-inquirers.

This aspect of enlightenment rationalism is, to be sure, not entirely "modern." In *De Utilitate Credendi* St. Augustine recounts that he was first

---

[23] "What is Enlightenment?" (1784), http://www.english.upenn.edu/~mgamer/Romantic/kant.html. Kant is an interesting and crucial figure in the story of enlightenment rationalism. On the one hand, his conception of enlightenment stands squarely within the movement initiated by the likes of Descartes and Locke. On the other hand, his Humean-inspired pessimism about the power of speculative reason prepares the way for postmodernist conceptions of inquiry.

attracted to Manicheanism by its disdain for credulity and its promise that no catechumen would have to accept on faith what could not be proved by "pure and simple reason."[24] After his conversion Augustine attributed this attraction to the sin of pride, which had blinded him not only to his own intellectual limitations but also to the fact that an appropriate sort of trust in others is essential to intellectual inquiry. In contrast, on the rationalist view all affective ties, taken indiscriminately, distort judgment and turn it into one or another form of self-deception. Hence, inquirers must habituate themselves to factoring out the affective ties they have as ordinary human beings when they assume the role of inquirers.

The earlier and more optimistic modernists believed that all careful reasoners of normal intelligence would find the very same first principles evident, and that they would likewise be able to discern the evident soundness of the arguments leading from those first principles to various important conclusions in metaphysics and moral theory.[25] For instance, in the *Discourse on Method* Descartes contends that even though not everyone has the creative talent to forge new intellectual paths, all human beings of normal intelligence have enough "good sense" (*le bon sens*) to perceive the evidentness of the first principles, arguments, and conclusions yielded by his new method of ideas—and this, presumably, regardless of their moral and spiritual condition, and regardless of the moral and spiritual condition of the cultures within which they practice intellectual inquiry. All that is needed for wisdom, then, is intellectual insight and good method on the part of the teacher and good sense on the part of the student. Moral and spiritual education are simply beside the point—no surprise, since they are instilled by just the type of communities whose influence rationalism seeks to banish from intellectual inquiry.

---

[24] *De Utilitate Credendi*, chap. 1, no. 2: "My purpose is to prove to you, if I can, that it is profane and rash for the Manicheans to inveigh against those who follow the authority of the Catholic Faith before they are able to intuit the Truth which is seen by a pure mind, and who, by having faith, are fortified and prepared for the God who will give them light. For you realize, Honoratus, that the only reason we fell in with such men was their claim that, apart from any intimidating authority, they would by pure and simple reason lead those who heard them to God and set them free from all error. For what else compelled me, for almost nine years, to spurn the religion instilled in me as a boy by my parents and to follow those men and listen to them diligently, except their claim that we had been made fearful by superstition and had been required to have faith before reason, whereas they would urge no one to believe unless the truth had first been discussed and made clear?" (my translation). See also *Confessions* Bk. VI, chap. 5.

[25] Descartes made this claim at least about foundational beliefs in physics and metaphysics, while it was extended to foundational moral beliefs by various modern moral philosophers.

The original modernist promise is that by using the correct methods, reason by itself can discover all the philosophical and scientific truths needed for both individual and communal human flourishing, and that, without reliance on faith of any sort, the general consensus of mankind will converge on just those truths. This was an exceedingly attractive prospect in the early seventeenth century, given the religious and political divisions that were plaguing Europe in the wake of the Reformation, and given the social and cultural accomplishments of the Renaissance. Nor did modernist bravado die easily. Despite the notable lack of consensus—or even progress toward consensus—on important metaphysical and moral issues among seventeenth- and eighteenth-century thinkers, and despite the pessimism about the powers of reason that had been trenchantly expressed by Hume, the same modernist optimism is evinced in Mill's spirited nineteenth-century defense of intellectual autonomy and freedom of inquiry in the second and third chapters of *On Liberty*.

Today modernist enthusiasm is largely confined to those scientifically-minded intellectuals who have devoted themselves to constructing wholly "naturalistic" (or "materialistic") worldviews. However, despite the dramatic recent achievements of the natural sciences, there are just too many deep and important questions about the human condition that the natural sciences cannot plausibly answer. They simply leave out too much that is important to us. As a result, materialistic worldviews fail to cohere with the fundamental attitudes and deep-seated first principles of most ordinary human beings. Moreover, when we turn to theoretical work in the human sciences, we notice that—for better or worse—this work seems to presuppose such first principles and hence cannot serve to discover them in the impartial manner promised by modernism.[26] But without rationalist-conceived human science there is no hope of constructing a unified rationalist account of reality, which would, at least in broad outline, integrate the disparate academic disciplines into a synthetic framework. Yet as the Pope insists in *Ex Corde Ecclesiae*, such an integration of knowledge is essential to our attaining a complete vision of the human person. To fail in our search for a unified and integrated account of reality is in essence to fail in our search for coherent self-understanding.[27]

Pope John Paul II notes with some concern that the recent past has seen the promise of the enlightenment fall on hard times and hard realities. For

[26] This claim is at the heart of the call for Christian-based social science that one finds in the work of the so-called "Radical Orthodoxy" movement, led by theologians such as John Milbank and Catherine Pickstock.

[27] This is a major theme of Walker Percy's fiction, which is in many ways a fitting literary complement to *Fides et Ratio*.

given the failure of modernists to provide a satisfactory comprehensive account of "how we ought to live," as Socrates was wont to say, there is a palpable sense in which pessimism and even cynicism with respect to the attainment of wisdom has been their cultural legacy. This will become clear as we turn to the postmodern alternatives.

The Pragmatist Conception of Inquiry

In the eyes of many, then, the so-called "enlightenment project" has failed as a path to sapiential certitude, despite its spectacular scientific and technological achievements. The possible reactions to this perceived failure are many, but two stand out as worthy of special attention because of their prominence in contemporary Western intellectual culture. Each in its own way not only rejects enlightenment rationalism but goes so far as to stand Socrates on his head.

The first, and more bourgeois, reaction to enlightenment rationalism might aptly be called pragmatism because of its association with John Dewey, though it finds a powerful early modern expression in Hume. According to this view, we should begin by simply admitting that the modernist search for sapiential certitude has been a failure and that such certitude has thereby been shown to be unattainable. As Philo puts it in the *Dialogues Concerning Natural Religion*, when we leave the arena of everyday human affairs and attempt to inquire into the deep foundational questions of metaphysics and moral theory, we are like "foreigners in a strange country,"[28] since our cognitive faculties, even when used as well as they can be, are not capable of yielding firm answers to these questions. Instead, we end up with competing comprehensive claims to wisdom, none of which has any more rational warrant than any other. Fortunately, even though we lack rational warrant for our sapiential claims, nature has endowed us with instinctive sentiments and beliefs which, if we do not corrupt them by either moral or epistemic fanaticism, are sufficient to guide us through ordinary life and even through scientific research conceived of empirically as a mere extension of ordinary thinking.

In the *Ethics* Aristotle had attributed the core of this position to the poet Simonides, who exhorted his readers to concern themselves just with things here below and not with the gods and heavens above. But the urgency with which pragmatism is defended today is a new phenomenon engendered by contemporary political realities.[29] The pragmatist emphasizes that the rationalist search for sapiential certitude is not only futile but especially dangerous

[28] David Hume, *Dialogues Concerning Natural Religion* (Indianapolis, Indiana: Hackett Publishing Co., 1983), p. 7.

[29] For an exposition, emendation, and defense of this "Rortyan" position, see Gary Gutting, *Pragmatic Liberalism and the Critique of Modernity* (Cambridge: Cambridge University Press, 1999).

within the framework of a pluralistic democratic society. For competing claims to comprehensive wisdom are frequently held with a high degree of what St. Thomas calls "certitude of adherence," and such firmness of commitment causes social division and undermines tolerance, the chief civic virtue required by such societies. So our best course is simply to abandon the search for wisdom as a general communal imperative. When it comes to ultimate moral and metaphysical questions, either we should train ourselves not to raise them at all or, if we find this psychologically impossible or otherwise undesirable, then we should at least refrain from insisting on the universal validity of our own sapiential preferences when we leave the private sphere and participate in public discourse. The role of the philosopher is not to raise these deep strategic questions, but is instead to engage in tactical "Socratic" irony, exposing the assumptions, pretensions, and incoherences of the wealthy, the famous, and the powerful.

The first thing to note about pragmatism as just described is that, despite its pretensions to the contrary, it in fact stands under the shadow of enlightenment rationalism. For according to the pragmatist, rationalism is mistaken not in its core conception of ideal intellectual inquiry, but merely in its optimism about the ability of affectless human inquirers to reach sapiential certitude by means of inquiry conceived rationalistically. Far from holding that rightly-placed affective commitment is essential to intellectual inquiry itself, the pragmatists see affective ties as kicking in, so to speak, only after inquiry properly speaking has failed in its task. Only from this perspective does it make sense to assign equal epistemic weight indiscriminately to all affective commitments (or at least to all politically tolerable ones), regardless of the intellectual content associated with those commitments. For instance, from this perspective the early Heidegger's commitment to the renewal of German culture under National Socialism is—*epistemically* at any rate—on a par with, say, Pope John Paul II's own commitment to the renewal of human cultures through what he calls the "new evangelization."

It is worth recalling that when Augustine became disillusioned with the Manichean guarantee of naturally grounded wisdom, his immediate temptation was to cling to his faith in pure reason and despair of ever reaching certitude about the ultimate meaning of human existence.[30] That is, he flirted with pragmatism as I have defined it. In the end, however, he altered his conception of inquiry instead, adopting the more classical approach explained above. So in the end the crucial issue for Augustine was not *whether* to make

---

[30] See especially *Confessions* Bk. V, chaps. 6, 11, and 14.

a faith-commitment *qua* inquirer but rather just *which* such commitment to make. And he came to believe that it was his own affective disorders that had tempted him, in effect, to assign equal epistemic weight to all such commitments after his disappointment with Manicheanism.

What drove Augustine beyond pragmatism was, in large measure, dissatisfaction with the thought that he should resign himself to abandoning the quest for wisdom as futile or, alternatively, to romanticizing it as an end in itself. In other words, he exhibited just the sort of moral urgency that John Paul II sets forth as one of the affective prerequisites for attaining wisdom. In contrast, the pragmatist seems content to recommend 1) the pursuit of a pleasant and comfortable life that avoids suffering as much as possible, and, within that stricture, 2) an effort to make other people's lives more pleasant, or at least less unpleasant. This was just the sort of life which Augustine abandoned after reading Cicero's *Hortensius* and which he had come to see as shallow, self-deceived, and indifferent to the deep human aspiration to commit oneself to noble ideals and deeds. In a passage that may very well have been aimed precisely at pragmatic postmodernism, Pope John Paul II speaks of nihilism:

> As a result of the crisis of rationalism, what has appeared finally is nihilism. As a philosophy of nothingness, it has a certain attraction for people of our time. Its adherents claim that the search is an end in itself, without any hope or possibility of ever attaining the goal of truth. In the nihilist interpretation, life is no more than an occasion for sensations and experiences in which the ephemeral has pride of place. Nihilism is at the root of the widespread mentality which claims that a definitive commitment should no longer be made, because everything is fleeting and provisional.[31]

The validity of applying this charge to pragmatism might not at first be obvious, since, after all, the pragmatist holds that people are free to commit themselves passionately and wholeheartedly to any kind of lifestyle they please, as long as they are tolerant of commitments that conflict with their own. But the very foundation of pragmatism implies that it is foolish to cling to any faith commitment with a degree of certitude that is not proportioned to what would be evident to any affectless inquirer, and yet this is precisely the sort of certitude that the virtue of faith confers on the Christian believer. To the pragmatist, then, the absolute certitude with which the Christian faithful adhere to their claim to wisdom can only seem foolish and dangerous. This is, after all, the certitude of the Christian martyrs, and these martyrs are precisely

---

[31] *Fides et Ratio*, no. 46.

the sort of "fanatics" whose influence in the public sphere pragmatism is anxious to minimize. Anyone who finds these martyrs, along with other saints, admirable will find pragmatism unsatisfactory. In fact, anyone who finds non-self-transcending conceptions of human fulfillment rather unfulfilling will likewise be dissatisfied with pragmatism's implicit disdain for the noble and heroic. Such people are looking precisely to make the sort of permanent and "definitive" commitments that the pragmatist views as silly and treacherous.

The Nietzschean Conception of Inquiry

If pragmatism is rather bourgeois, the same cannot be said of the Nietzschean brand of postmodernism. "Supposing truth to be a woman—what?" Thus begins Nietzsche's *Beyond Good and Evil*, and thus begins as well his relentless critique of the affectless rationalist inquirer. One finds hints of this view in Hume's darker moments, when his assertion of the ascendancy of non-rational sentiment over reason is particularly strong and his concomitant pessimism about reason is particularly intense.[32] But Hume still retains his ingenuous confidence that the most basic sentiments relevant to moral and scientific practice are universal, ineradicable, and predominantly benign, and so he manages—at least most of the time—to maintain his cheerfully ironic pragmatism. Thus it fell to the more serious, cynical, and persistent Nietzsche to launch a devastating critique of modernism and the bourgeois culture fostered by it. From Pope John Paul II's perspective, there is much to be learned from this critique,[33] but whereas Nietzsche's modernist predecessors had overvalued reason and rational discourse, so he himself undervalues them. In the end, it is the rhetoricians, and not the philosophers, who prevail.

As Nietzsche sees it, the classical search for wisdom is a movement of pure will or instinct, with reason serving only to rationalize the first principles that one already accepts or prefers without reason. To be sure, he chides the "neutral" or "value-free" modernist scholar for not being able so much as to appreciate the sentiments that have given rise to philosophy and religion across all human cultures.[34] Yet from his perspective all philosophical inquirers, classical as well as modernist, are operating in bad faith, since they

---

[32] The character of Philo in Hume's *Dialogues Concerning Natural Religion* is especially interesting in this regard, since he alternates—or so it seems to me—between a gleeful superficial disparagement of the search for wisdom (that is, pragmatism) on the one hand and a somber deep despair about the human condition (that is, Nietzscheanism) on the other.

[33] See *Fides et Ratio*, no. 91.

[34] A particularly entertaining example of this occurs at *Beyond Good and Evil* (New York: USA Viking Penguin, 1990), no. 59, p. 64, where Nietzsche pokes fun at the condescension of the "German scholar" toward religious people.

refuse to bring to the surface the various ways in which appeals to expert knowledge and to the so-called "authority of reason" have been and continue to be used as instruments of oppression.

Now one might find much truth in this attribution of bad faith even while insisting that intellectual inquirers equipped with affective rectitude have the ability to distinguish legitimate and benign from illegitimate and oppressive appeals to the authority of reason. (Ironically, given the context, Catholics might understand the interventions of the Church's teaching authority in philosophical matters to be aimed precisely at helping us make this distinction.[35]) But Nietzsche will hear of no such qualifications. On his view, all appeals to the authority of reason, whatever their provenance, should be viewed with suspicion. And, indeed, it is just such suspicion—in the beginning with respect to those who fall outside of one's own community of victims and in the end with respect to everyone, including one's own past selves—that marks Nietzschean inquiry.

In *Fides et Ratio* Pope John Paul II asserts that this attitude of universal suspicion—even if not wholly unjustified—leads straight to nihilism.[36] This might not at first be obvious, since there are highly-publicized communitarian versions of postmodernist inquiry that promote a sort of "secular fideism," complete with 1) "faith-communities" built upon the members' shared perceptions of being victimized by sinister and powerful outsiders and 2) an account of truth according to which truth as an ideal consists simply in the consensus of those who share the "faith" of the community. The radical intellectual perspectives generated by such fideism have, after all, produced some very insightful critiques of classical and modernist intellectual inquiry.[37]

Despite this veneer of communitarianism, however, the Pope is right on the mark in his assessment of the nihilistic tendencies of Nietzschean per-

---

[35] See chaps. 5 and 6 of *Fides et Ratio*, where the Holy Father defends magisterial interventions and also argues that the Catholic Church, because of the universality of its message, has been more successful than any other historical institution in interweaving the universalist claims of the Gospel with indigenous human cultures. This is not to deny that mistakes have been made along the way, and the present Pope has been the first to acknowledge them. But the intent has been to enhance indigenous cultures and bring them to perfection through the Gospel, and not to repress or replace them in the manner of, say, the Roman or British Empires or, more recently, imperialistic free-market consumerism.

[36] *Fides et Ratio*, no. 91.

[37] I have in mind, for example, certain feminist critiques of the history of science. This, by the way, is a game that Catholics and other Christians can play as well, since we are urged to see the world "through the eyes of faith." However, given that a fundamental stance of seeing oneself as a victim carries with it grave spiritual risks, it is probably better for Christians to employ this device very sparingly.

spectivalism. For the fact remains that Nietzsche's own analysis of bad faith can be turned back upon any such communitarian Nietzscheanism itself, and this "hermeneutic of suspicion" undermines the very communities that were initially held together by shared perceptions of victimization. It is no accident that the most salient characteristic of Nietzsche's "free spirit" is that he undergoes continual "dis-integration" as he uncovers and is disgusted by his own past self-deceptions. In the end the free spirit repudiates all attachments to people as individuals, to communities, to country, to pity, to science and philosophy, to his own virtues, and even to his own detachment.[38]

Interestingly, the free spirit's detachment is in some ways remarkably akin to the detachment of the Christian saint, whom Nietzsche both despises and grudgingly admires. But the detachment of the Christian saint is for the sake of friendship with God, and all the objects of detachment are in the end recovered to the extent that they can be re-ordered toward that friendship. The free spirit's detachment, in contrast, serves only to exclude him from genuine friendship with others and ultimately leaves him with only his suspicion, including his self-suspicion. No claim to objective or absolute wisdom will long survive inquiry of this sort. In short, given the foundational first principles of Nietzschean inquiry, there is ultimately no perspective—established either by faith or by reason—that can be both intellectually normative and a source of permanent friendship and harmony binding together the community of inquirers. So, once again, those looking to make permanent self-sacrificing and self-transcendent commitments will find Nietzschean inquiry less than satisfactory.

But whatever form postmodern nihilism might take, whether the passionate and suspicious nihilism of Nietzscheanism or the cheerfully ironic nihilism of pragmatism, it seems both to arise from and be sustained by an underlying despair about the human condition:

> The currents of thought which claim to be postmodern merit appropriate attention. According to some of them, the time of certainties is irrevocably past, and the human being must now learn to live in a horizon of total absence of meaning, where everything is provisional and ephemeral. In their destructive critique of every certitude, several authors have failed to make crucial distinctions and have called into question the certitudes of faith. This nihilism has been justified in a sense by the terrible experience of evil that has marked our age. Such a dramatic experience has ensured the collapse of rationalist optimism, which viewed history as the triumphant progress of reason, the source of all

---

[38] *Beyond Good and Evil*, nos. 31 and 41.

happiness and freedom; and now, at the end of this century, one of our greatest threats is the temptation to despair.[39]

It is undeniable that since the "collapse of rationalist optimism," philosophers have tended to be more guarded in their aspirations and less hopeful in their expectations, especially when compared to their predecessors in the great classical philosophical traditions. As Chesterton remarks, "[Modern philosophy's] despair is this, that it does not really believe that there is any meaning in the universe."[40] Still, even the classical pagan philosophers were in their own turn much less hopeful than Pope John Paul II is. Recall that Socrates' own conception of the best the philosopher could hope for even in the next life was the sort of perpetual philosophical conversation that Dante situated in the first circle of hell—a far cry from the intimate union with the Persons of the Triune God that John Paul II takes to be possible for us, at least in its beginnings, even in this life.

CONCLUSION

Pope John Paul II proposes a conception of intellectual inquiry which is radical by contemporary Western standards and yet which has preserved the classical quest for a unified rational self-understanding and an answer to the "mystery of personal existence." In this paper I have tried to suggest in inchoative fashion the main lines of argument by which this conception of inquiry might reasonably be defended as superior to its main competitors. What remains is to develop these arguments with greater rigor and specificity.

---

[39] *Fides et Ratio*, no. 91.
[40] G. K. Chesterton, *Orthodoxy* (San Francisco: Ignatius Press, 1995), p. 164.

The Spirit of Medieval Philosophy in a Postmodern World

Gavin T. Colvert

All these people ["modernists"] have simply ceased to believe in Truth, and believe only in verisimilitudes pinned to *some* truths. . . . One has to be quite naïve to enlist in the service of such a philosophy if one has Christian faith (which is nothing without the Word—infinitely independent of human subjectivity—of a revealing God who is infinitely independent of our mind). This is especially so if one belongs to the Catholic religion, which of all the religions . . . is most steadfast in recognizing and affirming the reality—irreducibly, splendidly, generously *in itself*—of the beings whom the Creator has made and the transcendence of this Other, who is the Truth in person and being itself subsisting by itself.[1]

FAITH, REASON, AND POSTMODERNISM

In his recent encyclical letter, *Fides et Ratio*, Pope John Paul II urges philosophy to recover its authentic vocation as responsible for "forming thought and culture" through the vigorous pursuit of truth.[2] Two striking features of this document are its optimism about philosophy's ability to answer fundamental questions and its overriding concern with the value of reason and truth.[3] This latter theme might well seem naïvely out of step with contemporary culture, in which the supremacy and autonomy of reason have

---

[1] Jacques Maritain, *The Peasant of the Garonne: An Old Layman Questions Himself about the Present Time*, trans. Michael Cuddihy and Elizabeth Hughes (New York: Holt, Rinehart and Winston, 1968), pp. 7–9.

[2] *Fides et Ratio*, intro., no. 5. Hereafter cited as *FR*.

[3] See, e.g., *FR*, intro., no. 6, "I feel impelled to undertake this task above all because of the Second Vatican Council's insistence that the Bishops are 'witnesses of divine and Catholic truth'. . . . In the present encyclical letter, I wish to . . . [concentrate] on the theme of *truth* itself and on its *foundation* in relation to *faith*."

been called into question.[4] Quite to the contrary, however, John Paul II is acutely aware of the so-called "postmodern" developments in culture, which tend as he says toward a "lack of confidence in the truth."[5] *Fides et Ratio* might well be termed the Pope's encyclical on the postmodern temperament.[6] As vital and contemporary as this document is, it repeats a theme made popular by certain Thomists long before the term "postmodern" was fashionable.

As the theme of his letter suggests, the Pope sees a solution to philosophy's discontent in the revitalization of a dynamic interrelationship between reason and faith. Echoing a thought expressed by many observers of modernity, including such unlikely intellectual compatriots as Étienne Gilson and Jacques Maritain on the one hand, and Richard Rorty on the other, he argues that modern philosophy in the wake of the Cartesian project turned increasingly inwards towards immanence and away from transcendence, especially transcendent truth.[7] This inward turn has wrought profound metaphysical and epistemological consequences. Metaphysically, philosophy lost its sapiential dimension, the ability to reach beyond the immediate focus upon reality as constrained to our experience of empirical phenomena.[8] Epistemologically, increased skepticism concerning reason's ability to know the truth about our world has arisen.[9]

For the Pope, on the other hand, faith provides access to truths that en-

---

[4] See John Caputo, "Commentary on Ken Schmitz: 'Postmodernism and the Catholic Tradition,'" *American Catholic Philosophical Quarterly* 73, no. 2 (Spring 1999), p. 254, "When I first read what Heidegger said about 'being-in-the-world' and how the question of whether there is a world makes no sense for beings whose Being is being-in-the-world, that struck a chord that resonated deeply with the 'realism' of my Catholic philosophical upbringing. We were all realists, afraid it seemed that someone was going to steal the world from us . . . I am sure the neoscholastic obsessiveness with 'realism,' with the epistemic defense of realism, is linked very closely to the Vatican defense of infallibility, both of which are distinctly 19th century events that reflect a lot of Cartesian, and very modern, anxiety."

[5] *FR*, intro., no. 5.

[6] See *FR*, chap. 7, no. 91.

[7] Ibid., "Modern philosophy clearly has the great merit of focusing attention upon man. . . . Yet the positive results achieved must not obscure the fact that reason, in its one-sided concern to investigate human subjectivity, seems to have forgotten that men and women are always called to direct their steps towards a truth which transcends them." See also chap. 7, no. 81, "[T]he human spirit is often invaded by a kind of ambiguous thinking which leads it to an ever-deepening introversion, locked within the confines of its own immanence without reference of any kind to the transcendent." John Paul II refrains from mentioning Descartes by name, but his brief presentation of the history of philosophy makes his view fairly clear. See chap. 4, nos. 45–46.

[8] See FR, chap. 7, no. 83.

[9] See FR, intro., no. 5 and chap. 4, no. 45.

hance the limited capacity of reason to establish truth demonstratively.[10] Thus, faith can enhance reason's self-confidence. But, more significantly, faith calls us to be open to self-transcendence. The modern habit of mind tended to eschew this as an appropriate philosophical starting point.[11] The postmodern habit of mind is hardly so unified. Postmodernists share a profound suspicion of modern philosophy's turn toward the self, but they do tend to accept the turn toward immanence in place of transcendence.[12] Some more secular postmodernists, such as Richard Rorty, view interest in the transcendent as the chief vice of their modern predecessors.[13] Catholic postmodernists may well recognize transcendence, but they tend toward a focus upon its unknowability.[14]

One particular epistemic shortcoming of the modern position, which relates especially to reason's interconnection with faith, is the failure to acknowledge the social dimension of knowledge. As John Paul II emphasizes, human persons find themselves in traditions of enquiry where "personal verification" must be complemented by "the truth of the person."[15] While the noetic quality of testimony may be less intrinsically perfect than personal verification, its fecundity and vital importance for human knowing are indisputable.[16] As Linda Zagzebski has cogently argued, modern epistemology tends to be excessively individualistic in its conceptions of knowledge and justification.[17] The upshot of this modern turn in the postmodern period is the rise of anti-realism and conceptual relativism. As John Paul II stresses, "legitimate plurality" has given way to "undifferentiated pluralism" and "widespread distrust of the human being's great capacity for knowledge."[18] The so-

---

[10] Maritain offers a complementary account of the relation between reason and faith in the *The Peasant of the Garonne*, pp. 142–43.

[11] See Descartes's letter of dedication which precedes his *Meditations on First Philosophy,* ed. Donald A. Cress, (Indianapolis, Indiana: Hackett, 1993), pp. 1ff.

[12] See Lawrence E. Cahoone, *From Modernism to Postmodernism: An Anthology* (Oxford: Blackwell Publishers, 1996), pp. 15–16.

[13] See Richard Rorty, "Pragmatism as Anti-Authoritarianism," *Revue Internationale de Philosophie* 1 (1999) pp. 7–20.

[14] See John Caputo, "Commentary on Ken Schmitz," pp. 255ff.

[15] See *FR*, chap. 3, nos. 31–32.

[16] See *FR*, chap. 3, no. 32.

[17] Linda Zagzebski, *Virtues of the Mind: An Inquiry into the Nature of Virtue and the Ethical Foundations of Knowledge* (New York: Cambridge University Press, 1996), p. 11 *et passim*. See also Linda Zagzebski, "Religious Knowledge and the Virtues of the Mind," in *Rational Faith: Catholic Responses to Reformed Epistemology*, ed. Linda Zagzebski (Notre Dame, Indiana: University of Notre Dame Press, 1993), pp. 199–225.

[18] *FR*, intro., no. 5.

lution according to the Pope, which Maritain and Gilson recognized so long ago, is to recover moderate realism by taking a more sensible epistemological course. We must recognize our nature as truth-seekers and interdependent beings with a capacity to realize that goal.[19] The truths acquired by faith provide an important support to this task.[20]

If John Paul II is correct concerning his diagnosis of the problem, we should therefore expect that a philosophical tradition that takes the interrelation between faith and reason seriously will have much insight to offer to our contemporary situation. The postulation of a fruitful relationship between faith and philosophic rationality was typical of the medieval intellectual project. Thus, the question naturally arises whether medieval philosophy can offer medication to an ailing postmodern world?

The purpose of this paper is to explore the viability of that idea. The scope of this exploration must unfortunately be placed within certainly narrowly defined limits. First of all, it will not be possible to offer an extended defense of John Paul II's assessment of the philosophical *status quo*. I will assume that he has correctly described the contemporary milieu and see if an alternative to postmodern fragmentation is possible. Second, any attempt to characterize *the* postmodern tradition would be tendentious. Rather than try to paint postmodernity with a single brush stroke, I will choose an illustrative example of a postmodern intellectual, Richard Rorty, who provides an interesting case in point. Nevertheless, Rorty's commitment to historicism, immanence, contingency and conceptual relativism could, in principle, be extended to other postmodern figures. Third, after a brief attempt to characterize the salient features of the tradition of medieval philosophy, attention will be given primarily to Aquinas's moderate realism and his conception of the complementarity of reason and faith.

THE MEDIEVAL PROJECT

The "Quid Sit" of Medieval Philosophy

If we are to understand how the spirit of medieval philosophy may have a constructive impact upon philosophizing in a postmodern world, we must have an account of the former's nature before we can see how it may be applied to the latter. Taking the concept "Christian philosophy" as an instance of medieval philosophy, Étienne Gilson observed that there is some doubt

---

[19] For instance, *FR* offers a refutation of skepticism along these lines; see chap. 3, no. 29. The following paragraphs take up the importance of testimony and the social dimension of knowledge. *FR*, chap. 3, nos. 31ff.

[20] *FR*, chap. 2, no. 20.

"whether the very concept of 'Christian Philosophy' has any real meaning . . . and whether there was ever any corresponding reality."[21]

This question is most difficult to answer because answering it depends upon our conception of what philosophy is. Furthermore, unless we regard "philosophy" as merely an accidental succession of incommensurable conversations, then we must conceive of medieval philosophy in terms of its continuity with the present.[22] If we have an arbitrarily narrow conception of what philosophy is about for us, then we will have a correspondingly provincial conception of whether medieval thought counts as philosophical. This is the crux of the problem, since modern philosophy until the midpoint of the present century generally regarded medieval thought as engaged in a self-contradictory endeavor. Postmodernity challenges the very conception of reason that sustained modernity's expulsion of the scholastics from the philosophical fold. But, it also accepts late modernity's flight from transcendence.

As we shall see, the medieval project provides a vantage point from which to critique not only modernity's conception of philosophical rationality, but also the late-modern skeptical presumption that attainment of truth could only occur according to those standards of rationality. The dynamic interrelation between faith and reason is an important source of this balanced view. If we are to see the contemporary value of medieval philosophy, we must open ourselves to the possibility of this constructive challenge.

The Connection Between Medieval
Thought and Christianity

The historical record indicates that throughout the medieval period, in addition to theological treatises, there were independent traditions of logical,

---

[21] Étienne Gilson, *The Spirit of Mediaeval Philosophy* (Notre Dame, Indiana: University of Notre Dame Press, 1991), pp. 1–2.

[22] This remark is intentionally cautious, precisely because Richard Rorty makes the opposite claim about the history of philosophy. See Richard Rorty, *Philosophy and the Mirror of Nature* (Princeton, New Jersey: Princeton University Press, 1979), pp. xiii ff., 3ff., and 389ff. This counter-claim is integral to his pluralistic attitude toward what counts as philosophical inquiry. The view of this analysis is that we can accept his critique of the Cartesian turn in philosophy without embracing his postmodern skepticism, which includes the incommensurable character of philosophical traditions. For an apparently contradictory remark, acknowledging the unity of philosophical experience, see ibid., p. 33.

natural scientific, jurisprudential and medical inquiry, to name a few.[23] One might argue that Gilson erroneously harnessed medieval philosophy to Christian philosophy and attempted to identify philosophy with those other sorts of intellectual activities.[24] Such an approach is conceivable but not satisfactory. As Gilson argued, the interaction between reason and religious faith was central to the intellectual milieu of the period.[25]

Consider, for instance, whether we should call Boethius a logician or a theologian? Or more importantly, is Boethius thinking as a Christian or a philosopher when he encounters Lady Philosophy in his cell and discusses with her the correct path to human happiness? Consider further how we shall draw precise boundaries between Aquinas's "philosophy" and his "theology." Some of his most fertile reflections on philosophical problems relating to free will and human agency can be found in those places where he discusses the will and sin of the angels.[26] Ockham provides another interesting case in point. There would arguably have been no treatise on quantity, as Ockham wrote it, without his concern to solve certain problems necessary for the explanation of the doctrine of the Eucharist. In fact, this point could be generalized to many important advances in natural philosophy, logic and other areas. Problems of foreknowledge and predestination, for instance, undoubtedly fueled careful reflections in modal logic. These examples not only indicate that there were "philosophic Christians" as Gilson put it, but that their Christian worldview frequently had an integral role to play in the formation of their philosophic outlook.[27]

---

[23] Gilson was also well aware of the contributions of Jewish and Islamic scholars. For the present purpose, it can be assumed that "Christian Philosophy," if it is intelligible, is an instance of a broader dialogue between reason and religious faith in the Middle Ages. Furthermore, while it must be granted that some thinkers, such as Averroes, drew sharp distinctions between reason and faith, those positions were still deployed within the context of such a dialogue.

[24] This was the position of some of Gilson's critics, notably Fernand Van Steenberghen. See Van Steenberghen, *Introduction à l'étude de la philosophie médiévale* (Paris: Béatrice-Nauwelaerts, 1974). More recent efforts have recognized, to various degrees, integral connections between philosophical and theological problems in medieval philosophers. For an excellent survey of these positions see Jan Aertsen, *Medieval Philosophy and the Transcendentals: The Case of Thomas Aquinas* (Leiden: Brill, 1996), pp. 1–24. This paper does not aim to critique any one of the current points of view in the debate, but rather to call critical attention to certain problematic assumptions that frame the debate, namely our understanding of what constitutes properly philosophical inquiry.

[25] See Gilson, *The Spirit of Mediaeval Philosophy*, pp. 2ff. *et passim.*

[26] See *Summa Theologiae* I, qq. 59 and 63. Hereafter cited as *ST.*

[27] Gilson, *The Spirit of Mediaeval Philosophy*, pp. 2ff.

We see the truth of this point both at the beginning and straight through to the end of the medieval period. St. Augustine, for instance, draws his *Contra Academicos* to a close with the following epistemological strategy:

> [N]o one doubts that we're prompted to learn by the twin forces of authority and reason. Therefore, I'm resolved not to depart from the authority of Christ on any score whatsoever. . . . As for what is to be sought out by the most subtle reasoning—for my character is such that I'm impatient in my desire to apprehend what the truth is not only by belief but also by understanding—I'm still confident that I'm going to find it with the Platonists, and that it won't be opposed to our Holy Writ.[28]

This strategy was to give birth to the project of "faith seeking understanding," which served as an important model for the pursuit of wisdom throughout the Middle Ages. Aquinas adopts a similar procedure at the beginning of the *Summa Contra Gentiles* when he proposes that, for those points which do not admit of demonstration, reason can adduce refutations of counter-arguments against them.[29] More significantly, in his own treatment of the intellect and the process of cognition, St. Thomas refers explicitly to Augustine's epistemological strategy.[30]

This strategy envisions fruitful cooperation between reason and faith as twin sources of access to truth. Faith not only provides the starting points for certain specific theological conclusions, but as Ralph McInerny has pointed out, it guides the sort of "research projects" which will seem worth pursuing to the Christian philosopher, and even suggests fruitful and pointless avenues of inquiry.[31] There is an important distinction between philosophy and sacred theology. The latter begins explicitly from revealed premises and reasons from them to specific conclusions as from authoritative starting points. Christian philosophy, on the other hand, begins with faith as forming a tradition of inquiry and providing an important external source of boundary conditions in the search for truth.[32] The Christian philosopher aims for consistency between the truths of reason and faith, but, he or she proceeds by the discipline's own internal standards of verification.

The result of faith's contribution to philosophy is seen in a certain kind of

---

[28] Augustine, *Contra Academicos* in *Against the Academicians / The Teacher*, trans. Peter King (Indianapolis, Indiana: Hackett Press, 1995), Bk. III, chap. 20, no. 43, p. 92.

[29] See *Summa Contra Gentiles* I, chap. 9.

[30] *ST* I, q. 84, a. 5.

[31] See Ralph McInerny, "Reflections on Christian Philosophy," in Zagzebski, *Rational Faith*, pp. 273ff.

[32] See ibid., p. 266.

epistemological optimism. At one level, faith provides confidence because reason has a companion to guide and sometimes to correct its own tentative steps. At another level, faith provides the Christian philosopher with evidence to support belief in the proper working order of reason's own truth-gathering capacities. That is, we know by faith that we were created by an intelligent being who has ordered us toward a *telos* which includes coming to know Him. This *telos* demands that the "research project" of radical philosophical skepticism must be misguided.[33]

Perhaps the most striking illustration of this point with regard to medieval Christian philosophy is none other than William of Ockham. Modern critics of Ockham's thought have accused the Venerable Inceptor's conceptualism not only of being responsible for unraveling the widespread medieval commitment to moderate realism, but also of being a form of proto-skepticism.[34] It is, no doubt, true that Ockham's refusal to countenance an isomorphic relationship between our general concepts and the structure of the external world raised very difficult questions about the relationship between thought and its object. It is also reasonable to hold that those profound difficulties contributed to the development of Cartesian dualism and the modern turn toward problems in epistemology, especially the skeptical worries generated by epistemic internalism. But, it is equally important to maintain that Ockham himself was not a skeptic. He was, in fact, confident about the human mind's capacity to know the external world through the certainty of intuitive cognition.[35] It is hard to see what could have sustained Ockham's optimism other than his commitment to the project of "faith seeking understanding," when we compare that commitment to the temperament of modern skepticism which followed his lead concerning cognition.

Postmodernists have rightfully pointed out that no philosophical project

[33] It is beyond the scope of the present inquiry to treat this point fully, since various Christian traditions have viewed the appropriate degree of confidence we should have in natural reason differently, due to divergent viewpoints concerning the corruptive influence of sinfulness. Zagzebski points out, for instance, that Catholic philosophers have tended to be more confident about our cognitive capacities than Protestant traditions generally (Zagzebski, *Rational Faith*, p. 207). But, even among Protestant philosophers, an argument can be made for a healthy degree of optimism about reason's capacities. See Caleb Miller, "Faith and Reason," *Reason for the Hope Within*, ed. Michael J. Murray (Grand Rapids, Michigan: Eerdmans, 1999), pp. 135–64.

[34] See Richard Weaver, *Ideas Have Consequences* (Chicago: The University of Chicago Press, 1984), p. 3. See also Josephus Gredt, O.S.B., *Elementa philosophiae Aristotelico-Thomisticae*, 10th ed., vol. 1 (Freiburg: Herder, 1953), pp. 94–96.

[35] This point is cogently argued for by Marilyn Adams in her magnum opus on Ockham's philosophy. See Marilyn McCord Adams, *William Ockham* (Notre Dame, Indiana: University of Notre Dame Press, 1987), especially vol. 1, pp. 495–550.

begins in a vacuum. Indeed, Alvin Plantinga, who is by no means a postmodernist, has argued that modern philosophy, which has tended to view the idea of tradition-bound inquiry as antithetical to philosophy, has its own set of traditions and boundary constraints.[36] Postmodernists have called our attention to this contextual aspect of philosophizing, but have further concluded that recognition of this point makes the attainment of transcendent truth an impossible ideal. Two questions then need to be answered. Can medieval philosophy as Christian philosophy challenge our loss of confidence in truth and can we make a space for medieval Christian philosophy as philosophy? In order to answer the first question, it is worth turning to a specific example: Aquinas's metaphysical realism.

Thomistic Moderate Realism

St. Thomas's moderate realism is an interesting case in point, because it lies in the middle ground between Platonic ultra-realism and nominalist minimalism. Like the Platonic realist and unlike the nominalist, Aquinas postulates an isomorphic relationship between concepts and the structure of extramental reality. Like the nominalist and unlike the Platonist, Aquinas holds there are only individual extra-mental existents.[37] Significantly, this position commits him to the view that there is a formal identity between the knower and the known, what John Haldane has recently labeled "mind-world identity theory."[38] As Haldane has argued, this form of metaphysical realism, precisely in virtue of its mind-world identity thesis, stands out as one of the best possible alternatives to contemporary versions of anti-realism late-modern skepticism.

In order to make this point, Haldane draws a useful distinction between three varieties of realism and anti-realism: ontological, epistemic, and semantic versions.[39] Ontological realism is a thesis about the mind-independence of reality and its underlying structure. Epistemological realism concerns our ability to use thought and language in order to represent accurately that mind-

[36] See Alvin Plantinga, "Christian Philosophy at the End of the Twentieth Century," in *The Analytic Theist: An Alvin Plantinga Reader*, ed. James F. Sennett (Grand Rapids, Michigan: Eerdmans, 1998), pp. 330ff. See also McInerny, "Reflections on Christian Philosophy," in Zagzebski, *Rational Faith*, p. 266.

[37] See e.g. *ST* I, q. 84, a. 1, and also *De ente et essentia*, IV, "non potest dici quod ratio generis, speciei, differentiae conveniat essentiae secundum quod est quaedam res existens extra singularia. . . ."

[38] For Aquinas's position see *ST* I, q. 84, aa. 1–4, 6. See also John Haldane, "Mind-World Identity Theory and the Anti-Realist Challenge," *Reality, Representation and Projection*, eds. John Haldane and Crispin Wright (Oxford: Oxford University Press, 1993), pp. 15–37.

[39] Ibid., pp. 15–17.

independent reality. The road to skepticism is paved with what appears to be a paradoxical tension between the demands of epistemological and ontological realism. The epistemological realist must hold that there is some intrinsic relation between thought and its objects that allows thought to identify them correctly.[40] The ontological realist must hold that the world exists independently of our capacity to grasp it or not.[41] The result is that the "evidence transcendence" of ontological realism and the required relation between mind and world of epistemological realism come into conflict. As Haldane points out, recent "semantic anti-realism" appears to be a response to this conflict, for it denies as unintelligible the thesis that the truth-conditions of thought and language may transcend our cognitional capacities.[42] It is no accident that worries about this tension have been the catalyst which has drawn some analytic philosophers closer to the postmodern fold.

Granted the viability of the semantic anti-realist's concerns, the only way out of this decline into skepticism is to hold together epistemological and ontological realism through the mediation of the world-directedness of our concepts to the very mind-independent structures of reality. As Haldane points out, Aquinas's metaphysical realism, which postulates the formal identity of the knower and the known, does precisely this.[43] The "mind-world identity thesis," if it can be accepted, therefore constitutes a potent response to postmodern anti-realism. It offers an account of cognition that can hold together epistemological and ontological realism, without turning to the failed project of Cartesian internalism. Moreover, because postmodernity has taught us to question the viability of putative naturalistic and positivistic reductions, we cannot therefore dispense *a priori* with the move to account for realism in terms of formal identity. Moderate realism holds out the prospect of restoring the world-directedness of our concepts and challenging the postmodern fragmentation of the mind's capacity to access transcendent truth. It is therefore most interesting to observe with Maritain and Gilson that Aquinas's stance as a philosophical realist is bound up with his Christian philosophical understanding of the complementarity of reason and religious faith.

Reason, Faith, and Realism

This point can be illustrated by a comparison of Descartes and Aquinas. For Descartes, the matter of the veracity of our knowledge of the external

[40] See ibid., p. 24.

[41] See William Alston, *A Realist Conception of Truth* (Ithaca, New York: Cornell University Press, 1996), pp. 170, 199ff.

[42] See Haldane, "Mind-World Identity Theory and the Anti-Realist Challenge," p. 17.

[43] See ibid., p. 19ff.

world was a persistent difficulty. It was not merely an impediment to a different project that could develop a constructive philosophy. Rather, it was the source of a philosophical principle, the Cartesian methodic doubt, which functioned as an explicit premise or background condition for every attempt at constructive philosophizing.[44] Descartes motivates this methodic doubt by examining numerous apparent paradoxes of perception, which highlight our tendencies to make erroneous judgments. For Descartes, the dubitability of perception requires us to reject the veracity of our sense powers and intellectual judgments until we can deduce their truthfulness from principles known with certainty.

Remarkably, despite the fact that they were aware of the very same perceptual difficulties and tendencies toward error, Aquinas and his predecessors were essentially innocent of this Cartesian problem. To be sure, Augustine experienced similar skeptical concerns as those that plagued Descartes, but as we have noted above, they did not issue in the methodic doubt.[45] Rather, Augustine made his best attempt to dispose of skeptical worries in the *Contra Academicos*, and then proceeded to philosophize in the light of faith. To be sure, there was ample room for a skeptical problem to emerge for Aquinas as well, even though it did not.[46]

In the *Summa Theologiae*, for instance, while discussing the question whether intellectual knowledge is derived from experience of the sensible world, he raises the point made by Augustine and later adopted by Descartes that it is difficult to offer a strategy for distinguishing internally dream states from waking ones.[47] In the *De Veritate* Aquinas demonstrates that he is aware of a subtle and complex range of more technical examples of perceptual error. Question 1, article 11, for instance, asks whether there is falsity in the senses. Aquinas presents an intriguing example in one of the *sed contra*'s to the article. He notes that when we regard an object through colored glass, the object appears to have the color of the glass, not its own color.[48] Hence, sensation can apparently be in error, even with respect to its proper object. Aquinas's resolution of this situation does not deny fundamentally the reality of perceptual and intellectual error.

It is therefore remarkable that he was simply not attracted by the sort of

[44] See e.g. René Descartes, *Meditationes de prima philosophia* in *Œuvres de Descartes*, eds. Adam and Tannery (Paris: Cerf, 1897–1913), vol. 7, p. 18ff.

[45] Gilson argues this point at length. See Étienne Gilson, *The Unity of Philosophical Experience* (New York: Charles Scribner's Sons, 1965), pp. 155–59.

[46] For Aquinas's explicit discussion of Augustine's strategy, see *ST* I, q. 84, a. 5.

[47] *ST* I, q.84, a. 6, obj. 1.

[48] *De Veritate*, q. 1, a. 11, sc 3.

internalist epistemological problems which captivated Descartes. We can be certain of this because he expressly treated a parallel case, namely whether the intelligible species or concept is that which we understand or that *by which* we understand. In *Summa Theologiae* I, q. 85, a. 2, he poses a series of objections that essentially profess the Cartesian view that we are immediately aware of our ideas and only indirectly aware of the external world. In response to this viewpoint Aquinas maintains that the Cartesian position is "manifestly false."[49] Significantly though, he does not offer any detailed argument in defense of his view. He just proposes two considerations that serve to reaffirm his commitment to mind-world identity theory. First, he notes that what we understand are the objects of science, and if we grant the "Cartesian" position, then there will be no science of extra-mental reality.[50] Second, he observes that granting the "Cartesian" position would lead to conceptual relativism, since the measure of truth would need to be the mind and not extra-mental reality.[51] Most importantly, these two considerations are not proofs of ontological and epistemological realism, they presume the truth of both standpoints.

We may therefore reasonably ask, why is it that Aquinas finds Cartesian representationalism, as well as the various forms of anti-realism and conceptual relativism, to be simply uninteresting and fundamentally misguided epistemological strategies? The answer that naturally suggests itself is that faith is providing important guidance to the sort of research projects which seem reasonable and worthy of pursuit. No other likely explanation is available, certainly not ignorance of the possibility of perceptual and cognitive error. Descartes's epistemological strategy is simply inconsistent with what Aquinas takes to be true about our nature as rational agents and our *telos* within the created order. Jacques Maritain puts this point succinctly in *The Peasant of the Garonne*:

---

[49] *ST* I, q. 85, a. 2: ". . . secundum hoc intellectus nihil intelligit nisi suam passionem scilicet speciem intelligibilem in se receptam. Sed haec opinio manifeste apparet falsa. . . ."

[50] Ibid., "Si igitur ea quae intelligimus essent solum species quae sunt in anima, sequeretur quod scientiae omnes non essent de rebus quae sunt extra animam, sed solum de speciebus intelligibilibus quae sunt in anima. . . ."

[51] Ibid., "Secundo, quia sequeretur error antiquorum dicentium 'omne quod videtur est verum,' et similiter quod contradictoriae essent simul verae. Si enim potentia non cognoscit nisi propriam passionem, de ea solum iudicat. Sic autem videtur aliquod, secundum quod potentia cognoscitiva afficitur. Semper ergo iudicium potentiae cognoscitivae erit de eo quod iudicat, scilicet de propria passione, secundum quod est; et ita omne iudicium erit verum."

Reason has its own domain, and faith hers. But reason can enter the domain of faith by bringing there its need to ask questions, its desire to discover the internal order of the true, and its aspiration to wisdom. . . . And
faith can enter the domain of reason, bringing along the help of a light
and a truth which are superior, and which elevate reason in its own
order—that is what happens with Christian philosophy. . . . Not only
does faith place in our path certain signals ("*Danger*: Winding Roads,"
etc.) thanks to which our little saloon-car runs less risks. But, above all,
faith can help us from within to overcome allurements and irrational
dreams to which, without assistance coming from a source superior to
reason, we would be disposed to yield.[52]

The force of Aquinas's commitment to rejecting the denial of mind-world
identity theory as "manifestly false" also makes greater sense when we consider his understanding of the virtue of faith. Considered formally, the
proper object of the virtue of faith is the first truth, namely God Himself.
But, considered materially, the virtue of faith extends to all those things, including the nature of the created world, which bear any relation to the first
truth and our attainment of it.[53] Two significant points follow from this.
First, faith is a cognitive habit, since its object is truth.[54] More specifically,
it is midway between science and opinion.[55] It shares the firmness of assent
with science, but incompleteness of understanding with opinion.[56] Faith's
firmness of assent comes not from reason being compelled by the force of
the evidence; rather it is strengthened by an appetitive component, an act of
choice.[57] This act of choice is of course voluntary, although assent is only
given to what is credible, and the will is sustained in its act by grace. Thus,
Aquinas's strength of commitment to metaphysical realism, by virtue of its
relation to more central matters of faith, despite the absence of a deductive
argument for it, should neither be surprising nor regarded as irrational. Second, the virtue of faith provides not only a certain type of cognition, but also
an ethical imperative. We assent to what faith entails in part because it is
fitting for us to do so in light of our interest in the attainment of our *telos* or
the goal of human fulfillment.[58]

---

[52] Maritain, *The Peasant of the Garonne*, pp. 142–43.

[53] See *ST* II-II, q. 1, a. 1.

[54] See *ST* II-II, q. 4, a. 2; See *ST* II-II, q. 2, a. 1.

[55] See *ST* II-II, q. 1, aa. 2, 4, 5.

[56] See *ST* II-II, q. 1, a. 4, See *ST* II-II, q. 2, a. 9, ad 2. For a good discussion of this
point see Laura García, "Natural Theology and the Reformed Objection," *Christian
Perspectives on Religious Knowledge*, eds. C. Stephen Evans and Merold Westphal
(Grand Rapids, Michigan: Eerdmans, 1993), pp. 127ff.

[57] Ibid.

[58] See *ST* II-II, q. 2, aa. 3–9, See *ST* II-II, q. 4, a. 5.

For Aquinas, then, skepticism and anti-realism not only fail to be fruitful epistemological strategies, they frustrate the attainment of the good of our nature. Thus, we have an ethical obligation to avoid such unproductive belief policies. In a remark which applies fittingly not only to his view of the need for faith with regard to specifically theological truths, but also with respect to human cognition generally, Aquinas explicitly endorses the Augustinian thesis that unless we believe we shall not understand. Interestingly enough, he credits it to Aristotle as a general thesis about knowledge. This constitutes a resounding reversal of Descartes's methodical doubt:

> Man becomes a participant of this discipline [the knowledge of natural and supernatural beatitude] not immediately, but successively, according to the mode of his nature. But for every human being to learn it is necessary that he should believe, so that he shall attain the perfect degree of scientific knowledge; just as the Philosopher says that "it is necessary to believe in order to learn."[59]

We can therefore see that Aquinas's commitment to epistemological and ontological realism in general are bound up with his view of the appropriate relation between reason and faith, a view which is characteristic of the medieval philosophical tradition.

Aquinas and Putnam: an Example

A striking example of how this tradition presents a constructive challenge, not only to the modern philosophical project, but also to postmodern anti-realism can be illustrated by comparing Aquinas to Hilary Putnam on the very subject of metaphysical realism. In his recent work *Realism with a Human Face*, Putnam speculates about the reasons for rejecting metaphysical realism.[60] His answer depends in part upon the possibility of what he calls "equivalent descriptions" or "notational variants" in scientific theories.[61] Simply put, there are some theoretical interpretations of physical phenomena which suppose very different ontologies, but which have negligible implications for "actual scientific practice."[62] Because of such "equivalent descriptions" Putnam reaches the quasi-Kantian conclusion that we are trapped in our conceptual schemes and that, in some sense, reality is theory-ladened.[63]

---

[59] See *ST* II-II, q. 2, a. 3.
[60] Hilary Putnam, *Realism with a Human Face* (Cambridge, Massachusetts: Harvard University Press, 1990), p. 39.
[61] Ibid.
[62] Ibid.
[63] See ibid., 40–41.

Remarkably, Aquinas was aware of similar circumstances, but did not feel compelled to draw the same anti-realist conclusions. On several occasions, for instance, he discusses the Ptolemaic theory of planetary epicycles.[64] Thomas observes that the Ptolemaic theory, which is discordant with the Aristotelian account, saves the phenomena, but remains a supposition because the discovery of some other theory, which accounts for the phenomena equally well, is a distinct possibility.[65] Significantly, his discussion of this case in the *Summa Theologiae*, occurs in the treatise on the Trinity. He compares the Ptolemaic theory of epicycles and eccentrics to the rational support for the doctrine of the Trinity. Granted the truth of each position, reason provides evidence lending confirmation to the viewpoint which should not be mistaken as sufficient proof that things are exactly as we suppose them to be.

This example is illuminating, because in the case of the Trinity, our concerns about the imperfection of our rational inquiry into the doctrine are tempered by the understanding that is acquired through faith. In the same way, the limitation of our ability to grasp the true nature of the planetary motions, does not present for Aquinas a test-case which catapults him into skepticism or anti-realism. Unlike the Trinity, of course, Aquinas's faith does not provide a ready-made set of metaphysical realist postulates, especially ones concerning the nature of the motions of the heavens. In fact, given the later history of this question, it is worth noting that Aquinas is careful to point out that the suppositions of the astronomers of his time must be regarded quite tentatively.[66] It does, however, provide him with the conviction that there is truth and that we can know and articulate it. That he could be mistaken about the true nature of this reality, Thomas was quite willing to entertain, but that he should be systematically deceived and incapable of articulating genuine knowledge claims about an independent world was simply not a reasonable alternative for him.

Interim Conclusions

Granted that the foregoing discussion of Aquinas and others is correct, we have reason to take seriously the constructive challenge to both modernism and postmodernism which medieval philosophy represents. As we shall see below, the modern habit of mind tends to deny medieval philosophy its proper place at the table, while the postmodern viewpoint is less exclusive,

---

[64] See *ST* I, q. 32, a. 1, ad 2; *Sententia de caelo et mundo*, Bk. I, lect. 3; Bk. II, lect. 17.

[65] See ibid., Bk. II, lect. 17.

[66] See ibid.

but at the high cost of denying transcendent truth. The spirit of medieval philosophy helps us to examine both those stances critically.

THE MODERN AND POSTMODERN PROJECTS

Gilson: Rationalism and the Spirit of Medieval Philosophy

While philosopher-theologians like Aquinas were acutely aware of their complicated relationship to classical learning, they quite properly regarded themselves as contributing to the conversation of the Western philosophical tradition, even as they sought to transform it into the wine of Christian wisdom.[67] Granting that we can reconcile the medieval thinker's self-images to the practice of philosophy, it is not clear that we ourselves can regard what they were doing as philosophical practice. Thanks to certain lines of thought popular in the early and middle portions of the 20th century, a consensus emerged about the nature of philosophy itself that was incompatible with doing so. The radical empiricist methods of figures such as A. J. Ayer, which banished as meaningless statements that do not admit of strict empirical verification, could not allow that medieval thought was properly philosophical.[68] Given their presuppositions, they were, of course, correct.

The question remains, was such an account of philosophy's essential nature provincial or purificatory? Gilson was cognizant of this problem, which he labeled "pure rationalism" in *The Spirit of Mediaeval Philosophy*. He took the positivist challenge so seriously that he made it the focal point of his departure, asking whether it was simply contradictory to speak of a spirit of medieval philosophy, precisely because collaboration between reason and faith was an impossible illusion.[69] He then astutely pointed out that medieval thinkers had their own internal understanding of the nature of rational evidence which guided their reflections in an ordered and predictable manner. To label this understanding as unphilosophical is to offer a questionable *a priori* criterion for the nature of such evidence.[70] Gilson concluded: "[W]hen reason starts making these arbitrary exclusions, it loses the right to judge."[71] Despite this strong stand in support of the charge of philosophical provincialism, he followed up the point immediately with the admission that, "I have no illusions as to the efficacy of my remark. . . . It will in no way change the

---

[67] See *Expositio super librum Boethii de Trinitate*, q. 2, a. 3, ad 5.
[68] See A. J. Ayer, *Language, Truth, and Logic* (New York: Dover, 1952).
[69] Gilson, *The Spirit of Mediaeval Philosophy*, p. 3.
[70] Ibid., p. 406.
[71] Ibid.

accepted outlook. . . ."[72] Gilson was correct on both scores. It was philosophical provincialism and the time was not ripe in the philosophical mainstream for his remarks.

The Turn to Postmodernity

Times have changed, however, and so has the mainstream philosophical landscape. The clearest indication of this fact is that critics of modernity have raised Gilson's principal concern about the *a priori* determination of standards of rational evidence by logical empiricism, and logical empiricism itself has thereby been called into question. With the move from provincialism to pluralism, however, other developments which threaten the continued relevance of important constructive strands in medieval thought, especially metaphysical realism, have arisen as well. Postmodernity saves a space at the philosophical table for medieval philosophy only by undermining the integrity of all traditional philosophical projects. It is beyond the scope of the present inquiry to defend that claim in its full generality, but, as we have mentioned above, it is well accepted that postmodernists share profound suspicions about representation and transcendent truth.

An interesting case that illustrates this point is Richard Rorty's skeptical presentation of the remaining task left to philosophy as concerning only hermeneutic "therapy." On the one hand, Rorty's critique of the Cartesian epistemological turn challenges the view of reason which allowed modern philosophy to dismiss the project of integrating faith and reason as intellectually second rate. On the other hand, he holds that we will not find a solution in a new and more successful metaphysical and epistemological stance from which we may guarantee access to truth. The task left for philosophy is to help us overcome this desire by entering into the clear light of pragmatism, where truth is replaced by utility.

If Rorty and his intellectual compatriots are correct, then not only Aquinas's moderate realism, but also Ockham's realistic conceptualism must be discarded as so much useless baggage. Two points need to be made about this development. First, the postmodern critique of modernity must concur with Gilson's assertion that the medieval project cannot be dismissed *a priori* as unphilosophical. Thus, postmodernity's confidence about its critique of transcendent truth may well be overstated, and postmodernists ought to take a much more serious look at *fides quaerens intellectum*. Second, it is also worth pointing out that such is the pluralism of the present state of philosophy, that voices like Rorty's are not the only ones to be heard. Within the an-

[72] Ibid.

alytic tradition from which Rorty takes his point of departure, for instance, some philosophers have even experienced a renaissance of interest in philosophical realism.[73]

Perhaps the best way to illustrate where the spirit of medieval philosophy may be placed with respect to the contemporary scene then is to examine two brief examples, Richard Rorty's project of hermeneutic therapy and the more hopeful case presented in John McDowell's recent monograph *Mind and World*. Remarkably, the latter work makes certain very promising moves in the direction of Aristotelian realism, which strengthen the suggestion that medieval thought may provide constructive assistance to our present intellectual circumstances.

Richard Rorty: Against the Cartesian Epistemological Turn

The benefit of examining Rorty's position is that it offers an argument that unequivocally acknowledges the philosophical character of medieval thought, even going so far as to allow that dynamic interaction between faith and reason may constitute properly rational and philosophical inquiry. Despite this benefit, Rorty's more pluralistic conception of philosophy is simultaneously useful and hostile to the spirit of medieval thought. In essence, Rorty salvages a place for medieval thought in the philosophical fold by detonating the project of philosophy itself. There are no *a priori* objections to counting "faith seeking understanding" as philosophy, because all systematic attempts to philosophize are socially constructed and ultimately unjustifiable themselves.

There is another relevant worry concerning Rorty's blurring of the lines between the disciplines that needs some brief consideration. That is, it may appear to clash directly with medieval conceptions of the distinction between philosophy and theology. In fact, medieval recognition of this distinction may appear to be a tacit endorsement of the logical empiricist position. The apparent difficulty here arises from failing to keep separate two notions: that of distinct starting points and that of incommensurable modes of inquiry.[74]

The Medievals were well aware of the difference between propositions depending upon human reason and those depending upon faith.[75] There was no simple-minded effort to mix reason and revelation indiscriminately. Aquinas, for instance, was careful to distinguish natural theology as a part of philosophy,

---

[73] See especially John Haldane, "Mind-World Identity Theory and the Anti-Realist Challenge." See *Essays on Moral Realism*, ed. Geoffrey Sayre-McCord (Ithaca, New York: Cornell University Press, 1988).

[74] For a similar line of argument see Maritain, *The Peasant of the Garonne*, pp. 141ff.

[75] See Gilson, *The Spirit of Mediaeval Philosophy*.

which takes its principles from human reason, and sacred doctrine which takes its principles from faith. He does, however, also affirm that sacred doctrine is a *scientia* and that it borrows from philosophical reasoning.[76] More specifically, sacred doctrine is a subalternate *scientia* because it takes its principles from another science inaccessible to human reason. The fact that it is subalternated renders it no less a *scientia*. Aquinas stresses this point by making a comparison to the learning process in many other sciences. It is sometimes the case that the pupil must take certain principles of a subalternate science for granted in order to progress in the understanding of that science.[77] He argues that this case is parallel to the case of sacred doctrine, where the principles of the higher science transcend human reason. Moreover, although ultimately understanding is the ground of every science, the proximate starting point of a subalternate science can be belief.[78] Once we have the principles in a subalternate science, whether proximately by reason or belief, we then proceed to reason from the principles to conclusions. In this latter respect, all the sciences are the same.

Our primary interest here is not in sacred doctrine considered in itself, but in the implications of these points for our understanding of the connection between philosophy and theology. Because sacred doctrine is a *scientia*, and one which can subsume philosophical principles, and because the mode of reasoning is the same as that of philosophical sciences, there is no reason to regard the two as incommensurable, even though their starting points are distinct. Hence, Aquinas's distinction is not that of modern empiricism, because he does not think there is a fundamental impenetrability of meaning between the two.

It is then plausible to maintain that we may extend Aquinas's argument from theology back to philosophy, although his remarks make the reverse point, by enlarging the notion of philosophical inquiry to include that which is made in the context of faith. This point is amenable to Rorty's argument insofar as he wants to call into question the artificial barrier between the two. It is not compatible with his position insofar as he detonates the distinction altogether by means of a social constructionist conception of knowledge. Because Aquinas is a realist and Rorty a conceptual relativist, the former can sustain the distinction between starting points whereas the latter cannot. It remains to be seen whether this latter aspect of Rorty's program can be resisted.

We can explore that point with help of an example, namely Rorty's diagnosis of a familiar historical incident, the debate between Galileo and Cardinal Bellarmine about the status of Galileo's astronomical theory. When Galileo

---

[76] See *Expositio super librum Boethii de trinitate*, q. 2, a. 3.

[77] Ibid. q. 2, a. 2, ad 5.

[78] Ibid., q. 2, a. 2, ad 6.

maintained that the heliocentric conception of the solar system was a true description of the way things objectively are, Bellarmine countered by suggesting that Galileo's theory might be a useful tool which saved the phenomena and had certain practical applications, but was open to question. In defending this suggestion, he appealed to scriptural evidence which he thought pointed to the Ptolemaic character of the universe.[79] We may now have good reason to think that Bellarmine had the losing side of the argument, both from the point of view of natural science and Aquinas's observations about the tentative status of the Ptolemaic theory mentioned above, but that is quite beside the point.

As Rorty comments: "Much of the seventeenth century's notion of what it was to be a 'philosopher,' and much of the Enlightenment's notion of what it was to be 'rational,' turns on Galileo being absolutely right and the church absolutely wrong. To suggest that there is room for rational disagreement here . . . is to endanger the very notion of 'philosophy.'"[80] Rorty offers the apparently startling conclusion that we must give up this conception of the limits of meaning in philosophy and with it our unshakable confidence in excluding Bellarmine and his evidence from the discussion.[81] But, given the alternative that Rorty tries to put in its place, this result has been established at a very high price. Rorty's diagnosis of the Galileo-Bellarmine struggle depends upon his acceptance of the model of change in scientific theories proposed by Thomas Kuhn in "The Structure of Scientific Revolutions."[82] According to Kuhn and Rorty, scientific paradigms do not have objective evidence which confirms or disconfirms them from a neutral standpoint; they are social constructions of their adherents.

In the final chapter of *Philosophy and the Mirror of Nature* Rorty proposes his hermeneutic project. We are faced with a dichotomy he argues: either modern rationalism is correct or everything is socially constructed. Faced with this dilemma, philosophy must become reactive and parasitic upon all forms of systematization, with its remaining task being one of "edification" rather than construction.[83] Edification does not consist in a search for truth, because it is outside the socially constructed paradigms within which we may speak about truth. With conceptual relativism, goes also the disintegration of philosophy. It becomes merely an accidental succession of turns in a conversation, no longer Gilson's *philosophia perennis*.[84]

[79] Rorty, *Philosophy and the Mirror of Nature*, p. 329.
[80] Ibid., p. 328.
[81] Ibid., p. 329.
[82] See T. S. Kuhn, *The Structure of Scientific Revolutions*, 2nd ed. (Chicago: The University of Chicago Press, 1970). See also Rorty, p. 324.
[83] Ibid., pp. 360–66.
[84] Ibid., p. 391.

With the replacement of systematization by therapy, the notion of the objectivity of truth also disappears. Rorty's commitment to this point has become even more emphatic in recent work after *Philosophy and the Mirror of Nature*. In "Pragmatism as Anti-Autoritarianism," for instance, he conceives of his task as a "protest against the idea that human beings must humble themselves before something non-human, whether the Will of God or the Intrinsic Nature of Reality."[85] Drawing upon the work of John Dewey, Rorty compares our ceasing to take the concept of truth seriously to the modern secular rejection of a divine being and a transcendent moral order. We must, he says, "set aside *any* authority save that of a consensus of our fellow humans."[86] When we do so, we will no longer look upon the world as an "authority" we must respect.

This attitude is a startling confirmation of John Paul II's thesis that postmodernism (at least of the Rortian variety) does not break with, but is an exaggerated continuation of the modern immanentist habit of mind. One must wonder seriously why some postmodernists see fit to shake Enlightenment rationality down to its foundations without challenging this perceived wisdom. Is there a loss of intellectual fortitude when it comes to breaking this taboo? More significantly, can such a position be a reasonable epistemological strategy? As William Alston has rightly observed, it looks like this attitude betrays a paradoxical unwillingness to accept our finitude, to accept the sometimes painful intrusion of reality into the ivory towers of our conceptual schemes. Perhaps the medievals, who lived in a less sanitized cultural space than ourselves, and who understood very well the reality of suffering and death, were better placed to see the mind-independent structure of reality.

Second, it is clear that Rorty's path offers a high price to pay for allowing medieval thought to return to the table of philosophy. But, perhaps we need not go down Rorty's path the same distance he has. Fortunately, there are a number of more hopeful alternatives to Rorty. Among them is the work of John McDowell.

McDowell: Mind's Answerability to the World

Both Rorty and McDowell agree that the present task of philosophy is therapeutic rather than constructive, in the sense that we must overcome the Cartesian picture of the world by rejecting it, rather than attempting to articulate another epistemological position within it.[87] Whereas Rorty disposes

[85] Rorty, "Pragmatism as Anti-Authoritarianism," p. 7.
[86] Ibid.
[87] Ibid., p. 7. See John McDowell, *Mind and World* (Cambridge: Cambridge University Press, 1996), pp. xxiii–xxiv, 85–86.

entirely with the idea of access to an independent world in favor of conceptual relativism, McDowell aims to replace this picture with an alternative conception of knowledge and experience that is answerable to the world. In this sense, a comparison can be drawn between McDowell and medieval realists such as Aquinas.

In his recent and influential monograph *Mind and World* he proposes to "diagnose" and offer a potential "cure" for some "characteristic anxieties of modern philosophy" concerning "the relation between mind and world."[88] From the start, it is clear that he wishes to unravel the heritage of Cartesian dualism in modern philosophy. It is therefore most significant that, while continually acknowledging the centrality of Kant for his own views, McDowell wishes to undo what Donald Davidson has called the "third dogma of empiricism," a "dualism of conceptual scheme and empirical content."[89] He argues that this dualism is closely bound up with two poles in modern thought described as "The Myth of the Given" (radical empiricism) and "frictionless spinning in a void" (idealism) which, when combined, give rise to an antinomy.[90]

McDowell's own favored solution for disposing of the antinomy between the empiricist and idealist tensions in modern thought, is especially interesting from the point of view of medieval realism. In order to dispose of the antinomy, he argues, we must reject both positions as illusory. The "empiricist" wants to privilege sensory experience as a tribunal for judgment, without allowing it to be infected by conceptual content. The "idealist" reacts by confining judgment to the sphere of reasons and insulating it thereby from answerability to the world. McDowell argues that we must regard sensible intuition itself as having conceptual content.[91] But, he also denies that this insulates knowledge from being a direct awareness of the world, such as it is:

> Conceptual capacities . . . can be operative not only in judgments . . . but already in the transactions of nature that are constituted by the world's impacts on the receptive capacities of a suitable subject. . . . Impressions can be cases of its perceptually appearing—being apparent—to a subject that things are thus and so. In receiving impressions, a subject can be open to the way things manifestly are."[92]

[88] Ibid., p. xi.

[89] Donald Davidson, "On the Very Idea of a Conceptual Scheme," in Donald Davidson, *Inquiries into Truth and Interpretation* (Oxford: Oxford University Press, 1984), pp. 183–98, especially pp. 187–89. See also McDowell, *Mind and World*, pp. xvi, 3–4.

[90] Davidson, "On the Very Idea of a Conceptual Scheme," pp. xii ff., 11ff.

[91] Ibid., p. ix.

[92] Ibid., p. xx.

This is a startling conclusion, for although it is open to a certain idealist interpretation, it would seem that McDowell is arguing for a form of direct realism that is hospitable to a realist epistemology of a Thomistic sort. That McDowell is adopting this sort of strategy, is further supported by his appeal to the Aristotelian concept of second nature in order to explain how it is possible that we experience the world as it really is, yet this experience already contains conceptual content. As he argues, human beings acquire certain conceptual capacities to discriminate and interpret features of the world.[93] The most appropriate model for these capacities is the Aristotelian conception of the acquisition of virtue and the enlightenment of our practical reasoning thereby.[94] Through the acquisition of virtues, practical reason becomes responsive to genuine requirements of reason that are independent of the moral agent. In the same way, McDowell argues we should regard understanding as becoming aware of independent intelligible aspects of reality that it previously was unable to discriminate through the acquisition of certain cognitive dispositions or a second nature.[95]

McDowell's conception of "answerability to the world" provides a very useful case in point for the present analysis, since he shares many sympathies with both the postmodern and pre-modern philosophical projects. With the postmoderns he shares the conclusion that the Cartesian epistemological turn and the poles of rationalism and empiricism to which it gave rise, have reached the end of the road. In answer to the failure of the modern project he does not propose skepticism, however, but a form of direct realism which borrows from the Aristotelian notion of virtue. Both aspects of this response offer a remarkable opening to the medieval intellectual project.

Virtue Epistemology

Given this fact, it is worth noting briefly in closing that in addition to McDowell's turn to the virtues in order to alleviate the modern epistemological predicament, there are currently a number of new full scale theories of knowledge which utilize the concept of intellectual virtue. One such example is that of Linda Zagzebksi's recent influential book *Virtues of the Mind*.[96] Several critical points of her approach are worth mentioning, since they signal a place for the spirit of medieval philosophy and constitute an answer to the loss of confidence in truth which John Paul II laments.

---

[93] McDowell, *Mind and World*, p. xx.
[94] Ibid., pp. 78–79.
[95] Ibid., pp. 79ff., xx–xxi.
[96] See Zagzebski, *Virtues of the Mind*.

Zagzebski fully agrees with the critique of the Cartesian turn in the account of knowledge, but she takes the point one step further.[97] The problem with the Cartesian legacy in epistemology, she argues, is much like that with modern rule-based ethical theories which neglect the character of the moral agent and focus almost exclusively upon the morality of individual acts. Modern epistemology, including the atomism of Descartes's own methodic doubt and procedure for justification, focuses almost exclusively upon individual beliefs and seeks the justifying conditions of those beliefs in the "phenomenological qualities of the mental state of believing itself."[98] Over against this proposal, Zagzebski argues that epistemology should focus primarily upon the character or intellectual virtues of the believer and hold that "knowledge is true belief grounded in epistemic virtue."[99] She further emphasizes that this calls for greater recognition of the social dimension of knowledge.[100]

Significantly, each of these features of the intellectual virtues provides an opening to the tradition of medieval Christian philosophy, a point which Zagzebski is well aware of. There are, of course, the obvious parallels between her use of the intellectual and moral virtues and their medieval counterparts. Indeed, she argues that special attention must be given to the revitalization of the virtues of understanding and wisdom once we get away from the conception of knowledge as merely piling up sets of individually justified beliefs.[101] But, perhaps most interesting for our present analysis, Zagzebski notes that emphasis upon the social dimension of knowledge fits especially well with the Catholic tradition's conception of the community as the locus of knowledge constituted by the deposit of faith.[102] In other words, not only our acquisition of moral and intellectual virtues depends upon the community, but often the content of belief depends upon the credible report of witnesses. This is true not only of religious faith, but of all types of "good believing."[103] It would seem that an inquiry into epistemology which focuses upon the intellectual virtues must therefore take account of what John Paul II has called "the truth of the person."

---

[97] See ibid., p. 11.

[98] Linda Zagzebski, "Religious Knowledge and the Virtues," p. 212.

[99] Ibid. p. 209.

[100] Ibid., p. 215. See Zagzebski, *Virtues of the Mind*, pp. 43ff.

[101] Zagzebski, *Virtues of the Mind*, pp. 43ff.

[102] Zagzebski, *Rational Faith: Catholic Responses to Reformed Epistemology*, p. 208.

[103] Ibid., p. 215.

CONCLUSIONS

Acknowledgment of this possibility brings us full circle to the question: Can medieval philosophy offer constructive advice and even challenges to an ailing postmodern world? The answer to that question depends in turn upon whether faith can credibly come to the aid of reason and whether commitments to moderate realism and transcendent truth can be sustained. Postmodernism has mounted a vigorous critique of the sort of conception of rationality which would exclude faith *a priori*, but we have argued that it should be equally critical of the modern turn toward immanence and away from transcendence. Furthermore, along with the skeptical voices in the present climate, there are also more hopeful ones. If we come to see the interminable struggle between empiricism and rationalism as misguided, John McDowell argues, we can engage in a therapeutic project which avoids the mistakes of the Cartesian turn, but preserves the notion of mind's answerability to the world. This move is remarkably like Aquinas's response to his version of the Cartesian problem. He is prepared to admit that perceptual and intellectual error are distinct possibilities, but not prepared to grant that systematic deception is a viable epistemic viewpoint. As we have seen, for Aquinas this position is bound up with his view of the relation between reason and faith. Zagzebski's call for a turn to the intellectual virtues and the social dimension of knowledge signals an important opening to just this sort of move. Thus, it is clear that there is much constructive work for medieval philosophy to do.

Natural and Supernatural Modes of Inquiry: Reason and Faith in Thomistic Perspective

Peter A. Pagan

"She hath sent her maids to invite to the tower. . . ." (Proverbs 9:3)

A topic of perennial interest, man's last end has been discussed by various seminal thinkers. Both Aristotle and Augustine, for instance, have written magisterial texts on this central issue. Interestingly, the Aristotelian and Augustinian theories of happiness coincide in important respects. Both deem the contemplation of the divine as essential to human perfection. Despite such striking similarities, however, these two theories are worlds apart. Aristotelian *eudaimonia* does not clearly extend beyond this life, whereas Augustinian *beatitudo* does. A fundamental reason underlying the substantive differences between their respective theories of happiness is that Augustine was guided by the light of divine revelation. Augustine's speculation on human finality is grounded in a distinctively Christian anthropology, an anthropology quite beyond the native range of the Stagirite's exceptional mind.

In *Three Rival Versions of Moral Enquiry*, Alasdair MacIntyre suggests a certain measure of incommensurability between the Aristotelian and Augustinian viewpoints.[1] Moreover, he proceeds to interpret Thomas Aquinas as a pivotal thinker who, relying on his sympathetic grasp of his predecessors'

---

[1] *Three Rival Versions of Moral Enquiry* (Notre Dame, Indiana: University of Notre Dame Press, 1990), pp. 105–26.

thought, transcended a seemingly unbridgeable chasm between the Aristotelian and Augustinian conceptual schemes. MacIntyre's fertile work merits careful reflection, but one may question whether Aristotle and Augustine held incommensurable conceptual schemes. Rather than play the incommensurability card, the faith-reason distinction seems more promising. This distinction may allow deeper insight into the Thomistic analogy of happiness, one that owes not a little to the Aristotelian and Augustinian legacies. The influence of these two intellectual giants may be observed vis-à-vis Thomas's distinction between perfect and imperfect happiness, for instance.

The fact that various commentators have offered diverse interpretations of Thomas's teaching on man's last end is hardly surprising. For if one compares the numerous Thomistic texts devoted to the question of human destiny, Thomas's thought can seem paradoxical. Some of these texts, Augustinian in inspiration, suggest that man's ultimate good cannot consist in anything short of the immediate vision of God. Other texts, more Aristotelian in tone, appear to suggest the contrary. One way to resolve this prima facie inconsistency would be to adopt a purely developmental approach to the relevant Thomistic passages. One might hold that Thomas gradually adjusted his understanding of man's ultimate end. Moreover, this way of resolving the apparent paradox would provide a neat solution to an important hermeneutical problem in the Thomistic synthesis. In view of the chronological proximity and interconnection of the seemingly inconsistent texts, however, a purely developmental solution to this difficult *aporia* would appear to require the admission of constant intellectual vacillation on Thomas's part, not to mention that it would sidestep the deeper philosophical issue. This dubious admission might be avoided by undertaking a chiefly metaphysical rather than historical analysis of Thomas's teaching on man's final end. The results of such an analysis will depend partly on how one construes Thomas's distinction between philosophy and theology.

In addition to that distinction, one must consider whether a certain type of hermeneutical approach to the Thomistic corpus tends to impose an unnecessary roadblock on the journey toward a more precise grasp of Thomas's seemingly inconsistent teaching on man's last end. Regarding hermeneutical approaches, one may distinguish two broad types: "externalist" and "internalist" hermeneutics. The impact of the former on Christian thought may be observed in relation to a key twentieth-century debate. This controversy involved several Catholic luminaries, including Maurice Blondel, Étienne Gilson, Jacques Maritain, and Fernand Van Steenberghen. A basic question in this debate was whether the idea of Christian philosophy is an oxymoron. In my judgment, an affirmative answer to this question will be difficult to avoid as long as an externalist hermeneutics dominates the field. Furthermore, an externalist hermeneutics inclines toward the view that Thomas remained internally divided with respect to his conception of man's ultimate destiny. It is my view that the idea of Christian philosophy properly understood is not an oxymoron, and that Thomas's teaching on man's final end was internally consistent.

In what follows, I will explore the distinction between philosophy and theology vis-à-vis a few key Thomistic texts on man's last end. In addition, I will explain and argue in favor of the superiority of internalist hermeneutics.

"[S]CIENTIA BEATA EST *QUODAMMODO* SUPRA NATURAM"

As I mentioned above, there are conflicting interpretations of Thomas's teaching on man's last end. Commentators agree that Thomas taught that man's *de facto* last end consists in the immediate vision of God. Disagreements arise, however, when considering Thomas's stance on whether unaided reason can know the possibility of this intrinsically supernatural end. Consider the following text:

> The beatific vision and knowledge are in a certain manner above the nature [*supra naturam*] of the rational soul, inasmuch as it cannot reach it of its own strength; *but in another way it is in accordance with its nature, inasmuch as it is capable of it by nature, having been made to the image of God*, as stated above.[2]

If reason can know in principle what man is capable of *by nature*, the foregoing text would suggest that a strictly philosophical analysis of human nature *qua imago Dei* can reveal the intrinsic possibility of the immediate vision of God. Moreover, this passage is only one of several texts that might leave one with the impression that Thomas regarded the possibility of the immediate vision of God as a philosophically demonstrable truth. One's interpretation of the text in question will depend in part on one's appreciation of Thomas's conception of the different methods employed in philosophical and theological inquiry.

The distinction between philosophy and *sacra doctrina* as articulated by Thomas is clearly foreign to pagan thinkers such as Aristotle. Yet this distinction seems indispensable to an adequate grasp of Thomas's authentic teaching on man's final end. Indeed, it seems that one reason why Thomas's teaching on man's last end has been interpreted in diverse ways is that the precise line of demarcation between philosophy and (sacred) theology is not always borne in mind. To avoid misconstruing Thomas's teaching on man's last end,

---

[2] *Summa Theologiae* III, q. 9, a. 2, ad 3 (hereafter cited as *ST*). Emphasis added.

one must be clear about his understanding of the difference between human *scientia* and the divine *scientia* in which believers participate through divine faith. Thus, I now turn to examine some points relevant to Thomas's teaching on the distinction between philosophy and theology.

MAN'S FINAL END AND THOMISTIC TEXTS

As noted earlier, Thomas's understanding of man's last end is expressed in many places. In his *Summa Contra Gentiles*, for example, he argues that a spiritual creature's last end can consist in nothing less than the immediate vision of God.[3] Similar reasoning is scattered throughout the Thomistic corpus.[4] For brevity's sake I focus here on the celebrated argument found in the *Summa Contra Gentiles* as a representative sample of Thomas's thought on man's last end.

Of special interest is the fact that the reasoning set forth in *SCG* III, chap. 50 has been the object of conflicting interpretations. Some commentators have suggested that this text provides hard evidence that Thomas thought that the possibility of the immediate vision of God is a philosophically demonstrable truth. For instance, Joseph Rickaby writes:

> If pure spirits and disembodied souls . . . have a natural desire . . . [for the immediate vision of the divine essence], and this natural desire . . . points to a corresponding possibility of realization; then either this vision can be attained by natural means . . . or man and angels, as such, require to be raised to the supernatural state, and could never possibly have been left by God to the mere intrinsic powers of their nature . . . making grace a requisite of nature. . . . [H]ow [does one] deliver Thomas from the dilemma? The usual escape is by saying that he writes . . . of human souls and angels . . . as they actually are in the historical order of Providence, elevated to the supernatural state. . . . But the Saint's arguments in this chapter are purely rational and philosophical, containing not the slightest reference to any fact presupposed from revelation.[5]

Since Thomas concludes this chapter with two biblical quotations (Ecclesiasticus 24:7 and Proverbs 9:3), presumably Rickaby means only that in this particular context no article of faith is an intrinsic element in Thomas's line of argument. This seemingly plausible reading of the disputed text assumes that Thomas's work contains a harmonious blend of strictly philosophical and

---

[3] See *Summa Contra Gentiles* III, chap. 50 (hereafter cited as *SCG*).

[4] See *Compendium theologiae* I, chap. 104; *ST* I, q. 12. In his detailed commentary on Aristotle's *Nicomachean Ethics* Thomas remarks that what Aristotle understands by man's ultimate end is equivalent in fact to imperfect beatitude.

[5] *Of God and His Creatures: An Annotated Translation*, trans. Joseph Rickaby, S.J. (Westminster, Maryland: Carroll Press, 1950), p. 223.

properly theological reasoning. In view of Thomas's understanding of the distinction between philosophy and *sacra doctrina* and his special conception of the intimate relationship between faith and reason, however, this assumption is not easily reconciled with the acknowledged purpose of the author of the *Summa Contra Gentiles*.[6] At the beginning of this work, Thomas avers:

> And so, in the name of the divine Mercy, I have the confidence to embark upon the work of a wise man, even though this may surpass my powers, and I have set myself the task of making known, as far as my limited powers will allow, the truth that the Catholic faith professes, and of setting aside the errors that are opposed to it. To use the words of Hilary: "I am aware that I owe this to God as the chief duty of my life, that my every word and sense may speak of Him."[7]

Here Thomas explicitly indicates that he intends the writing of the *Summa Contra Gentiles* to be a *theological* endeavor. In addition, the surrounding context of the reasoning set forth in *SCG* III, chap. 50 suggests that this text is to be understood in a properly theological sense. In the *Summa Contra Gentiles* his extended line of argument on man's last end begins at *SCG* III, chap. 25. There he states the following: "And so, it is said in Matthew (5:8): 'Blessed are the clean of heart, for they shall see God'; and in John (17:3): 'This is eternal life, that they may know Thee, the only true God.'" Moreover, at *SCG* III, chap. 52 Thomas declares:

> Thus, it is said: "The grace of God is life everlasting" (Rom. 6:23). In fact, we have shown that man's happiness, which is called life everlasting, consists in this divine vision, and we are said to attain it by God's grace alone, because such a vision exceeds all the capacity of a creature and it is not possible to reach it without divine assistance. Now, when such things happen to a creature, they are attributed to God's grace. And the Lord says: "I will manifest Myself to him" (John 14:21).

And at *SCG* III, chap. 53 Thomas argues that a spiritual creature would be altogether incapable of the immediate vision of God were it not for the supernatural light of glory.

Here one might underscore an important disagreement concerning the light of glory. It is well known that John Duns Scotus, among others, would

---

[6] For one interpretation of the purpose and method of the *SCG* see Jean-Pierre Torrell, O.P., *Saint Thomas Aquinas, Volume 1: The Person and His Work*, trans. Robert Royal (Washington, D.C.: The Catholic University of America Press, 1996), pp. 104–11. In this connection see also Anton C. Pegis's introduction to the *Summa Contra Gentiles, Book I* (Notre Dame, Indiana: University of Notre Dame Press, 1975), 39. Likewise, James A. Weisheipl, O.P., *Friar Thomas D'Aquino: His Life, Thought and Works* (Washington, D.C.: The Catholic University of America Press, 1983), p. 132.

[7] *SCG* I, chap. 2.

not concede that the immediate vision of God is altogether impossible without the superadded *lumen gloriae*. In this connection, Efrem Bettoni, commenting on views opposed to Scotus's understanding of the proper object of the human intellect, argues thus:

> From the point of view of Christian philosophy. . . . [i]f the intellect by its nature . . . cannot know anything apart from the essence of material things, it follows that as long as it keeps that nature, it will be impossible for it to know immaterial objects. In such a case, there is only one alternative: either we deny to man as such the capacity to enjoy some day the direct beatific vision of God, or we must admit that in heaven man changes his metaphysical nature. Recourse to the *lumen gloriae* is not a solution. For either the *lumen gloriae* changes the nature of our knowing faculty, and then our conclusion is granted, or it does not change it, and then the *lumen gloriae* will never be such as to confer on our intellect the capacity to know an object that in no way enters the sphere of its proper and natural object. Since both consequences are untenable, so also is the doctrine that logically leads to them.[8]

In a similar vein, Peter F. Ryan, commenting on Henri de Lubac's views concerning natural desire in relation to the idea of natural beatitude, remarks:

> De Lubac, *MS*, 78, n. 16, rightly points out that the nature lacking innate desire for supernatural beatitude could be fulfilled by it only by being so profoundly altered that it would become a completely different nature. As we have noted, the same is suggested by Scotus: "[I]f knowledge of the divine essence were above the nature of our intellect, the blessed will never see God; for no potency can be elevated above its specifying object, as vision cannot be elevated to understanding. Otherwise this potency would transgress the limits of its essence, and would not remain specifically the same."[9]

In reply to the foregoing Scotistic positions, one could note that, according to Thomas's understanding of grace and the theological virtues, supernatural habits (entitative and operative) render man's nature and spiritual faculties other; however, as Thomas points out, this supernatural elevation does not necessarily imply an essential transmutation or corruption of human nature.

---

[8] *Duns Scotus: The Basic Principles of His Philosophy*, trans. Bernardine Bonansea (Washington, D.C.: The Catholic University of America Press, 1961), p. 32. For a decidedly ambivalent affirmation of the *lumen gloriae* in a recent study that purports to offer a Thomist rather than Scotistic interpretation of supernatural acts, see J. Michael Stebbins, *The Divine Initiative: Grace, World-Order, and Human Freedom in the Early Writings of Bernard Lonergan*, (Toronto: University of Toronto Press, 1995), p. 216, and p. 354, n. 11.

[9] Peter F. Ryan, S.J., "Moral Action and the Ultimate End of Man: The Significance of the Debate Between Henri de Lubac and His Critics," Diss. Gregorian University, Rome, 1996, p. 278, n. 10.

Likewise, Thomas holds that the divine bestowal of the intrinsically super-natural *lumen gloriae*, a non-substantial form, does not entail a substantial transmutation of man's intellective faculty.[10] It is true that the creature's in-tellect is made other (*alterum*), but it is not changed specifically or numeri-cally into another thing (*aliud*). As Thomas observes:

> [A]ccidental differences make something other, while essential differ-ences make another thing. Clearly, this otherness, which results from ac-cidental differences, can in created beings belong to the same hypostasis or supposit, in that what is the same in number can be the subject of di-verse accidents.[11]

In part, then, the foregoing disagreement between Thomas and Scotus re-flects their differing conceptions of both the theological virtues and the rela-tionship between nature and grace.[12]

Thomas maintained that the *lumen gloriae* is strictly necessary if spiritual creatures are to participate in the divine vision. If Thomas is correct, then man's knowledge of the possibility of the divine vision as human act depends on his recognition of the superadded *lumen gloriae*. And if this special light is an intrinsically supernatural non-substantial form, then it is a divine gift that completely transcends the reach of created nature left to itself. Hence, the re-ality of this supernatural gift cannot be known apart from divine revelation.[13] It will not suffice to object that man's knowledge of the possibility of the im-mediate vision of God requires knowledge of the light of glory not as an ac-tual fact but as a mere possibility. For knowledge of the instrumental means, in this instance the *lumen gloriae*, is sought in view of knowledge of the de-sired end, in this instance the immediate vision of God. In other words, the intelligibility of the means to be used depends on the intelligibility of the end to be gained. But if the end is altogether unknown, there is no reason to in-quire as to the means without which the unknown end is strictly unattainable. And in this case no strictly natural end is commensurate with the *lumen glo-riae*. For Thomas, then, it appears that the very possibility of the immediate vision of God is a philosophically indemonstrable truth, a truth that necessar-ily eludes the noetic grasp of unaided human reason.[14]

If knowledge of this supernatural possibility exceeds the proper range of

---

[10] See *SCG* III, chaps. 53–54.

[11] *ST* III, q. 2, a. 3, ad 1.

[12] Scotus, for instance, thought that the difference between acquired love of God and infused charity is one of degree; in contrast, Thomas held that the difference is one in kind. Also see Romanus Cessario, O.P., *Christian Faith and the Theological Life* (Washington, D.C.: The Catholic University of America Press, 1996), p. 4, n. 6.

[13] See *De veritate,* q. 27, a. 2, ad 7.

[14] See *De malo*, q. 5, a. 3, resp; *ST* II-II, q. 1, a. 8, resp.

unaided reason, then it might seem that unaided reason cannot but reach one of the following two conclusions: either a) spiritual creatures are endless by nature, or b) they are necessarily ordained to nothing but a proportionate final end, an end which could not possibly be other than thoroughly fulfilling. *As a Christian theologian*, Thomas would maintain that the philosophical arguments leading to either conclusion would be unsound *in the present historical order*. That is not to say, of course, that an unbeliever could not persist indefinitely in holding either a) or b) as certain.

Another indication that the reasoning employed in *SCG* III, chap. 50 is theological rather than philosophical in nature is the fact that Thomas cites the same biblical passage in both *SCG* III, chap. 50 and *ST* I, q. 1, a. 5: "[Wisdom] sent her maids [*ancillas*] to invite to the tower."[15] In the latter text he addresses the question whether *sacra doctrina* is inferior or superior to other human sciences. In an objection, he states that *sacra doctrina* appears inferior to other human sciences, since the former depends on the latter. In his reply to the same objection (ad 2), he contends that *sacra doctrina* depends on human sciences not to prove its principles, which are indemonstrable, but to render its teaching more lucid to the human mind, which stands to the mysteries of faith as "an owl's eyes to the light of the sun."[16] And in his important commentary on Boethius's *De Trinitate*, he defends what some of his contemporaries regarded as a "controversial" position, namely, that the reasoning of (pagan) philosophers, when applied properly, can provide invaluable service to believers engaged in sacred science.[17] Given Thomas's own interpretation of Proverbs 9:3, it seems reasonable to hold that in *SCG* III, chap. 50 he employs philosophical reasoning as an ancillary, not to demonstrate in the philosophical sense that spiritual creatures can have no final end other than the immediate vision of God, but to indicate dialectically that Christian doctrine concerning man's ultimate end does not contradict any metaphysical principles or truths within the range of reason left to its own resources.[18]

---

[15] "Misit ancillas suas vocare ad arcem" (Proverbs 9:3).

[16] "[O]culus noctuae ad lumen solis" (*ST* I, q. 1, a. 5, ad 1).

[17] See *In Librum Boethii de Trinitate*, ed. Decker (Leiden: E. J. Brill, 1959), q. 2, a. 3, ad 7.

[18] "This science can in a sense depend upon the philosophical sciences, not as though it stood in need of them, but only in order to make its teaching clearer [sed ad majorem manifestationem eorum quae in hac scientia traduntur]. For it accepts its principles not from other sciences, but immediately from God, by revelation. Therefore it does not depend upon other sciences as upon the higher, but makes use of them as of the lesser, and as handmaidens [*ancillis*]: even so the master sciences make use of the sciences that supply their materials, as political uses military science. That it thus uses them is not due to its own defect or insufficiency, but to the defect of our intelligence, which is more easily led by what is known through natural reason (from which proceed the other sciences) to that which is above reason, such as are the teachings of this science" (*ST* I, q. 1, a. 5, ad 2).

These considerations provide grounds for questioning the claim that the arguments proposed in *SCG* III, chap. 50 are strictly philosophical in character. Still, one might object that at *SCG* III, chap. 54 Thomas seems to confirm the view that the reasoning contained in *SCG* III, chap. 50 is purely philosophical in nature.

> For these and similar reasons some men have been moved to assert that the divine substance is never seen by any created intellect. Of course, this position *both takes away true happiness from the rational creature, for it can consist in nothing other than a vision of divine substance, as we have shown, and it also contradicts the text of Sacred Scripture*, as is evident from the preceding texts. Consequently, it is to be spurned as *false and heretical*. (Emphasis added.)

Here it seems Thomas is saying that the denial of the possibility of the immediate vision of God contradicts *both* unaided reason *and* divine revelation. Why else would he distinguish here between what has been shown and what has been revealed? In reply, one could maintain that Thomas never intended the arguments in question to be interpreted as if they were altogether independent of the theological light of divine faith.[19] The impact of rationalism may predispose some readers to identify the relevant arguments as strictly philosophical demonstrations. Notice, however, that the unstated assumption here appears to be that arguments proceeding from the light of faith are rationally inferior to purely philosophical demonstrations. Accordingly, if one is not among the enlightened few who grasp philosophically man's *de facto* final end, one may yet have recourse to divine revelation. This Averroistic viewpoint, however, is fundamentally opposed to the Angelic Doctor's theological vision. For Thomas, rational arguments based on divine faith, that is, theological arguments, are superior in nobility to strictly philosophical demonstrations.[20] Thus, even if one does not know via *sacra doctrina* that man's *de facto* final end is the immediate vision of God, nevertheless faith in God's revealed word enables one to be infallibly certain that those who deny the theoretical possibility of the immediate vision of God are mistaken. For theological faith is not a weakness but a perfection of reason.

[19] "In regard then to knowledge of the truth of faith, which can be thoroughly known only to those who behold the substance of God, human reason stands so conditioned as to be able to argue some true likenesses to it: which likenesses however are not sufficient for any sort of demonstrative or intuitive comprehension of the aforesaid truth. Still it is useful for the human mind to exercise itself in such reasonings, however feeble, *provided there be no presumptuous hope of perfect comprehension or demonstration*" (*SCG* I, chap. 8). Emphasis added. See also *In Librum Boethii de Trinitate*, q. 2, a. 3, resp.

[20] "[A]lthough the argument from authority based on human reason is the weakest, yet the argument from authority based on divine revelation is the strongest" (*ST* I, q. 1, a. 8, ad 2). See *ST* I, q. 1, a. 5.

Here I should pause briefly to stress that I am not asserting that Thomas offers no arguments accessible to unaided reason. For many of his arguments, such as his proofs of God's existence, fall within the proper epistemic range of human understanding. But the soundness of some of his arguments transcends the noetic limits of unaided reason. The metaphysical landscape as it appears to elevated reason contains dimensions imperceptible to unaided reason confronted by the very same landscape. To use a rather lame analogy, unaided reason is like a color-blind person with monocular vision, whereas elevated reason is like a person with perfect vision. The perspective of the former is less complete than that of the latter. A strictly philosophic mode of inquiry is less perfect than that of *sacra doctrina*, and certain truths made visible under the theological light of faith remain invisible under the innate light of unaided reason.

INTERPRETING METAPHORS:
FROM PROFANE WATER TO SACRED WINE[21]

It seems fair to say that the Thomistic texts are luminous expressions of a believer engaged in a theological mode of inquiry, not of an unbeliever engaged in a purely philosophic mode of inquiry. Does this mean that Thomas could not employ philosophical reasoning in his theological arguments? In his *Commentary on Boethius's De Trinitate* Thomas answers an objection to the effect that anyone who mixes philosophical reasoning (symbolized by water) with sacred doctrine (symbolized by wine) corrupts the latter. In his reply he states:

> It can, however, be said that a mixture is not thought to have occurred when one of two items enters into the other's nature, but when both of them are changed in their nature [*a sua natura alteratur*]. So those who use the works of the philosophers in sacred doctrine, by bringing them into the service of faith, do not mix water with wine, but rather change water into wine.[22]

Commenting on this disputed text, Étienne Gilson maintains that Thomas is saying that sacred doctrine is not diluted when "mixed" with sound philosophy, for the latter is literally transformed into the former:

---

[21] See R. E. Houser, "Trans-Forming Philosophical Water into Theological Wine: Gilson and Aquinas," *Proceedings of the American Catholic Philosophical Association*, 69 (1995), pp. 103–16. Houser's article has proven helpful in sharpening my own ideas on this question.

[22] *In Librum Boethii de Trinitate*, q. 2, a. 3, ad 5.

Can [philosophy] be thus used by theology toward ends that are not its own without losing its essence in the process? In a way *it does lose its essence, and it profits by the change.* . . . *[T]heology* is not a compound, it is not composed of heterogeneous elements of which some would be philosophy and the rest Scripture; all in it is homogeneous despite the diversity of origin. "Those who resort to philosophical arguments in Holy Scripture and put them in the service of faith, do not mix water with wine, they change it to wine." *Translate: they change philosophy into theology, just as Jesus changed water to wine at the marriage feast in Cana.*[23]

Pace Gilson, one need not adopt his interpretation of Thomas's reply. Here I would press into service the distinction between externalist and internalist hermeneutics. An externalist hermeneutics, which refers to a certain way of approaching the written word in the search for knowledge, engenders a pre-disposition to treat written texts as if they were the focal point in the quest for understanding. In contrast, an internalist hermeneutics stresses the importance of *sapientes* within a living tradition, the interior activity of the intellect itself, and the cultivation of interior habits.

Now, from an externalist standpoint, Thomas's reply might mean that any passage extracted from a philosophical text loses its philosophic character the moment it is incorporated within a theological text. This reading, however, seems problematic. If the extracted passage loses its philosophic character when enveloped within a theological framework, then the original passage would not be of any service to *sacra doctrina*, since its original philosophic import would evaporate during the process of theological transplantation. Thus, philosophy would be useless to theology. But that is precisely the opinion against which Thomas argues. It would seem more tenable, then, to claim that any passage that was originally philosophic in character retains its philosophic nature, even within a strictly theological setting. This reading, however, does not seem to do full justice to Thomas's biblical metaphor.

To preserve the metaphor while retaining an externalist perspective, one might defend something like the following: A given passage can be either philosophical or theological in character depending on how it is construed by the interpreter. Thus, the same passage could be simultaneously philosophical and theological in character if one reader interprets it philosophically, while a second interprets it theologically. This proposal, however, will not persuade those who recognize that a given species of being cannot have more than one essential definition. For just as it is impossible for one and the same thing to

---

[23] Étienne Gilson, *The Philosopher and Theology*, trans. Cécile Gilson (New York: Random House, 1962), pp. 100–01. Emphasis added.

be a lion and a lamb simultaneously, it seems impossible for one and the same text, according to its very nature, to be philosophical and theological simultaneously. Of course a lion and a lamb can belong to the same genus—animal; however, since they are different in kind, they cannot possibly have the same specific differentia. Likewise, if a philosophy text and a theology text are truly different in kind, then no given text can be both a philosophical text and a theological text at once, unless the text exists exclusively in the interpreter's mind. But in that case there would be two essentially different notions, and now the two notions would lack a single ontological ground, namely, the physical text itself. Furthermore, if the text existed exclusively in the interpreter's mind, the externalist perspective as it is here understood would be inapplicable from the very start. The preceding externalist interpretations, then, seem inadequate. Either Thomas's biblical metaphor will be ignored, or the text's ontic unity will be lost. In either case, violence is done to the text itself.

Without either sacrificing the metaphysical integrity of texts or eliding the important distinction between philosophy and sacred theology, can Thomas's metaphor be preserved? Here an affirmative response would seem less than tenable as long as one does not venture beyond the theoretical boundaries of an exclusively externalist hermeneutics. If, however, one adopts an internalist hermeneutics, a new possibility surfaces. Thomas himself supplies an internalist hint. The very article in which he employs the enigmatic scriptural metaphor to advance his own position contains another key biblical reference:

> Those, however, who use philosophy in sacred doctrine can err in two ways. In one way by making use of teachings that are contrary to the faith, which consequently do not belong to philosophy but are a corruption and abuse of it. . . . In another way by including the contents of faith within the bounds of philosophy, as would happen should somebody decide to believe nothing but what could be established by philosophy. On the contrary, *philosophy should be brought within the bounds of faith, as the Apostle says in 2 Corinthians 10:5,* "We take captive every understanding unto the obedience of Christ."[24]

When philosophy is "brought within the bounds of faith," it enters into the service of *sacra doctrina*. The quotation from 2 Corinthians, interestingly, is also cited in a later work on the very same question, namely, whether philosophical argumentation has any place in *sacra doctrina*:

---

[24] *In Librum Boethii de Trinitate,* q. 2, a. 3, resp. Emphasis added.

Sacred doctrine makes use even of human reason, not, indeed, to prove faith . . . but to make clear other things that are put forward in this doctrine. Since therefore grace does not destroy nature but perfects it, *natural reason should subserve [subserviat] faith, just as the will's natural inclination subserves [obsequitur] charity.* Hence the Apostle says: "Bringing into captivity every *understanding* unto the obedience [*obsequium*] of *Christ*" (2 Cor. 10:5). Hence sacred doctrine makes use also of the authority of philosophers in those questions in which they were able to know the truth by natural reason.[25]

According to an internalist approach, the focal point of the quest for knowledge is not some inanimate text, an historical artifact. The focal point is the truth of things, truth that resides in persons and is the proper good of human understanding. But the special truth Thomas sought about man's *de facto* last end transcends the epistemic range of unaided reason.[26] In this instance what human reason must receive before it can even begin the supernatural quest for the prime truth of *sacra doctrina* is the theological virtue of faith. Through divine faith man's intellect submits unconditionally to the supreme authority of Self-revealed Truth and is thereby raised to share in the truth of the mind of Christ. In serving divine Wisdom human reason is joined through faith to Christ, the incarnate Truth sought by Thomas *qua theologian*.

Philosophy and theology are not mixed in Thomas's sense of the term, since each science retains its own essential character.[27] If they were mixed in his sense of the term, the two would be transformed into a third type of *scientia*, a hybrid. In fact, philosophy is not transformed into something else; rather, when it subserves the revealed mysteries of faith, philosophy is subalternated to theology in the order of final causality. Yet it is not a philosophical text that is subalternated to a theological text. Strictly speaking, from an internalist standpoint, neither philosophy nor theology is a text. Whether acquired or infused,[28] sacred theology is principally a *habitus* that perfects the intellect. This *habitus* issues in discursive activity based on divinely revealed truths grasped only through the theological virtue of faith. Philosophy, too, represents chiefly an acquired *habitus* of human reason. In the order of formal causality, this acquired *habitus* is not subalternated to theology. When human reason is transformed qualitatively by the infused light of divine faith, its essential nature is not thereby corrupted. Human reason becomes other

[25] *ST* I, q. 1, a. 8, ad 2.
[26] See *ST* I-II, q. 109, a. 1; *ST* II-II, q. 6, a. 1.
[27] See Houser, "Trans-Forming Philosophical Water into Theological Wine: Gilson and Aquinas," p. 115, n. 54.
[28] See *ST* I, q. 1, a. 6, ad 3.

(*alterum*), but it does not become another thing (*aliud*).[29] Reason (nature) and divine faith (the supernatural) are not separated; they are united in the most intimate fashion. But the real distinction between reason and faith, between philosophy and *sacra doctrina* is preserved. Nature remains nature; grace remains grace.

In short, the philosophical enterprise is understood better from an internalist standpoint than from an externalist perspective. From an internalist standpoint philosophical activity is related less to the idea of philosophy *qua* text than to the idea of philosophy *qua habitus*.

If one stresses the notion of philosophy *qua habitus* (internalist standpoint) over the notion of philosophy *qua* text (externalist viewpoint), what real advantage is to be gained vis-à-vis the blending of philosophical and theological arguments such as those found in the *Summa Contra Gentiles* and similar works? *Habitus* is not its own end, but is ordered to the perfection of operation. By stressing the notion of *habitus* one can see more clearly that philosophy in its fullness is not so much a text as it is an activity. Furthermore, in comparison with the subalternation of reason to the divine Word through faith, the subalternation of one ontologically independent text to a second seems more problematic so far as integration is sought.

From an internalist standpoint, one may now proceed to distinguish four types of speculative activity and thereby grasp how philosophy and theology can be integrated without confusion. First, there are rational acts that are strictly philosophical in nature. Speculative reason's operation is strictly philosophical in character if it is the operation of unaided reason. Second, there are rational acts that are properly theological in nature. In this case one or more revealed mysteries grasped through divine faith function as principles in human reason's syllogistic activity. Third, there are rational acts that are philosophical in essence and theological by participation. In this case reason serves formally as *ancilla theologiae* without incorporating revealed mysteries as principles of syllogistic argument. This type of speculative operation seems to be the kind of activity Thomas had in mind when he employed the biblical metaphor discussed earlier. Fourth, there are rational acts that are both philosophical and Christian simultaneously. Speculative reason's operation can be both philosophical in essence and Christian in mode only if the following three conditions are satisfied: 1) the act of reasoning is enhanced by the theological virtue of faith; 2) no revealed mystery is presupposed as a principle of syllogistic argument; 3) reason is not acting *qua ancilla theologiae*, as in apologetics.

---

[29] See *ST* III, q. 2, a. 3, ad 1.

This type of speculative activity is what may be called Christian philosophizing.[30] The Christian character of such argumentation resides primarily not in externalized proofs recorded in physical texts but in the Christian author of the arguments. Thus, these externalized arguments could in principle be produced by unaided reason. Such arguments, then, are philosophical in essence and, in some cases at least, derive from Christian minds.

Thus, one can preserve the biblical metaphor of water and wine without either eliding the real distinction between philosophy and theology or violating the metaphysical integrity of created being, the "text" of the divine Playwright. Still, one might object from an externalist viewpoint that an internalist approach to the problem is implausible. For it seems that the historical fact of philosophical and theological texts is denied. Moreover, the denial of the historical fact of philosophical and theological texts appears inconsistent with the earlier claim that the arguments contained in *SCG* III, chap. 50 are not purely philosophical but theological, and that the *Summa Contra Gentiles* is a theological rather than a philosophical work. In reply, an internalist could affirm that no text can be identified as philosophy or theology in the primary sense. Philosophy in its fullness is primarily the intellect's interior act of philosophizing. Similarly, theology is primarily the intellect's interior act of theologizing. Inasmuch as they bear the mark of virtue, these acts stem from interior habits, perfections rooted in the noetic faculty. Hence, one may speak of philosophical and theological habits. An internalist can also admit, however, that printed works are philosophical or theological *per extensionem*, inasmuch as they are the visible products of philosophical or theological activity within the spiritual creature's soul.

CONCLUSION

From an externalist perspective many expressed propositions and arguments are such that they can be interpreted as philosophical by some readers and theological by others, independently of the author's intent. From an internalist standpoint, however, the author's intent is central. If the author's internal speculative activity serves formally as *ancilla theologiae*, then his rational arguments need not be considered strictly philosophical arguments capable of eliciting necessary assent from unaided reason. One misconstrues the truly rational arguments found in *SCG* III, chap. 50 and in similar

[30] In this connection one may cite Joseph Owens's perspicacious remark: "[*Catholic* philosophy] is a kind of philosophy that is set up by the factual union of faith [the supernatural] and intelligence [the natural] in the same [created] person" (*Towards a Christian Philosophy* [Washington, D.C.: The Catholic University of America Press, 1990], p. 111).

Thomistic texts insofar as they are interpreted as instances of pure philosophy. Those arguments are actually superior to purely philosophical arguments, for the truth of some of their premises exceed the grasp of unaided reason.

The diversity of interpretations of Thomas's expressed teaching on man's last end is, in my judgment, partly a consequence of the fact that the specific character of any given text is not inherent to the material text itself. The philosophical or theological character of human words resides in thinking subjects primarily, and in inanimate texts by extension. In subtle cases the proper interpretation of a given text, the participated meaning of the written word, can elude more than a few readers. It is to be expected, then, that readers will sometimes fail to apprehend a particular writer's actual intent, unless the text's author, or a student intimately familiar with the author's thought, is available to amend faulty interpretations.

"Pati Divina":
Mystical Union in Aquinas

Heather McAdam Erb

T racing the development of modern atheism, Louis Dupré illumines a curious situation in which the Christian believer finds himself: Influenced
practically, though not theoretically, by the surrounding culture's fragmented, individualistic worldview, the Christian is obliged to turn inwards for
the source of sacralisation, to confront a sacred "sense of absence"[1] and an existential emptiness within his own heart, in order to reach the transcendent.
This confrontation of search and emptiness is for Dupré the "true significance
of the believer's current urge towards a spiritual life,"[2] and from it emerges an
intensive revelation of the infinite and a revitalisation of his religion.

Dupré's reply to a world which has lost its sense of divine presence is an
apophatic model of mystical experience where spiritual emptiness, transfigured in the night of divine absence, becomes a space of transcendence. The
transition from atheism's pure negation of the sacred to the paradox of divine
absence and presence in apophatic mysticism is a conversion from the modern "conquering, grasping" attitude towards the real to a contemplative receptivity to the core of being and selfhood at the heart of each creature.
Dupré's "mysticism of negation"[3] may have its inspiration in traditional

---

[1] Louis Dupré quotes Simone Weil in his article "Spiritual Life in a Secular Age,"
Daedalus (1982), p. 25.

[2] "The desert of modern atheism provides the only space in which most [believers
of our age] are forced to encounter the transcendent. It is a desert that in prayerful attention may be converted into the solitude of contemplation" (Dupré, "Spiritual Life
in a Secular Age," p. 27).

[3] "The more the awareness of God's presence increases, the more the idea of a
similarity between God and creature recedes. . . . Since the third century, the mystical
tradition of Christianity has recognized a theology in which all language is reduced to
silence. . . ." (ibid., p. 27). Dupré refers to Pseudo-Dionysius's "Dark beyond all light"
in this context, apparently distinguishing the night of closed ignorance (atheism) from
a night of spiritual plenitude in apophatic Christian mystics (ibid., p. 27).

Christian spiritualities such as Pseudo-Dionysius's translucent darkness or Eckhart's silence of the Godhead,[4] but emerges within an entirely different environment than traditional mystical theologies. In reply to the secularist rejection of the very possibility of a relation to the transcendent, Dupré stresses existentialist choice (the subjective pole of religious experience) and then grafts this attitude onto the objective system of interpretations—sacraments, Scripture and community, to structure the believer's living union with God.

An alternate account of the balance between the subjective and objective elements of mystical experience, and a different account of receptivity and passivity at the higher stages of religious consciousness, is found in Aquinas's spirituality texts, the theological precursors of John of the Cross's "science of love." For Aquinas, individual religious experience and the objective mysteries of faith are bound in a seamless unity, where the reference of experience is the mystery of God's love revealed in Christ. In Aquinas's thought, mystical experience is the natural crown of the life of grace, as a "shared similitude to the divine nature"[5] and a participation in God's inner life.

Aquinas's mystical apparatus of the infused virtues, gifts of the Spirit and discussions of prayer and the contemplative life, is embedded within the content of his moral theology, and not confined to treatments of paranormal phenomena such as ecstasy and rapture. The rupture between theology and spirituality in the seventeenth century was foreign to the medieval mind, as was the division between "mystical" and "ascetical" theology.[6] Mystical theology was pivoted on directing souls towards beatitude, through sharpening their contemplative gaze of love on divine beauty.[7] For Aquinas, mystical experience thus drew less on human subjective experience, the paranormal and technique, than on the divine invitation and process by which humanity is exalted from grace to glory.

In the discussion of the nature of mystical union in Aquinas's texts, one is led naturally to ask whether Aquinas himself was a mystic, according to acceptable scholarly definitions of the term "mysticism." Here, we must distinguish any documented mystical events of his life from the role that mystical

---

[4] Ibid., p.27.

[5] *Summa Theologiae* III, q. 62, a. 1 (hereafter cited as *ST*).

[6] The divide between spirituality (itself both "mystical" and "ascetical") and theology is traced to the seventeenth century in "Spiritual Theology" in *The New Catholic Encyclopedia*, vol. 13 (New York: McGraw-Hill, 1967–1989), p. 588.

[7] *ST* II-II, q. 180, a. 1. Cf. *ST* I, q. 12, a. 9: "God . . . is the fount and principle of all being and of all truth. He would so fill the natural desire of knowledge that nothing else would be desired, and the seer would be completely beatified."

theology plays in his writings. In his history of Western Christian mysticism, Bernard McGinn defines the mystical element in Christianity as "that part of its belief and practices that concerns the preparation for, the consciousness of, and the reaction to what can be described as the immediate or direct presence of God."[8] For McGinn, there is no possible separation between mysticism and mystical theology, for there is an interdependence between experience and its interpretation.[9] All mystical experiences are mediated by context, language and tradition, such that mysticism must be discussed under three aspects: as an element of religion, as a way of life, and as an expression of the direct consciousness of God's presence. Despite wide variation and interpretations, McGinn's definition of mysticism bears affinity with the definitions of Christian writers such as Carmody[10] and Egan,[11] as well as with secular experts such as Ellwood.[12]

The few mystical events in Aquinas's life do represent instances of "mysticism" thus defined, or as defined more specifically by those trained in the

[8] Bernard McGinn, *The Presence of God: A History of Western Christian Mysticism*, vol.1: *The Foundations of Mysticism* (New York: Crossroad, 1991), p. xvii.

[9] McGinn, *Foundations*, pp. xiii–xv. In this sense, McGinn falls under the "contextualist" school of mystical scholarship, as opposed to the "core/traditionalist" school. The former group sees mystical experience and interpretation as concurrent (since all mystical experience is mediated by a cultural and religious tradition); the latter group believes that a "core" identical mystical content can be found across all mystical experiences, regardless of religious tradition. On this distinction, see: Robert Ellwood, *Mysticism and Religion*, 2nd ed. (New York: Seven Bridges Press, 1999), pp.18–19.

[10] John and Denise Carmody, *Mysticism: Holiness East and West* (New York: Oxford University Press, 1996), p. 10: "[W]hat do we suggest as a working description of mysticism? We suggest: 'direct experience of ultimate reality.'" The Carmodys believe their approach to the study of mysticism to be more inclusive than the approach of McGinn. See ibid., p. 27, no. 5.

[11] Harvey Egan, *Christian Mysticism: The Future of a Tradition* (New York: Pueblo Publishing Company, 1984), p. 9: "My emphases and point of view agree totally with that remarkable scholar of mysticism, Evelyn Underhill, when she writes: '. . . mysticism is no isolated vision, no fugitive glimpse of reality, but a complete system of life carrying its own guarantees and obligations. . . . It is the name of that organic process which involves the perfect consummation of the Love of God: the achievement here and now of the immortal heritage of man. . . . It is an ordered movement towards ever higher levels of reality, ever closer identification with the Infinite.'" The quote from Underhill refers to E. Underhill, *Mysticism* (New York: Dutton, 1961), pp. 76, 81–82.

[12] See Ellwood, *Mysticism and Religion*, Preface, p. xi: "Mystical experience is experience in a religious context that is immediately or subsequently *interpreted* by the experiencer as a direct, unmediated encounter with ultimate divine reality. This experience engenders a deep sense of unity and suggests that during the experience the experiencer was living on a level of being other than the ordinary."

Thomistic tradition as a general thirst for the beatific vision,[13] as "the secret wisdom communicated to the soul through love,"[14] or as an "experimental knowledge of the deep things of God,"[15] or finally, as the "identification" with the supreme principle that is the aim and fulfillment of the universal spiritual effort.[16]

The most important biographical sources for the life of Thomas are the 1319 Naples canonization process and his biography by William of Tocco.[17] The few miracles associated with Thomas's life include his companion Reginald's cure from gout after Thomas gave him a relic of St. Agnes[18] and two instances of levitation and hearing Christ's voice in connection with prayer and devotion to the Sacrament.[19] Later in his life, he was known to become

[13] In his *A Preface to Metaphysics* (English translation of *Sept leçons sur l'être* (New York: The New American Library of World Literature, A Mentor Omega Book, 1961), pp. 15–16, Maritain distinguished three kinds of intellectual thirsts: a thirst for the water of science, a thirst for the water of created wisdom (for the various modes of being), and a thirst for the water of uncreated wisdom, or a desire for the vision of God. As Victor Brezik explains in his article "St. Thomas Aquinas and the Thirst for God," *Homiletic and Pastoral Review* 98, no. 9 (1998), p. 13, the thirst for uncreated wisdom bears fruit in the mystical wisdom of the saints, such that theology overflows into the mystical life.

[14] Here, Johnston is quoting John of the Cross, in the Thomist tradition. See: William Johnston, *Mystical Theology: The Science of Love* (London: Harper Collins, 1995), p. 4. Johnston also defines "Christian" mysticism as "nothing but a living of the Gospel at a deep level of consciousness" (*Mystical Theology*, p. 9). Johnston also asserts that "mysticism is the core of authentic religious experience" (William Johnston, *The Inner Eye of Love* [San Francisco: Harper & Row, 1978], p. 20).

[15] Maritain equates religious (vs. natural) mystical experience with Aquinas's experimental knowledge of the deep things of God in *The Degrees of Knowledge*, trans. G. B. Phelan (New York: Charles Scribner's Sons, 1959), p. 247.

[16] See Henri de Lubac, "Mysticism and Mystery," in Henri de Lubac, *Theological Fragments*, trans. R. Howell Balinski (San Francisco: Ignatius Press, 1989), p. 51.

[17] The sources for the life of Thomas, Tugwell tells us, are contained in *Fontes Vitae Sancti Thomae Aquinatis*, eds. Dominique Prümmer and Marie Hyacinthe Laurent, published in fascicles attached to *Revue Thomiste* (1911–37). See *Albert and Thomas: Selected Writings*, ed. and trans. Simon Tugwell (New York: Paulist Press, 1988), p. 291. We will be referring to the collection found in Angelico Ferrua, *Thomae Aquinatis Vitae Fontes Praecipuae* (New York: Alba, 1968), cited as *Ferrua*.

[18] *Ferrua*, pp. 363–4, cited in *Tugwell*, p. 233.

[19] Tugwell relates the story: "The sacristan at Naples, while Thomas was working on the *Tertia Pars*, is said to have seen Thomas raised above the ground in prayer; then he heard a voice coming from the crucifix saying, 'Thomas, you have written well of me; what reward will you take from me for your labors?' Thomas replied, 'Lord, nothing except you.'" (*Tugwell*, p. 265 and *Ferrua*, pp. 79–80, from Tocco). Tocco also told the account from Paris regarding Thomas's answer to the Masters' disputes over the Real Presence. Many of the brethren were called to witness Thomas floating in the air after some heard Christ assuring Thomas that his answer was as correct as was humanly possible. (*Ferrua*, pp. 100–101). Tugwell points to the questionable veracity of this second instance of levitation in *Tugwell*, p. 265.

so absorbed in the Mass that he had to be roused to continue, we are told.[20] The most famous mystical experience of Thomas is undoubtedly the divine encounter which occurred in or around December 6, 1273, during his celebration of Mass. Of this experience Thomas said nothing, but when urged to explain why he would neither dictate nor write another word, he replied, "Everything I have written seems like straw by comparison with what I have seen and what has been revealed to me."[21] As one scholar has noted, "straw" is a conventional image for the literal sense of Scripture. In his encounter with ultimate reality, Thomas approached the very object of theology, the reality to which the words of faith point but cannot grasp.[22] For Thomas, this stepping into the silence of the unfathomable God was not a departure from an academic life of abstractions but rather the earthly culmination of his unique fusion of logic and devotion, both harmoniously mingled in the *Summa*'s graceful architectonic and embodied in his Eucharistic hymns.[23]

Because Thomas's theological vision is balanced with the way of mystery and prayer, proofs of his personal sanctity cannot be divorced from the nature of his theological reflection. Despite its high precision and lucid clarity, theology remains a struggle of both mind and heart for the infinite mystery of God's light, the mystery which one does not master but adores. Torrell affirms that "growing reflection on the faith was a path to sanctity for Thomas," and that theology overflows into the spiritual life and into mysticism.[24] More precisely, Aquinas's mystical theology, that is, the apparatus of the mysteries of faith itself, including the gifts of the Spirit, is a branch of *sacra doctrina* as defined in *ST* I, q. 1, a. 1, that sacred teaching which exceeds human reason in its origin and nature.[25] For Aquinas, theological and

[20] *Ferrua*, pp. 73–74.

[21] The story is told by Tocco and found in *Ferrua*, pp. 318–20. See *Tugwell*, pp. 265–66.

[22] See Tugwell's interpretation of the event in *Tugwell*, pp. 266–67.

[23] "Adoro te devote, latens Deitas" ("Devoutly I adore you, hidden Deity") expresses this union, as does "Verbum Supernum" and "Pange Lingua." Aquinas's hymns also support the view that his mysticism is Eucharistic and thus Christological, for the soul is called from a participation in the passion of Christ to mystical union.

[24] Jean-Pierre Torrell, *Saint Thomas Aquinas: Vol.1: The Person and His Work*, trans. Robert Royal (Washington, D.C.: The Catholic University of America Press, 1996), p. xxi.

[25] *Sacra doctrina*, or sacred teaching, comprises the revealed content of Christian faith necessary for salvation. Although it does contain some truths accessible to human reason, *sacra doctrina* is provided as a remedy for human frailty, and proves necessary due to the brevity of human life. Human reason is used within sacred doctrine to provide clarity, as well as extrinsic and probable arguments. See *ST* I, q. 1, a.1; *ST* I, q. 1, a. 8, ad 1.

mystical contemplation coalesce in the unifying "contemplation of the truth of God," which encompasses the moral virtues, the philosophical and theological contemplation of God's effects, and the actual contemplation of the truth of God.[26] In the strictest sense, contemplation is not the struggle towards the light (theology) but a penetrating, direct gazing of the mind at the truth, which culminates in love.[27] All types of contemplation, however, are united in their first principle, and fulfill the intellect in view of the truth of God.[28] Thus, theology and the spiritual life are interdependent in Thomas's writings: theology is the essential condition of the spiritual life, and the spiritual life gives theology its guiding themes, its longing for the eternal light and awareness of its limits as the *theologia viatorum.*

THE "SUFFERING" OF DIVINE THINGS

In contrast to the speculative knowledge of God possessed by theologians, connatural knowledge of divine things springs from the supernatural gift of wisdom, which delivers an affective, experiential contact with God as the result of charity.[29] It is by the gift of wisdom that the believer comes to "suffer" the things of God, to taste the sweetness of His inner life, and to enjoy the incomparable delights of the contemplative life.[30] As a sensitivity to divine things based on connaturality, wisdom is an experiential love for the reality

---

[26] This dovetailing of religious and mystical contemplation occurs in his treatise on the Contemplative Life (*ST* II–II, qq. 179–82). See *ST* II–II, q. 180, a. 4: ". . . ad vitam contemplativam pertinet aliquid dupliciter: uno modo, principaliter; alio modo, secondario vel dispositive. Principaliter . . . pertinet contemplatio divinae veritatis, quia huiusmodi contemplatio est finis totius humanae vitae . . . Quae quidem in futura vita erit perfecta, quando videbimus eum "facie ad faciem"; unde et perfectos beatos faciet. Nunc autem contemplatio divinae veritatis competit nobis imperfecte . . . unde per eam fit nobis quaedam inchoatio beatitudinis. . . . Unde Philosophus *X Ethic.* in contemplatione optimi intelligibilis ponit ultimam felicitatem hominis. . . ."

[27] *ST* II–II, q. 179, a. 3, ad 1 and ad 3.

[28] *ST* II–II, q. 179, a. 4, ad 4.

[29] *ST* II–II, q. 45, a. 2; cf. *ST* II–II, q. 45, a. 4: "Dicendum quod sapientia quae est donum Spiritus Sancti, sicut dictum est, facit rectitudinem iudicii circa res divinas, vel per regulas divinas de aliis, ex quadam connaturalitate sive unione ad divina. Quae quidem est per caritatem. . . ."

[30] "Since, then, the contemplative life consists chiefly in the contemplation of God, of which charity is the motive . . . it follows that there is delight in the contemplative life, not only by reason of the contemplation itself, but also by reason of the Divine love. . . . Hence it is written (Ps. 33.9): 'O taste and see that the Lord is sweet'" (*ST* II–II, q. 180, a. 7). Cf. *ST* II–II, q. 97, a. 2, ad 2; *ST* II–II, q. 162, a. 3, ad 1, and other texts that will be reviewed.

known, an affective experience of love and spiritual sweetness which enables the just man to know God and creatures from the divine standpoint. And it is charity that joins taste or affectivity to the knowledge of wisdom, adding the experience of delight and spiritual sweetness.[31] In addition to the affective quality of wisdom which lends an "experimental" or "quasi-experimental"[32] character to the mystical experience proper to wisdom, Aquinas views the idea of "suffering" divine things through the lens of different types of knowledge:

> [W]isdom denotes a certain rectitude of judgment according to the Eternal Law. Now rectitude of judgment is twofold: first, on account of perfect use of reason; secondly, on account of a certain connaturality with the matter which one has to judge. . . . Accordingly . . . it belongs to wisdom as a gift of the Holy Ghost to judge aright about [divine things] on account of connaturality with them: thus Dionysius says (*Div. Nom.* ii) that "Hierotheus is perfect in divine things, for he not only learns, but suffers divine things."[33]

While wisdom is essentially in the intellect, it differs from the wisdom of philosophy in presupposing love as its principle,[34] which bathes the object in an intuitive light. Aquinas's understanding of the gift of wisdom as a dimension of experiential love of God, or "experimental" knowledge of God, then, is grounded in his division of the types of contemplation and wisdom.

Contemplatio is a term used analogously by Thomas to refer to three levels of intellectual vision: natural, revealed contemplation ("acquired" contemplation), and supernatural or "mystical" contemplation. In all cases, contemplation refers to divine truth and its related effects, and is the work of the speculative intellect.[35] Natural contemplation is the work of the philosophers, and ascends from creatures to grasp metaphysical truths about God. Revealed contemplation is the fruit of theological study, and attains God in Himself

---

[31] *ST* II-II, q. 45, a. 2, and ad 1: ". . . Augustinus loquitur de sapientia quantum ad suam causam. Ex qua etiam sumitur nomen sapientiae, secundum quod saporem quemdam importat." See *Scriptum super Sententiis* (Paris: Lethielleux, 1956), Bk. III, q. 35, a. 2, qla. 1, ad 3.

[32] A just man, Aquinas says, possesses a "quasi-experimental" knowledge of the divine Persons in his soul: I *Sent.*, d. 14, q. 2, a. 2, ad 3; I *Sent.*, d. 15, q. 2, ad 5; *ST* I, q. 43, a. 5, ad 2. A good study which proves both historically and contextually that Aquinas designated "quasi-experimental" knowledge as *affective*, and not as cognitive, is the article of John Dedek: "*Quasi Experimentalis Cognitio*: A Historical Approach to the Meaning of St. Thomas" *Theological Studies* 22 (1961), pp. 357–90.

[33] *ST* II-II, q. 45, a. 2. See *ST* I, q. 1, a. 6, ad 3.

[34] *ST* II-II, q. 45, a. 2; III *Sent.*, d. 35, q. 2, a. 1.

[35] *ST* II-II, qq. 179–82.

from revealed principles, but through the imperfect medium of faith.[36] Mystical contemplation, the preserve of those sanctified souls infused with charity, also attains God's inner life, but through a supernatural mode. Both the principle and term of this contemplation is in the appetite, for charity animates the mind and establishes immediate union with the object, and the ultimate perfection of the contemplative life is delight in the object loved.[37] Finally, the beatific vision, or the science of the blessed, is the knowledge of God through His own essence.[38]

For an understanding of Aquinas's mystical thought, an understanding of the divisions of wisdom and contemplation are central. Some scholars confuse mystical and natural contemplation in the claim that Aquinas's metaphysical discussions of God as *Ipsum Esse* are in fact apophatic mystical meditations.[39] Both Maritain and Garrigou-Lagrange, however, clearly grasp

[36] On the distinction between the contemplation of the *philosophi* and the *sancti*, see, e.g. I *Sent.*, prol.: "Contemplatio autem Dei est duplex. Una per creaturas, quae imperfecta est, ratione iam dicta, in qua contemplatione Philosophus, *X Ethic.*, cap. ix, felicitatem contemplativam posuit, quae tamen est felicitas viae. . . . Est alia Dei contemplatio, qua videtur immediate per suam essentiam; et haec perfecta est, quae erit in patrie et est homini possibilis secundum fidei suppositionem. . . ." See *ST* I, q. 1. a. 6; III *Sent.*, d. 35, q. 1, a. 2. On the division of theology into natural and revealed, see *In Librum Boethii de Trinitate*, ed. Decker (Leiden: E. J. Brill, 1959), q. 5, a. 4, ad 7 (Hereafter cited as *In de Trin.*). Although theology grasps God in Himself, it is not a quidditative knowledge, since Aquinas holds that in the present life it is impossible to know the essence of immaterial substances by either natural knowledge or by revelation (*In de Trin.* q. 6, a. 3; cf. John Wippel, "Quidditative Knowledge of God" in John Wippel, *Metaphysical Themes in Thomas Aquinas* [*Studies in Philosophy and the History of Philosophy*, vol. 10] (Washington, D.C.: The Catholic University of America Press, 1984), pp. 215–41.

[37] *ST* II-II, q. 180, a. 1: ". . . vita contemplativa illorum esse dicitur qui principaliter intendunt contemplationi veritatis. Intentio autem est actus voluntatis. . . . Et ideo vita contemplativa quantum ad ipsam essentiam actionis, pertinet ad intellectum; quantum autem ad id quod movet ad exercendam talem operationem, pertinet ad voluntatem, quae moves omnes alias potentias, et etiam intellectum ad suum actum. . . . Et propter hoc Gregorius constituit vitam contemplativam in 'caritate Dei,' inquantum scilicet aliquis ex dilectione Dei inardescit ad eius pulchritudinem conspiciendam. Et quia unusquisque delectatur cum adeptus fuerit id quod amat, ideo vita contemplativa terminatur ad delectationem, quae est in affectu, ex qua etiam amor intenditur." On the immediate union with God effected by grace, see I *Sent.*, d. 14, q. 2, a. 1; I *Sent.*, d. 14, q. 3; II *Sent.*, d. 1, q. 2, a. 2 and ad 4; *ST* I, q. 38, a. 1.

[38] *ST* I, q. 2 ad 3: "The object of the heavenly vision will be the First Truth seen in itself, according to 1 John 3:2: 'We know that when He shall appear, we shall be like to Him: because we shall see Him as He is. . . .'" On the impossibility of the wayfarer's quidditative knowledge of God, see, for example: *ST* I, q. 12, a. 11; *ST* I-II, q. 5, a. 3 (See n. 17 above).

[39] William Johnston implies this association in his book *Mystical Theology*: "The central problem of Greek philosophy—as it is the central problem of *mystical theology*—was the celebrated paradox of *the one and the many*. . . . How do we reconcile

Aquinas's distinction between an intellectual view of the First Cause, accompanied by wonder,[40] and infused contemplation, which operates according to the superhuman mode of the gifts of the Spirit.[41] The metaphysical gaze on divine truth stands "at the summit of the created world, and from that vantage point, it looks upon the inaccessible entrance towards which all created perfections converge."[42] Mystical contemplation, on the other hand, attains God's nature and selfhood and thus is the partial fulfillment of the experience of faith, and an affirmation of the promise that grace makes us sharers in the divine nature.[43]

The gift of wisdom, like the Aristotelian virtue of wisdom, has three functions, all of which permeate the interior life.[44] First, the gift of wisdom *contemplates* divine reality, for the Spirit moves the intellect to penetrate the deep things of God.[45] Because the motive and result of contemplation is charity (the love of God above all things), the process is one of ceaseless interaction of intellect and will, manifesting itself in an intuitive, loving gaze on divine beauty.[46] Thomas calls this act a "sight of the Beginning,"[47] a

---

the experience of unity with the experience of multiplicity? . . ." (W. Johnston, *Mystical Theology* [London: Harper Collins, 1995], pp. 47–48). Johnston goes on to describe the real distinction between existence and essence and their identity in God, and the inaccessibility of God's nature through human cognition. Richard Woods locates Aquinas's mystical thought in his "threefold way" (*via affirmativa, negativa* and *supereminentia*) in the attempt to illumine Aquinas's Dionysian heritage (Richard Woods, *Mysticism and Prophecy: The Dominican Tradition* [New York: Orbis, 1998], pp. 67–72).

[40] See, e.g., *ST* I, q.1, a. 6.

[41] See Réginald Garrigou-Lagrange, *Christian Perfection and Contemplation according to St. Thomas Aquinas and St. John of the Cross*, trans. Thomas Doyle (St. Louis, Missouri: Herder, 1954), pp. 221–23; p. 323, no. 44: "It would be a gross error to confound this infused contemplation with the philosophical meditation in which one thinks that the divine essence surpasses all our concepts." See Jacques Maritain, *The Degrees of Knowledge*, trans. Gerald B. Phelan (New York: Charles Scribner's Sons, 1959), pp. 248–51.

[42] Maritain, *The Degrees of Knowledge*, p. 251.

[43] See *ST* III, q. 62, a. 1: ". . . grace is nothing else than a certain shared similitude to the divine nature." See I *Sent.*, d. 14, q. 2, a. 1; I *Sent.*, d. 14, q. 3; I *Sent.*, d. 18, q. 3, a. 6; *ST* I, q. 38, a.1.

[44] For the three functions of the gift of wisdom, see *ST* II-II, q. 45, a. 1. The three functions are outlined well in *St. Thomas Aquinas: Summa Theologiae* [Blackfriars ed.] (New York: McGraw-Hill, 1974), vol. 35, appendix 4, pp. 200–02. Henceforth, all references to this edition of the *Summa* or to appendices therein, will be cited as *Blackfriars*, with appropriate pagination.

[45] *ST* II-II, q. 45, a. 3, ad 3.

[46] *ST* II-II, q. 180, a. 1. See *ST* II-II, q. 180, a. 6 on Aquinas's interpretation of Dionysius's threefold movement of the soul in mystical contemplation.

[47] *ST* II-II 180, q. 1, ad 2, where Aquinas quotes Gregory's phrase, "visio primi principii."

"sight of God's beauty,"[48] the "contemplation of divine truth"[49] or the "contemplation of divine things in themselves."[50]

The second function of the gift of wisdom is *judgment* of both divine and creaturely things, from the viewpoint of an affective experience of divine things.[51] In its function of speculative judgment, the intellect judges, through internal experience, the divine attributes, such as God's goodness, mercy or justice. As one scholar puts it, the soul becomes convinced of God's power because "it has been brushed by that power and sometimes almost crushed by [it]," or the soul understands God's peace by being immersed in that peace.[52] In its practical function, the intellect judges human actions in relation to the soul's participation in ultimate goodness, through tasting the mystery of God and drawing from the well of divine friendship.

Wisdom's third function is to put an *order* into things.[53] Thus, wisdom aligns the thoughts and actions of persons to ultimate beatitude according to priority and posteriority, and generates the peace which is the tranquillity of order.[54] Regarding all the functions of wisdom, it is by appreciating and entering into divine love that one is disposed to operate under the impulse of the Spirit, and exercise this supernatural gift.

MODE OF UNION WITH GOD

Through contemplation, God is present to the soul not in the order of substance or causality, but in an immaterial union of operation which is the intellectual act. While He is present to the whole of nature by essence, presence and power in a union of causality,[55] His personal gift of love to man is a Self-communication and call to share in His inner life, through becoming a new creation in grace.[56] In addition to willing the good of the rational being's

---

[48] Ibid.

[49] Ibid.

[50] *ST* II-II, q. 45, a. 3.

[51] *ST* II-II, q. 45, a. 2.

[52] *Blackfriars*, vol. 35, appendix 4, p. 201.

[53] "Sapientis est ordinare," *In Duodecim Libros Metaphysicorum Aristotelis Expositio* (Turin: Marietti, 1964), Proemium. Cf. *ST* I, q. 1; *ST* II-II, q. 45, a.1.

[54] Augustine's definition of peace as the tranquillity of order is found in *ST* I, q. 103, a. 2, obj. 3; *ST* II-II, q. 29, a. 1, ad 1; *ST* II-II, q. 45, a. 6. In the final text, Aquinas says that the seventh beatitude corresponds to the gift of wisdom, precisely in the fact that the role of the peacemaker is to create an order.

[55] *ST* I, q. 43, a. 3.

[56] See, e.g., *ST* I-II, q. 110, a. 4; *ST* I, q. 93, a. 4, ad 7–8.

nature, God wills His very self, His eternal goodness, to us,[57] so that He comes to dwell within the soul (*habitare in ea cum sicut in templo suo*), as the known is within the knower and the beloved within the lover.[58] Of the grace-relationship Thomas says,

> God is said to love all creatures in that he bestows on them the goodness of their natures. But there is love literally and completely, as being like friendship, when he loves a creature not as an artisan loves his work, but . . . as a friend loves a friend; a love by which God draws the creature into the fellowship of his own joy, so that the creature's glory and blessedness become those by which God himself is blessed.[59]

God calls the creature into glory, then, through the unconditional gift of Himself,[60] for love is the first gift we give to the one we love, and love is the first gift through which all gifts are given.[61] It should be noted that in positing a gulf between God's mode of presence to man and to nature, Aquinas is not denying the immanent causality of God in creatures through His constant willing of their being and operations, but rather distinguishing *non*rational "imaging" of God from *rational* "participation" in the divine life through the human acts of knowing and loving, which are the highest conceivable imitations of God.

While contemplation and the exercise of supernatural wisdom are intellectual operations, both start and end in charity and thus in the appetitive power. Since God can be loved better than He can be known in this life,[62] the affective union with God is more noble and yet more mysterious than the cognitive union, and is the most intimate.[63] As an effect of divine friendship, the connatural operation

---

[57] *ST* I-II, q. 110, a. 1: "According to that special love God draws the rational creature above the condition of his nature to share in the divine good. On the basis of such a love God is said to love someone in a literal sense (*simpliciter*), because in this love God wills to the creature literally the eternal good which is himself." See *ST* I-II, q. 26, a. 4 and ad 4; II *Sent.*, d. 26, q. 1, a. 1, ad 2.

[58] See *ST* I, q. 43, a. 3 on the indwelling of the Trinity in the soul: "There is one common way in which God is in all things by essence, power and presence, as a cause in the effects that share in the perfection of the cause. Over and above this common way, there is one special way that belongs to the rational creature, in whom God is said to be present as the known in the knower and the beloved in the lover. And because in knowing and loving the rational creature by its act reaches God himself, according to this special way God is said not only to be in the rational creature, but also to dwell there as in his temple."

[59] II *Sent.*, d. 26, q. 1, a. 1, ad 2. The translation is from *Blackfriars*, vol. 31, appendix 2, no. 14, p. 189.

[60] *ST* I, q. 38, a. 1.

[61] See *ST* I, q. 38, a. 2.

[62] *ST* I, q. 8, a. 3.

[63] *ST* I-II, q. 28, a. 1, ad 3: "Knowledge is perfected by the thing known being united, through its likeness, to the knower. But the effect of love is that the thing itself which is loved is in a way united to the lover. Consequently the union caused by love is closer than that which is caused by knowledge." See *ST* I-II, q. 27, a. 2, ad 2; *ST* II-II, q. 45, a. 3, ad 1.

of infused wisdom attains an immediate union with God, but is nonetheless an obscure, indirect knowledge of His essence, for it also rests on faith.[64] Like John of the Cross's "secret wisdom" infused into the soul through love,[65] Aquinas's divine contemplation is free from imagery, and passive not with respect to bodily forms but only with respect to the promptings of the Spirit.

In a text on the divine missions, Aquinas deftly combines the notions of the presence of God, the "experimental" or affective knowledge which is the Gift of Wisdom, and participation in the nature of God:

> The soul by grace is made like to God . . . and since the Holy Spirit is love, the soul is made like the Holy Spirit by the gift of charity. . . . The Son is the Word—not any kind of word, but a Word breathing forth love . . . knowledge with love . . . and that enlightenment of the intellect . . . breaks forth out into love. . . . And so Augustine says, "the Son is sent when he is known and perceived by anyone." Now perception denotes an experimental knowedge, and this is Wisdom, properly speaking.[66]

The language of *cognitio experimentalis* has received diverse interpretations by Thomistic scholars, but Thomas clearly says that the knowledge of the Son is followed by the love of charity, which gives experimental knowledge an *affective* meaning, not a cognitive meaning of being "quasi-perceptual."[67] John Dedek argues persuasively that the "quasi-experimental" knowledge of God attained by the gift of wisdom is experimental in a cer-

---

[64] *ST* I-II, q. 65, aa. 2–3; *ST* I-II, q. 66, aa. 2 and 6; *ST* II-II, q. 23, aa. 7–8, for example.

[65] John of the Cross gives several reasons for the "secrecy" of the wisdom which is divine contemplation: the wisdom is nonconceptual and infused into the soul through love; its effects are ineffable and not clothed in sensory or imaginative imagery; and it has the characteristic of "hiding the soul within itself," engulfing the person in a "secret abyss." See John of the Cross, *Dark Night of the Soul*, Book II, chaps. 17–18 (in *The Collected Works of St. John of the Cross*, eds. Kavanaugh and Rodriguez, trans. K. Kavanaugh (Washington, D.C.: Institute of Carmelite Studies Publications, 1973), pp. 368–73.

[66] *In De Trin.* Bk. IX, chap. 10. Many medieval writers, as also John of the Cross, are known to define contemplation as a "loving knowledge."

[67] On the debate among scholars this century, see Dedek, "*Quasi Experimentalis Cognitio*," especially pp. 383–85. Aquinas calls the knowledge of wisdom "quasi-experimental," Dedek argues, not to distinguish it from ordinary discursive knowledge, but to transfer the proper sense of *experientia* in the senses to its locus in the will, where an act of the appetite delights in its object: "Since the act of an appetitive power is a kind of inclination to the thing itself, the application of the appetitive power to the thing, insofar as it cleaves to it, gets by a kind of similitude, the name of sense, since, as it were, it acquires direct knowledge of the thing to which it cleaves, insofar as it takes complacency in it" [*ST* I-II, q. 15, a. 1] (p. 385).

tain sense (*quodammodo*)—in as much as it is joined to an *affective* experience of love and taste.[68]

Supernatural wisdom thus attains to a more intimate union with God than is possible through the mere virtue of wisdom, transforming the bitter into the sweet and labor into rest in human acts,[69] and springing from love, its effect is to melt the hardness of hearts.[70] While casting its rays across the soul's path, wisdom acts like the variety of colors reflected through a prism. It arrays a spectrum of realizations from a bright unknown world, extending and illumining one's consciousness, sometimes deliciously, sometimes painfully, in the process of revealing the divine mystery.

PASSIVITY AS RECEPTIVITY TO THE SPIRIT

Aquinas's doctrine of the infused virtues and gifts stands in stark contrast to the modern idea of mysticism as a set of supernatural experiences. The latter idea has been traced to Teresa of Avila[71] and the general cultural shift in the West away from mystical theology and the objective participation in the mystery of Christ, to an interest in individuals' subjective feeling states. The gifts are not transitory experiences but rather habits which perfect the infused virtues and render the soul more docile to the promptings (*instinctus*) of the Holy Spirit.[72] Two points stand out in Aquinas's study of the gifts in this connection: first, his insistence on the soul's passivity and receptivity in the texts on the gift of wisdom, and second, the difference between the apophatic emptying that is required for mystical ascent for Aquinas and the engrossment in subjective, supernatural phenomena that dominates modern accounts of mysticism and masquerades as interiority.

Regarding the first issue (the soul's receptivity to the Holy Spirit as an effect of the gift of wisdom), an explanation of the meaning of the "divine mode" as applied to the operation of the Gifts of the Spirit, is in order. Regarding this original teaching of Thomas,[73] various scholars have noted the similarity between Aquinas's teaching on the soul's surrender to the impulses of divine grace and John of the Cross's notion that higher mystical states are

[68] Ibid., p. 385.

[69] *ST* II-II, q. 45, a. 3, ad 1–3.

[70] On the four effects of love as a passion, see *ST* I-II, q. 38, a. 5.

[71] See Andrew Louth, "Mysticism" in *A Dictionary of Christian Spirituality*, ed. Gordon S. Wakefield (London: SCM Press, 1983), p. 273.

[72] *ST* I-II, q. 68, a. 3: "The gifts of the Holy Spirit are habits (or essentially supernatural, permanent qualities) whereby man is perfected to obey readily the Holy Spirit." Cf. *ST* I-II, q. 68, a. 2, ad 1; III *Sent.*, d. 34, q. 1, a. 1.

[73] On the development of this notion of docility to the Spirit, see *Blackfriars*, vol. 24, appendix 4.

marked by an increased passivity, occurring in the stage of ascent called the passive night of the spirit.[74] The passivity of the soul with respect to the movement of the Holy Spirit flows from the superhuman or divine mode of perfection of the Gifts: "In the gifts of the Holy Spirit, the position of the human mind is of one moved rather than of a mover."[75] And:

> The mode of an act is determined by its proper measure. Since the Gifts are for the sake of a superhuman mode of action, their activity must therefore be measured by a standard that is different from that of human virtue. This measure is the Divinity itself, in which man participates in his own mode so that he no longer acts humanly, but as one who has become God by participation.[76]

The type of inspiration is characterised as one of operating grace, by which the soul receives with docility the direction of the Spirit, which the soul could not produce by its personal efforts merely aided by grace.[77] Garrigou-Lagrange illumines the issue of the soul's docility under the influence of operative grace:

> When the divine predominates in an act or a state to such an extent that this act and this state cannot be produced by our industry or human activity aided by the actual grace required for the exercise of the virtues, then that state is called passive. For example, when the wind blows with such force that a boat advances without the necessity of rowing, its progress does not depend on the activity of the oarsmen.[78]

---

[74] On this comparison, see Leonard McCann, *The Doctrine of the Void as Propounded by St. John of the Cross in his Major Prose Works and as Viewed in Light of Thomistic Principles* (Toronto: Basilian Press, 1953) pp. 123–32; Jacques Maritain, *The Degrees of Knowledge*, pp. 343–44, quoting from John's *Spiritual Canticle*: "Even as the breeze stirs the hair and causes it to flutter upon the neck, even so does the breeze of the Holy Spirit move and excite strong love that it may make flights to God; for without this Divine wind, which moves the faculties to the practice of Divine love, the virtues work not. . . ." He says that John's teaching here echoes that of Aquinas and identifies this docility to the Spirit with the stage of spiritual betrothal in John's *Spiritual Canticle* (p. 343). Maritain also notes Teresa of Avila's connection between mystical ascent and passivity, noting that for Teresa, the "prayer of recollection" is still only "acquired" contemplation, since it follows the natural mode, in that it is still active, and not passive (p. 280).

[75] *ST* II-II, q. 52, a. 2, ad 1.

[76] III *Sent.*, d. 34, q. 1, a. 3.

[77] Garrigou-Lagrange, *Christian Perfection*, pp. 325–26, no. 51, in reference to *ST* I-II, q. 111, a. 2: "Hence in that effect in which our mind is moved and does not move, but in which God is the sole mover, the operation is attributed to God, and it is with reference to this that we speak of operating grace."

[78] Garrigou-Lagrange, *Christian Perfection*, p. 326. This mode differs in order, not degree, from the human mode, which accompanies the exercise of the infused virtues. In the latter case, divine inspiration operates like a breeze facilitating the labor of the oarsman (p. 326).

While the human exercise of virtue takes *reason* as its measure, man's participation in divinity confers a higher measure in the case of the Gifts, namely, the Spirit Itself. By imparting a divine mode to human activity, the Gifts exceed even the infused virtues, perfecting them by means of their elevated measure.[79] However, human reason and free will continue to operate during the exercise of the Gifts, since God moves each being according to its mode, says Thomas.[80] An analogy helps to show that the passivity with respect to the Spirit is not to be understood as "pure" passivity, but rather in the Aristotelian sense of "receiving," presupposing natural powers: Aquinas says that receptivity to the Spirit is the fruit of the Gifts, just as appetites' obedience to reason results from practising the moral virtues.[81] In both cases, reason and free will are operative, though under the influence of a higher source. Just as the moral virtues make the appetites obedient to reason, so the Gifts make the intellect and will amenable to the movement of the Spirit, and capable of performing the works called the "beatitudes."[82]

Connected to Aquinas's insistence on passivity at the higher reaches of spiritual development is the relative absence of supernatural phenomena in his accounts of mystical ascent. From the soul's special receptivity follows a gentle interiority that generates a deep peace, even in the midst of troubles, which radiates to others.[83] The gift of wisdom thus corresponds to the beatitude of the peacemakers, who contemplate all events within the hidden face of God, and communicate the tranquillity of order in proportion to their degree of charity. Far from a preoccupation with paranormal states or even with the charismata, Aquinas's ruling concern is the attainment of the freedom of surrender to God's action in the soul, and the soul's entrance into God's intimate inner life.[84]

In scholastic language, "sanctifying grace" is nobler than "gratuitous graces" or the charismata[85] on three counts, all of which involve the idea that

---

[79] See *ST* I, q. 34, a. 1; See *ST* I, q. 36, a. 3. Although the gifts exceed the infused virtues according to their divine *mode* (which confers passivity to the Spirit), they do not exceed the infused virtues in their nature. See *ST* I-II, q. 68, a. 8: "As the intellectual virtues . . . regulate the moral virtues, so the theological virtues . . . regulate the gifts of the Holy Spirit."

[80] *ST* II-II, q. 52, a. 1: "God moves each being in accordance with its mode. But it is proper to the rational creature to be moved to action through the enquiry of reason; and this enquiry is called counsel. . . ."

[81] For this analogy, see *ST* I-II, q. 68, aa. 3–5.

[82] See *ST* I-II, q. 70, a. 2 on the beatitudes.

[83] *ST* II-II, q. 45, a. 6.

[84] On this subject, see *In Librum Beati Dionysii de divinibus nominibus expositio*, ed. C. Pera (Turin: Marietti, 1950), chap. 7, lect. 4; I *Sent.*, d. 8, q.1, a. 1, ad 5.

[85] *ST* I-II, q. 111, a. 5. In *ST* I-II, q. 111, a. 1, Aquinas lists the charismata as found in 1 Cor. 12:8–10.

sanctifying grace unites a person immediately to God: This grace is at once more necessary, useful, and permanent than are graces *gratis datae*, he says.[86] The mystical life flourishes in the ardor of love, tasting and suffering the hidden life of God through an apophatic emptying of self. Aquinas says that the fusion of the soul to God, produced by love, "takes place when the soul, leaving all things and forgetting itself, is united to the splendors of the divine glory and . . . is illumined in the splendid depths of divine Wisdom."[87] This entry into what Dionysius termed "the transluminous darkness"[88] occurs through prayer and mortification, not through phenomenologically observed esoteric psychological states.[89] Aquinas sometimes even uses the term "dissolution" with respect to the soul's union with God,[90] and would thus agree with Turner's statement that "experientialism is . . . the 'positivism' of Christian spirituality. It abhors the experiential vacuum of the apophatic, rushing to fill it with the plenum of the psychologistic."[91]

For Aquinas, the apophatic element is found in the contemplation which joins us experimentally to a hidden God, Who discloses Himself through the new modality of the gifts and joins us to Himself connaturally through charity. Aquinas rejects the intellectual certitude so often craved by religious fundamentalists and asserts that the divine presence in the soul cannot be known with certainty in this life, but only through certain signs, which confer a security of the affections.[92] The apophatic element is also found in Aquinas's agreement with Dionysius's rejection of physical imagery and discursive reasoning in the three movements of contemplation.[93]

As well, Aquinas's apophaticism is located in his adoption of Augustine's and Dionysius's threefold way of purification, illumination and perfection[94]

[86] On this topic, see Réginald Garrigou-Lagrange, *Grace: Commentary on the "Summa Theologica" of St. Thomas, Ia IIae, q. 109–14*, trans. The Dominican Nuns (St. Louis, Missouri: Herder, 1952) pp. 157–81.

[87] *In Librum Beati Dionysii de divinibus nominibus expositio*, chap. 7, lect. 14.

[88] "Mystical Theology," in *Pseudo-Dionysius Areopagite: The Divine Names and Mystical Theology*, ed. and trans. John Jones (Milwaukee, Wisconsin: Marquette University Press, 1980).

[89] In this sense, Aquinas bears some similarity to the author of the *Cloud of Unknowing*, for the latter also denounces the varieties of what Denys Turner calls "experientialism." See Denys Turner, *The Darkness of God: Negativity in Christian Mysticism* (Cambridge: Cambridge University Press, 1995), p. 259.

[90] *ST* II-II, q. 24, a. 9

[91] Turner, *The Darkness of God: Negativity in Christian Mysticism*, p. 259.

[92] *ST* I-II, q. 112, a. 5 on whether a man can know that he has grace.

[93] *ST* II-II, q. 180, a. 6.

[94] See Pseudo-Dionysius, "The Ecclesiastical Hierarchy," in *Pseudo-Dionysii Aeropagitae De Caelesti Hierarchia*, ed. P. Henddrix (Leiden: Brill, 1959), chap. 5, *passim*. Like Dionysius, Aquinas applies the distinction to the diaconate, priesthood and episcopate (IV *Sent.*, d. 4, q.1, a.1).

which dovetails into his analysis of the three progressive degrees of charity exercised by the sanctified soul. The first stage in charity is exercised by beginners, whose main effort is to strive against sin (the purgative way). The second stage is practiced by those making progress in the virtues by the light of faith (the illuminative way). The third stage belongs to the perfect, who live in union with God through charity (the unitive way).[95] These three stages constitute the infancy, adolescence and adulthood of the spiritual life, and denote a gradual increase in the soul's passive purification and docility to the movement of the Holy Spirit.

Although Thomas lacks John of the Cross's elaborate apparatus of the active and passive nights of sense and spirit, his direct correspondence of the degrees of charity with the degrees in the moral virtues, as well as in the gifts and in contemplation,[96] derives from a similar insight. In both cases, the soul voids itself of all possible obstacles to complete union with God, and ascends from the level of self-interested passions[97] to complete similitude with God (and self-forgetfulness) through an initial mastery of the "social" virtues to a habit of the "perfecting" virtues and finally to the attainment of the "perfect" virtues.

One's success in negotiating this way of perfection is directly proportionate to one's degree of charity, which in turn corresponds to one's docility to the direction of the Spirit through the gifts. In this way, the infused virtues take on a divine character: prudence, for example, counts as nothing the things of the world, while the virtue of temperance neglects the needs of the body.[98] The radical exclusion of everything that would hinder the soul from belonging completely to God appears with equal clarity on the level of fraternal charity. In the most perfect degree of charity towards one's neighbor, one forsakes not only external goods, but also one's spiritual goods, and one's life if necessary.[99]

In conclusion, Aquinas's mystical theology can be said to labor under a double purification or negation. First, among his theological statements we find that the *intellect* labors under a darkness of "learned ignorance,"[100] to

[95] *ST* II-II, q. 24, a. 9; II *Sent.* d. 9, q. 2, ad 8.

[96] Aquinas speaks of the degrees of charity in *ST* II-II, q. 24, a. 9; of the degrees of the moral virtues in *ST* I-II, q. 61, a. 5, and of the movements or varieties of contemplation in *ST* II-II, q. 180, a. 6.

[97] The passions are progressively checked and silenced by these various virtues: *ST* I-II, q. 61, a. 5 and ad 2.

[98] *ST* I-II, q. 61, a. 5.

[99] *ST* II-II, q. 184, a. 2, ad 3, quoting *2 Corinthians* 12:15.

[100] The notion of *docta ignorantia* or "learned ignorance" (such that we fail to know God as He is in Himself) was developed in the fifteenth century by Nicholas of Cusa; and fourteenth century mystical writers such as the anonymous author of *The Cloud of Unknowing* also based their apophatic brand of mystical prayer on the unknowability of God, and the consequent failure of speech in reference to Him.

the effect that God cannot be known *sicuti est* even through the revelation of grace, so that we are united in this life with God as with something unknown to us.[101] Aquinas is equally insistent that infused contemplation is more perfect in proportion as it is freed from all sensible imagery.[102] Second, there is the progressive voiding of the *will* in its project of self-denial,[103] on two levels: first, in the self-motivated active asceticism of the way of purgation, where the gift of knowledge creates a night of the senses by illuminating the vanity of all creatures;[104] second, in the exercise of the higher, contemplative gifts of the Spirit, namely, understanding and wisdom, which render the soul progressively more passive and open to spiritual trials and consolations. In the gift of understanding, the mysteries of faith are penetrated by a supernatural light, strengthening faith, opening the soul to God's infinite grandeur and the depths of human wretchedness, and pointing to the excess of divine intelligibility.[105] In the gift of wisdom, the Spirit guides one's perception and ordering of human affairs, and unites the soul by experimental knowledge to the most exalted mysteries of faith.[106] This night of the spirit culminates in a participation in Christ's passion such that it experiences a divine peace and order amid tribulation, and wishes for complete self-transformation, rejoicing in infirmities and persecutions for Christ, and desiring only union and dissolution in Christ.[107]

One can begin to illumine the apophatic dimension of Aquinas's theology of spiritual transformation through its metaphysical moorings in the concept of love, which involve a dialectic of presence and absence of the beloved. Love both relates the appetite to the object in itself[108] and yet as an end or good which moves the will and draws it to itself,[109] the loved object escapes complete analysis, such that the unknown is still loved in the beloved.[110] The

---

[101] See *ST* I, q. 12, a. 13, ad 1; *ST* I, q. 13, a. 1, ad 2.

[102] *ST* II-II, q. 15, a. 3.

[103] In his theology of the infused virtues and supernatural gifts, Aquinas both complements the *via negativa* tradition and lays the theological framework for John of the Cross's development of the notion of active and passive nights of sense and spirit (which void the soul of inordinate desires).

[104] *ST* II-II, q. 9, a. 4.

[105] *ST* II-II, q. 8 *et passim*.

[106] *ST* II-II, q. 45, aa. 4–5.

[107] *ST* II-II, q. 45, a. 6 explains the connection between the gift of wisdom and the beatitude of the peacemakers; the text on dissolution is *ST* II-II, q. 24, a. 9.

[108] As opposed to proportioning the object to the intellect's power, although some initial knowledge is required for love; see *ST* II-II, q. 23, a. 6, ad 1.

[109] See *ST* I-II, q. 26, a. 2: ". . . the appetible object moves the appetite, introducing itself, as it were, into its intention. . . ."

[110] See *ST* I-II, q. 27, a. 2, ad 2: "[A] thing is loved more than it is known; since it can be loved perfectly, even without being perfectly known. . . ."

non-analytic character of appetite along with the existential unity of the appetible object require that the beloved be embraced as a totality, even in its factors which escape our gaze. The spirit's efforts at self-transformation through purgation or voiding are thus not a futile aim at making God the object of consciousness,[111] but are instruments aimed at creating a receptive passivity whereby the soul attunes itself to the divine action within it, rendering it docile to its inspirations (which proceed from a higher principle than human reason), and emptying it in order to be filled with the spiritual sweetness of quasi-experimental knowledge.

MYSTICAL UNION AND CHRISTIAN INTERIORITY

The hidden, detached, and dark aspects of the soul's simple gaze on divine truth are tempered by Thomas's depiction of mystical experience as both affective and as an ordinary part of the interior life of every Christian. Far from the notion that interiority is the product of technique or the manifestation of secondary phenomena, Aquinas speaks of the "mutual indwelling" of God and the soul as an effect of love, as an intimate response to the divine invitation,[112] and as the cause of ecstasy which impresses the beloved upon the soul.[113]

The contemplation which refers the soul directly to God increases in proportion with the degrees of charity,[114] and is the natural result of exercising the virtues and gifts in a life of grace.[115] Human sanctity, Aquinas says, requires the exercise of the infused virtues and the gifts,[116] and, as Garrigou-Lagrange explains, the basic principles of the interior life structure the mystical life as well.[117] Garrigou-Lagrange follows the lead of authors such as Saudreau, Lamballe and Arintero to reject the seventeenth and eighteenth century trend to separate "ascetical" from "mystical" theology. In that view, mystical union is not the culminating point of the normal development of the

[111] The soul can never know for certain whether it is experiencing union with God, but knows it is in a state of grace through certain signs (*ST* I-II, q. 112, a. 5).

[112] See *ST* I-II, q. 28, aa. 1–2 on love and "mutual indwelling."

[113] See *ST* I-II, q. 28, a. 3.

[114] See *ST* II-II, q. 24, a. 9, where Aquinas distinguishes three degrees of charity: that of the *incipientes*, the *proficientes* and the *perfecti*. This accords with his division between the levels of virtue in *ST* I-II, q. 61, a. 5.

[115] Both Maritain and Garrigou-Lagrange agree with this view. See Maritain, *The Degrees of Knowledge*, p. 259: "[M]ystical experience and infused contemplation are, indeed, seen to be the normal, rightful end of the life of grace . . . human life tends towards the Christian life since every man belongs by right to Christ, the head of the human race; and Christian life itself . . . tends to the mystical life." Cf. Garrigou-Lagrange, *Christian Perfection*, pp. 345ff.

[116] *ST* I-II, q. 61, a. 5; *ST* I-II, q. 68, a.1, ad 1.

[117] Garrigou-Lagrange, *Christian Perfection*, pp. 354ff.

life of grace, virtues and the gifts, but rather the province of a privileged spiritual elite.[118] Mystical theology is an integrated path towards spiritual perfection growing from an initial struggle against sin, through the practice of the virtues, towards perfect docility to the Holy Spirit. The human person is by nature oriented towards God, and the image of God inheres in humanity at three levels: nature, grace and glory.[119]

Four points converge to illustrate Aquinas's championing of the ordinary Christian in his mystical theology: First, his assertion that mystical union is the natural fulfillment of the life of grace; second, his non-Augustinian notion of prayer; third, his theory of charity as friendship with God; and fourth, his location of mystery in the ecclesial life of believers, specifically, in their participation in the objective reality of Christ through the Word and sacraments.

Regarding the first point, we cite Garrigou-Lagrange's two reasons for identifying the goal of the ordinary life of grace with mystical union: First, the basic principle of the mystical life and of the common interior life is the same, viz., the grace of the virtues and the gifts. While the interior life is dominated by the human exercise of the virtues, the mystical life is predominated by the superhuman mode of the gifts. Both the infused virtues and the gifts are possessed in degrees corresponding to charity, and in the normal progress of the life of grace, the superhuman mode of the gifts ends up dominating the individual's actions in a habitual manner.[120] Garrigou-Lagrange's second reason for identifying the two ends of the mystical and interior lives is that the spiritual purification required in the interior life requires the passive purifications proper to the mystical life.[121] Passive purification consists not in self-imposed mortification ("active" purification) but in spiritual cleansing flowing from the divine action within us.[122] The virtues of the purified soul are, for Thomas, refinements of the spirit, raising it from mere belief in the

[118] Ibid., p. 42: "[W]e find not only a continuity between ascetical and mystical theology, but also a certain compenetration. They are not two distinct divisions of theology, but two parts or two aspects of the same branch, which shows us spiritual life in its infancy, adolescence, and maturity."

[119] *ST* I, q. 93, a. 4.

[120] Garrigou-Lagrange, *Christian Perfection*, p. 349. Garrigou-Lagrange is quoting *ST* II-II, q. 184, a. 3 and I-II, q. 66, a. 2. He asserts a remote and general call of all souls in the state of grace to the mystical life.

[121] Ibid., p. 356.

[122] *ST* II-II, q. 8, a. 7; I-II, q. 69, a. 2, ad 3. Garrigou-Lagrange quotes the latter text, showing the connection between passive purification and the gift of understanding (ibid., p. 356). Of course it is John of the Cross who develops this notion and explores the active and passive purifications of the senses and spirit in *The Dark Night of the Soul*.

mysteries to a penetration and taste of them, so that one judges all things in them and lives in them with habitual docility.[123]

Aquinas's notion of mystical union also reflects a non-Augustinian idea of prayer which revives the original meaning of prayer as petition. One can point to three features of Thomas's idea of prayer which illustrate its direct application to the everyday Christian. First, he eschews the Augustinian tradition of prayer as an affective act of the will, which linked a prayer's efficacy to fervor and feeling. Second, he replaced this Augustinian understanding of prayer as affection with his own theory of prayer as an act of practical reason; and third, he opts for a theory of "parts" of prayer, whose end is impetration, over and against the tradition of "types" of prayer as a commentary on 1 Timothy 2:1, the classic text on the divisions of prayer. Now an analysis of these three points is in order.

While Augustine and the Franciscans identified and described prayer as an act of will consonant with the desire for beatitude,[124] Thomas broke with this tradition and described prayer as an act of practical reason, because it is in essence petition.[125] Of three effects of prayer (merit, consolation and impetration), only impetration is proper to prayer, he says,[126] while rejecting Augustine's idea that the efficacy of prayer is proportionate to one's fervent feelings, since prayer is an act of worship extending reverence to God.[127] Tugwell has noted that Thomas thus sets the stage for the sixteenth-century Dominican promotion of ordinary Christian piety, against the "encroaching

---

[123] On the virtues of the purified soul, see *ST* I-II, q. 61, a. 5: "There are the virtues of those who have already attained to the divine likeness: these are called the perfect virtues. Thus prudence sees nothing else but the things of God; temperance knows no earthly desires; fortitude has no knowledge of passion; and justice, by imitating the divine mind, is united thereto by an everlasting covenant. Such are the virtues attributed to the blessed, or in this life, to some who are at the summit of perfection."

[124] St. Augustine interpreted St. Paul's precept to "pray without ceasing" (1 Thes. 5:17) with reference to the desire for beatitude as meaning that the very desire to pray is one's prayer and if one's desire is continuous, so is one's prayer. By the twelfth century, the popular definition of prayer was a "devout inner affection towards God," and the tendency among thinkers is to replace the original meaning of prayer as a form of petition (see 1 Tim. 2:1, where prayer is comprised of "entreaties, prayers, pleas and thanksgiving") with a notion of prayer as an act of the will. While Francis connected prayer closely with "devotion," Bonaventure said that prayer should culminate in a fervent jubilation. For references and further explanation, see Simon Tugwell, "Prayer, Humpty Dumpty and Thomas Aquinas," in Brian Davies, ed., *Language, Meaning and God* (London: Biddles, Ltd., Guildford & King's Lynn, 1987), pp. 34–35.

[125] He goes against the "affectivity" emphasis and opts for identifying prayer as an act of reason in both IV *Sent.*, d. 15, q. 4, a. 3 and in *ST* II-II, q. 83, a.17.

[126] *ST* II-II, q. 83, a. 13.

[127] See IV *Sent.*, d. 15, q. 4, a.1; *ST* II-II, q. 83, a. 3. In these texts, Thomas details the meaning of prayer as an act of worship which is part of the virtue of religion.

tyranny of the new interioristic understanding of spirituality" flourishing among Carmelites and later among Jesuits.[128] Thus, in his gloss on 1 Timothy 2:1, which describes prayer as including "entreaties, prayers, pleas and thanksgiving," Thomas rejects the notion of "stages of prayer" or mystical stages of ascent[129] and takes Paul's division to refer to the "parts" of a "complete" prayer, exemplified by the parts of the Mass.[130]

Aquinas's theory of charity as friendship with God also illustrates his notion of mystical union to be one consonant with the ordinary Christian life of grace. Aquinas couches his discussion on charity as a union of perfect friendship with God in the language of the appetitive versus intellective powers. While *in se*, the intellect has a higher, simpler, and more universal object (being), in this life, the will's union with its highest object (God) is higher, for three reasons: First, it is the nature of the appetitive power to grasp things *in se*, whereas it is the nature of the intellect to grasp things in proportion to itself; second, where the object transcends the power, it is better to love it than to know it; and third, while knowledge ascends to God through creatures, love cleaves to God first, and then to other creatures through him, in the exercise of charity.[131] In the love which is divine friendship or charity, there is a sharing (*communicatio*) of God with us through a participation in His happiness,[132] which is concretized and affirmed by the Incarnation and celebrated in ecclesial life. Thus, it is the free reciprocation and delight of

---

[128] See Tugwell in Davies, *Language, Meaning and God*, pp. 47–48.

[129] The view that takes the biblical text as developing different levels of progress within prayer was introduced by Cassian and taken up by thinkers such as Bernard, William of St. Thierry, and Hugh of St. Cher. On the development of the idea of "stages of prayer," see Tugwell in Davies, *Language, Meaning and God*, pp. 28–29.

[130] IV *Sent.*, d. 15, q. 4, a. 3; *ST* II-II, q. 83, a. 17. Thomas adopts the traditional association between the list in 1 Tim. and the parts of the Mass. Tugwell has noted that Thomas's goal in his treatise on prayer is to explain its nature as an authentic religious activity. Thomas thereby "shores up prayer, precisely in the sense in which all Christians are commanded to practice it." See Tugwell, ed., trans., *Albert and Thomas: Selected Writings* (New York: Paulist Press, 1988), p. 278. While Aquinas does not use the "stages of ascent" properly speaking, he does implement the various stages of charity in *ST* I-II, q. 24, a. 9 and II *Sent.*, d. 9, q. 2, a. 8. The "purgative" way would correspond to the initial stage of striving against sin; the "illuminative" way would correspond to the progress in the virtues and initiates in contemplation; the "unitive" way would be reflected in the lives of the perfect, who live in union with God through the highest degree of charity. But the summit of charity is also the fulfillment of normal spiritual development and belongs not to the lower order of "gratuitous" graces (graces *gratis datae*, or charismatic graces such as prophecy, miracles, etc.) but to the ordinary order of sanctifying grace of the virtues and the gifts, which relate the soul directly to God.

[131] *ST* I, q. 82, a. 3 and *ST* II-II, q. 27, a. 4.

[132] *ST* II-II, q. 23, a. 1.

God's love that grounds mystical union and is the property of all souls in grace: Aquinas depicted charity as divine friendship, not as a rarefied, individualized mystical state isolated from the trials and concerns of the ordinary Christian journey or separated from the external communal expressions of ecclesiastical life.

The fourth indication of the appeal of Aquinas's mystical thought for ordinary Christians is his location of mystery at the heart of the ecclesiastical life of the believer. Christian mystical experience is essentially a deepening of faith for Aquinas, and a participation in, and interiorization of the reality of the objective mystery of Christ.[133] As de Lubac has asserted, "The mystery always surpasses the mystic. It dominates his experience, specifies it, and is its absolute norm."[134] The mystical life is entirely incarnational and sacramental for Thomas, and the basis of his mysticism is the stream of divine life that flows to man through a sacramental union. The Prologue to the *Tertia Pars* clearly states that union with God is effected by entering into the mystery of the Incarnation, and elsewhere he shows the path to union through contemplation of divine things in the humanity of Christ.[135] The ordinary believer's participation in the sacraments (the extension of the Word made flesh) launches the soul into the sacred mystery in the same way that a diamond, bending the sun's rays towards one's eyes, refracts breathtaking light, causing the stone to gleam. As the foundation of humanity's exaltation, it is the Incarnation which brings us to beatitude and a share in divinity,[136] and it is Christ's Passion, Thomas says, that opens the gates of Paradise and calls the exiles home.[137] Unlike pragmatic and psychologistic spiritualities of our times, satisfied with subjectivist varieties of "experience," Thomas's confidence in mystical ascent springs from a commitment to the traditions and strategies characterized by speculative theology and embodied in the whole of Christian life.

---

[133] Biblical texts which assert that the mystery is Christ Himself include Col. 1:27; 2:3; 1 Tim. 3:16, for instance. Louis Bouyer develops this point in *Introduction à la vie spirituelle* (Paris: Desclée de Brouwer, 1960).

[134] De Lubac, "Mysticism and Mystery," p. 54. De Lubac notes that mysticism is not "an attempt to escape through interiority, it is Christianity itself" (pp. 55–56).

[135] *ST* II-II, q. 28, a. 3, ad 9.

[136] *ST* III, q. 1, a. 2.

[137] *The Sermon-Conferences of St. Thomas Aquinas on The Apostles' Creed*, trans. Nicholas Ayo (Notre Dame, Indiana: University of Notre Dame Press, 1988), chap. 7, p. 70: "Sed Christus passione sua ianuam paradisi aperuit, et revocavit exules ad regnum. Aperto enim latere Christi, aperta est ianua paradisi; et effuso sanguine eius deleta est macula, placatus est Deus, ablata est debilitas, expiata est pena, exules ad regnum, revocantur."

CONCLUSION

Aquinas's mystical thought can serve as a corrective to introverted, individualist trends in both classical and modern spirituality. Hearkening back to the patristic ideal of mystical theology, Aquinas's mystical thought unites the spiritual and doctrinal elements of his theology. Thomas balances the subjective and objective poles of religious experience in having his sacramental and theological architectonic play its delicate counterpoint to the still voice of the Spirit's promptings. And throughout the soul's journey he entwines the thread of wisdom in its full range of characteristics—the affective or experimental union with God attained by the soul through charity and understanding; the receptive and apophatic emptying of self; and the diffusive peace stimulated by the sweetness of interior order. For Thomas, it is the divine Self-disclosure that initiates, guides and completes the mystical path, flooding the human plane with silent love and illumining the inner eye with supra-conceptual wisdom. In gathering up the aspects of Aquinas's mystical thought, spiritual landscapes open up that seemed hidden by discontinuity and crisis. For Aquinas, we have seen, the suffering of divine things radiates within a trans-luminous obscurity—a darkness not felt in the rarefied atmosphere of a mystical elite, but configured in ordinary acts of Christian believers, and unveiled to hearts rooted in both detachment and freedom in a loving responsiveness to the divine mystery.

The Shadow of Molinism: Reflections on Grace and Liberty in Maritain[1]

David Arias, Jr.

eminal thinkers cast lengthy shadows. To come after such a thinker is
often to stand in his shadow. But to work in the penumbra of another
can either protect one from damaging rays or hide one from nourishing
light. For, by its nature, the shadow can be either protective or obscurant (or
perhaps at times a little of both). What complicates matters is that most of us
stand in multiple overlapping shadows. More literally, standing in certain intellectual traditions may either protect one from certain errors or perhaps in-
hibit one from seeing the truth outside of one's own intellectual inheritance.
Whether the shadows in which one stands are helpful or harmful depends on
the qualities of the shadows themselves. These qualities, in turn, depend
largely upon the wisdom of the original shadow-casters.

For Maritain St. Thomas Aquinas is a seminal thinker whose shadow is
certainly protective. Maritain habitually follows St. Thomas in his writings
and styles himself a Thomist. However, St. Thomas's shadow is not the only
one in which Maritain stands. Indeed, in his *Existence and the Existent*,[2]
Maritain radically parts company with St. Thomas while standing well within
a shadow which resembles that of Luis de Molina. Despite the fact that Maritain, in his chapter "The Free Existent and the Free Eternal Purposes,"
claims to have "exorcised every shadow of Molinism"[3] from his worldview, I

[1] This thesis was originally inspired by private discussions with Dr. Christopher
Curry around 1997. I would like to extend my gratitude both to Dr. Curry and to Dr.
James Hanink for their helpful criticisms, corrections, and suggestions on an earlier
draft of this essay.
   [2] Jacques Maritain, *Existence and the Existent* (New York: Random House, 1948).
   [3] Ibid., p. 99.

will attempt to show that Maritain's views on predestination, as expressed in the same chapter, are metaphysically unjustifiable from a traditional Thomistic perspective and are essentially compatible with the theory of pre-destination advocated by Molina. That is, on the issues of grace, human lib-erty, and the divine *scientia* Maritain's views part company with St. Thomas's and fall victim to the very errors from which Maritain attempts to liberate them.

To defend my thesis I shall do three things. First, I will lay out what I take to be the essence of Maritain's view on predestination (which in-cludes his views on grace, human liberty, and the divine *scientia*) as it is expressed in chapter four of his *Existence and the Existent*. Second, I shall offer a critique of Maritain's views on these matters from the perspective of Réginald Garrigou-Lagrange's works on predestination and grace. Third, I shall conclude my essay by briefly arguing that Maritain's views on predestination, as found in chapter four of *Existence and the Existent*, agree with the essential tenets of Molina's theory of predestination. This essay should be seen as a cordial challenge to some of Maritain's meta-physical presuppositions.

Written in 1948, Jacques Maritain's *Existence and the Existent* constitutes a significant display, within the Maritain corpus, of this great thinker's meta-physical views on the created existent and his eternal Exemplar and Cause, *Ipsum esse per se subsistens*. This work, says Maritain, can be described "as an essay on the existentialism of St. Thomas."[4] Maritain is quick to note that there are two species of "existentialism." While they both affirm the primacy of existence, only the authentic (i.e., Thomistic) existentialism can be said to preserve essences or natures and, thus, manifest "the supreme victory of the intellect and intelligibility."[5] The inauthentic existentialism, on the other hand, says Maritain, destroys and abolishes essences or natures and manifests "the supreme defeat of the intellect and of intelligibility."[6] It is within this ex-istentialist context that Maritain, in chapter four, takes up the question of the relation between created finite liberty and uncreated infinite Liberty. The question to be addressed here is, in Maritain's words, the following: "What is the situation of man and of his fallible liberty in face of the absolutely free and absolutely immutable eternal plan established by the Uncreated in re-spect of the created?"[7]

[4] Ibid., p. 1.
[5] Ibid., p. 3.
[6] Ibid.
[7] Ibid., p. 85.

What then is Maritain's answer to this question? He begins by affirming the absolute immutability of the divine nature, the perfect comprehension by the divine *scientia* of all possible and actual creatures and created states of affairs (past, present and future, from the point of view of time), and the sovereign causality of God as the immutable One who sovereignly moves all created agents and their powers to act, including the human will.[8] In a word, Maritain holds that God, who is *Ipsum esse per se subsistens*, is the first exemplary, efficient, and final Cause of every iota of being and actuality in the created order.

But if *Ipsum esse* is the first efficient Cause of every iota of being and act in the created order, then it follows that He is the first Cause of every human act insofar as it has any ontological status whatsoever. Thus, Maritain says that in every morally good human act the given act proceeds wholly and entirely from God, as from the first efficient Cause, and wholly and entirely from the created agent, as from the secondary efficient cause, the latter being completely dependent upon and subordinated to the causal influx of the Former.[9]

Now, as Maritain points out, there is a "dissymmetry between the line of good and the line of evil."[10] In other words, when the question of moral evil enters into the human act one must say that while God is the first efficient Cause of that action, insofar as it stands out from nothingness, nonetheless, the created agent is the first deficient cause of the very same human action insofar as it is morally deficient and, thus, morally evil. In morally evil acts, just as in morally good acts, the act *qua* act proceeds wholly and entirely from God, as from the first efficient Cause, and wholly and entirely from the created agent, as from the secondary efficient cause. However, this same morally evil act *qua* deficient or privative act proceeds wholly and entirely from the created agent as from its first deficient cause. As Maritain shows, since *Ipsum esse* is the first Cause of all being and act, the only "thing" that a created agent can cause, insofar as it attempts to act autonomously from *Ipsum esse*, is nothingness.[11] For since the created agent is by nature defectible, it follows that insofar as the created agent "strays"from *Ipsum esse* (who is the ultimate Source of all efficiency) it must fall into deficiency and nothingness. On this point Maritain maintains:

---

[8] *Summa Theologiae* I, q. 105, a. 4 (hereafter cited as *ST*).
[9] Maritain, *Existence and the Existent*, p. 88.
[10] Ibid., p. 88.
[11] Ibid., p. 92.

It follows from this that whereas the created existent is never alone when it exercises its liberty in the line of good, and has need of the first cause for all that it produces in the way of being and good, contrariwise, it has no need of God, it is truly alone, for the purpose of freely nihilating, or taking the free first initiative of this absence (or "nothingness") of consideration, which is the matrix of evil in the free act—I mean to say, the matrix of the privation itself by which the free act (in which there is metaphysical good insofar as there is being) is morally deformed or purely and simply evil. "For without Me, you can do nothing"; which is to say, "Without Me you can make that thing which is nothing."[12]

After establishing this metaphysical vision of the human act and the causal relation that obtains between God and His created agent, Maritain addresses the doctrine of predestination, wherein he hopes to locate the resolution to his question regarding the situation of man and his fallible liberty in face of the immutable divine plan which God has regarding man and his actions. In addressing the doctrine of predestination Maritain first treats of what he terms the "divine activations" and thereafter takes up the nature of God's *scientia* and eternal plan. We shall briefly address each of these subjects in order.

By "divine activations" Maritain means those divine motions whereby God either makes the performance of a morally good act possible or actually produces a morally good act in the created agent.[13] Accordingly, Maritain holds that there are two kinds of divine activations. There is the "shatterable divine impetus" (i.e., sufficient grace) and the "unshatterable divine impetus" (i.e., efficacious grace). As is suggested by their denominations the "shatterable" divine impetus can be resisted whereas the "unshatterable" divine impetus is never in fact resisted, but rather is always efficacious in bringing about the divinely intended production of a morally good act.

For Maritain the way in which the shatterable and unshatterable divine impetuses are related is key. He maintains that every unshatterable divine impetus, which is received by any created agent, is always preceded by (by a priority of nature, not time) a shatterable divine impetus. If this shatterable divine impetus is not shattered or resisted, it naturally fructifies into an unshatterable divine impetus and the morally good act is actualized. Maritain holds that the unshatterable divine impetus is virtually contained within the shatterable one as the fruit is virtually contained within its flower. Just as if the flower is not destroyed, it will naturally make way for its fruit, so too if

---

[12] Ibid.
[13] Ibid., p. 94.

the shatterable divine impetus is not destroyed or shattered, it will naturally fructify into an unshatterable divine impetus.[14]

Since, as noted above, the only "thing" that a created agent can do by himself (i.e., independently from God) is nothing, Maritain says that there are only two possible responses that a created agent can make to the prompting of a shatterable divine impetus. Either the created agent can nihilate (i.e., resist) the shatterable divine impetus and thus introduce nothingness and deficiency into his act, or the created agent can remain perfectly still and not do anything whatsoever under the influence of the shatterable divine impetus.[15] If the agent nihilates the shatterable impetus, then he ultimately introduces sin into his act and destroys the possibility of receiving the unshatterable divine impetus, as regards his present act, since in destroying the flower he has robbed himself of its fruit. On the other hand, if the created agent remains perfectly still and does not do anything whatsoever under the influence of the shatterable divine impetus, then the shatterable divine impetus naturally flowers into an unshatterable divine impetus and, thus, the production of the morally good act is actualized.[16]

Maritain insists that, in the created agent's standing still under the shatterable divine impetus, the agent does not make even one iota of ontological

----

[14] Ibid., p. 97. Maritain describes the relationship between the shatterable and unshatterable impetuses within the context of the Thomistic doctrine of the "non-consideration of the rule." Maritain holds that the shatterable divine impetus is the resistible divine initiative which governs the human person in the process of deliberation. For it is in the process of deliberation, Maritain claims, that the human agent either will not do anything whatsoever, that is, will not stir under the divine touch and will thus effectively consider the rule which can and ought to be considered in this present deliberative process or he will attempt to act autonomously from *Ipsum esse* and will thus fail to consider the rule which can and ought to be considered in this present deliberative process. If the human agent chooses this second option and thus nihilates and resists the shatterable divine impetus, he will thereby deliberate defectively and, consequently, will consent to an evil option. Maritain maintains that if the human agent chooses the first option and does not shatter or resist the shatterable divine impetus, then the human agent will consider the rule aright in the act of deliberation and the unshatterable divine impetus will flower out of the shatterable impetus thus moving the agent to consent to the good moral option which he has concluded to in the process of deliberation. On this point Maritain says: "If we consider what is most important in this dynamism, the act itself of free choice or *election*, we can give the name of shatterable impetus to everything that prepares the way for it, including the good acts which, while arising out of free will, are not yet election (for example, everything good that falls within the *deliberation* which precedes election). We will then reserve the name of "unshatterable impetus" for that impetus which produces the good election" (ibid., p. 95).

[15] Ibid., p. 99.
[16] Ibid.

contribution to the efficacy of the fructification of the shatterable divine impetus into the unshatterable one. In his words Maritain says:

> But what is important to set forth here with unmistakable clarity is that the created existent contributes nothing of its own, does nothing, adds nothing, gives nothing—not the shadow of an action or of a determination coming from it—which would make of the shatterable impetus an unshatterable impetus or an impetus that comes to grips with existence. Not to nihilate under the divine activation, not to sterilize that impetus, not to have the initiative of making the thing we call nothing, does not mean taking initiative, of the demi-initiative, of the smallest fraction of the initiative of act; it does not mean acting on one's own to complete, in any way whatever, the divine activation. It means not stirring under its touch, but allowing it free passage, allowing it to bear its fruit (the unshatterable activation) by virtue of which the will (which did not nihilate in the first instance) will act (will look at the rule efficaciously) in the very exercise of its domination over the motives, and will burst forth freely in a good option and a good act.[17]

Maritain knows that here the "stakes are high." In order to preserve metaphysically *Ipsum esse's* sovereign causality and to remain free from the errors with which the Thomists have historically accused Molina and his followers, Maritain must insist upon the fact that the created agent can contribute absolutely nothing of his own, to the efficacy of its good acts, which it has not wholly and entirely received, as a grace, from *Ipsum esse*. Indeed Maritain is convinced that he has avoided the Molinist errors and successfully stood in the protective shadow of St. Thomas on this issue of the divine activations. In conclusion to his main explication of the divine activations Maritain says:

> [F]rom the moment we understand that the non-nihilating, which conditions the fructification of the shatterable impetus in unshatterable impetus, does absolutely not imply the slightest contribution made by the creature to the divine motion—from this moment we have beyond question exorcised every shadow of Molinism.[18]

Immediately following his treatment of the divine activations Maritain addresses the question of the divine *scientia*. As a Thomist, Maritain begins by affirming that God's act of knowledge is identical with *Ipsum esse*, that is, the divine essence itself.[19] But the divine essence is wholly independent of everything in the created order. Therefore, it follows that God's eternal act of knowledge is also wholly independent of everything in the created order.[20]

---

[17] Ibid., p. 100.
[18] Ibid., p. 99.
[19] Ibid., p. 105.
[20] Ibid.

Hereafter, Maritain makes the traditional distinction between God's *scientia simplicis intelligentiae* (wherein He eternally and perfectly knows all of the possible ways in which He can be imaged by creatures) and His *scientia visionis* (wherein God knows eternally and perfectly those creatures which He wills from all eternity actually to exist in the created order). It is Maritain's account of this latter type of divine knowledge, that is the *scientia visionis*, with which I am particularly concerned here. For God's *scientia visionis* is identical with His eternal plan and it is the eternal divine plan,[21] in particular, which bears upon the question of the relation between created finite liberty and uncreated infinite Liberty. In describing the *scientia visionis* Maritain holds that God does not *foresee* anything. Rather, since the eternal One is above time and since every moment of time, in its presentiality, is eternally present to Him, God *sees* in His comprehensive vision everything which He wills to create in the created order.[22] Citing a beautiful passage from St. Peter Damien, Maritain describes the *scientia visionis* as follows:

> This divine today is the incommutable, indefeasible, inaccessible eternity to which nothing can be added, from which nothing can be taken away. And all things which here below supervene upon and succeed one another by flowing progressively into non-being, and which are diversified according to the vicissitudes of their times, are present before this today and continue to exist motionless before it. In that today the day when the world began is still immutable. And nevertheless, the day is already present also when it will be judged by the eternal judge.[23]

Now that we have an idea of how Maritain envisions the *scientia visionis* let us ask him how exactly he thinks the free act of the created agent "enters into" God's eternal resolve to bring certain souls to glory in time. That is, how is it that the *scientia visionis* is related to the free acts of the elect which are actualized in time? There are at least three key texts in *Existence and the Existent* which well express Maritain's thought on this point. I cite them here in full:

> 1) The created existents which, according to the conception put forth by us, are ordained in all eternity to eternal life, *ante praevista merita*, by the primordial or "antecedent" will will be confirmed by the definitive or "consequent" will (from the moment they did *not* take the initiative of nihilating at the critical juncture) were by the definitive or "consequent" will *inscribed in the book of life before the world was created*.[24]

---

[21] *ST* I, q. 14, a. 16.

[22] Ibid., p. 87.

[23] Ibid., p. 86. From St. Peter Damien, *Opusculum De Divina Omnipotentia*, chap. 8. *P.L.* 145, 607.

[24] Ibid., p. 105.

2) Let us suppose . . . that at that instant [i.e., a given instant in time which is seen by God from all eternity] the free creature has the initiative of the thing that is nothing. Then, this is seen from all eternity in the free existent by the "science of vision"; and from all eternity God's definitive or circumstanced will (if it does not prevent the natural effect of this nihilating) permits the evil act of which this creature has the first initiative; and from all eternity the permission of this evil act, ordained to a better good . . . is immutably fixed in the eternal plan.[25]

3) Suppose that the eternal plan were a scenario prepared in advance. Suppose that in that scenario it was written that Brutus was to assassinate Caesar. Then, when Brutus steps forth upon the stage of the world, either the Stage Manager will leave him truly free to have or not to have the first initiative of sin, in which case Brutus might not murder Caesar and might frustrate the eternal plan—which is absurd; or else the Stage Manager will arrange in one way or another, with antecedent permissive decrees or supercomprehensions of causes, that Brutus really assassinate Caesar but still commit the murder freely. How then and by what subtleties, can one avoid the conclusion that God had the first initiative of the sin, and, were it merely a slackening His hand, caused the creature to fall into it? It was Brutus who had the first initiative of the free nihilating by which, God permitting, the decision of murder entered into his will and into the history of the world. If, at that instant in time, eternally present in the eternal instant, he had not had the initiative of nihilating, the immutable plan would have fixed things in another way from all eternity.[26]

From these texts two points become clear. First, Maritain holds that *antecedent* to His infallibly efficacious decree God sees from all eternity the nihilating or non-nihilating stances taken by His free creatures, whom He wills to bring into existence, in each set of their particular circumstances. Second, and as a consequence to this first point, Maritain says that God *does not* know the nihilating intentions of His created agents in His eternal permissive decrees. Rather, Maritain maintains that God's permissive decrees are *consequent* to God's knowing the nihilating intentions of His free creatures in their given circumstances.[27] It is God's prerogative, though, Maritain holds, to permit or not permit, from all eternity, His free creatures from carrying out their nihilating intentions. So stands Maritain's view of predestination and the way in which created liberty is related to uncreated Liberty and God's immutable plan.

What could be wrong, from a traditional Thomistic perspective, with what

---

[25] Ibid., p. 118.

[26] Ibid., pp. 118–19.

[27] That this is indeed Maritain's position can be seen in his *God and the Permission of Evil* (Milwaukee, Wisconsin: Bruce Publishing Co., 1966).

Maritain has said? How can he be charged with contradicting, in his view on predestination, some of his most basic principles, as a Thomist, when his views *seem* so Thomistic? I answer that Maritain can be interpreted as holding to at least two fundamental metaphysical errors. One of these errors is found in his position on the divine activations and the other one is in his position on the relation of the *scientia visionis* and God's permissive decrees to human acts.

Let us first turn to the error in Maritain's view of the divine activations. We saw that Maritain holds that when the created agent receives a shatterable divine impetus this same agent can either take a nihilating or non-nihilating stance towards the impetus. By taking a non-nihilating stance towards the shatterable divine impetus, that is, by remaining perfectly still under its influence and by not doing anything whatsoever the created agent adds absolutely nothing to the shatterable impetus but merely allows it to fructify into an unshatterable divine impetus. According to Maritain, it "depends solely" upon the created agent's decision as to "whether he will or will not take the initiative of nihilating."[28]

This view, however, is problematic for it attributes an unjustifiable ontological autonomy to the created agent. For is not the actual non-resistance of the shatterable divine impetus itself a good? Is not the created agent's actual continuation in the line of good itself a good?[29] For since the created agent's actual non-resistance is a mode of being, and since being and goodness are convertible,[30] it follows that the agent's actual non-resistance is a veritable good, albeit ontological and not moral.[31] But if the agent's actual non-resistance or actual continuation in the line of good is itself a good, then it can only be accounted for ultimately by the first exemplary, efficient, and final Cause of all created goods, *Ipsum esse*. And if the good of actual non-resistance can only be ultimately accounted for in terms of *Ipsum esse*'s sovereign causality, then it follows that Maritain is mistaken in claiming that this actual

---

[28] Ibid., p. 117.

[29] Réginald Garrigou-Lagrange, O.P., *Predestination* (St. Louis, Missouri: B. Herder, 1939), p. 332.

[30] *ST* I, q. 5. aa. 1, 3.

[31] Here I call the good in question an ontological and not moral good because the good in question, namely, a correct deliberation, wherein the rule which can and ought to be considered in the present deliberation is actually considered, is prior to and presupposed by the consent of the will to the correct final practical judgement. The Thomists hold that it is at the point of the will's consent to this final practical judgement that morality, properly speaking, enters into the scenario in question. See *Summa Contra Gentiles* III, chap. 10 (hereafter cited as *SCG*).

non-resistance of the shatterable divine impetus "depends solely" upon the decision of the created agent. To say that the good of non-resistance depends solely upon the created agent's decision is to maintain that there is a good which is accounted for ultimately by the causality of the created agent independently of *Ipsum esse*, who is infinite subsistent goodness itself. This, however, is to deny that *Ipsum esse* is the first efficient Cause of all things in the created order, which, of course, is absurd.

So, if in fact the created agent's actual non-resistance to the shatterable divine impetus is a good, and if this good can only be accounted for ultimately in terms of *Ipsum esse* who, by His sovereign causality, preserves the created agent in the line of good and keeps him from defecting, then how are we to understand the relationship between God's shatterable divine impetus (i.e., sufficient grace) and unshatterable divine impetus (i.e., efficacious grace)? Garrigou-Lagrange holds, as does Maritain, that in every sufficient grace granted by God efficacious grace is virtually contained therein as the fruit is virtually contained within its flower.[32] But, according to Garrigou-Lagrange, whenever a created agent does not actually resist God's grant of sufficient grace it is simply due to the fact that God's efficacious grace, which is now actually (and not *merely* virtually) present within the agent, is preserving the agent in question from resisting the sufficient grace.[33] This in brief is how Garrigou-Lagrange accounts for the preservation of the created agent in the line of good without compromising the sovereignty of God.

Maritain, however, not only knew of this position but also seemed to have objected to it in one of our citations of his work above. His basic objection seems to be as follows: If God's bestowal of efficacious grace is the cause of the created agent's actual non-resistance of sufficient grace, then God's refusal actually to grant efficacious grace to a given agent would seem to be the cause of the same agent's actual resistance to sufficient grace in which case God would be the Cause of sin, which is absurd. In answer to this objection, though, Garrigou-Lagrange holds that:

> It is true to say that man is deprived of efficacious grace *because* he resisted sufficient grace, whereas it is not true to say that man resists or sins *because* he is deprived of efficacious grace. He resists *by reason of* his own defectibility which God is not bound to remedy.[34]

This text is highly significant, for it illustrates that God's efficacious grace is the very reason for man's actual non-resistance whereas man's own de-

---

[32] Garrigou-Lagrange, *Predestination*, p. 331.
[33] Ibid., p. 332.
[34] Ibid., p. 333. Emphasis mine.

fectible nature is the very reason for his actual resistance. Indeed this view follows from Maritain's own principle, noted above, that while God is the sole ultimate Cause of all moral efficiency in the created order, creatures are the sole ultimate cause of all moral deficiency in the created order. For as the Angelic Doctor maintains:

> To sin is nothing else than to fail in the good which belongs to any being according to its nature. Now as every created thing has its being from another, and, considered in itself, is nothing, so does it need to be preserved by another in the good which pertains to its nature. For it can of itself fail in good, even as of itself it can fall into nothingness, unless it is upheld by God.[35]

Having briefly addressed this first error in Maritain's account of the divine activations, let us turn to what I interpret to be an error in his doctrine of the relation the *scientia visionis* and permissive decrees have to human liberty. As was stated above, when speaking on the relation that the *scientia visionis* and the permissive decrees have to human liberty, Maritain makes two points particularly evident.

First, Maritain holds that *antecedent* to God's infallibly efficacious decree He sees from all eternity the nihilating or non-nihilating stance of his free creatures, whom He wills to bring into existence, in each possible set of particular circumstances. Second, and as a consequence to this first point, Maritain says that God *does not* know the nihilating intentions of His creatures in His permissive decrees. Rather, Maritain maintains that God's permissive decrees are *consequent* to God's knowing the nihilating intentions of His free creatures in their given circumstances. It is God's prerogative, though, to permit or not permit, from all eternity, His free creatures from carrying out their nihilating intentions. On both of these points, though, Maritain ends up contradicting traditional Thomistic doctrine and, ultimately, compromising *Ipsum esse*'s sovereignty and absolute divine nature.

Garrigou-Lagrange says that it is impossible, both logically and ontologically, for God to see in the *scientia visionis*, from all eternity and antecedently to His efficacious decree, whether His created agents, in their particular circumstances, will to take a nihilating or non-nihilating stance towards the sufficient grace offered them.[36] This scenario is impossible precisely because it supposes that the *scientia visionis* is somehow independent from God's infallibly efficacious divine decree which, of course, is false.[37]

---

[35] *ST* I-II, q. 109, a. 2, ad 2.

[36] Garrigou-Lagrange, *Predestination*, p. 209.

[37] Réginald Garrigou-Lagrange, O.P., *God: His Existence and His Nature*, vol. 2 (St. Louis, Missouri: B. Herder, 1946), pp. 66–67.

Indeed, such a view, is a radical departure from St. Thomas himself who holds that God sees *in,* and not antecedently to, His infallibly efficacious decree those things which will infallibly come about in the created order.[38] This applies not only to those things which God wills directly (i.e., created goods) but also to those things which God wills indirectly (i.e., physical evils) and to those things which He wills merely to permit to occur (i.e., moral evils).

To hold that God knows what His creatures will do in their given circumstances *antecedently* to His efficacious divine decree and, thus, independently from His efficacious decree, as Maritain and the Molinists do, is tantamount to saying that God is a Spectator who views in His divine essence what His creatures will to do on their own and without reference to the divine will as the ultimate governing Standard of every iota of being and change in the created order. As a result, such a position denies that God's knowledge is the ultimate Measure of all things in the created order and alternatively holds that free creatures, who as yet do not even exist in the created order, are the measures of their Creator. But, as Garrigou-Lagrange shows, this view compromises the doctrine of God for it introduces a certain passivity into *Ipsum esse* Himself. He maintains that this view "ascribes passivity to Pure Act, that is, the divine intelligence is measured by the determination of our free will, which it must ascertain and wait upon."[39] But granted this, and granted that St. Thomas shows that God is Pure Act in whom there is no passive potentiality whatsoever,[40] it follows that this view of Maritain and the Molinists must be rejected as false.

Maritain's second point, which holds that God's permissive decrees are consequent to His knowledge of the nihilating intentions of his creatable agents, can likewise be shown to be false by the same argument just presented. That is, this second point of Maritain's which follows from his first also implies a passivity in the Pure Act that is *Ipsum esse,* which is impossible. This second point, though, raises an important question for Thomists. For, as we saw above, Maritain explicitly rejects Garrigou-Lagrange's position on this issue, which holds that God knows the nihilating intentions of his created agents from all eternity *in,* and not antecedently to, His permissive decrees.[41] Maritain thinks that this traditional Thomistic view amounts to saying that God is the Cause of sin.[42]

---

[38] *ST* I, q. 14, aa. 8–9.

[39] Réginald Garrigou-Lagrange, O.P., *Grace: Commentary on the Summa Theologica of St. Thomas, Ia IIae, qq. 109–14* (St. Louis, Missouri: B. Herder, 1952), p. 255.

[40] *SCG* I, chap. 16.

[41] Maritain, *Existence and the Existent*, p. 119.

[42] Ibid.

How then, are traditional Thomists, like Garrigou-Lagrange to respond to this charge? Garrigou-Lagrange himself offers one such response. He holds that the position which Maritain espouses fails to distinguish between necessary conditionality and causality.[43] The notion of necessary conditionality is far broader than that of causality. For while the notion of necessary conditionality is contained in the notion of causality, the converse is not the case. Thus, Garrigou-Lagrange teaches that God's permissive decrees are necessary conditions for sin to occur in time, for if God did not permit certain agents to fall into sin, then they would not do so.[44] Nevertheless, these same decrees are in no way the causes of sin.[45] Rather, as we saw above, the cause of sin is to be found exclusively in the deficiency of the created agent. Hence, Garrigou-Lagrange maintains:

> [A] man fails on his own account and he is sufficient unto himself when it comes to failing; but he requires the divine help preserving him in the good in order to persevere in it. To be preserved in goodness is a good and proceeds from the Source of all good; but to fall away from goodness presupposes only a deficient cause.[46]

In this essay I have argued that Maritain's views of grace, liberty, and predestination, as presented in his *Existence and the Existent*, are metaphysically problematic. In particular I have argued that his views of the divine activations and of the divine *scientia* and permissive decrees presuppose an ontological independence or autonomy, on the part of creatures, which compromises *Ipsum esse*'s sovereignty as the first efficient Cause of all created being and *Ipsum esse*'s nature as *Actus Purus*. While attempting to exorcise "every shadow of Molinism" from his worldview, Maritain seems, unfortunately, to fall into what have been seen by some traditional Thomists to be two of the most significant errors of Molinism.

The first Molinist error is that efficacious grace is not required in order to accept sufficient grace and that efficacious grace is not in itself efficacious but becomes efficacious by man's God-independent acceptance of it.[47] But, as we saw above, this view is precisely what Maritain seems to maintain when he holds that the non-resistance of the shatterable divine impetus "depends solely" upon the created agent and not upon *Ipsum esse*'s conserving

---

[43] Garrigou-Lagrange, *Grace*, p. 222.

[44] *ST* I-II, q. 79, a. 1.

[45] Garrigou-Lagrange, *Grace*, pp. 222–25.

[46] Ibid., p. 226.

[47] Maritain, *Predestination*, pp. 128–30. (For Molina's own words see the *Concordia*, q. 14, a.13, disp. 26.)

power and efficacious grace. This error ultimately denies that God is the first efficient Cause of all created good.

The second significant error of the Molinists, which denies God's nature as *Ipsum esse*, is that of the so-called *scientia media*.[48] The Molinists teach that "between" God's *scientia simplicis intelligentiae* and His *scientia visionis*, there exists the *scientia media* wherein God knows, from all eternity and *antecedently* to His infallibly efficacious divine decrees, what exactly His possible agents will do in all possible sets of determinate circumstances.[49] As we saw above, some traditional Thomists argue that this Molinist doctrine introduces a passivity into *Ipsum esse* for it implies that God's knowledge is actually measured by and thus determined by His possible creatures. Given the above texts from Maritain, it seems that he holds to this Molinist doctrine, albeit he attributes to the *scientia visionis* that which the Molinists attribute to the *scientia media*, thus fusing these two types of *scientia divina* into one. But to attempt to hold to both the Thomistic doctrine of the *scientia visionis* and the Molinist doctrine of the *scientia media* is to be in a state of contradiction since these doctrines are opposed as contradictories. As Garrigou-Lagrange holds,

> There is no alternative between the *scientia media* and the doctrine of the divine predetermining decree. Either God infallibly knows contingent futures, even conditioned futures, in His predetermining decree, which extends even to the free mode of our choices, or else He does not know them in this decree, that is, before this decree, which is precisely the theory of the *scientia media*.[50]

While meaning to exorcise the shadow of Molinism from his worldview Maritain seems to have essentially adopted it. While meaning to preserve both authentic human freedom and the sovereignty of *Ipsum esse* he seems to have compromised both. Garrigou-Lagrange often writes that every metaphysical or theological doctrine will end up affirming either that God determines all things in the created order or that God is determined by at least one thing in the created order.[51] There is no other alternative. Maritain's views on grace, human liberty, and predestination unfortunately seem to fall into the latter part of this dilemma.

[48] Ibid., pp. 131–33.
[49] Ibid., pp. 131–32. Again, for Molina's own words see the *Concordia*, disp. 52, sections 9, 19, and 29. The best recent summary of the Molinist position is Thomas Flint's, *Divine Providence: The Molinist Account* (Ithaca, New York: Cornell University Press, 1998).
[50] Réginald Garrigou-Lagrange, O.P., *The One God: A Commentary on the First Part of St. Thomas's Summa Theologiae* (St. Louis, Missouri: B. Herder Books, 1946), p. 472.
[51] Garrigou-Lagrange, *God: His Existence and His Nature*, pp. 558–62.

PART II

FAITH AND SCIENCE

The Mind of the Universe:
Understanding Science and Religion

Mariano Artigas

In the "Call for Papers" for the meeting of the American Maritain Association (2000), we read that papers might examine topics such as secular
humanism's impact on our understanding of the person and culture, and
also the resacralization of material culture. Both subjects can be considered
as two sides of the same coin, which is closely related to the progress of empirical science. In its beginnings, the new science was seen as a road from nature to its Maker, promoting natural theology. Later on, however, it was interpreted as favoring a "disenchantment" of the world. I will comment on some
proposals of "reenchanting" the world, and will refer to my own proposal,
which has recently been published in my last book.[1]

THE DISENCHANTMENT OF THE WORLD

The term "disenchantment" of the world can be traced to the Romantic
movement, where it was considered to be a consequence of scientific
progress. Friedrich Schiller spoke about the "de-divinization" of the world,
which was translated by Max Weber as the "disenchantment" of the world.
Two alternative ways of overcoming this "disenchantment" were suggested,
namely supplementing the scientific image with spirituality or changing
science itself. Hegel, for example, intended to change the concepts of the
physical science, but had very little success. This line of thinking, in spite
of the repeated setbacks it has suffered, exercises a strong fascination also
today. This is perhaps due to the fact that complementing science from the
outside may seem a too weak remedy, because apparently it leaves un-

---

[1] Mariano Artigas, *The Mind of the Universe: Understanding Science and Religion*
(Philadelphia & London: Templeton Foundation Press, 2000).

touched the claim that empirical science is the only valid road to objective knowledge.

It is important to recall that the de-divinization of the world possesses two different meanings. It means first that the world is neither a part of God nor can be identified with Him. This central tenet of Christianity, which contrasts with pantheism, favored the birth of modern natural science. In a second and completely different sense, de-divinization means that there are no traces of God to be found in the world. This is the meaning used by Schiller and Weber. "Disenchantment" translates the German *Entzauberung*, and expresses that, as a result of scientific progress, the world cannot be considered anymore as a clue to discover the hand of God acting in nature.[2] According to Weber, the disenchantment of the world is closely related to a process of "rationalization," which replaces the ancient "magic" features of thinking with scientific naturalist explanations. The disenchantment of the world, Weber concludes, steadily grows as scientific thinking grows.[3]

This evaluation resembles the three-stage law of Comte's positivism, and is presented even today as if it were the result of an objective account of history. I completely disagree with this. Fighting religion in the name of science is as old as human history. In every epoch, naturalism presents itself as if it were the result of human progress. The anti-religious arguments of Lucretius, a century before Christ, are basically the same that are used now. They attempt to overcome religion in the name of science by reducing all explanations to these two questions: "What is this made of?" and "How does it work?"

Empirical science concentrates on the study of natural patterns. It should not be used to derive assertions for or against spiritual realities. To interpret naturalism as "the ontology of science" is meaningless. The causes of secularization in Western societies are complex. In any case, scientific progress should not be blamed as favoring secularism. Ultimate questions involve personal commitments. I do not think that scientific progress has changed the nature of this problem. Therefore, it is unfair to present scientific progress as a major cause of the disenchantment of the world. Even an agnostic like Karl Popper recognizes that "science does not make assertions about ultimate questions—about the riddles of existence, or about man's task in this world";

---

[2] "*Entzauberung* refers mainly to the 'contents' aspects of culture and describes the demystification of the conception of the world connected with growing secularism, with the rise of science, and with growing routinization of education and culture" (S. N. Eisenstadt, "Introduction," in Max Weber, *On Charisma and Institution Building* [Chicago: The University of Chicago Press, 1968], p. li).

[3] Max Weber, "Science as a Vocation," in *On Charisma and Institution Building*, p. 298.

that "science has nothing to say about a personal Creator"; and that "argument from design may not be within the reach of science."[4] Scientific progress is not a major cause of the disenchantment of the world.

RE-ENCHANTING THE WORLD

Now I shall refer to two positions that coincide in their criticism of the disenchantment of the world, but advance different proposals to overcome it.

The first position is inspired by Alfred North Whitehead and Charles Hartshorne, but has now a postmodern orientation. John B. Cobb, Jr., and David Ray Griffin are two preeminent representatives of this position, presented in a collective work entitled *The Reenchantment of Science*, an introduction to a series in constructive postmodern thought.[5] Griffin proposes to change science itself. This involves a most difficult task. In fact, a major difficulty arises: What would the reenchanted science look like? What would be a reenchanted physics, for example? Griffin tells us that we can no longer admit that science is value-free, as today it is widely held that the social factors affect science essentially, not just superficially. The corresponding footnote includes a list of writings, the first of which is Paul Feyerabend's *Against Method*, which is not a reliable reference. Griffin also says that science is inherently imperialistic, which is not a description of science but of the abuse of science usually called "scientism." According to Griffin, natural science should include a kind of natural philosophy, but this means mixing two different levels of knowledge. I think it is much safer to leave the scientific community to decide its standards. Empirical science is a human construct, but it aims at a knowledge of natural patterns that exist independently of our constructions. Error or bad philosophy may enter into the citadel of science, but open windows and intersubjective criticism are the best antidote against them. The source of confusion is scientism, not science. Scientism is not science, but a mistaken philosophy that presents itself as if it were science. It is a kind of pseudo-science. Scientism should be fought on the philosophical level, showing that it consists of unjustified extrapolations and leads to contradiction.

My second example is the "Intelligent Design" theory (IDT), recently proposed by Michael Behe, William Dembski, and others.[6] They say that

---

[4] Karl R. Popper, "Natural Selection and the Emergence of Mind," in *Evolutionary Epistemology, Rationality, and the Sociology of Knowledge*, eds. Gerard Radnitzky and William W. Bartley (LaSalle, Illinois: Open Court, 1987), pp. 141–42.

[5] *The Reenchantment of Science. Postmodern Proposals*, ed. David Ray Griffin (Albany, New York: State University of New York Press, 1988).

[6] Michael Behe, *Darwin's Black Box* (New York: Simon & Schuster, 1996); William Dembski, *Intelligent Design. The Bridge Between Science & Theology* (Downers Grove, Illinois: InterVarsity Press, 1999).

progress in biology reveals the existence of many contrivances that suggest the idea of an intelligent design. This is true. In the name of a mechanistic approach, teleology was expelled from physics first and afterwards from biology too, but recent progress shows that nature is full of teleological dimensions. Nevertheless, I do not agree that intelligent design forms part of science itself. The reason is that an explicit reflection on finality is a philosophical task. A central tenet of the IDT is that specified complexity is a reliable empirical marker of intelligent design. Probably this is true, but this kind of argument is philosophical, not scientific. A transformation of current science is proposed also in this case, introducing within science philosophical elements. Nothing will be gained, however, if we label as scientific something that is not really science.

In order to avoid the evils introduced by the disenchantment of the world we should, first of all, respect the autonomy of natural science. Then we must criticize scientism, which is the real cause of misunderstanding. Finally, we could try to bridge the gap between the sciences and the humanities in a rigorous way, presenting philosophical thinking as such. This can be done in different ways. I will present now my own proposal, warning that I do not claim it to be the only viable approach.

BRIDGING THE GAP

When we try to relate the sciences and the humanities we should notice, first of all, that there exists a methodological gap between the natural sciences on the one hand, and the humanities and spirituality on the other. To bridge this gap we need to find something which is common to both sides. A serious candidate is represented by the so-called "boundary questions." John Polkinghorne refers to them saying: "There are questions which arise from science and which insistently demand an answer, but which by their very character transcend that of which science itself is competent to speak."[7] Those questions should be closely related to science, as we are told that they "arise from science." However, they would not be, properly speaking, scientific questions. But, what does it mean that, although they are not scientific, they "arise from science?" It is much easier to understand that they cannot be answered by science, because if they are not strictly scientific, it is impossible to answer them by using the methods of science. I dare say that, properly

---

[7] John Polkinghorne, "A Revived Natural Theology," in *Science and Religion. One World: Changing Perspectives on Reality*, eds. Jan Fennema and Ian Paul (Dordrecht: Kluwer, 1990), p. 88.

speaking, genuine boundary questions cannot arise from science. Scientists are human beings, and they may pose themselves metaphysical questions in connection with their work. But then they are acting as philosophers or theologians, and cannot solve their problems by using only the methods of their sciences.

Dialogue between science and religion requires a common partner that can be neither science nor religion. Philosophy is a good partner, probably the only real candidate. That is why Ian Barbour says:

> Any view of the relationship of science and religion reflects philosophical assumptions. Our discussion must therefore draw from three disciplines, not just two: *science* (the empirical study of the order of nature), *theology* (critical reflection on the life and thought of the religious community), and *philosophy*, especially epistemology (analysis of the characteristics of inquiry and knowledge) and metaphysics (analysis of the most general characteristics of reality).[8]

My proposal focuses on one kind of boundary question: *the presuppositions and implications of scientific progress*. Empirical science includes not only factual knowledge, but also its necessary conditions, which can be considered as general presuppositions the analysis of which constitutes a philosophical and theological task.

There are three kinds of such presuppositions. The first refers to the intelligibility or rationality of nature: it can be labeled as ontological, and is closely related to natural order. The second refers to the human ability to know the natural order: it can be labeled as epistemological, and includes the different forms of scientific argument. The third refers to the values implied by the scientific activity itself: it can be labeled as ethical, and includes the search for truth, rigor, objectivity, intellectual modesty, service to other people, cooperation, and other related values.

There is moreover feedback from scientific progress on these presuppositions, because the progress of science retrojustifies, amplifies and refines them. These presuppositions are necessary conditions for the existence of science; therefore scientific progress is a sufficient condition for their existence, and enables us to determine their scope.

Seen under the light of that feedback, the analysis of those presuppositions can provide a clue to the philosophical meaning of scientific progress and, therefore, to its theological relevance. This analysis stands on its own feet, but it also provides good reasons against naturalism, as it shows that scien-

---

[8] Ian Barbour, *Religion in an Age of Science* (San Francisco, California: Harper, 1990), p. 3.

tific progress is most coherent with a theistic and spiritualist perspective. Now I will consider those presuppositions, and the feedback of scientific progress on them.

SELF-ORGANIZATION AND DIVINE ACTION

The ontological presuppositions of science refer to natural order. Empirical science studies natural patterns, which means order. The concept of order is so general that it can be considered a quasi-transcendental, as any conceivable state of affairs possesses some kind of order.

The more the sciences progress, the better we know how the natural order is structured. In classical physics order means regularities and laws. In recent times the progress of the physical sciences has made possible a big advance in the life sciences, where we find a higher type of order, namely organization. Our knowledge of natural order now includes cosmic and biological evolution, from the Big Bang up to the present. Therefore, we dispose now of a scientific picture of the world which includes the regularities of physics, the complexity of biology, and the evolutionary perspective of origins. I dare say that now, for the first time in history, we have a scientific worldview which provides a complete and unified picture of the world, because it includes all natural levels (micro- and macro-physical, as well as biological), their mutual relations, and their evolution. I do not mean that we know everything about the world. There is very much left for future generations. But we already know some basic features of the different natural levels and their mutual connections.

The new worldview is centered around a dynamic process of self-organization. Our world is the result of the deployment of a dynamism that produces different natural levels with new emergent characteristics. Nature is creative in a real sense.

In the new worldview the concept of information plays a relevant role. I used to say that information is "materialized rationality." It includes plans that are stored in spatio-temporal structures. It guides the successive formation of increasingly complex patterns. Information is stored, displayed, integrated, coded and decoded in the different natural systems and processes. In this perspective we can say that an electron "knows" physics and chemistry much better than us, as it will act in different circumstances according to the immensely varied potentialities it contains.

The corresponding idea of God is that of a Creator who has conceived the natural dynamism, and uses it to produce, according to the natural laws created by Him, a world of successive levels of emerging novelties. Our world does not exhaust the possibilities of creation. God usually acts respecting and protecting the natural capacities of his creatures, and He has given them marvelous potentialities which are never exhausted, so that new results can always be produced. Nature is full of organization, directionality, synergy (cooperativity), and very sophisticated activities. All this is most coherent with the "continuous" activity of divine wisdom.

These ideas are contained in a definition of nature provided by Thomas Aquinas, which is really good and surprisingly modern. Commenting Aristotle, Aquinas surpasses him and writes: "Nature is nothing other than the *ratio* of a certain art, namely, the divine, inscribed in things, by which things themselves move to a determinate end: just as if the master shipbuilder could impart to the wood something from which it could move itself to taking on the form of the ship."[9] Now we can say that God acts this way and we can provide many striking examples. Scientific progress turns order into self-organization, and helps us to consider the role that natural and divine creativity play here.

Evolution is often invoked as an argument for naturalism. Some people counterattack denying the very existence of evolution or criticizing the theories that try to explain it, but nothing of this sort is required. Although theories of evolution contain many unexplained enigmas, evolution is a scientifically respectful subject. Moreover, it can help us to understand better divine action in the world. In fact, evolution supposes self-organization. Therefore, it supposes the existence of a big chain of successive potentialities, that have been actualized thanks to a corresponding chain of adequate circumstances. All this is, to say the least, strikingly impressive, and is very coherent with the existence of a divine plan. In this line, Marie George comments:

> The fact that random processes can result in living things arising from non-living things presupposes the existence of not just any sort of matter, but one which has the potency to be formed into living things; further, not just any sort of agents will do, but there must be ones apt to impart the appropriate forms to the appropriate matter. In addition, in order for these supposedly randomly formed living things to survive and reproduce, there must be a habitat favorable to them, and the possibility of its development also needs explanation. Just as it is luck that one gets a royal flush, but not that one can get it—the deck is designed that way, so too it may be luck that this or that organism appear, but it cannot be luck

---

[9] "Natura nihil est aliud quam ratio cuiusdam artis, scilicet divinae, indita rebus, qua ipsae res moventur ad finem determinatum: sicut si artifex factor navis posset lignis tribuere quod ex se ipsis moverentur ad navis formam inducendam" (Thomas Aquinas, *In octo libros Physicorum Expositio* [Rome: Marietti, 1965], II, chap. 8: lect. 14, no. 268).

that it is able to appear. And this is true even if there are many universes. For even if the combination of factors which gives our universe its life-bearing potential have been "dealt" into it alone, and not to any others, these factors still must have a specific design if they are to make life possible. If there are no queens and kings, having five billion card games going instead of just one still won't get one any closer to drawing a royal flush.[10]

I will return to the many universes soon. Now I want to highlight that chance is not opposed to divine plan. The role that chance plays in evolution is sometimes interpreted as an argument against the existence of a divine plan. I will quote again Marie George who says on this point that "a difference of levels, however, leaves room for the same event to be both chance and intended without this involving a contradiction."[11] Aquinas himself argued that the divine government of the world is compatible with the existence of contingency,[12] and it can be shown that chance is required for the great variety of things in this world to be produced by natural means. Another typical confusion arises when the agency of secondary causes is seen as incompatible with divine agency.

Now I return to the many worlds. The ultimate argument against teleology eventually stems from the possible existence of many worlds. We should not be surprised by the specific organization of our world, so the argument runs, as it would only be the chance result of the evolution of an infinity of possible worlds. This criticism has been used routinely against the existence of purpose in the universe.[13] I must confess that I am not very impressed by this argument. In fact, if our world, as the result of an immense evolutionary process of self-organization, has the high degree of specific organization we perceive, this requires the existence of the chain of potentialities and circumstances I have already referred to: in this respect, it does not matter whether there is only one world or many of them.[14] Actually, our world is so specific that we could even think that God, wanting to form it according to natural

---

[10] Marie I. George, "On Attempts to Salvage Paley's Argument from Design," in *Science, Philosophy, and Theology*, forthcoming (South Bend, Indiana: St. Augustine's Press).

[11] Ibid.

[12] See Thomas Aquinas, *In duodecim libros Metaphysicorum Aristotelis* (Rome: Marietti, 1964), VI, chap. 3: lect. 3, nos. 1191–222; *Summa Theologiae* (Rome: Marietti, 1952), I, q. 19, a. 8.

[13] Brian Zamulinski, "Review of: M. A. Corey, *God and the New Cosmology: The Anthropic Design Argument*," *Australasian Journal of Philosophy* 72 (1994), p. 405.

[14] Marie George presents a similar argument, and quotes Arthur Peacocke in the same line ("On Attempts to Salvage Paley's Argument from Design").

principles, created a self-organizing universe so immense that our little world could be formed. As Joseph Zycinski puts it:

> Cosmologists for a long time have been intrigued by the question of why life appeared so late in a universe which has been expanding for 20 billion years, and why the density of matter in the universe is so small that successive generations continually relive Pascalian anxiety in their experience of the emptiness of infinite spaces. Modern cosmology supplies a partial explanation. Even if life were to develop in only one place, a large and old universe would have been required. Billions of years of cosmic evolution are necessary for the appearance of carbon producing stars, an indispensable element for the rise of known forms of life.[15]

Scientific progress provides us with a basis that is richer than ever for teleological reasoning. The present worldview does not by itself prove any meta-scientific thesis. It cannot be used, under the form of anthropic principles, as a substitute for metaphysical and theological reasoning. It does, however, show that our world is full of directional dimensions, of tendencies and synergy, of rationality. It introduces information, which is materialized rationality, as a concept that plays a central role in explaining our world. It represents our world as the result of a gigantic process of self-organization, where successive specific potentialities have become actualized, producing a series of increasingly organized systems that have culminated in the human organism, which provides the basis for a truly rational existence. Therefore, the present worldview amplifies the basis for teleological reasoning, which is one of the main bridges that may connect the natural and the divine.

SCIENTIFIC CREATIVITY AND HUMAN SINGULARITY

There is also a feedback from scientific progress on the epistemological presuppositions of science, which refer to the human ability to know nature's order. This is also related to the search for truth, which is the highest among the values that give meaning to the scientific enterprise.

Nature does not speak. In natural science we build sophisticated languages in order to question nature and interpret the answers provided by our mute partner. This shows that, although we are a part of nature, nevertheless we transcend it.

To achieve new knowledge of nature we must formulate new hypotheses, plan experiments in order to test them, interpret the results of experiments,

[15] Joseph Zycinski, "The Anthropic Principle and Teleological Interpretations of Nature," *The Review of Metaphysics* 41 (1987), p. 318.

and judge the value of the hypotheses. All this requires creativity. There are no automatic methods for achieving interesting results.

Scientific creativity is a proof of our singularity. It shows that we possess dimensions that transcend the natural ambit. They can be labeled as spiritual. The very existence and progress of the natural sciences is one of the best arguments for our spiritual character. The success of empirical science also shows that our spiritual dimensions, related to creativity and argument, are intertwined with our material dimensions, so that we are a single being constituted by both aspects. All this is coherent with the view that man is a co-creator who participates in God's plans, and has the capacity of carrying the natural and the human ambits to more and more evolved states.

Also at this level we can appreciate that scientific progress retro-justifies, enriches and refines the epistemological presuppositions of science. Thanks to this progress, we know better our own capacities, and we are able to develop them in a line of increasing creativity which corresponds to God's plans.

Jacques Monod used science to conclude that "man knows at last that he is alone in the universe's unfeeling immensity, out of which he emerged only by chance."[16] Christian de Duve, a biologist and Nobel laureate like Monod, comments:

> This is nonsense, of course. Man knows nothing of the sort. Nor does he have any proof to the contrary, either. What he does know, however—or, at least, should know—is that, with the time and amount of matter available, anything resembling the simplest living cell, let alone a human being, could not possibly have arisen by blind chance were the universe not pregnant with them.[17]

I have already noted that chance is compatible with a divine plan and, therefore, should not be used to argue against the existence of that plan.

Moreover, the evolutionary origin of man does not conflict with human spirituality. Speaking of the emergence of the human being, the agnostic Karl Popper wrote: "Now I want to emphasize how little is said by saying that the mind is an emergent product of the brain. It has practically no explanatory power, and it hardly amounts to more than putting a question mark at a certain place in human evolution. Nevertheless, I think that this is all which, from a Darwinian point of view, we can say about it."[18] Naturalism interprets

---

[16] Jacques Monod, *Chance and Necessity. An Essay on the Natural Philosophy of Modern Biology* (New York: Alfred A. Knopf, 1971), p. 180.

[17] Christian de Duve, *A Guided Tour of the Living Cell* (New York: Scientific American Books, 1984), pp. 357–58.

[18] Karl Popper (with John Eccles), *The Self and Its Brain* (New York: Springer, 1977), p. 554.

scientific progress as a proof that no dimensions other than those studied by the sciences can be considered on objective grounds. Instead, the role played by creativity, argument, and interpretation in science shows that the contrary is true.

The meaning and relevance of science reach their highest peak when we consider its ethical presuppositions. Empirical science is, above all, a human enterprise directed towards a twofold goal: a knowledge of nature that can be submitted to empirical control, and thus one that can provide a dominion over nature. Therefore, the meaning of science is also twofold: the pursuit of truth and the service to humankind. In this case, it is obvious that scientific progress retro-justifies, enriches and refines these goals, and provides better means for their implementation. Besides, scientific work requires an entire set of values, such as love for truth, rigor, objectivity, intellectual modesty, cooperation, interest to solve practical problems (medical, economic, and so on), so that scientific progress contributes to the spread of these values.

Searching for truth is a most relevant human value, central to the scientific enterprise. Speaking against scientism, Popper says: "The fact that science cannot make any pronouncement about ethical principles has been misinterpreted as indicating that there are no such principles; while in fact the search for truth presupposes ethics."[19] This is very important. Empirical science is meaningful above all as a search for truth, and this is a central ethical value in human life. The term "truth" is one of the most frequently used in the encyclical *Fides et Ratio*; in the English text it appears 365 times (without counting terms derived from truth). Pope John Paul II, in a few words full of philosophical meaning, writes: "One may define the human being, therefore, as *the one who seeks the truth*."[20]

There is another passage of *Fides et Ratio* which can easily remain unnoticed but is most important for my purpose. In the very beginning of the encyclical we read:

> In both East and West, we may trace a journey which has led humanity down the centuries to meet and engage truth more and more deeply. It is a journey which has unfolded—as it must—within the horizon of personal self-consciousness: the more human beings know reality and the world, the more they know themselves in their uniqueness, with the question of the meaning of things and of their very existence becoming ever more pressing.[21]

---

[19] Karl Popper, "Natural Selection and the Emergence of Mind," p. 141.
[20] Pope John Paul II, *Fides et Ratio*, 14 September 1998, no. 28.
[21] Ibid., no. 1.

This coincides with my emphasis on the anthropological feedback of scientific progress on human self-knowledge.[22]

Sometimes it is said that quantum mechanics has reintroduced the subject in the physical sciences. The real situation is much more interesting. There is always a reference to the subject in science. Only, this reference is not explicit: it remains implicit, unless we reflect on it. When we do this, we carry out a philosophical task that reveals the singularity of the subject who does science.

Alasdair MacIntyre says that empirical science should be considered a moral task because its aim is the pursuit of truth, and he adds: "The building of a representation of nature is, in the modern world, a task analogous to the building of a cathedral in the medieval world or to the founding and construction of a city in the ancient world, tasks which might also turn out to be interminable."[23] In this context, to be a realist, in the epistemological sense, is not indifferent.

THE MIND OF THE UNIVERSE

The new worldview presents a creative universe inhabited by creative human beings who are, at the same time, bearers of insignificance and of grandeur. This worldview is most coherent with the emphasis on God's respect towards creation. The resulting model of God and divine action underlines God's involvement with creation and God's respect for human freedom.

Just as in philosophy of science we speak of the empirical under-determination of theories by facts and, therefore, of the role of our interpretations, so too we find here God's transcendence over any particular data or representation. For instance, we can know that there should be a divine plan, but it is left to our free responsibility to recognize it, and to venture towards its implementation with a sense of ethical responsibility. Nobody can substitute us. There is an essential openness in nature, in human affairs and in the construction of our future.

God can also be viewed as an artist. The universe, and personal beings such as ourselves, participate in his creativity. This is most consistent with the self-organization of nature and with human freedom. Our world does not

[22] The particular emphasis ("the more . . . the more . . .") is absent in the Spanish version, while it is explicitly present in the Polish, Latin, French and German versions, and more or less explicit in the Italian version. Cf. Miroslaw Karol, "«Fides et ratio» n° 1: ¿Cuál es el texto correcto?", *Anuario Filosófico* 32 (1999), pp. 689–96.

[23] Alasdair MacIntyre, "Objectivity in Morality and Objectivity in Science," in *Morals, Science and Sociality*, eds. H. Tristram Engelhardt, Jr. and Daniel Callahan (Hastings-on-Hudson, New York: The Hastings Center, 1978), pp. 36–37.

exhaust God's creativity and perfection. Any representation of God will always be partial and imperfect. Nevertheless, we can know and experience those features of divine wisdom and love that we need in order to find the meaning of our lives.

I refer to God as "the mind of the universe" not in a pantheistic sense, but to express that our universe exhibits rationality, information and creativity; that it makes possible the existence of human beings who are strictly rational and creative; and that all this requires a divine foundation: a participation in God's creativity. Old and new ideas converge. In fact, I have borrowed the expression "the Mind of the Universe" from the Stoic Seneca who wrote:

> What is God? The mind of the universe. What is God? The whole that you see and the whole that you do not see. Thus we render to him his magnitude, because we can think of nothing greater, if he alone is everything, if he sustains his work from within and from without.[24]

Seneca's words were borrowed fifteen centuries later by Luis de Granada, one of the Spanish classical writers of Christian spirituality, who adopted them without any qualms, and even used them as a part of the argument that leads us from the contemplation of nature to the knowledge of its Creator.[25] At that time only small fragments of modern empirical science existed. The progress of science has changed our view of nature in a number of significant ways. We can safely conclude, however, that a philosophical reflection on this progress goes hand in hand with a religious view of nature and man.

[24] "Quid est deus? Mens universi. Quid est deus? Quod vides totum et quod non vides totum. Sic demum magnitudo illi sua redditur, quia nihil maius cogitari potest, si solus est omnia, si opus suum et intra et extra tenet" (Lucius Annaeus Seneca, *Quaestiones naturales* [Paris: Les Belles Lettres, 1961], vol. 1, Bk. I, chap. 13, pp. 10–11).

[25] "¿Qué cosa es Dios? Mente y razón del universo. ¿Qué cosa es Dios? Todo lo que vemos, porque en todas las cosas vemos su sabiduría y asistencia, y desta manera confesamos su grandeza, la cual es tanta, que no se puede pensar otra mayor. Y si él solo es todas las cosas, él es el que dentro y fuera sustenta esta grande obra que hizo" (Luis de Granada, *Introducción del Símbolo de la fe*, Part I, chap. 1, ed. José M. Balcells [Madrid: Cátedra, 1989], pp. 129–30).

Science, Postmodernism, and the Challenge of Philosophy in the New Century

Warren Murray

T he profound changes in philosophy in the last four centuries, particularly its ever narrowing field of inquiry, is in part a result of the rise of the experimental sciences. But we should not forget that philosophy was itself a cause of that rise, at least in the particular way it occurred. Both Bacon and Descartes insisted that natural philosophy should henceforth be practical, and this practical approach corresponded to the method of the new experimental sciences, leaving no place for the old theoretical philosophy of nature.

Having thus excluded itself from the field of nature, philosophy has had to seek out other areas and other approaches to knowledge in an effort to justify its existence. The impact of the new sciences it spawned quickly became so great that philosophy has had all it could do to remain in existence. It tried the critical approach and various versions of claims to absolute knowledge; unable to compete with them, it tried to synthesize the sciences, or put their houses in order, or, full of envy at their prestige, to deny to the sciences any real value. But progressively, philosophy has generally become simply the history of philosophy, and philosophical reflection has given way to scholarship. We have come to a point where it is either assumed that philosophy should be dependent on the sciences or on history or philology and their methods, or that its field should have nothing to do with any objective or systematic knowledge of things.

Indeed, contemporary philosophy, whether in its wildest postmodernist expressions, or in the half-way houses of a Gadamer or a Rorty, attests to its own incapacity to answer the perennial philosophical questions, or sometimes even to recognize them as valid. In their place are proposed questions to which, it is maintained, there are not even any answers. Yet we are told that asking such questions, and discussing them with others, without, however, any hope of ever resolving them, is the ultimate goal of philosophy. Obviously, such an attitude, based on the belief that truth is unobtainable, can only lead to skepticism, cynicism and solipsistic system building.

There is no serious reason to expect that the present-day skepticism and solipsism in philosophy will simply disappear on their own as new methods of analysis are supposedly found; it is more likely that before they do, the mind-set that engendered them will have spread its poison to all aspects of the intellectual life, and that even the sciences, with their resultant technologies, will fall victim to their own success. The war now being waged between the extremes of scientism and of postmodernism (e.g., the "Sokal Affair") could likely destroy all the middle ground as well, and philosophers of a realist bent (if there still are any in a few years) will find themselves without an audience and without jobs.

It is easy enough to understand why modern philosophy, in its historical mode, has tended to substitute erudition for thought: where skepticism has excluded universal truth, there can remain but conventional truth or opinion, along with, perhaps, some more or less well-established individual facts. And if one is not sure about the truth of some philosopher's doctrine, one can perhaps try to decide what he meant at least, or failing that, what he wrote, or when he wrote it, etc. Finally, there need remain nothing more than the text itself, which in this context might mean anything.

Now, philosophers can either continue to follow this slippery slope of system building, or they can return to the great Greek tradition and build upon it by applying its principles to the problems of today. What Chesterton said about Christianity can also be said about traditional philosophy in the present age: it has not been tried and failed, it has simply not been tried.

The great English writer and apologist, C. S. Lewis, had a pet peeve about Christians who felt obliged to always affix to their Christianity some other doctrine in order to make it fashionable: Christianity and X; Christianity and Y. Instead of such efforts to try to make Christianity more relevant by associating it with some fashionable enterprise, he preferred what he called "Mere Christianity," believing that Christianity itself sufficed. Well, I would like to propose that the tradition incarnate in such philosophical schools as "Thomism" and "Aristotelianism" is sufficient to supply future generations with the principles of solid philosophical thought, as they did in the past, without the addition of any other principles, and without mixing them up with radically incompatible schools of modern philosophy.

Nothing in such a proposal, however, ought to be taken as implying that there is no need to correct the details of this perennial philosophy, but adding on new discoveries and removing opinions found to be clearly erroneous is not at all the same thing as trying to correct the very principles and basic teachings of this philosophy. To fail to make this distinction is to fail to see the difference between common experience and what can be derived from it with certitude, and particular experience, which necessarily leads us to less certitude as it leads us to more detail. Analyzing the common concepts derived from common experience is the privileged sphere of philosophical reflection, whereas the expansion of experience into more and more particular forms, and the subsequent efforts to explain this experience by the use of *a priori* hypotheses, is especially the domain of the experimental sciences. And just as common experience comes before and is prerequisite to particular experience, so too philosophy must come before and be in some way prerequisite to science. I say "in some way," since it is obviously not necessary to have done philosophy in order to do the sciences, but it is necessary to have done philosophy in order to understand what is being done in science and what the knowledge obtained in these particular disciplines is worth. In point of fact, natural philosophy, with its general considerations of nature, causality, motion, time and place is wisdom in respect to the experimental sciences. These principles are the only ones that allow for anything more than an accidental and *ad hoc* understanding of what science is doing and what scientific knowledge is worth.

This role of philosophy as wisdom is so intrinsic to what philosophy is that we could well maintain that either philosophy is the queen of the sciences, or it is nothing—nothing, that is, but empty rhetoric. To hold that its only legitimate task in respect to other disciplines is to synthesize their findings is to beg the question of its nature and role. In virtue of what particular competence can philosophy claim this task as its own unless it is first of all antecedent to the sciences and wisdom in respect to them? Unless it already has some more general principles and a more general method, it can do no synthesizing. It is, in fact, because philosophy has abandoned the study of reality that it can no longer have a role to play in respect to the more particular disciplines.

Indeed, one crucial place where philosophy has abandoned its claims to being able to know a fundamental part of reality is with respect to nature. The modern world has more and more firmly rejected the idea of nature, that is, that things have a distinctive constitution which is a principle of their activities and which determines their end or ends, and that the knowledge of this is the most important kind of knowledge about them that there is. We have come so far as to deny that even we human beings have a nature and thus some pre-ordained end. Such a denial manifestly subverts any attempt to establish a uniform and unvarying moral code, and destroys the science of ethics and politics.

Even those who, influenced by religious belief, will continue to try to keep reason in the service of the truly human good, being deprived of natural philosophy, will also end up in systems of thought that they cannot justify and will thus cease to have any impact outside of the narrow circle of their disciples.

The ultimate bankruptcy of philosophical thought will leave a void that will soon become filled with ideas of another kind, coming from ill-digested science or pseudo-science, and this will poison theology and ethics beyond any hope of immediate recovery. Or, worse yet, the reaction against the abuses of reason will reach a paroxysm and society will revert to barbarism.

Things are already well-advanced along both of these fronts. But, someone might well object: What good all this rhetoric if in fact these ancient doctrines have been shown to be false? Must we not learn to live with the truth, however disagreeable? Should we not rather be seeking alternate bases for philosophy—ones more compatible with the discoveries of the modern sciences?

I would suggest that such projects, however sincere, are ill-conceived and destined to failure. For one, I have seen no proof that the basic concepts of Aristotelian-Thomistic philosophy, such as nature and causality, have been refuted by anyone. Their rejection is not a refutation, although we would be well-advised to ask why they were rejected, or why other concepts were put in their place. And although we may have no difficulty in seeing that the rejection of traditional principles almost always comes from failing to even understand them, this itself calls for an explanation.

I would further hold that it is not science that is to dictate to philosophy its principles, but the inverse, however much our modern ways of thinking may make such a proposition seem preposterous. To return to true philosophy does not at all imply a negation of experimental science or of its technology. It rather places these disciplines in their proper framework and allows them better to serve humankind.

In trying to understand the differences between philosophy of nature and the experimental sciences in respect to the kinds of knowledge they give us of nature, it is good to reflect on the fact that science, in its attempts at explanation, can at best shadow nature and natural phenomena. It can, it is true, thanks to its mode, arrive at the discovery of many new and detailed facts about nature. But these facts themselves, the more they are particular and detailed, the less they will be certain. We may, for example, be fairly well-assured that when quantum physics talks about virtual particles and quantum voids in space that these expressions do correspond in some way to observables, but we have no assurance that what they correspond to is really what they claim to have described. What the scientist observes, as many great physicists, such as Niels Bohr, Werner Heisenberg, Arthur Eddington and Albert Einstein, were often wont to insist on, are always simple things at our level of observation. We do not experience elementary particles, we see traces of water droplets in a cloud chamber; we do not observe biological evolution, we find fossils in the rocks, etc. These so-called factual entities beyond our ken are, in fact, largely theoretical entities.

It is also true to say that the knowledge that philosophy of nature gives us is a very general one indeed. So much so that we, habituated as we are to the more detailed knowledge furnished by the experimental sciences, may be inclined to dismiss it as without much worth. What such philosophical knowledge lacks in detail, however, it more than makes up for in both its fundamental character and in its certitude. The philosophy of nature does not shadow reality, it talks directly about it; it does not limit itself to the measurable and quantitative aspects of nature, it considers nature in all its aspects, and most importantly, it seeks to know what natural things are.

Certainly, it does not get to such knowledge for particular things in nature. We can hardly know what a man is, never mind a horse or a tulip. But it does aim at this. Furthermore, it has become evident through the last few centuries that natural philosophy cannot come to know these things all by itself; it must take as an ally the experimental sciences, but it must do so, so as to remain wisdom for them. Without the detailed knowledge which biology, chemistry and physics supply about natural things, we will never complete the project that Aristotle set as a task for natural philosophy: namely, to reach to the very elements of things. On the other hand, if we do not admit the role that the more general and philosophical part of the study of nature must play, our knowledge of nature will remain without interpretative principles, without direction, and seriously fragmented.

In order to understand more clearly what I am trying to say, let us examine some of the consequences that have arisen from the break with the tradition of Greek philosophical thought:

1) As I mentioned earlier, one of the biggest differences between philosophy in our age and that of the Greek tradition concerns the concept of nature. Now, modern thought denies or ignores nature as an intrinsic principle of movement and rest. For many centuries now, the word *nature,* although retaining some of its original senses in common usage, has been more and

more restricted in philosophical and scientific writings to signifying either the totality of sensible things, or a vague principle derived from a sort of distillation of the combined activities of these natural things, or a force acting throughout the universe in a rather blind way, or as some vague intention attributable to this force. Even where the word is used to express the essence of something, it is taken less as a principle of motion and rest than as something static and inert. And this is one reason for the misunderstandings about Aristotle's concept of nature, since many moderns seem to think that if a thing has a determinate nature, then it must differ from any other creature with a different nature in the same way that a triangle differs from a circle, or one number from another. Aristotle's nature is form and it is matter. And from the combination of these two there arises a natural being which, although it may share a common nature with others, still retains particularities due to its matter. Its nature might also tend towards that of another kind, even to the point where it may become difficult or even impossible to distinguish clearly between the two. This flexibility in nature, this gradual passage between one nature and another, need not lead to a blurring of the distinctions between things, which would be the case if the modern notion of nature were accepted.

2) Something closely related to this denial of nature is the denial of many forms of causality, chief among which is the final cause, and this also amounts to the denial that there is any transcendence in nature. It is indeed in seeking to understand how the final cause is a possible cause that we are led to see something beyond the purely material and sensible world. Now, this denial stems from more than an intellectual problem, and more often than not finds its roots in a desire to abolish any transcendence from the world. Those who want no God behind the world must leave no place for Him, whereas to admit finality quite obviously leaves the door open to His intrusion in our neat little machine-world.

3) The second of the causes that are denied—and this will sound strange indeed—is a true efficient cause. This is so since no efficient cause can operate without an end. The efficient cause has been replaced in modern physics by forces which, ironically, are always necessarily violent, that is, that always act from the outside and against the resistance of the bodies they act upon. Now this is precisely what Aristotle would criticize: there can be no violent motion if there is no natural one, and no natural one without an end. One of the results of this modern position is that motion itself is denied in what is most essential to it: the existence of a mobile that is not only able to change, but that is in fact changing. With inertial motion, as this has been defined since Descartes, we cannot even decide what is moving or how.

4) There is a third kind of cause that is not entirely denied, but is rather seriously limited, and this is the material cause; all that is kept of it is a matter considered as an already existing component of things. This is what an Aristotelian would call "secondary matter." What is eliminated is matter as potency or ability to be things. And this is what matter most of all is.

5) Now, all that really remains is the formal cause. Can we at least say that modern thought, and science in particular, has at least left this cause intact? Unfortunately not. Even the formal cause of natural things is not really retained. As an example, let us take the case of the soul. Now, according to Aristotle, the soul is the form of the living thing. The modern mind, on the other hand, would find this far too abstract a form. Form, for the moderns, is either the exterior shape of something, or some accidental aspect of it, or a representation of the thing, as is a portrait or a symbol, or a mathematical equation. What science has done to explain things is to introduce extrinsic formal causes, which are *a priori* representations of reality. In physics, these are principally to be found in mathematical equations.

6) Looking now at another fundamental philosophical question, namely, how the mind is related to things, we find two essential traits that are reversed in modern thought. First of all, it is now generally held that the mind is an active principle which measures the things we know, rather than being a passive ability measured by the things it knows. This doctrine was developed in some continuity with the teachings of the Latin Averroists, but was strongly influenced by the *a priori* method of the sciences; it reached its consecration as a principle in Kant's version of the Copernican revolution, and then this doctrine gradually gave way to an even more subjective concept of knowledge for which the mind creates in total freedom the concepts it uses.

7) Concomitant with this concept of the knowing mind was the reversal of the relation between the will and its object, the good. Whereas traditional philosophy held that the good measures the will and that, hence, a will is only to be called good if it is fixed in the good, the modern spirit found this too constraining and decided that it was rather the will that measured the good. Although these two positions had antecedents (they are, in fact, the ultimate triumph of Protagoras's doctrine that man is the measure of all things), in modern times the main force in establishing these ideas came from Kant. This strange doctrine about the anteriority of the will to its object reached its ultimate consecration in the philosophy of Jean-Paul Sartre, who accords to man the kind of absolute freedom that even God could not have.

8) Furthermore, given that the good was no longer considered to be the measure of the will, and given that in art it is we who are the measures of the works that are produced, it was only inevitable that there should come about

a substitution of art (technique) for prudence, both for the individual and for political society. Now, traditional philosophy held that art must be subject to prudence, since the latter is concerned with all the means to the ultimate end of man.

9) Another of the consequences of the above changes in mind-set is that theoretical knowledge has become subordinate to practical knowledge, whereas the tradition placed practical knowledge after, and considered it inferior to, the theoretical. Both Francis Bacon and René Descartes were insistent on claiming that the ancients, Aristotle especially, had produced but sterile philosophical reflections, whereas the new natural philosophy must be practical. For Descartes, this meant that although metaphysics and physics itself constituted the roots and the trunk of the tree of knowledge, its branches and fruits were to be sought further out, and consisted of knowledge of a practical nature, such as medicine, mechanics and ethics. Bacon, for his part, proclaimed that "knowledge is power." And indeed this is what it has become. The very idea today of a science of nature which is not productive seems strange to us. Yet this was the ideal of the Greek tradition.

10) Another major transformation of thought concerns logic. Whereas logic for an Aristotelian is the art or science of directing the mind in coming to truth, and whereas it was thought that for that purpose it had to be concerned with concepts, the modern mind (started with Galileo, Descartes and Leibniz, and reaching a certain perverse perfection in Frege and Russell) has succeeded in conflating logic and mathematics. This has come about for many reasons, chief among which are confusions about the nature and purpose of logic, on the one hand, and the nature of mathematics, on the other. If mathematics is seen to be purely instrumental, yet, in a sense, tautological, and logic is thought to be the same, what would distinguish them? If words and symbols are the same, what could distinguish an art of using words from one that manipulates symbols? Besides, the use of symbols in science has long proved to be not only important, but indispensable. Therefore, all of logic should follow the same path.

In addition, the tendency to nominalism, which started already in the late Middle Ages, amounts to a denial of the universal, of essential definitions, and of categorical reasoning, as well as of dialectic. Such a conception of thought, although false on every score, is tied in some ways to the scientific method, since the latter is not really trying to get to the essences of things. A clear sign of this, for example, is to be found in the modern schools of biological taxonomy, all of which tend to be nominalistic.

11) Finally, having denied and reversed all the principles of ancient philosophy, what should be more natural than that the end itself of this discipline—

wisdom—should be denied. There is no transcendence in modern philosophy. Everything is this-worldly. Being is no longer sought for its own sake, nor are its causes. So, after having eliminated natural philosophy, mathematics, logic and ethics, modern thought takes on metaphysics.

We must conclude, then, that it is not only a few differences of opinion that separate ancient philosophy from the modern, but an entire world-view. Perhaps, in fact, the word "philosophy" comes close to being purely equivocal.

Without the knowledge that a solid and independent philosophy can furnish, many philosophers and scientists will feel free to impose on reality, ourselves included, whatever they desire and whatever technology allows. Without such a basis for thought and action as a correct conception of nature allows, philosophers will continue to hold that the mind is not measured by truth and can thus think whatever it wants, and that the will is not measured by some objective good, but should exercise a radical freedom and attempt to specify its own object, and then call this object the good.

If philosophers forget that philosophy is first and foremost wisdom and not game-playing, and that what is proper to wisdom is to direct, then they will necessarily lose their rightful place among the disciplines and leave a vacuum that will be filled otherwise.

In point of fact, the malaise that pervades the modern mind and that has spawned such monsters as postmodernism, has at least the justification of its origin in the absence of principles that might have allowed the sciences to find their proper place, instead of falling into the hubris of scientism. Postmodernism is simply a reaction to a bad situation—a blind reaction, indeed, but a partly understandable one. If we as philosophers would like to see something more serious on the philosophical menu, perhaps it is up to us to put it there.

To do so, philosophers will have to return to the independence and common sense of the Greek tradition, to master well its wisdom, and to use this thought to answer the modernist and postmodernist problems with objective knowledge, and the "scientistic" contention that outside of science there is no truth. Concretely, this will mean a return to a study of Aristotelian logic, natural philosophy, ethics and metaphysics, for only in so doing will philosophy be able to answer the various forms of reductionism and the despair of finding any truth that have progressively taken hold of the discipline in the last century or so.

The Catholic Faith, Scripture, and the Question of the Existence of Intelligent Extra-terrestrial Life

Marie I. George

T he vastness and beauty of the heavens evoke feelings of awe and wonder, and have led people throughout the ages to ask: Are we alone in
the universe? This question has enjoyed increased popularity in recent
times. Aside from the many writers of fiction who earn their living by popu-
lating the skies, a fair number of contemporary scientists have been engaging
in speculations about extra-terrestrial life, some even searching for it. The positions advocated by scientists in turn have stimulated the thought of theologians and philosophers of science. A wide variety of positions has been
adopted, one of which I intend to examine here. It has to do with a question
which arises if one concedes that intelligent ET life may exist, namely, if intelligent ET life exists, does that mean that Christianity which proclaims that
the Son of God became a human being to save us from our sins is merely an
anthropocentric story? A common response to this question is that the discovery of ET life[1] poses no threat to Christianity—it would simply be the case
that the universe turned out to be bigger than the Scriptures led us to believe.
What is often not made clear is exactly why someone might think that the existence of ETs would relegate Christianity to the realm of mythology. Correspondingly, the grounds for the claim that there is no incompatibility between
the beliefs are often more hinted at than explicated.

The purpose of this paper is to clarify what if any incompatibility there is
between Catholic Christian beliefs and the existence of ETs. I am not going
to examine the scientific investigations which bear upon the likelihood of ET

---

[1] Hereafter ET life is to be understood to refer to intelligent ET life.

life, partly because many others are more knowledgeable than myself in this area, and partly because these discussions have little direct bearing on my main purpose. If there are grounds for maintaining that there is or is not a conflict between Christian belief and the existence of extra-terrestrial life, these grounds are not going to disappear because of what science says one way or the other about the likelihood of extra-terrestrial life.

The existence of extra-terrestrial life could conflict with the Catholic faith in three ways. First, it could directly conflict with official Church teaching.[2] Second, it could conflict with Scriptural passages. Sometimes the latter conflict coincides with the former, but this is not always the case since Catholicism is not a "religion of the book," and not all passages of Scripture have an official interpretation. Finally, belief in ET life could also conflict with traditional beliefs which the faithful are not bound to adhere to (beliefs such as limbo). The latter two forms of conflict are less acute; such Scriptural passages are subject to reinterpretation, and such traditional beliefs sometimes go out of vogue. I will limit myself here to considering official Church teachings, and the most relevant and most problematic of the passages of Scripture which do not have an official interpretation.

The Good News is that the Second Person of the Trinity became a human being in order to save human beings from sin,[3] both original sin and personal sin. Christ realized our salvation by his death on the cross and his resurrection from the dead. Since Christ's sacrifice does not save us without cooperation on our part, a substantial amount of Christian doctrine concerns what we must do in order to obtain eternal life. The supposed conflict with Christian belief and belief in ETs is not with the teachings about Christian behavior, but with those concerning the Incarnation and Redemption.

One kind of argument regarding the existence of ETs is based on the failure of Scripture to mention them. From this omission people have argued to opposite conclusions. Those who are convinced of the reliability of Scripture conclude that ETs do not exist. Whereas those who lack this prior conviction, and who are inclined to admit the existence of ETs, conclude that Scripture is unreliable.

Both of these arguments base themselves either on a faulty supposition as to the purpose of Scripture or as to its completeness, or on an unjustified assumption about the relation of ETs to humans, and sometimes on more than

---

[2] "[T]he Christian faith is not a 'religion of the book'" (*Catechism of the Catholic Church* [Bloomingdale, Ohio: Apostolate for Family Consecration, 1994], no. 108). (Hereafter cited as *CCC*.)

[3] See *CCC*, no. 457.

one of these. The purpose of Scripture is not to instruct us about the constitution of the cosmos, but to teach us things that we need to know to save our souls. Thus, when Scripture does not speak of something, the probable conclusion to be drawn is that knowledge of that thing does not pertain to our salvation. I say "probable conclusion" because not every article of the faith is found in Scripture, the Immaculate Conception being a case in point. What is found in Scripture is written for our salvation; what is not found in Scripture may or may not pertain to our salvation. Thus those who reason that Scripture says nothing about the existence of ETs and therefore they do not exist, first assume that knowledge of ET existence pertains to our salvation, and second that everything that pertains to our salvation is necessarily in Scripture. Those who reason that Scripture is unreliable because it does not speak of ETs, either mistakenly think that the purpose of Scripture is to give a course in cosmology, or while acknowledging its purpose regards our salvation, assume, as their opponents do, that knowledge of ET existence pertains to our salvation, and that everything pertaining thereto is spoken about in Scripture.

A probable case, however, can be made that if ETs exist, the reason why Scripture omits any reference to them is because such knowledge is unimportant for our salvation. A reference to Catholic belief concerning another type of intelligent being is helpful here. The *Catechism of the Catholic Church* states that "Angels are a truth of the faith."[4] Angels played and still play a role in regard to our salvation, and are repeatedly mentioned in Scripture: our first mother sinned at the instigation of a fallen angel; the new Eve at the announcement of an angel became the Mother of God; Christ speaks about children having angels, etc. If ETs had a similar impact on our salvation it is reasonable to expect to hear about them in Scripture just as we hear about angels, with oral tradition remaining an alternate means of our knowing about them. Factually no extra-terrestrial has had any known effect on any human individual whatsoever. Moreover, salvation has already been effected through Christ's death and resurrection. Whence: "'The Christian economy, therefore, since it is the new and definitive Covenant, will never pass away; and no new public revelation is to be expected before the glorious manifestation of our Lord Jesus Christ.'"[5]

The discovery of ETs would not be reason to revise God's saving plan for humanity, nor would ETs bring us some new revelation. Any future interactions we might have with them would not be radically different than those with our fellow humans, and thus how we should treat them and how we

---

[4] *CCC*, no. 328.
[5] *Dei Verbum* 4, quoted in *CCC*, no. 66.

should expect them to treat us is already known to us through the Ten Commandments and the other moral teachings of the New Testament. ETs as rational material beings would have the same rights as we do to life, property, good name, etc.[6] And they would have a similar potential to impact on our lives as others humans do, by exhorting us to do good, by giving good example, etc. or by the opposite, leading us astray, giving us bad example, granted they may perhaps be more helpful or pernicious than our fellow humans if they are more intelligent than they.

It is noteworthy that Augustine and Aquinas seriously entertained the possibility that there exist intelligent beings in the universe in addition to humans and angels, namely, animated celestial bodies. These theologians did not immediately reject this possibility because Scripture makes no mention of such beings.[7] This is reasonably ascribed not only to their conviction that Scripture did not teach everything there could be known about the cosmos, but also to their confidence that there could be no conflict between faith and reason. God could certainly create other intelligent beings if he wanted to, and if they were discovered their existence was not going to conflict with God's teaching about himself which comes to us through the Christian Faith. But let us return to making plain what the purported points of conflict are.

Some thinkers do not see a problem in Scripture's lack of mention of ETs, but instead discern a conflict between the teachings of the faith and certain consequences of ET existence. Among these are Abbé Joseph Émile Filachou who sees accepting ET life as incompatible with Christian belief on three counts: "the importance presupposed [in Scripture] of the role of man on earth, the supreme dignity attributed to the Divine founder of the Christian Church, and finally the grandeur attributed to the Church itself."[8]

The first point can be answered by saying that the existence of ETs does not as such prejudice the role of humans on earth as having dominion over

[6] Note that a question arises as to whether they should be baptized.

[7] "Whether, however, some incorporeal substances are united to the celestial bodies as forms, Augustine leaves in doubt and so does Origen. Which nevertheless seems to be rejected by many moderns for the reason that since the number of the blessed according to divine Scripture is made up from human beings and angels alone, those spiritual substances cannot be counted among human souls nor among Angels who are incorporeal. But nevertheless Augustine even leaves this in doubt. . . ." (Thomas Aquinas, *De Quaestiones Disputatae de Potentia* in *Quaestiones Disputatae*, ed. P. Bazzi et al. [Turin: Marietti, 1965], vol. 2, q. 6, art. 6, resp.).

[8] *De la pluralité des mondes*, p. 100, quoted by Michael J. Crowe in *The ET Life Debate 1750–1900: The Idea of a Plurality of Worlds from Kant to Lowell* (New York: Cambridge University Press, 1986), p. 411. (Hereafter cited as *The ET Life Debate 1750–1900*.)

the earth. Even if ETs were superior to us in intelligence, we as rational creatures would not be their slaves any more than one human is the slave of another human who is significantly more intelligent; nor would ETs have any right to our property from the simple fact they are more intelligent. ET immigration would raise the same sorts of problems human immigration raises, e.g., perhaps we would be obligated to share the earth with them.

Filachou's other two questions regarding the relation such beings would have to Christ and to his Church, however, are not so easily resolved. As to their relation to Christ a wide variety of scenarios has been proposed, and evaluated in the light of Christian teaching.[9]

One possibility is that these beings never sinned, and thus are not in need of a redeemer.[10] That such occur does not seem excluded by any Catholic teaching. Christ would be the head of these beings, as he is head of the angels, and knowledge about Christ would be of interest to them in the same way it is of interest to the angels.[11]

Another possibility is that the ETs did not sin, are not in need of a redeemer, and yet the Word becomes incarnate as one of them for reasons other than redemption. Although human redemption is the chief reason given for the Incarnation of Christ as a human being, other reasons for his Incarnation are given as well. If God so chose he could certainly become incarnate as another human-type being for reasons other than redeeming that people. (I say "human-type" being because the ETs are supposed not to be pure spirits, but

---

[9] See C. S. Lewis, "Religion and Rocketry," in *Fern-Seed and Elephants and Other Essays on Christianity*, ed. Walter Hooper (London: Fontana, 1975).

[10] Another possibility proposed by some is that ETs were created for a purely natural happiness and were never offered grace so as to be able to live a supernatural life. In this case, at the end of time there would be upright intelligent beings existing in separation from the Church triumphant. This accords poorly, if at all with Eph. 1:8–10 which says that "He has let us know the mystery of his purpose, the hidden plan he so kindly made in Christ from the beginning to act upon when the times had run their course to the end: that he would bring everything together under Christ, as head, everything in the heavens and everything on earth." The possibility that the first ET parents did not sin, but some of their offspring did does not demand separate analysis.

[11] "[James] Beattie's . . . final reply posits extended effects from the redemption. He states that extraterrestrials 'will not suffer for our guilt, nor be rewarded for our obedience. But it is not absurd to imagine, that our fall and recovery may be useful to them as an example; and that the divine grace manifested in our redemption may raise their adoration and gratitude into higher raptures and quicken their ardour to inquire . . . into the dispensations of infinite wisdom.' Moreover, he suggests that this view is 'not mere conjecture [but] derives plausibility from many analogies in nature; as well as from holy writ, which represents the mystery of our redemption as an object of curiosity to superior beings, and our repentance as an occasion of their joy'" (Crowe, *The ET Life Debate 1750–1900*, p. 102).

to have a body as well.)[12] However, a complication arises with the possibility that Christ become incarnate more than one time, namely, passages from Scripture indicate that there is one Lord, Jesus Christ:

> And even if there were things called gods, either in the sky or on earth—where there certainly seem to be "gods" and "lords" in plenty—still for us there is one God, the Father, from whom all things come and for whom we exist; and there is one Lord, Jesus Christ, through whom all things come and through whom we exist (1 Cor. 8:5–6).

> His state was divine, yet he did not cling to his equality with God, but emptied himself to assume the condition of a slave, and became as men are; and being as all men are, he was humbler yet, even to accepting death, death on a cross. But God raised him high and gave him the name which is above all other names, so that all beings in the heavens, on the earth and in the underworld, should bend at the name of Jesus and that every tongue should acclaim Jesus Christ as Lord, to the glory of God the Father (Phil. 2:6–11).

If the Second Person became incarnate on another planet as an ET, there would appear to be a Lord other than Jesus Christ, true God and true man, since what would be true of the Second Person as having an ET nature would not be true of the Second Person as having a human nature. One solution proposed is that "one Lord" applies to Christ in his divine nature alone.[13] Thus, the Second Person incarnate as an ET would not be a Lord other than our Lord Jesus Christ. However, this interpretation does not accord well with the passage just cited from Philippians, which implies that it is the Word incarnate (as man) who is given the name "Lord."[14] The Word

[12] Scripture excludes the possibility that there existed on earth other races of human beings that were not descended from Adam. "If it is certain that death reigned over everyone as the consequence of one man's fall, it is even more certain that one man, Jesus Christ, will cause everyone to reign in life who receives the free gift that he does not deserve, of being made righteous." (Rom. 5:17) See also Pope Pius XII, *Humani Generis* (Boston: Daughters of St. Paul, ca. 1950), no. 37.

[13] "At another point [Terrasson] counters the claim that Scripture explicitly states that there is but one Lord by interpreting it as applying only to the divine part of Christ's nature. Admitting that Christ's terrestrial incarnation and redemption have sufficient merit for the entire universe, he nonetheless suggests that because Christ has a role both as savior and as teacher, his incarnation as teacher on sinless planets is fully appropriate" (Crowe, *The ET Life Debate 1750–1900* , p. 135).

[14] Note that the manner in which the Father gave this name to a man is through the grace of union, by which Christ would be at the same time God and man. The incarnation was not a reward for Christ's passion, but preceded it. However, sometimes in Scripture something is said to happen, when it becomes known. Christ's divinity was much more manifest after the resurrection. Therefore, the Father does not give Christ the name "Lord" as if Christ did not have it from the time of his incarnation, but he is said to give it when Christ comes to be commonly venerated as Lord. See Thomas Aquinas, *Super Epistolas S. Pauli*, ed. P. Raphaelis Cai, O.P. (Rome: Marietti, 1953), vol. 2, nos. 70–71.

in his divine nature is eternally Lord as begotten by the Father. Although perhaps it is ultimately correct that a supposed Lord of the ETs would not be a lord other than Our Lord Jesus Christ because of the unity of the person assuming those two natures, still in light of the natures assumed being two, it is at very least counter-intuitive to say that there would not be two Lords.

A number of other passages from Scripture pose a similar sort of problem.[15] They refer to Christ as the head of all things:

> Such is the richness of the grace which he has showered on us in all wisdom and insight. He has let us know the mystery of his purpose, the hidden plan he so kindly made in Christ from the beginning to act upon when the times had run their course to the end: that he would bring *everything together under Christ, as head, everything in the heavens and everything on earth* (Eph. 1:8–10). [Emphasis mine]

A question pertinent for our purposes is whether Christ is the head of the angels in his humanity or only in his divinity. Aquinas maintains that:

> The head causes an influx of sensation and motion to all members of the body. . . . [S]omeone can understand "to flow into" ("influere") in two ways according to the spiritual sense and mode. One mode as principal agent: And thus it belongs to God alone to provide an influx of grace in the members of the Church. In another mode instrumentally: And thus even the humanity of Christ is a cause of the said influx; because as Damascene says . . . as iron burns on account of the fire conjoined to it, so were the actions of the humanity of Christ on account of the united divinity, of which the humanity itself was an instrument. Christ, nevertheless, according to the two last conditions of head [governance, influence] is able to be called head of the angels according to human nature, and head of both according to divine nature; not, however, according to the first condition [namely, sameness in nature], unless one takes what is common according to the nature of the genus, according as man and angel agree in rational nature, and further what is common according to analogy, according as it is common to the Son along with all creatures to receive from the Father, as Basil says, by reason of which he is said to be the first-born of all creatures, Col. 1:15.[16]

Aquinas maintains, then, that it is the union of the human nature to the divine nature in the person of Christ which makes that human nature an

---

[15] To be "lord" and to be "head" are closely related, but not exactly the same thing. One is called "Lord" in virtue of one's power, whereas one is denominated "head" by likeness to certain features of a bodily head. These features include perfection (the head being the seat of all five senses), sublimity (the head is the highest member), influence (in a certain manner sensation and motion flow to the other parts of the body from the head), and conformity of nature with the other members. See Thomas Aquinas, *Super Epistolas S. Pauli*, ed. P. Raphaelis Cai, O.P., vol. I (Rome: Marietti, 1953), 1 Cor., no. 587.

[16] *Quaestiones Disputatae de Veritate*, in *Quaestiones Disputatae*, ed. Raymundi M. Spiazzi, O.P. (Turin: Marietti, 1964), vol. 1, q. 29, art. 4, resp. The question addressed is: "Whether to be the head of grace belongs to Christ according to his human nature."

instrument of governing and causing in regard to all creatures. Before that union Christ "would have been the head of the Church only according to his divine nature, but after sin [which Aquinas takes to be the main reason for the Incarnation] it is necessary that he be head of the Church also according to his human nature."[17]

An ET nature united to the divine nature in Christ would then also be an instrument of governing and causing in regard to all creatures. Would there then be two heads (and two Churches), if "head" refers to the Word in both his divine and in his several assumed natures?

Questions which pertain to the hypostatic union are of the greatest difficulty, and I do not pretend to be able to resolve them. I note that Thomas Aquinas on the related question of whether the Word would be two men if he assumed two human natures gives two somewhat different answers. In the *Commentary on the Sentences* he says that:

> "[A]lthough Jesus and Peter [the name given to the Word in his supposed second incarnation] would be one supposit, nevertheless they would be called two men on account of the plurality of the natures assumed, but keeping the unity of the supposit, the diversity of natures would not impede that one would be predicated of the other, [i.e., it could be said that Jesus is Peter]; because the identity of supposit suffices for the truth of the predication."[18]

Yet in his later work, the *Summa Theologiae*, Aquinas maintains that "if a divine person would assume two human natures, he would be called one man having two human natures on account of the unity of the supposit."[19] Our hypothetical case, unlike the one Aquinas takes up, involves two different natures, and so Aquinas's latter solution, even if correct, does not seem applicable.[20]

Perhaps there is some way of resolving the apparent conflict between Scripture's affirmations that there is one Lord and one head of the Church, and what would obtain if the Word became incarnate a second time as an ET. The supposition that a second incarnation took place for the purpose of *redeeming* fallen ETs, however, runs up against an additional and more telling difficulty. Colossians 1:15–20 states that:

---

[17] Ibid., q. 29, art. 4, ad 3.

[18] *Scriptum super Sententiis*, (Paris: Lethielleux, 1956), d. 1, q. 2, a. 5, resp.

[19] *Summa Theologiae*, ed. Instituti Studiorum Medievalium Ottaviensis (Ottawa: Commissio Piana, 1953), III, q. 3, a. 7, ad 2.

[20] A further incongruity that would result from the supposition that the Word assumed an ET nature in the same manner in which he assumed human nature is that he would have two mothers. For the Catholic Church teaches that Mary is "Mother of the Church" and "Queen over all things." (See *CCC*, no. 963 and no. 966.) Yet an ET mother of God would seem to have equal claim to these titles.

> As he is the Beginning, he was first to be born from the dead, so that he should be first in every way; because God wanted all perfection to be found in him and all things to be reconciled through him and for him, everything in heaven and everything on earth when he made peace by his death on the cross.[21]

This passage says Christ reconciled all through his death on the cross. Thus fallen ETs, if they are redeemed, are not redeemed by any one other than Christ.

An alternate position that does not conflict with Scripture in the said way is that Christ's sacrifice on the cross on earth makes satisfaction for the fallen ETs as well as for us. Although Scripture says that it is befitting that Christ belong by blood to the race he came to save,[22] it remains the case that Christ did not have to become man, nor having done so did he have to die in order to redeem us, but rather the human race could have been saved in many other ways. Similarly, there are many different ways that God could have saved fallen ETs. However, Scripture indicates that in fact all who are saved are saved by the death of Christ. It is possible that ET salvation was accomplished by means of the one sacrifice of Christ on the cross, since it is a sacrifice which is infinite in its saving power.[23] As Beilby Porteus puts it:

> [I]f the Redemption wrought by Christ extended to other worlds, perhaps many beside our own; if its virtues penetrate even into heaven itself; if it gather together all things in Christ; who will then say, that the dignity of the agent was disproportioned to the magnitude of the work . . . ?[24]

[21] This also rules out the possibilities that another person of the Trinity became incarnate to save ETs or that God saved them in some way apart from the death of Christ.

[22] "As it was his purpose to bring a great many of his sons into glory, it was appropriate that God, for whom everything exists and through whom everything exists, should make perfect, through suffering, the leader who would take them to their salvation. For the one who sanctifies, and the ones who are sanctified, are of the same stock. . . ." (Heb. 2:10–17).

[23] See also Thomas Paine's views cited by Crowe, *The ET Life Debate 1750–1900*, p. 163. Thomas Paine rejects Christianity in favor of many inhabited worlds on the grounds that if there were a large number of human-like civilizations, Christ would thus be very busy traveling from world to world in an endless succession of deaths. This straw-man argument is based on the gratuitous assumption that Christ would have to die over and over. Paine fails to consider the alternative that Christ's death on Calvary was applied to all intelligent beings in need of redemption. (A question would remain as to how Christ may have bestowed knowledge of his redeeming act and of his Church to ETs.)

[24] Quoted by Michael J. Crowe, *The ET Life Debate 1750–1900*, p. 103. See also p. 412: "Montignez in his fourth essay develops the thesis that although Christ came only to the earth, he is nonetheless Lord of the universe, and moreover 'the blood which flowed on Calvary has gushed out on the universality of creation . . . has bathed not only our world, but all the worlds which roll in space. . . .'"

One might argue further that in keeping with the dignity of the agent it would be fitting that the redemption extend to more beings than human beings.

Some other thinkers, such as William Whewell, reject the above views for the reason that:

> The earth . . . can not, in the eyes of any one who accepts this Christian faith, be regarded as being on a level with any other domiciles. It is the Stage of the great Drama of God's Mercy and Man's Salvation. . . . This being the character which has thus been conferred upon it, how can we assent to the assertion of Astronomers, when they tell us that it is only one among millions of similar habitations . . . ?[25]

One could, however, concede that there are millions of similar habitations without rejecting the uniqueness of our planet if the dwellers of those other habitations were saved through Christ's sacrifice on earth. And to Whewell's objection that if there are innumerable worlds there is no reason to think that God is more concerned about the earth than about other ones,[26] Monseigneur de Montignez responds that:

> Because our earth is of insignificant size and contains "probably the most disgraced" creatures in the cosmos, it served as the ideal locale for that "annihilation of the divinity" which is the incarnation. As Christ chose "Bethlehem . . . the least among the cities of Judah" for his birthplace, so also he selected the earth as the location for the founding of his Church and his redemptive actions.[27]

Montignez offers an argument by fittingness for why the earth would be privileged by God. However, God's good will and pleasure are unfathomable to us, and thus our inability to know with certitude why God condescended to become incarnate on planet earth is not a reason for denying that a special dignity has been conferred on the human race.

We see then that Filachou did not exhaustively examine the scenarios possible on the supposition of ET existence. Both the scenario just outlined as well as that in which ETs are not in need of redemption is consistent with the "supreme dignity attributed to the Divine founder of the Christian Church." Both of them are also consistent with "the grandeur attributed to the Church itself."[28] If the ETs are redeemed by Christ's death, they belong to the same Church that humans do. If the ETs did not fall, they would be in a situation

---

[25] William Whewell, quoted by Crowe, *The ET Life Debate 1750–1900*, p. 285.

[26] Cf. Crowe, *The ET Life Debate 1750–1900*, p. 283.

[27] Monseigneur de Montignez, quoted by Crowe, *The ET Life Debate 1750–1900*, p. 412.

[28] From Filachou's *De la pluralité des mondes* cited earlier.

similar to that of the good angels[29] who along with human saints are counted as members of the same Church triumphant.[30]

In conclusion: I have tried to show that there is no necessary incompatibility between the Christian faith and the possible discovery of other intelligent beings. And I have intentionally done so while showing why people take diametrically opposed views on this question in order to bring out oversights on both sides. The extreme views in the ET-Christianity debate are that either the discovery of ETs would spell the end of Christianity, or it would have no more impact on it than the discovery of a new species of butterfly. Though the purpose of Scripture is to teach us things that pertain to our salvation and not to catalogue the beings in the universe, it does make statements about Christ's nature, mission, and relation to creation that lead to conclusions as to how Christ would relate to other material rational beings. (The discovery of a new species of butterfly would raise no question as to the relation of the individuals of this species to the Church of which Christ is the head.) While the existence of ETs as such is not in disaccord with what is said in Scripture, nonetheless further assumptions concerning the status of the supposed beings do in some cases pose difficulties. There are scenarios which would square poorly or not at all with Church teaching and/or Scripture, such as that the Word became incarnate as an ET in order to redeem them. A proper explanation of the Christian view on ET life should not ignore such conflicts, but rather while recognizing them, should show that there are alternate scenarios which do not conflict with Church teaching or Scripture. The most likely of the compatible scenarios are either the ETs are not in need of redemption, or if they are, they are saved through the one sacrifice of Christ on Calvary. One should not forget, however, that possibility is one thing and probability another.

[29] "Both angels and humans are ordered to one end, which is the glory of divine fruition. Whence the mystical body of the Church is made up not only of humans, but also of angels" (*Summa Theologiae* III, q. 8, a. 4, resp.).

[30] Note that another alternative is that the ETs were made for a purely natural happiness, and so though they successfully resist temptation, they never are rewarded with glory. However, one might question whether the creation of such a rational creature would be in keeping with God's goodness.

Is There a Need for
Catholic Identity in Bioethics?
(A Young Layman Questions Himself
About The Peasant of the Garonne)

John F. Morris

O ne of the growing fields of applied ethics is bioethics. The practice and delivery of health care have given rise to numerous ethical questions over the last thirty years, and rapidly developing new technologies promise to continue to challenge our ethical thinking. The Catholic Church has maintained a presence in health care from its inception as part of the healing ministry of Jesus. Even in the midst of the current crisis in which many hospitals and medical facilities are merging or closing due to financial constraints, the Catholic mission in health care remains strong—although not without its challenges. As a natural consequence, Catholic scholars have regularly addressed moral issues relating to health care long before the term "bioethics" was coined. Certainly, the roots of a Catholic approach to bioethics can be found in the work of St. Thomas Aquinas. One could also point to the influential Spanish Dominican, Francisco de Vitoria, who in the 1500s developed the work of Aquinas in regard to withholding and withdrawing medical treatment, and the difference between ordinary and extraordinary means. Today this work is carried on in the United States by the American Bishops, by groups such as the Catholic Health Association and the National Catholic Bioethics Institute, as well as by ethics committees in local Catholic hospitals, and by Catholic women and men across the country.

But this involvement is coming under fire today. In our culture dominated by secular humanism, the views and arguments of Catholics appear to have no place, at least in so far as they come from our Catholic identity. Following upon the political notions of separation between Church and State, it would seem reasonable to some in bioethics that debates must involve only secular ideas, which presumably will appeal to all parties involved. I would suggest that this notion of "secular" is beginning to be taken rather strongly in bioethics, excluding any arguments coming from a religious tradition—whether specifically scriptural or theological in nature or not—as inappropriate in the public discourse. These thoughts raise the question of whether or not a specifically "Catholic" approach to bioethics is legitimate? I would like to consider this question from a slightly different perspective: *Is there a need for a Catholic identity in bioethics?*

In my paper, I want to examine the growing attitude of resistance to arguments with religious associations, both in the political and public arenas, and more specifically within the field of bioethics. Then, I will raise a challenge to such resistance as unjust and unreasonable. Finally, I want to end with a personal reflection on the need for a "Catholic" identity in bioethics as part of the temporal mission of Catholic scholars. It is my belief that a Catholic presence does not destroy the pluralism of public debate, but rather enriches it, in that the spirit of Catholic scholarship is a search for truth.

PUBLIC DISCOURSE AND RELIGIOUS PERSONS

Can a person, as a Catholic, participate actively in America's public discourse and debate of bioethical issues? The typical answer is often, "It depends what you mean by "as a Catholic."

Lying beneath the surface of the question of what it means to be "a Catholic" is the deep cavern of debate regarding the separation of Church and State. I do not mean to imply that such debate is unimportant—in many ways it may be all-important to the future of our country as a land of moral conviction. But the scholars writing on this issue offer little consensus as to the original intent of the Framers of the Constitution, and they indicate wide divergence of opinion as to the purpose of the Establishment Clause in the First Amendment, and conflicting visions as to the height, breadth, and width of Jefferson's "wall of separation." Should the application of the Establishment Clause protect religion and religious institutions from interference and persecution from the State? Or, should any application of the Clause aim solely at protecting the integrity of the democratic political process in this country from the influence, and some would say corruption, of religious institutions? To an extent, the divergence of opinion is unsettling: How does the separation of Church and State in America impact those who accept a specific religious tradition? Do we have a place in public discourse in this country, or must we live with a separated psyche—private religious beliefs and secular-ized public ideas?

It is interesting to note that forty or more years ago several scholars did not think this would be an issue any longer—that is, the question of Church and State should have disappeared by now (not settled, just vanished as an ir-relevant concern). Consider one prominent example, *The Secular City*, pub-lished by Harvey Cox in 1965. Cox and others[1] anticipated that human soci-ety would become increasingly secularized as a result of scientific and technological development. What was heralded as the overcoming of myth and superstition (Cox's view of religious faith) would eventually be ex-plained away by modern disciplines such as psychology and neurology—in short, scientific rationality would lead to the demise of organized religion. One gets the sense that this was supposed to occur through a direct correla-tion—the more we learned, the less we were supposed to believe. Cox and the others were wrong, and Cox admits this in a paper he published in 1996, "Religion and Politics after *The Secular City*": "We are in the midst of a reli-gious resurgence all around the world, and without realizing, measuring, and weighing in the importance of this resurgence, we don't understand the world we are living in."[2] Of interest is the fact that Cox claims this "resurgence" was unanticipated:

> So here we are at the end of the twentieth century which was supposed to see the withering away or the marginalization of religion, but some-thing quite different is happening. . . . [I]t was unanticipated because the scholars who were thinking about religion forty years ago were still steeped in the myth of modernity, in the idea of progress, of the gradual overcoming of superstition by science and technology and rationality. They were *so* sure that religion could be explained away on the basis of sociological, psychological, or neurological theories that they really did-n't appreciate how profound—and I would say ineradicable—the reli-gious dimension of human life is. It is not going away.[3]

---

[1] For some illustrative examples see: Bryan Wilson, *Religion and Secular Society* (London: C. A. Watts, 1996); Peter L. Berger, *The Sacred Canopy: Elements of a So-ciological Theory of Religion* (Garden City, New York: Doubleday, 1967); Thomas Luckmann, *The Invisible Anthropological View* (New York: Macmillan, 1967); and Anthony F. C. Wallace, *Religion: An Anthropological View* (New York: Random House, 1966).

[2] Harvey Cox, "Religion and Politics after *The Secular City*," in *Religion and the Political Order: Politics in Classical and Contemporary Christianity, Islam and Ju-daism*, ed. Jacob Neusner (Atlanta, Georgia: Scholars Press, 1996), p. 4.

[3] Ibid.

Now it would be hard to say just how many "scholars" really believed this, or if this idea was truly anything more than a hope for some of them, but the general consensus today is that religion does matter in human society.

The corollary to this is that it does not seem possible, for better or worse, to keep religion entirely out of the public and political arenas, even given current debates regarding the Establishment Clause. Cox himself offers the following remarks in the conclusion of his essay:

> Our present religious resurgence . . . marks a tidal change in human spirituality. It is a recognition that modernity has in some measure failed, and that for many people, the bright promise of what science was supposed to do for us has now turned to ashes. The scientists themselves, perhaps more than anyone else, now recognize that we should count on science for a much more limited role. We are thankful for what science can do, but we don't count on it as the Messiah. The age of scientific and technological messianism is over, and now the door is open for something else. I think that religions are going to play an important role in whatever that "something else" is. But it is going to be good news *and* bad news.[4]

Not exactly a ringing endorsement for religion and people of faith, but an endorsement nonetheless.

In the volume in which Cox's essay was published, many scholars consider the implications of religion in the public and political arenas. They question how they misjudged religion, why it has resurrected itself, and what impact this new resurgence will have in contemporary society—all the while noting that religion, for better or worse, is here to stay and will be part of public discourse. Other authors on religion and politics make similar claims. For example, in his essay, "Religion as a Political Interest Group," Anthony Champagne writes:

> Religion is a powerful force in the lives of the American people, far more powerful a force than political scientists have traditionally been willing to grant. Religious concerns include a vast number of political, social, and economic issues, ranging from compulsory vaccination laws to sex education to nuclear proliferation. Today, that which is the domain of the state and that which is within the domain of religious faith substantially overlap.[5]

Such scholars are hard at work, trying to clarify how religion should function in our pluralistic society, what role it should have in politics, what its limits

---

[4] Ibid., p. 10.

[5] Anthony Champagne, "Religion as a Political Interest Group," in *Religion and Politics*, ed. W. Lawson Taitte (Austin, Texas: University of Texas Press, 1989), p. 117.

are, how far it should extend, and so forth. A noble cause to be sure, but one which has yet to arrive at consensus.

However, I believe it is important to emphasize that simply because religion seems to be resurging, and that in some sense religion seems to be more recognized in the political sphere now, these developments do not ensure that religious people are allowed to be a part of public discourse—at least in a *substantial* manner. Frank Guliuzza, in his work, *Over The Wall: Protecting Religious Expression in the Public Square*, captures this concern vividly:

> [A]lthough religious believers are becoming ever more active in politics and political debate, many academic and cultural elites dismiss religious-based argument from dialogic politics. If I am correct, then the frequency of political activism by religious believers does not mean that they are taken seriously, or even welcome in the marketplace, by many academic and cultural elites.[6]

The danger here is that even though things may seem fine and peaceful on the surface, religious voices and attitudes may be getting silenced and neutralized in more subtle ways in this country. Guliuzza explains the danger further:

> What a growing number of scholars are telling us is that the complex relationship between religion and politics has been damaged. The problem, they maintain, is that the two institutions do not fully interact in contemporary American society. Specifically, religious voices are neutralized and are thus restrained from many parts of American public life. Even though religion permeates the political and social environment, it is abrogated effectively by the actions of many cultural and intellectual elites.[7]

What is particularly troubling is that the religious voice is being silenced *qua* religious—without any regard for the merits or truth of the claims brought forth by religious people. As Guliuzza notes:

> It is staggering to fathom the general contempt with which religion and religious people are held on college and university campuses. . . . This contempt might be understandable if intellectuals had reached their conclusions after serious study, but often scholars react to "religion" without employing the careful inquiry they devote to their own areas of expertise. Consequently, it is not uncommon for academics to casually dismiss religious argument as unworthy of serious discussion.[8]

I believe that part of the problem here is that the difference between a "religious argument" and "an argument from a religious person" is becoming more

---

[6] Frank Guliuzza, *Over the Wall: Protecting Religious Expression in the Public Square* (New York: State University of New York Press, 2000), p. 5.

[7] Ibid., p. 12.

[8] Ibid., pp. 15–16.

and more blurred. If our current understanding of the separation of Church and State does not allow the former, is there any room left for the latter?

The emphasis on the academic and intellectual level, then, is significant. It would be hard to prove that religious people are not welcome in the public arena, for there seems to be ample evidence to the contrary. Religious people and religious groups are gaining in numbers and presence. Cox's "resurgence" suggests itself everywhere. But does *mere* presence matter? Not really—not when it comes to public discourse. At a time when America is recognizing the need to empower disadvantaged groups in our communities, and to provide more open and public forums because of our diversity, the religious voice seems to be effectively "marginalized" from those very forums. But this "marginalization" is subtle, as Guliuzza explains:

> The pressure to privatize religion is more subtle than an overt restriction on political participation. Remember I am distinguishing between the treatment religion receives by intellectual elites from the public at large. Citizens who are religious are welcome to the political debate as *citizens*. They can bring whatever intellectual arrows that are in their quivers to the fray—with one exception. Increasingly, religious argument is unwelcome.[9]

Without necessarily accepting Guliuzza's whole thesis, I think he makes some valid points regarding the religious person in public and political discourse. The religious person is welcome as a citizen—that, on the surface seems appropriate. But if, at the same time, religious argument is dismissed by cultural and intellectual elites without even being heard, what value does the participation by religious people in public debates hold for both the religious person himself, and for the public? Very little I am afraid. Even worse would be the rejection of any arguments that come from religious people, simply *because* they come from religious people, and regardless of whether such arguments are based upon theological or scriptural sources versus arguments based on valid reasoning which happens to concur with a person's religious beliefs. It is the latter attitude that I see gaining momentum in the field of bioethics—the marginalization of arguments from religious persons without any serious consideration of the merits of those arguments.

THE SECULARIZATION OF BIOETHICS

In terms of the political implications of the separation of Church and State, and the impact of prevailing attitudes for public discourse and debate, much more could be (and will need to be) said. But I want to narrow down

[9] Ibid., p. 26.

my focus specifically to the field of bioethics. Even though Cox and others have conceded that religion has not died, there is no mistaking the increase in secularization in cur country and the impact such secularization has had on what we believe public discourse should look like.

In bioethics, for example, issues are still treated largely in terms of their technical dimensions, and to a certain degree on their legal implications. Some mainstream ethicists will discuss "values," but values-talk is embedded in the private lives of those involved, not in the public discourse of the "issues." Certainly, the "secularization" that has been occurring in American society has also touched the public discourse of bioethics. In 1990 Daniel Callahan noted this development:

> The most striking change over the past two decades or so has been the secularization of bioethics. The field has moved from one dominated by religious and medical traditions to one increasingly shaped by philosophical and legal concepts. The consequence has been a model of public discourse that emphasizes secular themes: universal rights, individual self-direction, procedural justice, and a systematic denial of either a common good or a transcendent individual good.[10]

This "systematic" rejection of transcendent ideals is evidenced in recent texts in bioethics, which are more and more taking on a legalistic flavor, as well as in the media on shows such as *20/20*, *Dateline*, and *Frontline* when they feature bioethical issues. When cloning, the human genome project, or reproductive technologies are addressed, the focus is scientific. Even the "Health Minute" reports that are part of nightly newscasts primarily focus on technological breakthroughs, with little serious effort to engage in any ethical considerations during the reporting. There is evidence to suggest that Guliuzza's claim is correct, and that religious voices are being neutralized within the field of bioethics, as well as in other aspects of our society.

As an illustration, I want to point to two examples from the discourse of bioethics which reflect this "marginalization" of the religious voice. First, consider the remarks of Justice Stevens in his dissenting opinion on *Webster v. Reproductive Health Services* (1989), one of the landmark abortion cases following the wake of *Roe v. Wade* in 1973. The Supreme Court was considering the constitutionality of a Missouri law that prohibited the use of public funds for counseling a woman to have an abortion that was not necessary to save her life, that also prohibited the usage of public facilities for abortions except in cases where the mother's life was at risk, and which required abortion doctors

---

[10] Daniel Callahan, "Religion and the secularization of bioethics." *Hastings Center Report*, July–August, 1990, p. 2.

to test the viability of fetuses over twenty weeks gestation. In part, however, attention was drawn to this case because a preamble had been affixed to the law which stated that: "life begins at conception and that unborn children have protectable interest in life, health, and well-being."[11] Note Justice Steven's discussion regarding this point from the law's preamble:

> I am persuaded that the absence of any secular purpose for the legislative declarations that life begins at conception and that conception occurs at fertilization makes the relevant portion of the preamble invalid under the Establishment Clause . . . the preamble, an unequivocal endorsement of a religious tenet of some but by no means all Christian faiths, serves no identifiable secular purpose. That fact alone compels a conclusion that the statute violates the Establishment Clause. . . . Bolstering my conclusion that the preamble violates the First Amendment is the fact that the intensely divisive character of much of the national debate over the abortion issue reflects the deeply held religious convictions of many participants in the debate. The Missouri Legislature may not inject its endorsement of a particular religious tradition into this debate, for "[t]he Establishment Clause does not allow public bodies to foment such disagreement."[12]

It is important to note, however, that in the actual bill that was signed into law by the Governor of Missouri in 1986, no religious arguments were included. That is, the statement in the preamble to which Justice Stevens reacts is not offered as a religious argument *per se*—but rather as a conclusion of medical science and reason. However, because of associations that were suggested by certain *amici* for Reproductive Health Services, it was concluded that the point regarding conception was an endorsement of religion, and thus invalid under the Establishment Clause. Justice Stevens did not even consider this as a point worthy of consideration on its own merits. There are numerous people who would accept the statement regarding life beginning at conception on purely scientific grounds. The idea of "life at conception" has been excluded from the public discourse on abortion—at least at the highest levels of the Supreme Court where, unfortunately, it matters most.

A second example comes from the recent debate over physician-assisted suicide. One of the leading proponents of assisted suicide is Timothy E. Quill, M.D. In his various discussions of this topic, Dr. Quill has addressed the Principle of Double Effect, which is often employed in arguments against his view that assisted suicide is morally permissible. Double Effect helps to explain why allowing a person to die under certain circumstances (i.e., when

---

[11] Missouri Senate Committee Substitute for House Bill No. 1596 (1986), preamble.
[12] Justice Stevens, dissenting opinion, *Webster v. Reproductive Health Services*, 492 U.S. 490 (1989).

treatment is medically futile or there is the presence of a grave burden for the patient) may be permissible, when the intention is not to kill the person, but rather to act for some other important good. At the same time, Double Effect rather clearly shows that assisted suicide is impermissible, because the actual "assistance" here requires that one intend to kill the patient. Now, Quill objects to this principle at many levels. Note, however, the first reason Quill offers for rejecting the Principle of Double Effect in a 1997 "Sounding Board" article in *The New England Journal of Medicine*:

> The rule of double effect has many shortcomings as an ethical guide for either clinical practice or public policy. First, the rule originated in the context of a particular religious tradition. American society incorporates multiple religious, ethical, and professional traditions, so medicine must accommodate various approaches to assessing the morality of end-of-life practices.[13]

Quill does go on to present other reasons to reject this Principle, at least as it might apply to assisted-suicide. But what is striking is that his very *first* claim against Double Effect is that it comes from a "particular religious tradition," which he notes earlier in the article specifically as the Roman Catholic tradition. Quill's remaining comments hark back to this initial remark, albeit rather subtly. In explaining the development of the Principle of Double Effect Quill makes note that it developed in the Middle Ages. Later, suggestions are made that the Principle rests on an ambiguous and old-fashioned notion of intentionality, one which modern psychology suggests does not reflect the complexity and ambiguity of the human psyche. The implication is one of the religious medieval tradition versus modern psychology—or more strongly, superstition versus science. Quill also notes that philosophers and theologians who attempt to apply the Principle often have trouble doing so clearly. Dr. Quill's consideration of the Principle of Double Effect seems tainted by his perception of it simply as a religious concept. It is again worth noting that in current applications of Double Effect, no religious or theological arguments are asserted in its defense. It is offered as a rational Principle in its own right, but people like Quill would marginalize its application because of its religious association.

Many other examples could be offered in further support of this marginalization of the religious voice in public debates on issues in bioethics. Religious health care institutions are coming under greater pressure to perform

---

[13] Timothy E. Quill et al., "The Rule of Double Effect—A Critique of Its Role in End-of-Life Decision Making," in *The New England Journal of Medicine* 337, no. 24, December 11, 1997, p. 1770.

treatments that secular society deems necessary and important—with religious objections being viewed less and less favorably in the media. Religious hospitals and health care facilities are charged with being unresponsive to the needs of the community, especially in regards to reproductive rights and women's health issues. The reasons for not providing certain treatments and drugs are characterized as "Catholic reasons"—not just "reasons." How can religious institutions respond if their voice is marginalized in the public debate? Do religious health care facilities have a place in the public forum? If yes, how much of their "religious" side can they bring into the public realm? Does it depend on what one means by "Catholic"? Is the Catholic role only valid if it is first secularized?

A CHALLENGE IN THE NAME OF JUSTICE

Even granting that some levels of separation between Church and State are valid within the American political system, the presence and participation of religious believers in public discourse must be allowed in the name of justice.

To support this, it must be noted that there is a distinction between the *political* realm and the *public* realm that needs to be drawn out more clearly. Modern *political* debate has been setting the tone for *public* discourse—but the two are not co-equal. What may not be appropriate for a State to do, is not necessarily, *de facto*, inappropriate for society—especially a society that claims to be genuinely pluralistic and diverse. As Richard McBrien notes in his essay, "The Future Role of the Church in American Society":

> The discussion of the general topic of religion and politics, and of the more specific topic of church and politics, is confused when the distinction between society and state is collapsed. The separation of religion-church and state is not the same as the separation of religion-church and society.[14]

Given this distinction, I would argue that to achieve justice at the *political* level, where direct theological and scriptural argument would not seem appropriate, there must be a correlating openness to a plurality of views at the *public* level, within the rules of civil discourse. How else could our country achieve the common good, unless all parties are allowed a presence at the discussion table? This in no way implies that we have to meet all the interests that come forth in our society—*political* policies will have to discriminate in some sense. But to achieve fairness in a pluralistic society, the *public* forum

---

[14] Richard P. McBrien, "The Future Role of the Church in American Society," in *Religion and Politics in the American Milieu*, ed. Leslie Griffin, published under the auspices of *The Review of Politics* (Notre Dame, Indiana: University of Notre Dame Press, 1986), p. 87.

will need to be open—and open in a genuine manner, not just to those views and causes deemed politically correct. To exclude some voices (those of traditional religious backgrounds or the religious right) in the name of allowing others to speak more freely is simply discrimination in the very worse sense. We must also become more careful about lumping all groups into one—all religions and religious people do not bear the burden of the acts of a few who claim to be following God's commands. Each case, each act, each idea must be considered on its own merits.

And so, it would seem perfectly legitimate for religious institutions and religious persons to participate in *public* discourse within society, even if more direct *political* activity was not likewise legitimate. As McBrien explains:

> Although the activity of the U.S. Catholic bishops on nuclear weapons and abortion, for example, is concerned with policies which are established by the *state*, the bishop's involvement in these issues occurs in and through the channels a democratic *society* provides for public debate. In such a society voluntary associations play a key role, providing a buffer between the state and the citizenry as well as a structured means of influencing public policy. The church itself is a voluntary association. As such, it has the constitutional right to raise and address what it regards as the moral dimension of public issues, and to encourage its own members to engage in the same public discussion of these issues. . . . Whatever Thomas Jefferson's metaphor about a "wall of separation" may mean constitutionally for the relationship between church and state, it can have no inhibiting impact, constitutional or otherwise, on the relationship between church and society.[15]

In short, accepting the limitations of our *political* system in terms of religion does not mean that we must accept the marginalization of the religious voice *and* the religious person that is occurring in contemporary *public* discourse.

The same concerns were reflected in an article written by Daniel Sulmasy and Edmund Pellegrino in response to Quill's arguments against Double Effect. In their well reasoned and thorough essay titled, "The Rule of Double Effect: Clearing Up the Double Talk," these authors address Quill's claim that the religious association of Double Effect is a hindrance to its effectiveness as a moral guideline:

> This is a very odd position. Should the commonly held position that stealing is morally wrong be rejected simply because it can be found (Exodus 20:15) in the commandments of a particular religious tradition? The religious origins of a moral principle or rule should not preclude its

[15] Ibid., pp. 87–88, 92.

discussion in civil society. Nor should the congruence between a moral argument's conclusions and the teachings of a religion undermine the validity of the argument. An exhortation to exclude such rules and principles in the name of tolerance seems itself highly intolerant.[16]

The crucial point that Sulmasy and Pellegrino underscore is that whereas the Double Effect was developed by religious people, no specific theological or scriptural arguments are asserted in its defense:

> There is nothing about the rule of double effect that is inherently religious. The fact that it was developed by theologians does not vitiate the fact that it might be morally true. Nothing about the rule presumes any knowledge of scripture or the teachings of any religion. All that is required is a belief that certain actions are absolutely morally prohibited, or, more controversially, at least a belief that consequences are not the sole determinants of the morality of an action. . . . A logically rigorous argument against the rule of double effect would deal with the rule on its own terms.[17]

Having made the point that Double Effect needs to be considered on its own merits in public discussions of bioethical issues, the authors go further and call Quill to task for this inappropriate attack. They do not let Quill get away with this attempt to marginalize the principle simply because of its religious origins:

> To raise the question of the origins of the rule as a reason to discredit it is a form of the logical fallacy of the *ad hominem* argument—to claim to discredit an argument because of who states it. . . . The argument that it should be rejected out of hand simply because it originated with a particular religious tradition is completely unwarranted.[18]

Sulmasy and Pellegrino get to the heart of the problem here, and challenge Quill's blatant *ad hominem* remarks. One wonders whether or not these important points were given due attention—Pellegrino is a well-known Catholic doctor, and Sulmasy, who has a Ph.D. and M.D., happens to be a Franciscan. I can only hope their article was considered on the merits of its arguments and not simply on its origins.

Nonetheless, I believe that we must continue to challenge such *ad hominem* attacks raised against the arguments of religious persons, and call for serious consideration and discussion in their place. This is the only

---

[16] Daniel P. Sulmasy and Edmund Pellegrino, "The Rule of Double Effect: Clearing Up the Double Talk," in *The Archives of Internal Medicine*, 159, March 22, 1999. See p. 548.

[17] Ibid., pp. 548–49.

[18] Ibid., p. 549.

way we can hope to reach Truth. Whatever *political* needs our country may have for separation of Church and State, I do not believe there is a corresponding need for such a strong secularization of ideas in *public* discourse—certainly not to the extent of marginalizing the arguments of religious persons without further consideration. Our country has come such a long way in regards to recognizing the dangers and injustices of exclusion, with women and minorities for example, that it seems a shame to forget what has been learned.

BUT WHY SPECIFICALLY CATHOLIC?

If one grants the arguments given thus far, a further question remains. Why insist on a specifically "Catholic" approach to bioethics? Is there really a need to make such an explicit identification? Indeed, if what has been said thus far is true, perhaps insisting on a "Catholic" identity would be counterproductive in today's public climate—that is, if the voices of religious persons are being marginalized, would it not be more effective to voluntarily secularize the "Catholic" approach so that the ideas would be more acceptable? One might even wonder if specifically "Catholic" positions, for example on birth control and assisted reproduction, should be withheld from public debate in the hope of fostering better cooperation within our diverse society? I find this line of reasoning troubling for Catholic scholars and Catholic institutions. I believe that such an attitude accepts the *ad hominem* attacks that are made within public discourse as legitimate criticisms of the ideas of religious persons, rather than recognizing such attacks as fallacious attempts to neutralize the questioning of morally troubling positions. And so, I recognize two significant reasons why there is, indeed, a need for a "Catholic" approach to bioethics within contemporary American society. First, I would insist that the Catholic approach brings a unique perspective to the table that is founded on a carefully thought out understanding of the human person—an understanding that is lacking within the general arena of bioethical discussion. Second, I believe that developing a specifically "Catholic" approach to bioethics is appropriate for Catholic philosophers as part of fulfilling their temporal mission as Christians. To aid my reflections on these points, I turn to the work of Jacques Maritain in his final reflection, *The Peasant of the Garonne*, and to John Paul II's encyclical letter, *Fides et Ratio*.

Let me begin by noting that, while one may speak at times of "Catholic bioethics," the Church, as noted consistently in official documents and teaching, cannot have an authoritative bioethics. Bioethics is an applied field of philosophy, and as John Paul II reminds us in *Fides et Ratio*, there is no "official philosophy of the Church, since the faith as such is not a philosophy."[19] However, as Maritain notes in *The Peasant of the Garonne*: "[F]aith itself demands to be completed by a . . . theology. And theology cannot take shape in us without the help of that natural wisdom of which human reason is capable, whose name is philosophy."[20]

For Maritain, this statement is a reflection of his belief that there could be a genuine "Christian philosophy." Much has been debated regarding the notion of a "Christian philosophy," but I want to focus specifically upon Maritain's explanation of how natural such a development would be in the Christian who also happens to be a philosopher—the two roles are not antithetical:

> After all, a Christian can be a philosopher. And if he believes that, in order to philosophize, he should lock his faith up in a strongbox—that is, should cease being a Christian while he philosophizes—he is maiming himself, which is no good (all the more as philosophizing takes up the better part of his time). He is also deluding himself, for these kinds of strongboxes have always poor locks. But if, while he philosophizes, he does not shut his faith up in a strongbox, he is philosophizing in faith, willy-nilly. It is better that he should be aware of it.[21]

Simply put, I would say that Catholic philosophers are not two people, but one. And as one person, it is certainly possible to develop oneself as a philosopher and be true to the demands of philosophical inquiry, without at the same time offending one's fundamental religious beliefs. In fact, I would claim that in the name of philosophical consistency, a Catholic philosopher must carry out this task.

In *Fides et Ratio*, John Paul II also addresses the notion of "Christian philosophy." He notes that there can be a genuinely

> Christian way of philosophizing, a philosophical speculation conceived in dynamic union with faith. It does not therefore simply refer to a philosophy developed by Christian philosophers who have striven in their research not to contradict the faith. The term Christian philosophy includes those important developments of philosophical thinking which would not have happened without the direct or indirect contribution of Christian faith.[22]

John Paul II is not naïve to the demands of philosophy which require it to be independent and autonomous. However, he expresses in his letter a belief

---

[19] John Paul II, *Fides et Ratio*, no. 76.

[20] Jacques Maritain, *The Peasant of the Garonne*, trans. Michael Cuddihy and Elizabeth Hughes (New York: Holt, Rinehart and Winston, Inc., 1968), p. 85.

[21] Ibid., p. 142.

[22] John Paul II, *Fides et Ratio*, no. 76.

that philosophy and the Christian faith are compatible: "[P]hilosophy must obey its own rules and be based upon its own principles; truth, however, can only be one. The content of Revelation can never debase the discoveries and legitimate autonomy of reason."[23]

In addition to the compatibility of philosophy and faith, there is a practical role that the development of a "Christian philosophy" can serve, which was recognized by both Maritain and John Paul II. In *The Peasant of the Garonne*, Maritain explains:

> It seems clear that in its very capacity as philosophy, Christian philosophy is, on its own level, better "situated" than theology for the dialogue. . . . Dogmatic differences are not philosophy's concern, at least not directly. The object of its investigation belongs to the natural order and has to do with that natural ecumenism the desire for which, however frustrated, naturally haunts the human mind. Not only is dialogue with non-Christians much easier for philosophy, since each of the parties can more easily receive from the other valuable contributions for his own thought, but the possibilities for intellectual agreement in this field are also of much vaster scope.[24]

In *Fides et Ratio*, John Paul II echoes this important "bridging" role of philosophy:

> Philosophical thought is often the only ground for understanding and dialogue with those who do not share our faith. . . . Such a ground for understanding and dialogue is all the more vital nowadays, since the most pressing issues facing humanity—ecology, peace, and the co-existence of different races and cultures, for instance—may possibly find a solution if there is a clear and honest collaboration between Christians and the followers of other religions and all those who, while not sharing a religious belief, have at heart the renewal of humanity.[25]

The recognition of the practical value of philosophy for the Church in no way undermines the value and validity of philosophy as an activity in and of itself. Rather, this is simply a recognition of the applicability of philosophical reflection and insight for day to day life.

What, then, does the Catholic philosopher bring to the "real world" of public discourse regarding issues in bioethics? First, I believe, is the focus on the human person that is inherent within the philosophical and theological traditions of the Church, and the primacy of the person over the community. As Maritain explains:

---

[23] Ibid., no. 79.
[24] Jacques Maritain, *The Peasant of the Garonne*, p. 165.
[25] John Paul II, *Fides et Ratio*, no. 104.

> In that community of human persons which is a society, the Church, in keeping with the demands of truth, gives primacy to the person over the community; whereas today's world gives primacy to the community over the person—a highly interesting and significant disagreement. In our age of civilization the Church will increasingly become—bless Her—the refuge and support (perhaps the only one) of the person.[26]

I find these words both true and stirring. There is ample evidence that in the years since Maritain wrote these words, the world has not reformed her ways. Nor should one mistake the current emphasis on "autonomy" in American bioethics for a genuine respect for the person. Abortion, euthanasia, assisted suicide, genetic manipulation, cloning, stem cell research all pose serious threats to the dignity of persons. The Church, and specifically Catholic philosophers interested in bioethics, have an important duty to continue to call attention to the dignity of human persons.

The affront to the dignity of human persons is due, in part, to the lack of a clear understanding of human nature in the contemporary arena, especially within scientific discourse. In his own time Maritain made note of this lack:

> I am told by trustworthy friends, the best representatives of the world of technicians feel much more concern for the mystery of the *true* man, and are much more open to a genuine realism, than are those who belong to the intelligentsia. What they lack is a thorough idea of man, which no one in the intelligentsia furnishes them, and which it would be up to philosophers and theologians worthy of the name to propose them.[27]

This need has only become more pressing in contemporary American society. Indeed, with developments in the Human Genome Project we may be on the verge of changing what it means to be human, yet few in the scientific community seem concerned. They simply do not understand the seriousness of what we are doing because they lack a critical understanding of what they are working upon. Biology, neurology, psychology, sociology, and genetics are setting the tone for public discourse, none of which can offer a complete understanding of human nature. Nor have the various philosophies of modernism and postmodernism offered anything to help our understanding.

In sum, Catholic philosophers have something truly important to share in this debate, if only the intelligentsia will allow the arguments of religious persons to be heard. The secularized and largely scientific attitudes that dominate public discourse simply do not address all the questions relevant to human society. As Maritain explains:

---

[26] Jacques Maritain, *The Peasant of the Garonne*, p. 51.
[27] Ibid., p. 171.

> It is clear that science as such has nothing to tell us about the problems which matter most to us, and about the idea of the world, of man, perhaps of God, which we cannot escape forming for ourselves, any more than about the torment of the absolute, the "why were we born?"; the "to what can we wholly give our hearts?"; the desire for that fire which will burn us without consuming us, which as hidden as they may be, are there, in our very depths. All of this remains completely outside the scope of science.[28]

And if the strong notions of separation between Church and State continue to set the tone for public discourse, these issues will not be brought to the forefront at the very time when they matter most to us as a society—on the brink of so many long lasting and deeply impacting decisions. The philosophical conclusions of Catholic philosophers who are drawn to such issues because of their faith background are indeed relevant for our society as we consider where we are heading in the next millennium. It would be a terrible tragedy to simply allow American society to continue unknowingly into the future with so many important questions and issues left unconsidered because of the "religious associations" of those questions and issues.

In addition to these reasons for developing a specific "Catholic" approach to bioethics, I want to offer one final reflection. These last thoughts are more subjective in nature, and are drawn from Maritain's own reflections on the temporal mission of the Christian in *The Peasant of the Garonne*. Early in the book, Maritain makes the following remarks:

> The age we are entering obliges the Christian to become aware of the temporal mission which he has with respect to the world and which is like an expansion of his spiritual vocation in the kingdom of God and with respect to it. Woe to the world if the Christian were to isolate and separate his temporal mission (then it would be wind only) from his spiritual vocation! The fact remains that this temporal mission requires him to enter as deeply as possible into the agonies, the conflicts, and the earthly problems, social or political, of his age, and not hesitate to "get his feet wet."[29]

However, as we jump into the water, Maritain reminds us that this temporal mission is not the only duty of the Christian. One must be careful, he notes, to avoid "kneeling before the world."[30] Rather, the Christian must always remain dedicated to his spiritual calling. Thus, a Christian is required to: "love the world with that love which is charity as a creature of God on the way to its own natural ends, and therefore to cooperate in its temporal

---

[28] Ibid., p. 113.
[29] Ibid., p. 43.
[30] Ibid., p. 56.

struggle against injustice and misery."[31] The mission to work within the world is not a subsequent call to abandon Truth in order to make living in society more convenient, and with less conflict:

> Charity has to do with persons; truth with ideas and with reality attained through them. Perfect charity toward our neighbor and complete fidelity to the truth are not only compatible; they call for one another. . . . It has never been recommended to confuse "loving" with "seeking to please."[32]

The Catholic philosopher must in fact remain dedicated to Truth if he is to manifest true charity.

Finally, Maritain does not suggest that all Catholics who engage in philosophy must carry out this temporal mission in the concrete. Rather, he suggests that there are those among the laity who will be drawn to such work, for example in the field of bioethics, as "a calling." This notion of "a calling" seems echoed in *Fides et Ratio*, when John Paul II issues a challenge to Catholic philosophers—which he admits is daunting—to help people "come to a unified and organic vision of knowledge":[33]

> I appeal also to *philosophers*, and to all *teachers of philosophy*, asking them to have the courage to recover, in the flow of an enduringly valid philosophical tradition, the range of authentic wisdom and truth—metaphysical truth included—which is proper to philosophical enquiry. They should be open to the impelling questions which arise from the word of God and they should be strong enough to shape their thought and discussion in response to that challenge. Let them always strive for truth, alert to the good which truth contains. Then they will be able to formulate the genuine ethics which humanity needs so urgently at this particular time.[34]

This "call" is issued by the Pope to those philosophers who are interested in the specific tasks he is addressing in this letter. There is no demand for all Catholic philosophers to carry out these tasks—the freedom of philosophical enquiry will undoubtedly call some towards other philosophical tasks. But I believe that this call from the Pope for Catholic philosophers to work in a genuinely philosophical manner for the betterment of humanity serves as the ultimate foundation for a specifically "Catholic" approach to bioethics. It certainly embodies the spirit of my own involvement in the field.

---

[31] Ibid., p. 62.
[32] Ibid., pp. 90–91.
[33] John Paul II, *Fides et Ratio*, no. 85.
[34] Ibid., no. 106.

CONCLUSION

In many ways, the goal of this paper was simple: to justify the need for a specifically "Catholic" approach to bioethics. In public debates on bioethical issues there is a need to support and promote the unique perspective that the Catholic Church has on the primacy and dignity of the human person. Contemporary thinking about human nature needs to be revitalized by the philosophical wisdom embodied in the Catholic tradition. Here lies one manner in which Catholic philosophers can fulfill their temporal mission in the world today—a mission that is further supported by the Pope's encyclical, *Fides et Ratio*.

Discussion of the above points required an examination of the current milieu of public discourse on bioethical issues, in which it was argued that the voices of religious persons are being marginalized, without due consideration for the positions and ideas being espoused. I believe that such current intolerant attitudes need to be challenged by philosophers at all levels, and within all fields of study. It will be important to continue to distinguish political needs for separation from public and social needs for openness in the pursuit of truth.

In the end, to reflect back upon Cox's former belief that religion would eventually be replaced by science, I believe that Cox and others who shared his position, were wrong because they were only looking at religion and religious institutions, all the while underestimating the religious *person*. For example, as a lay person, it is my understanding that what makes Catholic health care "Catholic," is not the fact that there may be a chapel in the hospital, nor that there may be crucifixes in patient rooms, nor that a religious order may run the institution and have members sit on the Board of Directors—none of these factors represents the totality of Catholic health care. Catholicism is about a *way of life*—a life that is in touch with the present, yet not disconnected from the past. The *way of life* embodied in Catholicism is connected with the tradition of Christianity—a living tradition represented in Church teaching, council documents, papal letters, the writings of holy women and men, the Gospels, and the Word, Himself, Jesus Christ. To think of Catholic health care as something offered by certain people, or in certain buildings, is to impoverish what in its deepest reality is a healing ministry. In sum, being "Catholic" is not limited to following certain rules and rituals, but rather encompasses the totality of one's life in an imitation of the life of Christ.

Life involves action, and action is the arena of ethics. Hence, the need for a "Catholic" approach to bioethics flows from the *way of life* to which all Catholics and Christians are called. Even if there did not exist a single hospital in this country affiliated in any formal way with the Catholic Church, there should still be Catholic health care wherever there are Catholic nurses, doctors, therapists, administrators, etc. In a similar fashion, I believe that a "Catholic" approach to bioethics should exist wherever Catholic philosophers apply their philosophical training to the field of bioethics. The "calling" here is a personal one—part of the mission of a Christian in the world today, and as genuine as the calling of Catholics to any vocation. However, the actual presence of Catholic hospitals, health care facilities, and academic institutions, especially those devoted to the study of bioethics, allows for a more concrete, physical presence—that is, a sacramental presence—in our communities, states, and nation. Catholic philosophers today have inherited a tremendous gift from the tradition they work within, as well as an incredible opportunity to foster the living presence of Christ and the search for truth within the world today. Perhaps the greatest strength we have to stand on is that the wisdom of the Catholic tradition strives to be reasonable—this is the heritage left to us by the great Church fathers and doctors. Not that we will ever know the mysteries of this life fully, but that there is reason here—the reason of God. If this is the case, as Catholics believe, then we find an answer to our question, "Why the need for a *Catholic* identity in bioethics?" Truth!

Time in Relation to
Self, World, and God

Teresa I. Reed

T he modern conception of time separates us from self, world, and God. It separates us from self by replacing the irregular, lived time of human events with the regular, uniform time of the clock. It separates us from the world by reinforcing the mechanical model of the universe. Finally, it separates us from God by eliminating sacred time and eternity and by removing God's presence from the world.

An understanding of time is one of the most deeply held assumptions of human culture. Time awareness tends to be internalized, and people are reluctant to make it explicit because so many other values depend on it. We set our priorities and organize our activities within our lived temporality of consciousness, events, and acts. Now, it is possible to think of time and to experience time in a variety of ways.[1] Three kinds of time will be discussed here: clock time, lived time and sacred time. I will first discuss clock time and its advantages. After distinguishing clock time from lived time, I will discuss the application of clock time to the self, in terms of schedules and functions. I will then discuss how the use of clock time in natural science reinforces the mechanical conception of the universe and of the self, and appears to support philosophical naturalism. Finally, I will show how clock time and the mechanical conception of the universe challenge the very existence of sacred time and religious experience, and I will make a few recommendations about our task with respect to all of this in the twenty-first century.

---

[1] On time and culture, see Edward T. Hall, *The Dance of Life: The Other Dimension of Time* (New York: Doubleday Anchor, 1983), and Alfred Gell, *The Anthropology of Time: Cultural Constructions of Temporal Maps and Images* (Oxford: Berg, 1996). Hall focuses on differences, whereas Gell focuses on similarities.

The path taken by Western culture depended heavily on the mechanical clock. When we think of time, we usually think of clock time. Clock time is regular, uniform time, divided into hours, minutes, and seconds. We are raised to think that clocks "tell time," but that expression is highly ambiguous. A clock is really only a uniform motion machine to which we can compare other motions and changes. The units of what is usually called "time measurement" are conventional; it does not matter, for example, how long a minute or a second is taken to be, so long as we agree on the definition.[2] Western culture welcomed the regularity and uniformity of the mechanical clock. The advantages of clock time were apparent almost immediately and contributed to its dominance. The scientific advantages of precise time measurement are immediately obvious. Increasingly accurate clocks permitted laboratory sciences to measure the duration of physical, chemical and biological processes. Social advantages include the benefits of synchronizing human activities such as political meetings, university classes, musical events, family gatherings, religious rituals, athletic competitions—anything that people gather together to do at the same time. Socio-economic advantages begin with regularized hours of labor, and progress along with industrialization through multiple shifts and wages based on time, to an increasingly elaborate infrastructure of scheduled transportation, utility, and communication networks.[3] Precise timekeeping provides the solution to practical problems such as navigation, from the longitude problem (solved by Harrison to within a few seconds) to our global positioning system (GPS, which is accurate to within billionths of a second).

Many of the structures of contemporary human life are highly abstract, and they rely on the use of clock time which is itself an abstraction. I use the term "abstract" in contrast to the term "concrete." From the realist point of

[2] Aristotle convincingly argues (against Zeno) that time must be continuous, and because it is continuous, it is actually divisible into conventional units that are potentially infinitely divisible. See Aristotle, *Physics* VI, 1, 231a21–231b20. There is no natural smallest unit of time (or length or motion). Therefore, we are free to subdivide time as much as we like. The Cs-133 atomic clock subdivides the second by defining it as "the duration of 9,192,631,770 periods of the radiation corresponding to the transition between the two hyperfine levels of the ground state of the Cesium-133 atom."

[3] On the social effects of the mechanical clock, see G. J. Whitrow, *Time in History: Views of Time from Prehistory to the Present Day* (Oxford: Oxford University Press, 1989); Gerhard Dohrn-van Rossum, *History of the Hour: Clocks and Modern Temporal Orders*, trans. Thomas Dunlap (Chicago: The University of Chicago Press, 1996); David S. Landes, *Revolution in Time: Clocks and the Making of the Modern World* (Cambridge, Massachusetts: Belknap Press of Harvard University Press, 1983); Mark M. Smith, *Mastered by the Clock: Time, Slavery, and Freedom in the American South* (Chapel Hill, North Carolina: University of North Carolina Press, 1997).

view, the "concrete" world is the world of real things in everyday experience. "To abstract," as St. Thomas Aquinas tells us, is to separate out in thought.[4] "Abstraction" occurs when we select out features or patterns that individual things have in common. This process pays attention to the generic and leaves behind, or even discards, the particular. Modern thought tends to assign priority to abstract systems and to devalue particular, concrete individuals. Existential philosophers of the nineteenth and twentieth centuries have criticized this tendency. Kierkegaard, Sartre, Marcel, and others warn us against the modern preference for abstract systems and rational constructions. They warn us that we ourselves are particular, concrete individuals endangered by an emphasis on generic, abstract systems. To the modern mind their warning comes across as vaguely anti-scientific. Modern thought assigns to natural science the task of knowing reality best. The practice of natural science is said to require intellectual objectivity. This objectivity is taken to mean detachment or abstraction from all that messy personal stuff, including opinions, preferences, moral values, purposes and the like. Objective, quantitative science requires precise measurement, including time measurement, and the clock provides an objective standard for uniform periods of time. The clock reinforces the modern preference for objectivity, and the modern preference for objectivity reinforces an emphasis on clock time. Clock time, then, is an abstract structure that applies generally to all events regardless of their particular features. The advantages of relying on clock time conceal the disadvantages of forgetting that clock time is an abstraction from lived time.

Lived time, or time as we experience it in everyday life, differs considerably from clock time. In contrast to the uniformity and evenness of units we find in clock time, lived time is uneven. We experience time as passing more quickly or more slowly, depending on the significance of the events through which we are living. Precise schedules are simply inappropriate and irrelevant when it comes to birth, death, joy, suffering, illness, grief, the creative process, and profound life changes of all kinds. You know what it means to experience an accident in slow motion or see your life flash before your eyes. We say "What a difference a day makes," "Those were the longest three days of my life," and so on. Notice that instead of describing some abstract structure of time, these examples describe real events. We experience real events as belonging within a network of intersubjective relationships. "Intersubjective" here means partly subjective and partly objective; it means "personal" but not "relative to the individual" (because there are essential structures of

---

[4] St. Thomas Aquinas, *ST* I, q. 85, a.1, ad 1. This is abstraction through simple and absolute consideration, where we consider one thing without considering another.

intersubjectivity). Intersubjectivity indicates the presence of a real relation or interaction between a person and anything else, and so the term "intersubjective relationship" is partly redundant although I use it sometimes in order to emphasize the relational character of intersubjectivity.[5] Any description of lived time focuses on the events through which one lives, and describes the experience or passage of time relative to those events. Lived time occurs within real experiences which are relational and intersubjective and which vary considerably in significance. This non-arbitrary significance is embedded in the relational character of the experiences, and produces the unevenness of lived time.

It would be easy from a purely objective point of view to dismiss this unevenness and to say that this apparent unevenness is purely subjective and therefore illusory. Why? From the purely objective point of view, clock time is the only "real" time, because it appears to be objective and measurable. However, clock time is an abstraction from time as we live it. The experience of lived time is uneven because lived time gives priority to concrete human events rather than abstract schedules. Clock time, on the other hand, gives priority to abstract schedules rather than concrete human events.[6] Cultural differences come into play here. Is it more important, for instance, to talk with someone you know or to be on time for an appointment? We rarely notice, much less challenge, our cultural preference for clock time. When we rely on the clock to order human affairs, we apply clock time to ourselves. The lived time of human events and of our own self, a temporality which we experience as profoundly uneven, becomes forced into an abstract and uniform structure. The clock time of abstract schedules displaces the lived time of human events and intersubjective relationships.

When lived time is subsumed under clock time, the self disintegrates into a collection of functions. Gabriel Marcel calls this "the functionalized world." The functionalized world compartmentalizes the person into sets of

---

[5] This account uses Husserlian intentionality to describe our being in the world. Josef Pieper expresses a similar idea: "[T]he 'internal' is the ability to have a real relationship, a relation to the external; to have an 'inside,' means [to be able] to be related, and to enter into relationship. . . . A world means the same thing, but considered as a whole field of relationships. Only a being with an 'inside' has a 'world'; only such a being can exist in the midst of a field of relations" (*Leisure, the Basis of Culture*, trans. Gerald Malsbury, intro. Roger Scruton [South Bend, Indiana: St. Augustine's Press, 1998], p. 81). The terminology of internality and externality, however, can be misconstrued into modern subjectivity and objectivity.

[6] Different sports reflect the difference between giving priority to schedules and giving priority to events. For example, football and basketball are time-driven, whereas baseball and tennis are event-driven.

functions (primarily social and biological), and reduces our experience to "elements that are increasingly devoid of any intrinsic value or significance." "Precise amounts of time are allotted for various functions," including sleep and recreation, and the person loses a sense of the whole of oneself; Marcel calls this the fragmentation of personality.[7] Similarly, Josef Pieper argues against the priority of the world of total work.[8] The clock makes possible the world of total work: we live to work, not work to live. This modern reversal of ends and means gives priority to the abstract system over the concrete individual, and dissolves the individual into the system. Many examples illustrate this point. We define our selves by our paid occupation and our value by our function within the economic system. Our function within the economic system, to get a job and make money, is the purpose of life (our students have internalized this). Efficiency is the greatest virtue. Productivity requires doing the greatest amount of work in the least amount of time. The appropriate answer to the question "How are you these days?" is "Busy." We are counseled about "time management." Salaried people are "off the clock" but are expected to work unpaid overtime. "Time is money." It is hard to get time off to care for others, and you are in real trouble if you use up your "sick days." People feel lucky when allowed to take "personal days" (Who do your days belong to, anyway?). Hospitals bill by the day and insurance companies mandate a length-of-stay for a medical condition. Attorneys bill by the quarter hour. "Quality time" attempts to compress significant human interaction into a short span of clock time, making up in quality for what we cannot have in quantity. We tend not to notice the weirdness of these things because we tacitly assign priority to the abstract structures regulated by clock time. In other words, insofar as we live by the clock, we *are* moderns.

Nietzsche understood modernity rather well when he proclaimed the death of God. "God is dead" because the everlasting busyness of a modern life leaves no room for God. Modern people, as modern, embed their identity into their functions and live outside of themselves. Nietzsche says of modern people, "They feel they are already occupied . . . ; it seems that they have no time at all left for religion, especially as it is not clear to them whether it involves another business or another pleasure. . . . They are not opposed to religious usages; . . . it is only that they live too much aside and outside even to feel the need for any for or against in such things."[9] The externality of the functionalized world

---

[7] Gabriel Marcel, "Concrete Approaches to Investigating the Ontological Mystery," in *Gabriel Marcel's Perspectives on the Broken World*, trans. K. R. Hanley (Milwaukee, Wisconsin: Marquette University Press, 1998), pp. 173–75.

[8] Pieper, *Leisure, the Basis of Culture*, pp. 3–60.

[9] Friedrich Nietzsche, *Beyond Good and Evil*, trans. R. J. Hollingdale, intro. Michael Tanner (New York: Penguin, 1990), Part Three, no. 58, p. 83.

leaves no room for relational experience. We are too busy with our scheduled activities to belong to ourselves, or in the world, or to God. The modern functionalized world is actively hostile not only to relational experience in general, but also to religious experience in particular. The rule of clock time displaces not only the lived time of ordinary human events, but also the sacred time of prayer and contemplation.

It is one of the ironies of history that the invention of the mechanical clock can be traced to the bells used to tell the hours in monasteries.[10] The bells tolled the monastic hours in order to orient one's life away from ordinary lived time toward God. The discipline of interrupting one's activity at scheduled times served to detach time from ordinary human events in order to lead the soul closer to God. However, and this is the irony, it also contributed to the abstract and objective conception of time that fostered the conception of the mechanical universe. Spiritual withdrawal practices a kind of detachment from ordinary human events, but that detachment is not the same as the detachment of scientific observation.[11] The application of clock time to the world, especially through natural science, separated us from the world and contributed to the modern decline of religion.

Modern science depends on clock time. Science aims at explanation, prediction and control of natural things and processes, and these activities require precise measurement. For example, the gravitational constant was measured first by Galileo, who used an inclined plane and a pendulum. The uniform motion of the pendulum allowed him to quantify the pattern he observed. The goal of quantification is to discover the rational structure of the universe; according to Galileo, the book of Nature is written in mathematics.[12] Galileo's contemporary, René Descartes, was one of many thinkers

[10] See, for example, Whitrow, *Time in History*; Dohrn-van Rossum, *History of the Hour*; Landes, *Revolution in Time*.

[11] According to Lewis Mumford, "[The mechanical clock] dissociated time from human events and helped create belief in an independent world of mathematically measurable sequences: the special world of science" (*Technics and Civilization* [New York: Routledge & Kegan Paul, 1934], p. 15, quoted in Whitrow, *Time in History*, p. 127).

[12] "Philosophy is written in that great book which ever lies before our eyes—I mean the universe—but we cannot understand it if we do not first learn the language and grasp the symbols, in which it is written. This book is written in the mathematical language. . . ." (*Opere Complete di Galileo Galilei*, (Florence, 1842, vol. 4, p. 171, cited in E. A. Burtt, *The Metaphysical Foundations of Modern Physical Science* [New York: Doubleday, 1954], p. 75). See also Edmund Husserl's analysis of Galileo's mathematization thesis, in *Husserliana* VI, ed. Walter Biemel (The Hague: Martinus Nijhoff, 1954), Part II, pars. 8–10; *The Crisis of European Sciences and Transcendental Phenomenology*, trans. David Carr (Evanston, Illinois: Northwestern University Press, 1970), pp. 21–61.

who used the mechanical clock as a model for the physical universe.[13] This idea goes far beyond the usefulness of the clock for making precise measurements. The mechanical model of the universe functioning like a giant clock reinforces the uniformity of time, and the uniformity of time reinforces the model. Causality is reduced to efficient causality, because an explanation of how a clock works is a complete scientific explanation of the clock; form follows function. The removal of teleology from the universe for the purposes of scientific investigation becomes the removal of teleology from the universe altogether.

As the devaluation of lived time progresses, clock time becomes longer, more abstract and more remote from human life. Many examples can be taken from geology, physics, and biology. Geological science discovered evidence of a far distant past—through examining tree rings, rock strata, fossils, ice cores, etc., people learned about the ancient prehistory of the earth. Eternity, understood as outside of time, vanished and was replaced by the indefinite extension of clock time stretching back into the past and forward into the future. The calculation of time began to take place on a vast scale: 100 million years ago X happened, 5 billion years from now Y will happen.[14] Astrophysics developed theories about not only the formation of stars and planets, but also the generation and destruction of our physical universe as a whole, through "the big bang" and either "the big crunch" or eventual entropic exhaustion (that's "the big whimper"). People now tend to think it makes sense to talk of order emerging by chance from chaos, because "over time" it could happen—as if an event does not need a cause if a very long time is involved. Throw chance and time together, and anything can happen. In a similar way, evolutionary theory postulated the anonymous operation of natural selection; organisms are supposed to adapt "over time" to their environment. Genetics now attempts to calculate the date of a species' origin, based on the number of genetic changes, and a postulate about the amount of time required for a change. Relativity physics did not relativize time; it took the speed of light as

[13] René Descartes, *Discourse on the Method*, Part Five, and *Meditations on First Philosophy*, Sixth Meditation. See *The Philosophical Writings of Descartes*, vols. 1–2, trans. John Cottingham, Robert Stroothoff, and Dugald Murdoch (Cambridge: Cambridge University Press, 1984, 1985).

[14] It became very hard for Western people to prevent themselves from calculating time in terms of fixed and uniform intervals. For example, fundamentalist interpretations of time in the Old Testament, in opposition to geological "deep time," presuppose that biblical mentions of time must refer to our uniform intervals. That is a modern assumption, just as the calculation of precise time intervals is a modern concern. A "day" is our most immediate and natural "unit" for measuring the order and duration of events, especially in the absence of reliable timekeeping devices.

a constant because that is thought to be necessary for clock time to function normally (that is, uniformly) in *all* frames of reference. In all of these cases, we see that time is only clock time, eternity is only an infinite or indefinite extension of clock time, and the calculation of time expands to vast intervals that are unimaginable and irrelevant to a human life.[15]

At this point comes the shift from natural science to philosophical naturalism. Natural science appears to provide an objective view of time that tells us we are nothing. It appears that the real experience of an ordinary human life amounts to nothing when measured against the immense scale of the universe. Human life loses its place, its purpose and its significance. Pascal describes our modern situation brilliantly in his *Pensées*, when he shows how we are suspended between the infinitely large and the infinitely small: "Anyone who considers himself in this way will be terrified at himself . . . seeing his mass, as given him by nature, supporting him between these two abysses of infinity and nothingness. . . ."[16] Personal past, present and future have no relation to the past, present and future of the vast universe.[17]

The plausibility of philosophical naturalism depends largely on clock time and its abstraction from lived time. Without noticing the limitations of scientific method and the abstraction upon which it rests, the philosophical naturalist takes the anonymous and autonomous functioning of physical laws to be the only norm in the universe. It is one thing to argue that the immense scale of the universe dwarfs the span of a human life; it is another to argue from that to the cosmic insignificance of a human life—the life of the human who purports to discover the immense scale of that universe. Although it is possible to practice natural science without being a philosophical naturalist, scientific abstraction as a way of thought encourages people to discard every aspect of life that cannot be understood in scientific terms.[18]

So far I have discussed the implications of clock time for lived time and the real self. Clock time overwhelms lived time and the real self in two ways:

[15] The vastly small Planck distance (1.61×10^{-33} cm) and Planck time (5.36×10^{-44} sec) are also unimaginable and irrelevant.

[16] Blaise Pascal, *Pensées, Les Provinciales* (Paris: Bookking International, 1995), p. 34, 72–199; *Pensées*, trans. and introd. A. J. Krailsheimer (New York: Penguin, 1966), p. 90, 199 H9.

[17] Versions of the anthropic principle require consciousness in our universe, in more or less strong ways, but that requirement has nothing to do with an ordinary human life.

[18] The abstraction practiced by scientific method cannot be described within that method; it is an abstraction forgetful of itself. This leads to problems about the nature of theory, and to self-contradictory views such as logical positivism. Many aspects of life are vulnerable to the overextension of scientific thought, especially morality.

first, through assigning priority to abstract schedules over concrete lived events, and secondly, through supporting a mechanical and naturalistic view of the universe that appears to trivialize human life. Now I will examine the consequences of clock time for sacred time and our relation with God. The modern abstraction from real intersubjectivity reduces lived time to clock time, reduces the living world to the machine, and separates us from God.

A mechanical and naturalistic view of the universe, ruled by the clock, removes God from the world. In a naturalistic universe, there is no room for the presence of God. For modern thought, the world is only a collection of purely natural things obeying scientific laws. Everything "real" has a purely natural explanation and, conversely, anything without a purely natural explanation in principle cannot be admitted to be real. If the world is purely natural and objective, then a God, if one exists at all, cannot act through the world; there can be no sacraments, no signs of God's providence, no analogies between Creator and created being, no redemption of the machine. The modern clocklike universe functions quite well on its own. This view of the universe is opposed by sacramental religion. Sacramental religion is inherently and essentially anti-modern, with regard to the world, religious experience, and sacred time.[19]

Sacramental religion affirms God's presence through the world and affirms the validity of religious experience. A spiritual life is much more than an intellectual assertion of a First Cause or an emotional hope in redemption; a spiritual life requires a relationship with God through prayer and contemplation, and/or through the world as a sacramental. From the viewpoint of faith, God sustains the being of all creatures; "in Him we live and move and have our being."[20] According to the Roman Catholic catechism, "The sacraments are efficacious signs of grace, instituted by Christ and entrusted to the Church, by which divine life is dispensed to us. The visible rites by which the sacraments are celebrated signify and make present the graces proper to each sacrament."[21] God's grace makes possible the transformation of nature. The Holy Spirit acts through the Church, through our activity of living and spreading God's Word. The world, in addition to its natural character, embodies the

---

[19] The anti-modern aspect of sacramental religion explains some of the affinities between Roman Catholicism and Native American spirituality. These affinities were documented recently in the brilliant museum exhibit "Sacred Encounters." See Jacqueline Peterson with Laura Peters, *Sacred Encounters: Father DeSmet and the Indians of the Rocky Mountain West* (Norman: University of Oklahoma Press, 1993).

[20] Acts 17:28. St. Paul, in his debate with the Stoics, uses this quotation from Epimenides.

[21] *Catechism of the Catholic Church* (New York: Doubleday Image, 1995), no. 1131, p. 320; see also no. 1084, p. 307. According to the Baltimore catechism, "A sacrament is an outward sign instituted by Christ to give grace."

goodness and love of the Creator and requires our stewardship. Religious experience, then, is relational and intersubjective; it depends on real interaction with God through the vehicle of the world and our imperfect, embodied human life.[22]

The sacramental view of the world just described stands in sharp contrast to the naturalistic view of a purely objective world. Given the modern dichotomy between the purely objective and the purely subjective, the naturalistic thesis drives God and religion out of the objective world and into the realm of subjective psychology. Since God has no place within the purely objective world, the only place left for God in modern thought is within the purely subjective self. So Kierkegaard argues that the only truth Christianity can have is subjective truth, the terrible risk taken by the isolated individual in making the irrational leap of faith.[23] Religion for a Pascal or a Kierkegaard must be a matter of inwardness alone, and an individual's relationship with God answers to no objective or intersubjective criteria whatsoever—no criteria for one's action, from religious doctrine, or from a faith community. The loss of a sacramental view of the world, then, pushes religion into irrationalism. The modern reduction of rationality to scientific rationality does away with the rationality of religious belief. The modern believer, in attempting to reject the mechanical self, is thrust into the odd position of defending religion by insisting on its irrationality. Although it may appear that religion can be preserved by relegating it to the purely subjective self, that move is self-defeating for the person of faith.[24] The isolated, purely subjective self lacks connection with others and with the world.[25] Moreover, it is hard to defend the existence of a purely subjective self. From the naturalistic point of view, the point of view of clock time and the mechanical universe, that purely subjective self must be reducible to an objective mechanism, i.e., the brain. So the human self, like everything else in the universe, would be a purely natural and mechanical thing. Clearly, however, that mechanical self would be incapable

[22] This paper does not address the related issue of community.

[23] Søren Kierkegaard, *Fear and Trembling and Concluding Unscientific Post-script*, in *The Essential Kierkegaard*, eds. Howard V. Hong and Edna H. Hong (Princeton, New Jersey: Princeton University Press, 2000), pp. 93–101, 198–215.

[24] The problem of discernment then becomes insoluble. Even Kierkegaard, who criticized modern thought so perceptively on "The Present Age," could not overcome the modern isolation of the self. See *The Essential Kierkegaard*, pp. 252–68.

[25] The purely subjective self is the Cartesian *cogito*, distilled by Descartes for the purpose of proving to the intellect alone that the world exists, and taken seriously by Sartre thanks to his misinterpretation of intentionality. Descartes' method produced the modern dichotomy between subjectivity and objectivity, and the untenable view of the human person as "the ghost in the machine."

of genuine religious experience. The person is missing, and so is the possibility of any relational experience. Therefore, the modern view of the world must either reject religion entirely or subjectivize it, and the subjectivizing of religion cannot succeed in defending a religious life, or the presence of God in the world, or the reality of the sacraments.

The purely subjective self, however, is not the real self in lived time. The purely subjective self was conceived as the counterpart to the purely objective world, and both of them are artificial constructs of modernity. The real self lives an intersubjective and relational life in a multidimensional world. I have argued so far that religious experience requires an intersubjective relationship with spiritual reality, and that modern thought makes this experience impossible in principle because of the modern abstraction from lived time. Religious experience also requires an intersection between lived time and eternity, which can be described as "sacred time." Sacred time is the time of religious experience, the time of prayer, contemplation, and liturgy.[26] Sacred time cannot be confined to Sunday or a holy day, although it is true that we need to set aside some time specifically for religious activity in order to maintain its importance in our lives. The holy day or festival as sacred time achieves much more than a scheduled break from everyday work. As Josef Pieper says, "The holding of a festival means: an affirmation of the basic meaning of the world, and an agreement with it, and in fact it means to live out and fulfill one's inclusion in the world, in an extraordinary manner, different from the everyday."[27] Modern thought tends to eliminate holy days altogether, because clock time recognizes no significant difference between one day and another. Whereas clock time abstracts from lived time, sacred time transforms ordinary lived time and renders it qualitatively different. Sacred time opens onto eternity and enables the soul to experience a communion with God, often through liturgy and with others, but also through contemplation. Of course this communion occurs on unequal terms, but it involves the deepest levels of one's true self, the real self capable of intersubjective relationships. Religious experience heightens our grasp of reality and the source of our being. The transformation of a human life through religious experience is literally incomprehensible to modern thought. Modern thought abstracts from the real person and makes the self

---

[26] Mircea Eliade's work on sacred time and profane time distinguishes different but related meanings of sacred time for archaic religion and historical religion. See *The Myth of the Eternal Return*, trans. Willard R. Trask (Princeton, New Jersey: Princeton University Press, 1974).

[27] Pieper, *Leisure, the Basis of Culture*, pp. 33–34.

incapable of any intersubjective relationship, much less a transcendent one. This modern self could use a tune-up every now and then, perhaps a vacation filled with scheduled activities, and of course there are all sorts of self-help books that tell us how to adjust ourselves and create the connections that we lack. All of that is very far removed from spiritual renewal, the relational act of contemplation that opens up the soul to its eternal validity.

Despite our rightful interest in coordinating human events, despite the success of scientific time-measurements of physical events, the modern conception of time separates us from self, world, and God. Modern thought practices an unacknowledged abstraction, that promotes the dissolution of self, alienation from the world, and the decline of religion.[28] The dominance of clock time results from its success in measuring natural events and coordinating human activities. It would be unreasonable to give up the advantages given to us by our abstract systems and technological devices. However, we must find a way to undo the modern reversal of ends and means. To do that, we must promote an explicit discussion of ends, i.e., reinstate teleology. We must describe the different kinds of wholes and parts, in order to prevent the over-extension of scientific thought. We must refute the modern dichotomy between subjectivity and objectivity and explore the essential structures of intersubjectivity. We must listen to the experience of other cultures that do not elevate clock time over lived time. We must promote and defend metaphysical realism, to affirm the priority of the everyday life which is presupposed by all inquiry. We must show how it is possible to integrate everyday life, scientific discovery, and religious experience. We must defend the faith by addressing the core issues challenging the very existence of a religious life. We must promote urban planning that emphasizes social relationships and fosters the development of real connections among real people. We must be able to explain how "leisure is the basis of culture" to a society obsessed with *technē*. Our work in the 21st century, then, must challenge the reign of clock time and reinstate both the lived time of real human activities and the sacred time of prayer and relation to God.

---

[28] This unacknowledged abstraction also promotes the loss of community, both the ordinary community of family, friends, and other non-abstract groups, and the community of the mystical body of Christ, i.e., the Church.

PART III

SCHOLARSHIP AND EDUCATION

How Reason Can Survive the Modern University: The Moral Foundations of Rationality

Dallas Willard

When I speak of reason surviving the modern university, I refer to reason as a living, social practice. Reason as a human faculty or as a mental function, and all that essentially pertains to it, is perhaps in no danger. It is we, it is the university and education generally, that are in danger because of the loss of the *practice* of reason.

By "reason" I refer to the capacity to apprehend truth itself, as truth is displayed in any true thought, judgment or statement. That capacity involves, among other things, the capacity to grasp logical relations and thereby appreciate evidence for truth. The primary function of reason is to see truth as a property of judgment or representation and to see the simpler laws of truth that govern truth-values as necessarily distributed over judgments that are logically related to one another by such relations as strict implication and logical contradiction. The ideal of the intellectual, artistic and academic life as the pursuit of truth, or of just being thoroughly logical, is far beyond being in "deep trouble" in the university today, and in many places is approximating the status of a "lost cause."[1]

---

[1] I will not try to demonstrate this here, or discuss it at any length. I take it as a given. But those who would like to pursue it can certainly consult Robert Nisbet, *The Degradation of the Academic Dogma* (New York: Basic Books, 1971), for an older work; or, among most recent works, Edward Tingley, "Technicians of Learning," *First Things* (August/September 2000), pp. 29–35, or the Fall 2000 edition of *The Hedgehog Review: Critical Reflections on Contemporary Culture*, entitled "What's the University for?"

Of course truth is inseparable from the being (reality, existence) of that which the true judgment is about. So reason is intimately linked to the comprehension of *being*, of *how things are*. It is a capacity for insight into reality or what is. Maritain says in one place, "If I . . . am a Thomist, it is in the last analysis because I have understood that the intellect sees, and that it is cut out to conquer being. In its most perfect function, which is not to manufacture ideas, but to judge, the intellect seizes upon existence exercised by things. And at the same time it forms the first of its concepts—the concept of being, which metaphysics will bring out, in its own light, at the highest degree of abstractive visualization."[2]

Reason is therefore indispensable to knowledge, which, it was thought in other times, the university and the intellectual life was primarily about. No longer. We now have *research* universities, but not *knowledge* universities. Our goal is "information" and its use, or possibly only novelty. What this all means is well laid out in Lyotard's book, *Knowledge: The Postmodern Condition*.[3] As a description of the actual processes of university life in general, and the professionalized life that goes on around and within it, this book is not a totally misguided representation of the facts of academic life and of what is regarded and rewarded as "good work."

The book shows how little is said about truth today in our "research" centers, and perhaps less still about logic as anything other than rules to be built into a computer to manipulate symbols of "information." Sometimes "logic" is now used to characterize actual processes of thought which some individual or group tends to carry out. But logic has no weight beyond actual processes that can be technologically or socially sustained, and it has no tight connection (if any at all) with truth in its correlation with reality.

Reality in academe is the social (including the technological) "flow," and whatever is spoken of as truth or logic must not transcend the flow. Knowledge, accordingly, which cannot completely shake its connections with truth and logic (evidence) in some sense, also now becomes a matter of the "flow." Knowledge becomes what, for the time being, passes for or is accepted *as* "knowledge." It becomes a kind of practice—perhaps the "best professional practice." It is *belief* in a certain social setting. No wonder we turn from "knowledge" to "research" with a sigh of relief, as from something boring to something adventuresome and exciting. Research still has at

2 Jacques Maritain, *The Range of Reason* (London: Geoffrey Bles, 1953), p. 9.
3 Jean-François Lyotard, *The Postmodern Condition: A Report on Knowledge* (Minneapolis: University of Minnesota Press, 1984).

least a mild connotation of finding out something of reality as it exists independently of our mental and social states.

By contrast, Maritain says: "Nothing is more important than the events which occur within that invisible universe which is the mind of man. And the light of that universe is knowledge. If we are concerned with the future of civilization we must be concerned primarily with a genuine understanding of what knowledge is, its value, its degrees, and how it can foster the inner unity of the human being."[4] Most students and faculty in my acquaintance would draw a complete blank on this statement.

If knowledge is power, as we have by now long been told, and power is what we really want, we will find many ways to power, and will no doubt discover that knowledge and claims to knowledge can actually *hinder* the pursuit of power. I think something like this "discovery" has happened: People generally, the "masses," want many things, along with the status of having a university education. They would like to be "right," of course, and to have social status, along with opportunities in life—especially occupational and social opportunities. The life of reason in any traditional sense is not necessarily required for any of these, and may even be opposed to them. It is, in any case, a life of sustained labor. The academic community finds many ways to make itself useful to its public and exciting to its inhabitants other than pursuing a life of reason and knowledge.

But let us go a little deeper into what reason is. I have already said that it is the capacity to apprehend truth itself and the laws of truth (and falsity), along with the realities corresponding to truth. Truth itself is "correspondence" of thought (proposition, belief, statement) with what the thought (etc.) is about. A proposition is true provided that what it is about is as that proposition holds or indicates it to be. The many so-called theories of "truth" that have arisen in the last century and a half are not theories of *truth* at all, but are efforts to change the subject, driven by failures of representationalist accounts of mind and language.[5] Their aim, nonetheless, surely is to represent truth as it is, not to present theories that are "true" of truth in the non-correspondence senses of "true" they themselves spell out. Reason is our ability to bring that peculiar structure of truth with which a child is familiar before consciousness, and, in simpler cases at least, to gain insight into or understanding of it and of the necessary relations between propositions and their truth values.

We take the simplest of illustrations of these relations. With very little

---

[4] Maritain, *The Range of Reason*, p. 3.
[5] See Frederick F. Schmitt, *Truth: A Primer* (San Francisco: Westview Press, 1995).

reflection on experience and thought one can see that the proposition *Swans are living things* is true, that what a swan is involves or requires any particular swan to exemplify life. (Try giving a dead or plaster "swan" to someone you have promised a swan.) But even if this were not so, it is easily seen that *if* all swans are living things, no thing that lacks life would be a swan (obversion), or that no things lacking life are swans (contraposition). Reason here enables you to know something about everything in the entire universe—something that in this case is fairly uninteresting, to be sure. But the point is the process, and the triviality of the case may help us see the process more clearly.

By contrast, the truth of the proposition that all swans are living things leaves undetermined whether all living things are swans. Conversion "without limitation" is a logically illicit move. This too is an insight of reason. Realization of a *non sequitur* is as much a rational insight as is insight into an implication or contradiction between thoughts or propositions. The grasp of what does *not* logically follow or is irrelevant is often a triumph of reason.

Now I have taken the simplest possible cases to illustrate the use of reason, because I want to make *what reason is* very clear on the basis of thought experiences which everyone can have. (The reader must do the necessary, reflective thinking to achieve the experiences in question.) It is, to repeat, the capacity for insight into truth (or falsity) and truth-value relations between propositions. Similar simple insights of reason underlie basic rules of the logic of propositions (e.g., the distributive laws or De Morgan's laws) and of quantification, as well as systems such as that in Russell and Whitehead's *Principia Mathematica*, with its rules of substitution and detachment. Rational insight into the systems of logical rules allows reason to extend its reach far beyond anything that it can directly grasp in the manner of the simple cases.

(Reason also displays its nature in grasping evidential and conceptual relations other than implication and contradiction, of course; but I shall not undertake to discuss these matters here.)

Now let us try to say something about the reasonable *person* and the life of reason. And here we are, of course, primarily concerned with persons in the context of academic or scholarly life, as lived on our university campuses and carried on in our professional associations. Who is the reasonable person? What is a life of reason? We can, I think, say a few things that are true and important about being a reasonable person, without trying to establish necessary and sufficient conditions of rationality—a difficult if not impossible task.

We can perhaps agree that persons are reasonable in the degree to which they conform their thinking, talk and action to the order of truth and understanding. Reasonable persons will characteristically reason soundly, not contradict themselves, and be open-minded and inquiring about the issues with which they deal. They will seek to employ the best concepts, classifications and hypotheses, testing them by interrelating them and by reference to their experience and the experiences of others. They will be open to criticism, and even seek it, knowing how hard it is to secure truth on most subjects. People are unreasonable to the degree in which they are not reasonable. No one will turn out to be perfectly reasonable or unreasonable.

The main point in all of this, to my mind, is simply that the reasonable person—the one who acts in accordance with reason in life as well as in their academic or other profession—is the one who governs his or her beliefs and assertions by insight into truth and logical relations. In particular, they are *not* mastered by how they *want* things to be, by the beliefs they happen to have, or by styles or currents of thought and action around them. If they advance claims as true or justified they do so on the basis of such insight, and are very careful to be sure that that basis is *really there*. The difficulty of securing such a basis will make any reasonable person quite humble in their claims and willing (indeed, happy, even solicitous) to be corrected when they are mistaken. Thus the reasonable person is not close-minded or dogmatic, or insistent on having their own way, but just the opposite. And that attitude is, indeed, based upon insight into the truth about the nature of scholarly or intellectual work itself. Positively, of course, the reasonable person will be devoted to *method* for determining truth and the soundness of reasoning, and will carefully observe such methods. They will be conscious and explicit about moving beyond such methods if that is, for some reason, unavoidable in their practice and statements. Life sometimes pushes us beyond where evidence reaches.

The unreasonable person, by contrast, will pursue the "right" conclusion at the expense of rational method and will aim at the achievement of certain pre-preferred effects and outcomes as their primary goal rather than at adherence to rational method. They will judge method as good or bad in terms of the conclusions reached rather than judge the conclusion as good if it emerges from rational method or sound reasoning. They will freely judge and assert without logical discipline.

It is at the point, I think, that we can see and state what has happened in the university setting in recent decades. Generally speaking, rational method, understood in traditional terms where the weight is relentlessly placed on truth and logical relations, either leads to conclusions which are thought, on other grounds, to be "unacceptable," or at least it cannot be found to support the conclusions which *are* acceptable or desired. Now this is not a particularly new phenomenon, but in the distant past it more commonly led to the evasion or distortion of truth and logic rather than their repudiation or attempted replacement with "methods" or "logics" that yielded more gratifying results. Indeed, truth and logic has throughout history often been *forced* to support positions that could not, in truth, be rationally supported. Temptation to intellectual irresponsibility is strong. Truth is often bitter, and the path down which "standard" logic would lead us may doom us or our dearest commitments.

That brings me to my next point, which is perhaps the main point of what I have to say here. The life of reason is not, generally speaking, *self-sustaining*. The values inherent in it are not by themselves enough to secure its institution and perpetuation. This brings out the pointlessness of teaching logic as part of a liberal education without illuminating and emphasizing our *duty* to be logical. Only a strong *moral* commitment to being a reasonable person can effectively produce routine conformity, or will to conform, to truth and logic in action and assertion. We see such commitment in outstanding examples such as Socrates, Jesus and Spinoza, and certainly Maritain.

We all have tendencies to want certain things to be true or things to turn out in a certain way. Or sometimes, perhaps, we are just in a hurry to some end. Moreover, our feelings and imagination, as well as our will, have the power and often the habit of obscuring truth and sound reasoning from our intellect. Perhaps our intellect itself is impaired by our overall mental and moral condition or our social setting. To be a reasonable person, to live the life of reason, is therefore not an easy, much less an automatic, thing, but a strenuous life, an uphill battle, involving constant watchfulness, effective precautions, and many failures and humiliations. Unless there is more in us than the mere appreciation of truth and logic, we will not be able routinely to conform our thought and action to them—especially in the social setting. (Consider only the frequency of explicit lying. It is one form of disregard of the truth and its laws.)

Being reasonable, or living the life of reason, as here explained must be incorporated into our moral identity, must be a part of what we understand as being a good person, if it is to have power to direct our lives and govern our thinking and speaking. Only so can reason survive in the modern university—or anywhere else. Willful disregard of truth and the laws of truth must also be recognized as expressions of a morally evil will and person, if they are to be routinely excluded from life. Moral evil is hardly ever discussed in academic ethics today, and the same is true of being a good person. Using one's professional vocation as an avenue of moral realization, of becoming and being a good person is even less discussed. But the scientist or journalist who falsifies data to achieve their various ends betrays the goodness of heart which, I am sure, everyone in their sober and thoughtful moments recognizes as the essence of moral goodness. And such betrayal is hardly less evident in the teacher or scholar—or parent or pastor—who is careless or intentionally negligent of truth and sound reasoning and method, in order to secure ends or outcomes that they cherish for other reasons than their intellectual integrity.

The morally good person, let us say, is a person who is intent upon advancing the various goods of human life with which they are effectively in contact, in a manner that respects their relative degrees of importance and the extent to which the actions of the person in question can actually promote the existence and maintenance of those goods.

The person who is morally bad or evil is one who is intent upon the destruction (or non-maintenance) of the various goods of human life with which they are effectively in contact, or who is indifferent to the existence and maintenance of those goods. Truth and solid reasoning are among the important human goods.

Here, I submit, is the fundamental distinction within moral phenomena: the one which is of primary human interest, and from which all the others, moving toward the periphery of the moral life and ethical theory, can be clarified. We can call it, simply, "good will." For example: the moral value (positive and negative) of acts; the nature of moral obligation and responsibility; virtues and vices; the nature and limitations of rights, punishment, rewards, justice and related issues; the morality of laws and institutions; and what is to be made of moral progress and moral education, and so on. A coherent theory of all these matters can, I suggest, be developed only if we start from the distinction between the good and the bad will or person—which, we have already admitted, very few philosophers are currently prepared to discuss.

But I don't want to get side-tracked here. We can allow some latitude on exactly how the basic moral distinctions are to be understood, as long as we don't try to derive moral principles from some version of *formal* rationality alone. An Aristotle, a St. Thomas and a Kant—perhaps even hedonistic utilitarianism of the John Stuart Mill or Sidgwick varieties—could all say what I am saying here, that being reasonable is an essential element in moral excellence, and that one who does not incorporate being reasonable, and living a life of reason, into their moral identity will not be able to sustain routine reasonableness in their practice. We have a moral duty to be as intelligent as possible, and that incorporates adherence to truth and sound reasoning.

In order for reason as a practice, or reasonableness, to survive as a governing principle in life and profession, a certain awe and reverence for truth and logical relations is required, one that goes beyond whatever utilitarian value they may have—which itself is very great—and accepts their unconditional claim as human goods on our judgment and our behavior. And that awe and reverence will inevitably be associated with a strong sense of moral shame for the individual or group that does not comply with that unconditional claim. This shame will accompany the realization that I have not been the person I ought to have been because, in my non-compliance, I have not honored truth and reasoning according to strict logic, and have not acted to the benefit of those effected by my judgment or action—regardless of whether or not I am found out. Of others, such as those scientists who falsify data or journalists who make up juicy news, we will regard their behavior as morally shameful, as diminishing them from what they ought to be. We will say, "How could they do that?"—even though we very well know how they could. Commitment to truth and reason is not a governing force in their life, not a point of their moral identity, no matter how they may "spin" it. And that is why we appropriately think they are not good persons—even though in our current moral confusion we may think it morally wrong of us to think any person not good.

Strangely, perhaps, one of the strongest threats to being reasonable today is the desire to be or to appear to be scientific. Certainly if "scientific" were understood in a more classical sense, it would come down to precisely the same thing as being reasonable. Brentano had this sense in mind when he in the mid-nineteenth century urged that philosophy become scientific.[6] But "scientific" has increasingly been understood to mean conformity with the findings and assumptions of existing sciences, or, really, of existing scientists. And the will to come out scientific in this sense, or to appear so, is a primary obstacle to the life of reason in our time—and especially on the campus. Other obstacles fall in social, political and religious areas. I think of the attempt to relativize conceptualization, logic and evidence to race and gender. But I won't try to go into that here.

But now we confront a startling possibility. Perhaps the weakening of the life of reason which, if I and others are right, we are now experiencing in the midst of the academic world is the result of the disappearance of any accepted body of moral knowledge from our intellectual as well as our general culture. Is there a credible and widespread understanding today of who is a good (or evil) person, especially in the university context? If there is, I cannot identify it. In fact, as already noted, we don't even allow ourselves to talk about such things. How, then, could the life of reason as described be fostered

---

[6] For elaboration of this point see my "Who Needs Brentano," in *The Brentano Puzzle*, ed. Roberto Poli (Brookfield, Massachusetts: Ashgate Publishers, 1998).

and sustained within a moral identity if there is no recognizable body of moral knowledge within which moral identity can be cognitively identified as an objective reality in human life? Rationality today cannot find a moral foundation.

Non-cognitivism in ethical theory has triumphed in the twentieth century. In its original form, simple emotivism, it has long been rejected. But the conclusion which that original form established in academic and cultural consciousness still holds the field, and all the book-length blustering about justice and virtue theory has not budged it an inch. But then there *cannot* be an acknowledged body of moral knowledge, because the very possibility of such knowledge is ruled out. And so no moral support for the practice of rationality in life and profession can come from moral knowledge. Its support, such as it may be, must come from itself or from various utilitarian considerations or from feeling favoring it.

Now for my part I believe there is moral knowledge accessible to any thoughtful person, even though there is now no generally *acknowledged* body of moral knowledge, especially on campus. This accessible moral knowledge is rooted in our non-empirical awareness of the will and its properties—we have no better term for this than the unfortunate word "intuition"—in self-knowledge and abstraction directed upon the properties of intention, will and character. Like logical knowledge itself, basic moral knowledge does not in its beginnings depend upon reasoning, though, along with logic, basic moral knowledge lays the foundation for a body of moral knowledge derived largely through reasoning. The most elemental moral knowledge is quite direct. It is strongly presented, for example, by what Lévinas has to say about the face of the other and its immediate claim on me,[7] as well as what Maritain says about connatural knowledge of the virtues.[8] So while I am sure that moral knowledge has disappeared from *view* in our culture in general, I do not say it does not exist. It is just not available as a basis for a social enterprise such as education or the direction of the intellectual or professional life.

Well, what if anything might be done? A few comments:

If rationality and the life of reason is sustainable only as a part of what it means to be a morally good person, and if, as I believe, being a morally good person is sustainable in a social setting only within a framework of accessible moral knowledge that can serve as a guide to life and a background for holding people responsible, then one concerned about a rational life must seek to

---

[7] Emmanuel Lévinas, *Totality and Infinity* (Pittsburgh, Pennsylvania: Duquesne University Press, 1969), especially pp. 77–81 and 187–204.
[8] Maritain, *The Range of Reason*, p. 23.

make accessible to the public an appropriate body of moral knowledge. Can that be done, and, in particular, can it be done in our current social context or anything close to it?

This is a very difficult question to answer, because it is, at bottom, a question of social causation: a notoriously difficult type of question. But perhaps such transformations have been accomplished from time to time in the human past, at least to some significant degree. I have already mentioned Socrates. He and those who gathered around him and came afterward do seem to me to have put in place a powerful version of moral excellence that included devotion to truth and right reasoning sufficient to sustain the life of reason as an ideal and a practice in the lives of many who learned of it. Perhaps I am too hopeful about that period, and certainly it had its problems and failures, but reading the history of many public figures in the centuries during and after Socrates is impressive, as are the writings and influence of people such as Epictetus or Seneca.

More impressive still, in terms of effect, is the view and experience of the moral life and devotion to truth in the Christian tradition, which gave rise to the universities in the Western world, and sustained them up until the end of the nineteenth century or so. One might think of trying to renew that tradition, and not pass it off as irreparably undermined by its critics and opponents. After all, it is not an exaggeration to point out that no alternative to the Christian tradition has yet been discovered as a satisfactory basis for life.

I am haunted periodically by the words with which Alasdair MacIntyre closed *After Virtue* years ago—still, to me, the most profound words in the book. He says, you may recall, that the barbarians are already within the gates—one wonders who they might be—and that we are not now waiting for Godot, but for another and no doubt very different, St. Benedict. [9]

I'm sure I have never fully understood what MacIntyre had in mind with this statement, but I believe he intends to say that community must come, somehow, *before* virtue, and subsequently provide the support for rationality and the life of reason, among other things. But the community itself, so far as Benedict was concerned, certainly had to be a product of the transcendent reality of Jesus and the Kingdom of God, including the Church. I really doubt that this is what MacIntyre had in mind, at least at the time he wrote those words, but it may now be time to ask if there is really any serious alternative to it.

The details are far from clear to me, but I think something like the development of a community of moral understanding in the Christian tradition

[9] Alasdair MacIntyre, *After Virtue*, 2nd edition (Notre Dame, Indiana: University of Notre Dame Press), p. 263.

must be the answer to our current situation. This seems to me the only thing capable of redeeming reason, of providing the moral substance and understanding that can make the life of reason possible. Though I do not share MacIntyre's philosophy of mind and logic, and believe that the understanding and practical appropriation of moral insight is much freer of specific communities than he supposes (There is a human nature, in my view, and it is fairly obvious.), I am sure that the restoration of moral knowledge to our academic culture will require a certain community of professionals, academics and intellectuals devoted to that cause over a lengthy period of time.

Perhaps the Maritain Association could serve as the center for such an effort. It does not seem to me that success in this enterprise would necessarily be a miracle or an expression of special graces, but it would require the lives of many excellent thinkers in concert over a long period of time. It would require much institutional support from a wide variety of sources as well as powerful intellectual leadership. Success would not be guaranteed, but it surely could be achieved, and perhaps grace and miracle would assist in appropriate ways. Surely no one has greater responsibility to attempt the restoration of moral knowledge to academic culture, or better prospects of achieving it, than the people who identify themselves with Jesus Christ and the intellectual and academic tradition deriving from him. Perhaps it is time to say that, if reason is to be salvaged, the academic life must be seen as a spiritual calling, and the moral character that can routinely support the life of reason with integrity must be a life in the spirit of Christ.

It is fair to say that Maritain represented in his work and life such a posture toward moral wisdom and the life of reason. The last words in the article on him in Edward's *The Encyclopedia of Philosophy* read as follows:

> Maritain is admired even by those who may be of very different philosophical convictions. He is admired not only for his life-long zeal for truth and impassioned commitment to freedom, but also for his exceptional qualities as a person—his humility, his charity, his fraternal attitude toward all that is. Increasingly he is being recognized as one of the great *spirituals* of his time.[10]

As arrogant as it will seem to many in the academic culture of today, can we aim at anything less than what we saw in Maritain himself, if we are to be responsible human beings concerned with the redemption of reason today?

---

[10] Paul Edwards, ed., *The Encyclopedia of Philosophy*, vol. 5 (New York: Macmillan Publishing Co. & The Free Press, 1967), p. 164.

Maritain as Model
of the Catholic Scholar

Ralph McInerny

A VISIT TO MEUDON

O n September 14, 1932 four German philosophers, who had come to
France for the *Journée d'études de la Société Thomiste* meeting on
the theme of phenomenology, paid a visit to the Maritain house at
Meudon. Jacques was then fifty years old but he already had an international
reputation as a Christian philosopher. Jacques recorded the visit in his diary:
"Wednesday 24. Exaltation of the Holy Cross. Visit of Edith Stein, Dom
Feuling, Rosenmoeller and Soehngen."[1] It was more than gallantry that
caused him to list the woman before the men. Edith Stein, like Raïssa, was
Jewish and a convert to the Catholic faith. It would be nearly a decade after
her conversion that she would enter the Carmel of Cologne where she took
the religious name of Teresa Benedicta of the Cross. It was a shared sense of
the nature of Christian philosophy that created immediately a special rapport
between the Maritains and Edith Stein.

The conversion of the Maritains had taken place more than a quarter century earlier and it was not long afterward that they came to blend their pursuit
of sanctity with their pursuit of truth under the tutelage of Thomas Aquinas.
Edith Stein would say that it was while reading Thomas Aquinas that she first
saw the unity of the spiritual and intellectual lives, that the pursuit of truth
was a way of loving God. "It became clear to me in reading Saint Thomas,"
she wrote, "that it was possible to place knowledge at the service of God and
it was then and only then that I could resolve to take up again my studies in a

---

[1] Jacques Maritain, *Notebooks*, trans. Joseph W. Evans (Albany, New York: Magi
Books, 1984), p. 165.

serious manner."[2] Her meeting with the Maritains could be brought under the heading: *Spiritus ad spiritum loquitur.*

In Jacques Maritain there was an intimate bond between who he was and what he taught.

LES CERCLES D'ÉTUDES THOMISTES

A student of Jacques Maritain who fell during World War I surprisingly named his old professor as a beneficiary of his will. This unexpected money created new opportunities for the philosopher. The Villard bequest not only enabled him to continue his philosophical work. He would also be able to conduct a center of spirituality at Meudon in a large house the Maritains were able to buy with their new and unexpected post-war windfall. But both objectives were pursued at the same address. It was at Meudon that Maritain began the Thomistic Study Circles.

An indication of the importance Maritain attached to the study circles and retreats that were held at his house in Meudon is the fact that he devotes nearly one quarter of his *Carnet de Notes* to the subject. This project, which would continue until the beginning of World War II when Jacques and his wife left France for the United States, represents one of the most sustained efforts on Maritain's part to influence the culture of his native land as a convert to Catholicism. The effort met with both successes and failures.

The meetings at the Maritains' seem to have begun without any thought of regular recurrences. Jacques tells us that he found in a notebook this entry, "First reunion of Thomistic studies at the house, with Picher, Vaton, Barbot, Dastarac, Massis."[3] The date of the entry was Sunday, February 8, 1914. There was no immediate sequel to that meeting, not surprisingly: World War I broke out in 1914. It was five years later, in the fall of 1919, that regular meetings devoted to Thomistic studies began at the Maritain home in Versailles. Jacques

---

[2] In a letter written February 12, 1928, she said, "It was through St. Thomas that I first came to realize that it is possible to regard scholarly work as a service of God. Immediately before, and a long time after my conversion, I thought living a religious life meant to abandon earthly things and to live only in the thought of the heavenly realities. Gradually I have learned to understand that in this world something else is demanded of us, and that even in the contemplative life the connection with this world must not be cut off. Only then did I make up my mind to take up scholarly work again. I even think that the more deeply a soul is drawn into God, the more it must also go out of itself in this sense, that is to say in the world, in order to carry the Divine life into it" (Edith Stein, *Self-portrait in Letters, 1916–1942* in *The Collected Works of Edith Stein*, vol. 5 [Washington, D.C.: Institute of Carmelite Studies, 1993], p. 54).

[3] Jacques Maritain, *Notebooks*, p. 133.

had been on leave of absence from the *Institut Catholique* during the academic year 1917–18 (the last year of the war), engaged on writing two introductory books in philosophy.[4] The names mentioned as attending the first meeting were hardly household words, and Maritain describes the participants of the second meeting, which would indeed begin a series, as personal friends and students of his from the *Institut Catholique*. It was still an informal gathering, and stayed that way until 1921 when the decision was made to formalize the meetings and to stabilize their focus. The participants were those "for whom the spiritual life and the pursuit of wisdom (philosophical and theological) had major importance. . . ."[5]

From the time of their conversion, the Maritains' household had lived on a schedule that took its rationale from a dual purpose—the pursuit of truth and the pursuit of sanctity. In Germany, there had been only an accidental connection between the two, with prayer merely surrounding studies more or less unrelated to the goal of the spiritual life. The discovery of Saint Thomas had opened up the possibility of a more integral connection between the life of the mind and the spiritual life. This was exactly the discovery that Edith Stein too would make.

When the Maritains became Oblates of St. Benedict, their regimen of prayer and study had taken on a particular stamp, but the Thomistic Study Circles acquired their own character. There was the continuation of the conviction that laymen too were called to sanctity, but the spirit of Versailles was more Dominican than Benedictine, a movement prefigured in a way in Thomas Aquinas's move from Montecassino to the Order of Preachers.

Most of the participants were lay people—old and young, male and female, students and professors—but there were priests and religious as well. The lay people represented a wide range of vocations, not just professional philosophers, but doctors, poets, musicians, businessmen, scientists. Catholics were in the majority but there were also unbelievers as well as Jews, Orthodox, and some Protestants. As for Thomas, some were already experts in his thought, others mere beginners. It was interest in the thought of Thomas Aquinas, albeit of different degrees, that brought them together.

What was the atmosphere? It was not a class or a seminar, the participants did not come as students in that sense, nor was it a soirée with drinks

---

[4] Jacques Maritain, *Éléments de philosophie, I: Introduction; II: Petite logique.* These appeared in English as *An Introduction to Philosophy,* trans. E. I. Watkin (New York: Sheed & Ward), and *An Introduction to Logic* (New York: Sheed & Ward, 1937).

[5] *Notebooks*, p. 184.

and cigarettes, although people came as guests to a home. Jacques insists on the need for feminine influence for the success of such a venture, and characterizes the participants as guests of Raïssa. There were three women hostesses, Raïssa, her sister Vera, and their mother. The samovar was readied and later there would be dinner. Writing as a lonely widower many decades later, Jacques insists that Raïssa was the "ardent flame" of the reunions, taking an active if discreet part in the discussions. And she prayed constantly for the success of the reunions. "It is clear that without her—or without her sister—there would have been no Thomistic Circles, anymore than there would have been a Meudon (or for that matter a Jacques Maritain)."[6]

The discussion would go on throughout the afternoon, through tea and on into dinner, though not all stayed for that. At midnight, the hosts bade goodbye to the last guest, then collapsed with fatigue.

It is significant that Jacques insists on the role of Raïssa in the reunions. The motive was certainly the dissemination of the thought of Thomas Aquinas, but of course there was also a wife promoting her husband's career and influence. As time went on, the reunions became the occasion for conversions to Catholicism, and the relevance of Thomism for all aspects of culture gave the reunions the air of a salon which sought to exert influence on the artistic and literary life of Paris. The very public *contretemps* with Jean Cocteau and the effort to rival the literary influence of André Gide are facets of this. But all that was far in the future when the effort began.

For the first ten or twelve years, the topics were the great problems of philosophy and theology, treated technically. Texts of Thomas would be read, the great commentators consulted—special mention is made of John of St. Thomas, of course—and an effort made to "disengage from the intramural disputes of Second Scholasticism the truths whose appeal transcended the prison-like setting of the texts."[7] What were the themes? Faith and reason, philosophy and theology, metaphysics, poetry, politics, indeed all the issues raised by the culture around them.

Jacques was the leader, as we learn when he tells us that he prepared his expositions of the texts the night before or Sunday morning, "hastily, but carefully." Among his papers, he found notes for the meetings and we are not surprised to hear that these took the form of synoptic tables and great schemata on large sheets that could be affixed to the wall. The subjects he treated, by way of analysis of texts, included the following. Angelic knowledge. How

---

[6] *Notebooks*, p. 135.
[7] Ibid.

angels know future contingents, singulars and secrets of the heart. Intellectual knowledge. The agent intellect. Knowledge of the singular. The vision of God and the light of glory. The desire for that vision. Theoretical and practical knowledge. Is sociology a science? In what sense? Medicine. Politics. Justice and friendship. The Trinity: subsistence, person, the divine persons. Original sin. The Incarnation. The human nature of Christ. Free will. . . .

Maritain recalled these topics from the first decade of the reunions, which should mean through 1929. These were tumultuous years—the public flap with Cocteau, the attempt to dissuade Gide from publishing *Corydon,* the establishment of *Roseau d'or,* the Golden Reed, a series of books meant to rival Gide's influence on French culture. And it was also during this decade that *L'Action Française,* with which Jacques had long been associated, was condemned by Rome.

Perhaps there is no better way to get a sense of the flavor of this effort than by examining the little book Jacques and Raïssa co-authored to express the vision of the intellectual life which lay behind the Circles as well as the Constitution that governed its meetings.

PRAYER AND INTELLIGENCE

The Statutes governing the Thomistic Study Circles can be found in an appendix of Maritain's *Carnet de Notes,* published many years afterward, in 1964. Section 1, which states the general principles of the Circles, is of more interest than the section devoted to organization.

"In making Saint Thomas Aquinas the Common Doctor of the Church, God has given him to us as our leader and guide in the knowledge of the truth."[8] Maritain's mind had been formed by the philosophy of the day, negatively, for the most part, but more positively in the case of Bergson. After his conversion, he did not immediately see the significance of Thomas Aquinas in the intellectual life of the Catholic. It was nearly four years after his conversion that he began to read the *Summa Theologiae.* Doubtless motivated by docility at first, he quickly became personally convinced of the wisdom of the Church's designation of Thomas as chief guide in philosophy and theology. Thomas has pride of place among the Doctors of the Church and professors should present his thought to their students. Maritain's characterization of Thomas's doctrine stresses its formality. "It addresses the mind as a chain of certitudes demonstratively linked and is more perfectly in accord with the faith than any other."[9] It carries with it the pledge of a sanctity inseparable

8 Ibid., p. 290.
9 Ibid.

from the teaching mission of the Angelic Doctor who all but effaced his human personality in the divine light. However attractive the person of Thomas is, however much a model of the Christian life, Maritain quotes with enthusiasm the statement of Leo XIII in *Aeterni Patris: Majus aliquid in sancto Thomas quam sanctus Thomas suscipitur et defenditur.*" "*There is in Thomas something greater than Thomas that we receive and defend.*"[10] It is because of his sanctity as well as his intelligence that Thomas can be a vehicle of the truth and a model for the pursuit of it.

One of the purposes of the *Cercles d'études* was to enlist lay people in the Thomistic Revival. The aim was not to obtain members of a philosophical or theological sect within the Church or indeed beyond it. Maritain taught us to see Thomism, not as a rival of other equally valid ways of doing philosophy, but as the name for doing philosophy rightly—philosophy *tout court.* It is sometimes said that Thomas was not a Thomist, and of course he was not. No more was Aristotle an Aristotelian. Neither man saw what he was doing as hewing to a party line and narrowing his interests. The most notable thing about the thinking of Aristotle is the attention it pays to whatever had been said on a topic before he took it up. This led him to look for truths lurking in doctrines which on the surface might seem merely bizarre. A good example of this is the careful analysis and balancing of early naturalists in Book One of the *Physics.* He discerns beneath the jumble of conflicting claims a common recognition. It is facetious to see in this a tendency to hold that his predecessors were lisping Aristotelians, inchoate Stagirites. Philosophy is a common enterprise, no person alone can do it well, and everyone has standard cognitive equipment and could scarcely miss the truth entirely. In much the same way, what is called the Thomistic synthesis is an effort to bring together what strike the historian of ideas as radically different systems and find in them contributions to the common task of the pursuit of truth.

John Paul II, in *Fides et Ratio,* confronts the scandal of philosophy, the bewildering variety of philosophical systems and asks how one might adjudicate between them. His answer is found in paragraph four—there is an implicit philosophy held by all which provides criteria of acceptance and rejection. Anyone who reads the list of components of that Implicit Philosophy will recognize the starting points and principles from which Aristotle and Thomas proceed. Since these principles are a common human possession, philosophizing that moves off from them—rather than doubting, denying or ignoring them—will not be a *kind* of philosophy, but simply philosophy. No one owns the starting points.

[10] Ibid.

Maritain's vast and many-faceted *œuvre* reveals this same anchorage in what anyone may know and an interest in what every philosopher has said—at least in principle. Thomism is unique in this unlimited openness—what other philosophy seeks sustenance anywhere and everywhere? The result is not a pastiche, an eclectic hodgepodge. Nor does this openness preclude rejection of what has been said. Well, one could go on. But my topic now is different.

To be a Thomist is to follow the lead of one whose intellect was strengthened by supernatural grace and whose study was a species of prayer. So Maritain wrote, "[W]e think it is impossible that Thomism can be maintained in its purity and integrity without special recourse to the life of prayer."[11] If the intellectual life has its virtues, it also has its vices. It is to avoid the latter and acquire the former that prayer must be an integral part of the life of a Thomist. Maritain suggests that we are called to have intellectual reparation to God for the errors the human intellect has committed lest we add to them ourselves. "It is important that intellectuals dedicate themselves in a special manner to give to God the homage that modern philosophers refuse to give and at the same time to intercede for the voluntary and involuntary victims of error."[12] Lay Thomists are asked to commit themselves to at least an hour of prayer each day.

De la vie de l'oraison has two parts: The Intellectual Life and Prayer, and The Spiritual Life. Anyone acquainted with the *opusculum* called *De modo studendi,* attributed to Thomas Aquinas, will be reminded of it when he opens this little book by Jacques and Raïssa Maritain. Each of the nine chapters, three in part one, six in part two, bears as its title a Latin citation on which the text is a brief commentary. But, of course, it is the conjunction of the intellectual and spiritual lives that gives the book its stamp, and one which, in the modern world, causes surprise.

The progressive secularization of philosophy has had its effect on the sense of what the vocation of a philosopher is. Of Descartes's account of knowledge Maritain famously remarked that it bore a peculiar similarity to Thomas Aquinas's account of angelic knowledge. Methodic doubt led Descartes to his first certainty that, even if he were deceived about any and everything he might think, of one thing he could not be deceived, namely, that he was thinking. From this starting point the Cartesian project of reconstruction began. Descartes regards himself as a thinking something, a *res cogitans,* and his project is to see if he can get outside his mind, mind being

---

[11] Ibid., p. 293.
[12] Ibid.

all he is at this point. This is the origin of the so-called mind-body problem. It is not surprising that such an understanding of the philosophical task has influenced the philosopher's notion of his calling. It is almost exclusively cerebral, the pursuit of knowledge unrelated to the wider life which, presumably, the philosopher leads.

This impoverishment of the pursuit of truth is something to which Maritain responded in a variety of ways. The later discussions of Christian Philosophy are obviously related to it. The distinction between the nature and the state of philosophy, between philosophy and philosophizing, obviously addressed this issue. But from the beginning, after their conversion and consequent pursuit of a spiritual life under the guidance of a director, any philosophizing by the Maritains would necessarily be seen in the context of the spiritual life. The book on the life of prayer—in English it would be called *Prayer and Intelligence*—was first published anonymously in 1922, reprinted under the names of the authors in 1925, and then with changes in 1933 and with more changes still in 1947. The basic text of the book remained the same, with the variations occurring in the notes and addenda. This history of the book may be taken to underscore that its subject represents a profoundly abiding concern of the authors. "O Wisdom, which proceeds from the mouth of the Most High, reaching from end to end mightily and sweetly disposing all things, come and teach us the way of prudence," is the book's motto, followed by an excerpt of Peter Calo's *Life of Thomas Aquinas*:

> After the death of the Doctor, Brother Reginald, having returned to Naples and resumed his teaching, cried out while weeping copiously: My brothers, while he lived my master kept me from revealing wonderful things of which I had been the witness. One is that he acquired his knowledge not by human effort but by the merit of prayer, for each time that he wanted to study, to dispute, to lecture, write or dictate, having recourse to prayer first of all, he begged with tears to find in the truth the divine secrets, and by the merit of this prayer, having been prior to it in uncertitude, he arose instructed. . . .

> *Verbum spirans amorem*: the Word breathing forth love. It is necessary that in us too love proceeds from the Word, that is, from the spiritual possession of the truth in Faith. And just as whatever is in the Word is found in the Holy Spirit, so too what is in our knowledge must pass into the affections by way, and to rest only in it. Let love proceed from truth, and knowledge be made fruitful in love. Our prayer is not what it should be if either of these two conditions be lacking. By prayer we mean above all that which takes place in the secret of the heart and is ordered to the contemplation of and union with God.

That is the complete first chapter of the little book and it sets its tone. The Christian vocation is one of union with and contemplation of God, who is Truth. Any pursuit of truth should be linked to the primary goal. It is by acting under the impulse of grace or some more mystical gift, that the soul will attain this ultimate end. The soul must depend totally on the divine action, suspending its human mode of acting. Until God favors us with repose in Him, we must work to dispose ourselves for the reception of this gift. Our intellectual efforts must therefore be ordered to knowing God and our will to the love of Him. Only when fortified by prayer can intellect develop its highest virtualities, and the closer a soul approaches God in love, the more simple and luminous will intellectual vision become.

There is, moreover, a quite special relation between the intellectual life and the life of prayer, in that prayer requires the soul to leave the realm of sensible images and rise to the purely intelligible, and beyond, and, reciprocally, the activity of intellect is more perfect to the degree that it is freed from these same sensible images.

Only a life of prayer can give us an absolute fidelity to the truth, without diminution and diversion, and a great charity towards our neighbor, especially a great intellectual charity. Only it allows us, by naturally rectifying our faculties of desire, to pass from truth to practice.

CONCLUSION

I have already suggested how foreign such thoughts would seem to a typical contemporary philosopher. He is trained to think of himself as pure intelligence, uninfluenced by any antecedent convictions, with religious faith being the first thing to be put in escrow. The privatization of religion could be said to follow from the privatization of thought, the turn to the subject which makes the first philosophical problem: How can I go out of my mind? The Cartesian project is of course make-believe. Kierkegaard wrote an unfinished story *Johannes Climacus,* or *De omnibus dubitandum est,* in which he followed the fortunes of someone who tried to follow this advice, forgetting that he was a creature of flesh and blood, an incarnate spirit. It was one of Maritain's canniest insights that the intellectualism of Descartes falsified the pursuit of holiness.

Of course, any mention of pursuing holiness rings tinnily in the contemporary philosophical ear. Doubtless some of the resistance to the resurgence of interest in the virtues stems from uneasiness at the thought that even in philosophy character matters. Of course, one can be good as gold and dumb as a post and not every scoundrel fails to catch hold of a truth or two. But the ideal is to unify our lives in terms of an ample understanding of the ultimate end. The Greeks in their wisdom saw contemplation as the goal of the philosophical life. For the Christian that truth is transformed by its elevation to the supernatural order and the realization that we are called to friendship with God, to seeing Him even as we are seen.

The divorce between life and thought began under Christian auspices—Descartes was a good Catholic—and it led to the almost complete secularization with which we are surrounded. Surrounded, and therefore influenced by. There are many benefits to be had from turning to the thought of Jacques Maritain. But surely one of the greatest is that he makes impossible for us to separate study and the pursuit of truth from its orientation to our ultimate end, the vocation to which we have been called. When Maritain worked a variation on St. Paul—*Vae mihi si non thomistizavero*—he had in mind, not membership in a club, joining one philosophical sect among many, but the unified pursuit of truth and holiness that characterized Saint Thomas Aquinas and Jacques Maritain.

Augustine versus Newman on the Relation between Sacred and Secular Science

John Goyette

T he aim of the present paper is to compare St. Augustine and Cardinal
Newman on the nature of a Catholic education. The context of my remarks is the crisis in Catholic higher education which occasioned the
much debated document, *Ex Corde Ecclesiae*. According to this document,
Catholic universities should educate under the light of faith. It does not specify, however, exactly how the faith ought to function as the organizing principle of a Catholic university. In attempting to ascertain how *Ex Corde* envisions that a university be made Catholic, one must turn to St. Augustine and
Cardinal Newman, the two authors most frequently cited in *Ex Corde* aside
from previous papal statements and other Vatican documents on education. In
reading *Ex Corde*, one finds that it treats the teaching of Augustine and Newman on Catholic education as generally compatible. This paper will show,
however, that they importantly differ regarding the aim and scope of Catholic
education. This will contribute to a more adequate understanding of *Ex Corde*
and the current Pontificate's efforts to restore a true Catholic education.

The appeal to Augustine and Newman is not surprising: they present perhaps the two best known models for the integration of a Catholic education
and a liberal education. St. Augustine's articulation of a program of Christian
education in *On Christian Doctrine* is the first of its kind in the Latin West
and it served as a model for the medieval university.[1] And Newman's *Idea of*

---

[1] For a discussion of how Augustine's *De Doctrina Christiana* served as a model
for the medieval university see Eugene Kevane, *Augustine the Educator: A Study in
the Fundamentals of Christian Formation* (Westminster, Maryland: Newman Press,
1964), especially pp. 137–41, 257–67, 369–70.

a University is perhaps *the* modern statement of how a university education rightly understood ought, nay must, be one that is Catholic. When one compares the program of studies outlined by St. Augustine and Cardinal Newman, however, one will find that they disagree regarding the purpose of studying the secular disciplines and the extent to which they ought to be included within a Catholic education. In *On Christian Doctrine*, Augustine asserts that the secular sciences should be studied only to the extent that they are useful for the study of divinely revealed truth, i.e., as ancillary to theology, and warns against studying such disciplines for their own sake lest the charms of pagan culture impede the attainment of heavenly beatitude. Newman argues, on the other hand, that the two main branches of a liberal education—science and literature—are neither useful nor necessary for the study of theology; nevertheless, despite their worldly charms, he insists that a liberal education be pursued primarily for its own sake. A careful study of Newman, then, will show that his account rejects the view of St. Augustine and of his medieval followers that the secular sciences are to be understood as handmaidens of theology. One is forced to ask, then, whether Newman's break from the tradition enables him to better address the current crisis in Catholic higher education or whether the idea of a university he embraces contributes to the present problem.

AUGUSTINE'S *ON CHRISTIAN DOCTRINE*

Let me begin by examining Augustine's program of studies outlined in *On Christian Doctrine*. What sets Augustine apart from some of his contemporaries is his answer to a question that troubled many of the early Fathers, namely: How should one approach the classical culture of the Greeks and Romans? Should one simply reject philosophy and the liberal arts developed by the pagans as something profane or should one attempt to salvage what one can from classical culture? The answer of Tertullian—encapsulated by the famous question what does Jerusalem have to do with Athens?—is to reject the whole of pagan culture and learning. Now Augustine and many of the other Fathers take a different tack: their approach is to adopt whatever is serviceable to the faith in pagan culture and to reject the rest. As Augustine puts it, "[E]very good and true Christian should understand that wherever he may find truth, it is the Lord's."[2] Augustine argues that the secular sciences should not be shunned by the Christian but should be viewed like the gold

[2] All quotations from Augustine's *De Doctrina Christiana* are from *On Christian Doctrine*, trans. D.W. Robertson, Jr. (Upper Saddle River, New Jersey: Prentice Hall, 1958). Bk. II, chap. 18, no. 28.

and silver vessels that the Jews took with them when they fled Egypt. Just as the gold and silver were rightly appropriated by God's chosen people, so secular learning in truth belongs to Christ.[3] Now as I noted, Augustine was not alone in asserting that one ought to appropriate whatever is useful among pagan learning; we find a similar view in Justin Martyr, Clement of Alexandria, Basil, Gregory, Jerome, Ambrose and other early Fathers. Indeed, one even finds St. Paul appealing to pagan authors. What makes Augustine unique is his attempt to formulate a whole program of studies that incorporates pagan learning into a Christian education.[4]

How, then, does Augustine, organize his program of studies? For Augustine, the organizing principle is the end of Christian education, the knowledge of God attained through an understanding of the wisdom contained in Sacred Scripture. In appropriating the treasures found in the secular sciences, Augustine argues that only those disciplines that can be put to a higher use should be appropriated, viz., whichever are useful either for the discovery or teaching of the knowledge of the Scriptures. In light of this principle Augustine surveys the whole of pagan knowledge in Bk. II of *On Christian Doctrine*, identifying those disciplines that are useful for discovering and teaching the truth of the Scripture and those that are not.

To accomplish this task Augustine makes a somewhat elaborate division of the whole of pagan culture and learning in order to determine what is serviceable to the faith, and what ought to be rejected as dangerous or lacking in utility. He begins by distinguishing between knowledge of things that are instituted by men, on the one hand, and knowledge of those things that are "firmly established or divinely ordained."[5] In other words, knowledge of things that are merely conventional is to be distinguished from knowledge of those things that are not merely conventional but are what they are by nature, or nature's God. Knowledge of things instituted by man is then divided into superstitious and non-superstitious knowledge.

Superstitious knowledge includes knowledge of the making and worshipping of idols, knowledge pertaining to the worship of any creature as if it were God, knowledge of charms, amulets and other cures condemned by the medical art, and consultations and arrangements concerning signs and leagues with devils, e.g., magical arts. Also are included the arts of divination, such as

[3] Ibid., Bk. II, chap. 40, no. 60.

[4] On the unique position of Augustine in regards to the adoption of pagan learning, see Donald A. Gallagher, "St. Augustine and Christian Humanism," in *Some Philosophers on Education*, ed. Donald A. Gallagher (Milwaukee, Wisconsin: Marquette University Press, 1956).

[5] Augustine, *De Doctrina Christiana*, Bk. II, chap. 18, no. 29.

astrology and the books of haruspices and augurs. Superstitious knowledge is wholly rejected by Augustine not only because these disciplines are what he calls "nullities," i.e., knowledge pertaining to things that are false or empty, but also because all such practices lead, in the end, to fellowship with demons.

As for the non-superstitious knowledge of humanly instituted things, Augustine divides this into the knowledge of things pertaining to what is useful or necessary and knowledge pertaining to superfluity or luxury. Those things that are necessary or useful include such things as weights and measures, money, and bodily dress and ornaments used for the sake of distinguishing sex or rank.[6] Of particular utility for the study of Scripture is knowledge of the various languages employed in Scripture which are especially valuable for discovering the meanings of names and other words that arise in Sacred Scripture. Those human institutions that are superfluous or luxurious include pictures and statues, and "the thousands of imagined fables and falsehoods by whose lies men are delighted."[7] Now all of those human institutions that are useful or necessary are, according to Augustine, to be learned and adopted. As for those things made by man that are superfluous, they should be rejected or dismissed. Note that Augustine here puts aside nearly all of what we would call the fine arts. And, in addition, he appears to exclude nearly the whole of classic literature.

So much for knowledge of things made or invented by human beings, let us now turn to the other main branch of heathen learning, knowledge of those things that are not humanly instituted. The first thing Augustine includes in

[6] Although Augustine does not mention knowledge of moral and political institutions in his catalogue of the sciences in Book II, in Book III he makes clear that knowledge of these things is of the utmost necessity in interpreting Scripture since it is needed to determine whether a passage is to be taken literally or figuratively. His rule that whatever is contrary to virtuous behavior should be taken figuratively presupposes a thorough knowledge of human laws and customs since men are inclined to estimate sins "on the basis of their own customs, so that they consider a man to be culpable in accordance with the way men are reprimanded and condemned ordinarily in their own place and time" (Bk. III, chap. 10, no. 15). They ought, instead, to attend to what is proper to a particular time and place: "Careful attention is therefore to be paid to what is proper to places, times, and persons lest we condemn the shameful too hastily" (Bk. III, chap. 12, no. 19). The practice of polygamy in the Old Testament, for example, ought not to be condemned since this custom proceeded from the necessity for a sufficient number of children (Bk. III, chap. 12, no. 20). Augustine notes, however, that while the interpreter of Scripture must be familiar with the various laws and customs that differ from one place and time to the next, he must also be able to distinguish those things that are merely human institutions and those things that are naturally just (Bk. III, chap. 14, no. 22).
[7] Ibid., Bk. II, chap. 25, no. 39.

this division is knowledge of history, which he asserts is not humanly instituted since "those things which are past and cannot be revoked belong to the order of time, whose creator and administrator is God."[8] Augustine approves of this knowledge because it is very useful for the study of Scripture, especially for refuting certain false assertions pertaining to things found in Scripture, e.g., those who claim that the sayings of Christ were taken from the books of Plato.

Having spoken of things past, Augustine turns to the knowledge of things that are present. "To this class," Augustine says, "belong things that have been written about the location of places, or the nature of animals, trees, plants, stones, or other objects."[9] Knowledge of natural things is very useful because Scripture uses natural things as signs of those things that are invisible. It is tempting to describe the knowledge Augustine speaks of as natural science, but this is much too broad. Augustine is not talking about the systematic investigation of the causes and principles of natural things; rather, he is talking primarily about the specific properties of the various species of animal, vegetable and mineral acquired by means of simple observation. This is what we would call natural history. Indeed, Augustine will later assert that the labor expended in discovering knowledge of natural things might be dispensed with "if [a] capable person could be persuaded to undertake the task for the sake of his brethren, to collect in order and write down singly explanations of whatever unfamiliar geographical locations, animals, herbs and trees, stones, and metals are mentioned in the Scripture."[10] The knowledge of nature useful for the study of Scripture can be obtained by means of an encyclopedia of natural history with entries corresponding to Scripture.

Also included among knowledge of present facts is the knowledge of the stars, viz., astronomy. Now although Augustine is careful to distinguish between astronomy and astrology, he nonetheless rejects it as useless or unprofitable: "Knowledge of this kind in itself, although it is not alloyed with any superstition, is of very little use in the treatment of the Divine Scriptures and even impedes it through fruitless study.[11] The stars are rarely mentioned in Scripture, Augustine notes, and "since it [viz., astronomy] is associated with the most pernicious error of vain prediction it is more appropriate and virtuous to condemn it."[12]

[8] Ibid., Bk. II, chap. 28, no. 44. It is unclear whether Augustine means to suggest that certain human institutions, once they are safely in the past, become legitimate subjects of study (e.g., the various forms of idolatry found in the ancient world).

[9] Ibid., Bk. II, chap. 29, no. 45.

[10] Ibid., Bk. II, chap. 39, no. 59.

[11] Ibid., Bk. II, chap. 29, no. 46

[12] Ibid., Bk. II, chap. 29, no. 46.

Augustine then turns to the manual arts such as the art of housebuilding, medicine, and agriculture. One might at first be surprised to find Augustine classifying the manual arts among knowledge of those things not instituted by men. I think the reason why Augustine does this is that these arts are found in virtually every culture and to that extent they do not exist merely by convention, as do weights and measures, style of dress and the fine arts, shoemaking, housebuilding and medicine, but rather are found in every culture and follow the same basic principles. But what does Augustine say about these arts? They can be useful for the study of Scripture, he says, but they need not be incorporated into a program of studies since the knowledge of them we acquire through the ordinary course of life is sufficient to understand the meaning of Scripture when it employs images based upon them.

Having dealt with the knowledge of corporeal things that are not instituted by men, Augustine deals with the knowledge of those things that cannot be understood or attained by means of the senses but only by reason. Included in this class are the science of reasoning and mathematics. Knowledge of mathematics is of great utility because numbers are frequently employed as signs of spiritual things in Sacred Scripture. As in the case of the knowledge of natural things, however, we should not be led to believe that Augustine is here calling for a thorough study of arithmetic and geometry, since the knowledge useful for the study of Scripture might easily be satisfied if, as in the case of natural objects, someone were to collect together and explain the meaning behind the various numbers that are mentioned in Holy Scripture. As for the science of reasoning, Augustine indicates that its utility surpasses all of the other pagan disciplines. Indeed, he asserts that the knowledge of reasoning is "interwoven throughout the text of Scripture like so many nerves" and "is of more use to the reader in solving and explaining ambiguities . . . than in clarifying unknown signs."[13]   Unlike the knowledge of numbers, then, the knowledge of reasoning required for the study of Scripture cannot be attained by simply collecting together the rules of logic.

There is another science closely related to logic that Augustine says is useful, viz., rhetoric. It is useful not so much for the discovery of the wisdom contained in the Scriptures, as it is for teaching the truth to others. Augustine does not recommend that one study the rules of rhetoric, however; rather, one should learn the art of rhetoric by reading and studying the speeches of eloquent men.[14] Now we might be tempted to take this remark as a recommendation to study classic literature, e.g., the speeches of Cicero or the works of

[13] Ibid., Bk. II, chap. 39, no. 59.
[14] See ibid., Bk. IV, chap. 3, no. 5.

Virgil. By this means we can apparently save the study of literature that Augustine appeared to dismiss as useless luxury. Yet, we ought to note that Augustine draws the bulk of his examples of the art of rhetoric either from Scripture itself or from the writings and sermons of noted Christian teachers such as St. Ambrose and St. Cyprian. Indeed, Augustine argues that Sacred Scripture possesses its own peculiar kind of eloquence that befits the seriousness of its subject matter and the divine authority with which it speaks.[15] It is perhaps also worth noting that Augustine waxes eloquent about the dangers of pagan eloquence in other places, e.g., the *Confessions*.

Lastly Augustine speaks of the utility of philosophy. "If those who are called philosophers, especially the Platonists, have said things which are indeed true and are well accommodated to our faith, they should not be feared," Augustine notes, "rather, what they have said should be taken from them as from unjust possessors and converted to our use."[16]

Let us summarize Augustine's program for a Christian education. Broadly speaking, for Augustine a Christian education is one in which theology orders all the other disciplines by directing them to itself. Only those disciplines should be contained in a Christian education which contribute either to the discovery of the wisdom contained in Sacred Scripture or to the teaching of what has been discovered to others. Pagan learning and culture is never to be pursued for its own sake; it is to be pursued only as ancillary to sacred theology.[17]

Now before we turn to Newman we ought to locate the reason why Augustine is so adamant in rigorously excluding the study of the secular sciences as

[15] See ibid., Bk. IV, chap. 6, nos. 9–10.

[16] Ibid., Bk. II, chap. 40, no. 60.

[17] One should note that although Augustine recommends the study of the secular sciences only to the extent that they can immediately be brought to bear upon the interpretation of Scripture, a brief glance at his writings, including those that come after *De Doctrina Christiana*, make clear that he does not confine the study of Scripture to biblical exegesis in the narrow sense of the term. Interpretation of Scripture for Augustine includes not only line-by-line commentaries, but also the systematic investigation of doctrines found in the Scriptures, and the discussion of disputed questions arising from the study of Scripture. Thus, the systematic study of God by means of divinely revealed principles that characterizes, for example, the *Summa Theologiae* of St. Thomas is in fundamental agreement with Augustine's understanding of theology. The continuity between Augustine and the theology of the Middle Ages is perhaps most evident, however, from the fact that in the Middle Ages the masters of theology were know as *magistri in sacra pagina*. Indeed, the principal duty of St. Thomas himself at the University of Paris consisted in lecturing directly upon the pages of Sacred Scripture. And although we find a much broader study of the secular sciences in the medieval university, these sciences were understood as subservient to theology. Hence, although St. Thomas recommends a study of nearly all of the secular sciences, he justifies this on the grounds that it is useful or necessary for the study of theology: "[A]ll the other sciences are so to speak ancillary and propaedeutic in its coming into being" (*Commentary on the De Trinitate of Boethius*, q. 2, a. 4, ad 7).

an end in itself. The reason is found in Bk. I of *On Christian Doctrine*, where Augustine explains that God alone is to be enjoyed, i.e., pursued as something good in itself; everything else should be used for the sake of God, otherwise it will impede our journey towards, or deflect us altogether from, our true end. Augustine makes the point very elegantly using the image of the wanderer:

> Suppose we were wanderers who could not live in blessedness except at home, miserable in our wandering and desiring to end it and to return to our native country. We would need vehicles for land and sea which could be used to help us to reach our homeland, which is to be enjoyed. But if the amenities of the journey and the motion of the vehicles itself delighted us, and we were led to enjoy those things which we should use, we should not wish to end our journey quickly, and, entangled in a perverse sweetness, we should be alienated from our country, whose sweetness would make us blessed. Thus in this mortal life, wandering from God, if we wish to return to our native country where we can be blessed we should use this world and not enjoy it, so that the "invisible things" of God "being understood by the things that are made" may be seen, that is, so that by means of corporal and temporal things we may comprehend the eternal and spiritual.[18]

Thus we should never take delight in the secular sciences for their own sake since this impedes our ability to arrive at our true end; rather, they should be pursued only to the extent that they contribute to an understanding of God. It is with this thought in mind that Augustine asserts that Christian students, especially those who are intellectually gifted, should be warned against thinking that we can attain the end by means of the secular sciences themselves: "[S]tudious and intelligent youths who fear God and seek the blessed life might be helpfully admonished that they should not pursue those studies which are taught outside of the Church of Christ as though they might lead to the blessed life."[19] Unless the secular sciences are completed by sacred theology, the knowledge they provide can make us neither wise nor happy.[20] Indeed, Augustine even suggests that when men take delight in the secular sci-

---

[18] *De Doctrina Christiana*, Bk. I, chap. 4, no. 4.

[19] Ibid., Bk. II, chap. 38, no. 58.

[20] This is a noticeable change from Augustine's view of the liberal arts when composing earlier works such as the *De Ordine* where Augustine speaks as if we can attain the happy life by means of the liberal arts and describes the conversion to Christ as almost synonymous with the conversion to philosophy. This change prompted Augustine to note in his *Retractions* (1. 3. 2) that he attributed too much to the liberal arts in the *De Ordine*. For a discussion of the change in Augustine's view of the liberal arts from his earlier writings to *On Christian Doctrine*, see Frederick Van Fleteren, "St. Augustine, Neoplatonism, and the Liberal Arts: The Background to *De Doctrina Christiana*" in *De Doctrina Christiana: A Classic of Western Culture*, eds. Duane W. H. Arnold and Pamela Bright (Notre Dame, Indiana: University of Notre Dame Press, 1995).

ences they are not delighting in the truth so much as they are taking delight in themselves and their own learning.[21] When divorced from the Truth that is Christ, the secular sciences culminate in pride and vanity not *gaudium de veritate*. This is why Augustine concludes his program of education in Bk. II of *On Christian Doctrine* by warning us against the dangers of pride: "When the student of Holy Scripture, having been instructed in this way, begins to approach his text, he should always bear in mind the apostolic saying 'Knowledge puffs up, but charity edifies.'"[22]

NEWMAN'S *IDEA OF A UNIVERSITY*

Having outlined Augustine's program of Christian education in *On Christian Doctrine*, let me now turn to Cardinal Newman's *Idea of a University*.[23] In the Discourses that make up the *Idea* Newman argues for the compatibility of a liberal education and Catholic education. According to Newman, a university cannot claim to fulfill its mission if it does not include Catholic theology within the university curriculum: "[A] University cannot exist externally to the Catholic pale, for it cannot teach universal knowledge if it does not teach Catholic theology."[24] Indeed, Newman argues not only that theology must be included within the university, but also that it makes an important contribution to the unity and integrity of the liberal arts curriculum.

In Discourses II–IV of the *Idea of a University*, Newman proposes three distinct reasons for including theology within the university curriculum and these three arguments suggest, in turn, three ways in which theology might exert a curricular influence within the university. In Discourse II Newman argues that theology ought to be included among the subjects of university teaching: 1) because a university cannot claim to teach universal knowledge if it excludes the science of theology; 2) since each of the various sciences are partial and incomplete, and become distorted when studied in isolation

[21] See *On Christian Doctrine,* Bk. II, chap. 38, no. 57, along with Bk. II, chap. 13, no. 20. For an excellent discussion of how the problem of pride factors into Augustine's treatment of the secular sciences in *On Christian Doctrine* see John C. Cavadini, "The Sweetness of the Word: Salvation and Rhetoric in Augustine's *De doctrina christiana*," in *De Doctrina Christiana: A Classic of Western Culture*.

[22] *De Doctrina Christiana*, Bk. II, chap. 41, no. 62.

[23] Much of what is said in the following discussion concerning Newman's view of the relation between theology and the secular disciplines is treated more fully in John Goyette and William Mathie, "The Idea of a Catholic University: Newman on the Role of Theology in a Liberal Education," *Maritain Studies* 16 (2000): pp. 71–91.

[24] All references to Newman in this essay are taken from *The Idea of a University*, ed. Martin J. Svalgic (Notre Dame, Indiana: University of Notre Dame Press, 1982), p. 163.

from all the rest, theology is needed to supplement or complete the view of the whole afforded by the secular sciences; and 3) since each science has a natural tendency to exceed its proper limits (a tendency, that is, to make claims that are not only partial and incomplete but altogether false), the inclusion of theology is necessary to prevent the other sciences from usurping the territory that rightly belongs only to theology.

Although Newman makes a powerful case for the presence of theology within the curriculum, emphasizing the need for theology to complete the secular sciences and to prevent them from going beyond their proper bounds, he rejects the notion that the secular sciences should be pursued for the sake of theology.[25] While he speaks of theology as the highest and most important science, he does not claim that the secular sciences should be seen as subservient to theology. In fact, he mostly avoids speaking about the sciences in a manner that suggests that they are hierarchically ordered.[26] Newman prefers instead to speak of "the circle of the sciences," an image that highlights the mutual influence of one science upon another. Thus, while Newman insists that theology is needed to complete the secular sciences, he also maintains that the secular sciences are needed to complete theology. Moreover, to the extent that the circle of the sciences is in need of an organizing principle, this role is filled not by theology, but by philosophy:

> [T]he comprehension of the bearings of one science on another, and the
> use of each to each, and the location and limitation and adjustment and
> due appreciation of them all, one with another, this belongs, I conceive,

[25] Newman occasionally speaks about theology in a way that seems to imply that it operates as a final cause. He asserts, for example, that all of the other sciences, when pursued to their furthest extent, converge upon the study of God: "[A]ll knowledge forms one whole, because its subject-matter is one; for the universe in its length and breadth is so intimately knit together, that we cannot separate off portion from portion, and operation from operation, except by a mental abstraction; and then again, as to its Creator, though He of course in His own Being is infinitely separate from it, and Theology has its departments towards which human knowledge has no relations, yet He has so implicated Himself with it, and taken it into His very bosom, by His presence in it, His providence over it, His impressions upon it, and His influences through it, that we cannot truly or fully contemplate it without in some main aspects contemplating Him" (ibid., p. 38). Despite the suggestion in the above passage that all of the other sciences are ultimately ordered towards theology, Newman makes clear in other places, notably Discourse IX, that the secular disciplines, especially literature and natural science, tend to diverge from the science of theology.

[26] In one passage in Discourse III Newman asserts that the sciences are ordered the way that the art of bridle-making is subordinate to the art of strategy, a description that suggests that the various sciences form a hierarchical structure. Despite occasional remarks of this kind, however, he much more frequently speaks about the sciences in a manner that eschews the notion of their being hierarchically related to one another.

to a sort of science distinct from all of them, and in some sense a science of sciences, which is my own conception of what is meant by Philosophy, in the true sense of the word, and a philosophical habit of mind, and which in these Discourses I shall call by that name.[27]

That Newman is opposed to the inclusion of the secular sciences on the grounds that they are useful or necessary for the study of theology becomes especially clear in the case of science and literature. These disciplines are not only unnecessary for the study of theology, they even exhibit a marked tendency to be hostile to theology.[28] One might think that the truths of science, by which he means modern natural science, might be useful for establishing the existence of God or defending other truths of theology, but Newman is very much opposed to this use of science. He does not deny that certain conclusions about God can be drawn from natural science, but he claims that the theological speculation that grows out of natural science does more harm than good to theology. In Discourse II he argues that "physical theology," the drawing of theological inferences from scientific truth, arrives at the notion of a God responsible for the laws of nature, but this notion of God differs from, and even tends to be in opposition to, a God that exercises particular providence and who is, therefore, capable of revealing himself to man. The God of the natural scientist is a God "who keeps the world in order, who acts in it, but only in the way of general Providence, who acts towards us but only through what are called laws of Nature, who is more certain not to act at all than to act independent of those laws. . . ."[29] Moreover, Newman argues in Discourse IX that although physical science may give us a sense of God's power, wisdom and goodness, it does not point to God as the author of the moral law, nor does it indicate God's mercy and the economy of salvation. This is because the physical sciences are mostly concerned with the heavens and the earth, those parts of the whole that exist "before the introduction of moral evil in the world."[30] "[T]he Catholic Church," however, "is the instrument of a remedial dispensation to meet that introduction."[31] Science, therefore, is blind or indifferent to those aspects of God with which Revelation is primarily concerned.

But what of literature which, according to Newman, "stands related to man as Science to Nature"? Does literature, as the study of man, contribute to

---

[27] Ibid., p. 38.
[28] Newman discusses the hostility of natural science and literature at length in Discourse IX.
[29] Ibid., p. 38.
[30] Ibid., p. 171.
[31] Ibid.

the understanding of Revelation and the remedial dispensation of the Church? According to Newman, it cannot. If science ignores moral evil, literature suffers from the opposite tendency "of recognizing and understanding it too well."[32] "[W]hile Nature physical remains fixed in its laws, Nature moral and social has a will of its own, is self-governed, and never remains any long while in that state from which it started into action. Man will never continue in a mere state of innocence; he is sure to sin, and his literature will be the expression of his sin, and this whether he be heathen or Christian."[33] Literature, then, is "the science or history, partly and at best of the natural man, partly of man in rebellion."[34] Nor does Newman think that the dangers of literature can be remedied by a Christian literature. "[I]f Literature is to be made a study of human nature, you cannot have a Christian Literature. It is a contradiction in terms to attempt a sinless Literature of sinful man. . . . Such is man: put him aside, keep him before you; but whatever you do, do not take him for what he is not, for something more divine and sacred, for man regenerate."[35] According to Newman, literature cannot contribute to the subject of theology because it necessarily studies the nature of fallen man, not the nature of man in the state of his original innocence or as regenerated by grace. Nor is it possible to view literature as a helpful propaedeutic to theology by portraying the nature of fallen man as fallen and in need of grace. According to Newman, literature portrays fallen human nature not in all of its ugliness and despair as can be seen, for example, in the daily newspapers, but in a manner that is captivating and seducing, hence the remark that it knows moral evil "too well."

Newman denies, then, that science and literature, which for him are the two main branches of liberal education, are either useful or necessary in explicating the faith. Why, then, does the Church take an interest in these secular disciplines? According to Newman, the Church takes an interest in these disciplines because they are essential elements of a liberal education. And the Church desires that its members receive a liberal education so that they may be better fit for the world and more capable members of society since an educated mind possesses "the faculty of entering with comparative ease into any subject of thought, and of taking up with aptitude any science or profession."[36] The educated Catholic, because he is more capable of filling his respective post in life, will be a better representative of the faith simply because

---

[32] Ibid., p. 174.
[33] Ibid., p. 173.
[34] Ibid., p. 174.
[35] Ibid. pp. 174–75.
[36] Ibid., p. xliv.

he appears more credible to his otherwise worldly auditors. But not only does a liberal education enable a man to appear respectable in the eyes of the world, it also enables him to better understand and defend the faith. It does so by enlarging the mind of the student, enabling him to think more clearly and consistently and to express his own views in a manner that is coherent and persuasive. Indeed, Newman notes that if a university education enables a man to understand and defend his opinions more energetically even if he be in error, how much more will it aid the defense of truth?

> Men who fancy they see what is not are more energetic, and make their way better, than those who see nothing; and so the undoubting infidel, the fanatic, the heresiarch, are able to do much, while the mere hereditary Christian, who has never realized the truths which he holds, is unable to do any thing. But, if consistency of view can add so much strength even to error, what may it not be expected to furnish to the dignity, the energy, and the influence of Truth![37]

According to Newman, the uneducated Christian fails in some sense to realize the truths which he holds because he lacks a consistency of view: he fails to fully grasp the principles he holds and the conclusions that follow from these principles.[38] The development of the mind that results from a university education, then, indirectly aids one's understanding of the faith as well as any other subject to which one applies the mind.

For Newman, then, the secular disciplines contained within a Catholic university are pursued as part of a general cultivation of the mind, not because they are necessary or useful for the study of theology. But this is not the only respect in which Newman differs from Augustine. Whereas Augustine cautions against taking delight in classical culture as something that will impede the journey to our native country, Newman argues in Discourses V–VII that liberal education, by its very nature, is knowledge pursued for its own sake. He notes that the meaning of the term "liberal" in liberal education indicates that it is to be contrasted with what is "servile." In the first instance, "servile" refers to any kind of bodily labor or mechanical employment, as opposed to activities involving mind or intelligence. Newman points out, however, that not every bodily activity is regarded as servile since military contests and certain games of skill are regarded as liberal. Similarly, not every

[37] Ibid., p. xliv.

[38] In light of the hostility of science and literature articulated in Discourse IX, Newman may also be suggesting that the Christian who lacks a liberal education, having never studied science and literature, is unaware of how the truths of the faith stand in relation to the world presented by science and literature. It may be that the study of science and literature is necessary if one is to fully grasp the mysterious and miraculous nature of faith.

work of intelligence is regarded as liberal since the practice of many arts serves some further end, e.g., medicine has traditionally been regarded as servile since its end is health. What is "liberal," then, is what is not in the service of another. What is "servile," on the other hand, is for the sake of another. Liberal education, then, aims at intellectual cultivation not because it is useful but because it is intrinsically satisfying.

But what kind of knowledge is pursued for its own sake? According to Newman, the universal knowledge that a university claims to impart is the kind of knowledge that is intrinsically desirable. This knowledge does not consist, however, in the superficial knowledge of a great many subjects. Such an education, according to Newman, is little more than "a sort of passive reception of scraps and details."[39] Universal knowledge is an enlargement of the mind that is only attained when one seizes and unites a multitude of diverse facts and stamps them with a single form:

> The enlargement consists, not merely in the passive reception into the mind of a number of ideas hitherto unknown to it, but in the mind's energetic and simultaneous action upon and towards and among those new ideas, which are rushing upon it. It is the action of a formative power, reducing to order and meaning the matter of our acquirements; it is a making the objects of our knowledge subjectively our own, or, to use a familiar word, it is a digestion of what we receive, into the substance of our previous state of thought; and without this no enlargement is said to follow. There is no enlargement, unless there be a comparison of ideas one with another, as they come before the mind, and a systematizing of them.[40]

The enlargement of mind that is the goal of liberal education is what Newman calls "philosophy" or "a philosophic habit of mind." According to Newman, it is this form of knowledge that is "sufficient for itself, apart from every external and ulterior object."[41] However useful this knowledge may be, it is first and foremost something good in itself. And in his discussion of liberal education in Discourses V–VIII, he reminds us that "we are inquiring, not what the object of a Liberal Education is worth, nor what use the Church makes of it, but what it is in itself."[42] Although Newman grants that a university education is useful and that its utility motivates the Church to found Catholic colleges and universities, he argues that it should, nay must, be pursued primarily, or initially, as something good in itself.

Newman is not naïve, however, about the dangers that Augustine warns us

[39] Ibid., p. 111.
[40] Ibid., p. 101.
[41] Ibid., p. 84.
[42] Ibid., pp. 92–93.

of in *On Christian Doctrine*. In the Ninth Discourse he points out that "Liberal Knowledge has a special tendency, not necessary or rightful, but a tendency in fact, when cultivated by beings such as we are, to impress us with a mere philosophical theory of life and conduct, in the place of Revelation."[43] Indeed, Newman goes on to indicate that the pursuit of liberal knowledge within the university will inevitably do harm to sacred theology:

> Knowledge, viewed as knowledge, exerts a subtle influence in throwing us back on ourselves, and making us our own centre, and our minds the measure of all things. This then is the tendency of that Liberal Education, of which a University is the school, viz., to view Revealed Religion from an aspect of its own,—to fuse and recast it,—to tune it, as it were, to a different key, and to reset its harmonies,— to circumscribe it by a circle which unwarrantably amputates here, and unduly develops there; and all under the notion, conscious or unconscious, that the human intellect, self-educated and self-supported, is more true and perfect in its ideas and judgments than that of Prophets and Apostles, to whom the sights and sounds of Heaven were immediately conveyed. A sense of propriety, order, consistency, and completeness gives birth to a rebellious stirring against miracle and mystery, against the severe and the terrible.[44]

It is precisely the fact that liberal knowledge, or philosophy, consists in the active power of seizing and uniting diverse facts and stamping them, in some sense, with our own form, that is responsible for the danger liberal education poses to the faith. In the end, Newman's analysis appears to agree with Augustine's suggestion that taking delight in the secular sciences inevitably leads to pride: "Knowledge, viewed as knowledge, exerts a subtle influence in throwing us back on ourselves, and making us our own centre, and our minds the measure of all things."[45] But whereas Augustine attempts to remedy this problem by admonishing us not to take delight in the secular sciences for their own sake and to study them only insofar as they aid us in the pursuit of sacred theology, Newman makes no attempt to discourage the pursuit of liberal knowledge for its own sake, nor does he attempt to exclude those sciences that do not appear to contribute to theology.

Where then is the remedy to be found? Given the dangers that a university education poses to the faith not only because of the hostile tendencies of science and literature but also, and perhaps more importantly, the dangers inherent in the pursuit of liberal knowledge for its own sake, Newman does not look to the presence of theology within the curriculum as a sufficient guarantee that a university be Catholic:

[43] Ibid., p. 165.
[44] Ibid.
[45] Ibid., p. 165.

> [I]t is no sufficient security for the Catholicity of a University, even that
> the whole of Catholic theology should be professed in it, unless the
> Church breathes her own pure and unearthly spirit into it, and fashions
> and moulds its organization, and watches over its teaching, and knits to-
> gether its pupils, and superintends its action.[46]

What is needed to insure the Catholicity of the university is an extra-curricular influence, the pure and unearthly spirit of the Church. Newman does not
articulate precisely how this is to be accomplished but he suggests that the
Church confront the dangers inherent in liberal learning in the same way
which St. Philip Neri confronted the dangers of the Renaissance, "an age as
traitorous to the interests of Catholicism as any that preceded it, or can follow
it."[47]   How does St. Philip face the dangers presented by the discovery of
classic literature and art, which Newman compares to an enchantress luring
"the great and the gifted" into an abyss? According to Newman, it is "not
with argument, not with science, not with protests and warnings, not by the
recluse or the preacher, but by means of the great counter-fascination of purity and truth."[48]   It was St. Philip's personal charm, albeit an otherworldly
charm, that was able to counteract the charms of the newly discovered classics of science and literature. The key to St. Philip's charm was due in large
part, however, to the fact that he did not appeal to doctrine and authority, but
Christian charity and humility:

> [H]e preferred to yield to the stream, and direct the current, which he
> could not stop, of science, literature, art, and fashion, and to sweeten and
> to sanctify what God had made very good and man had spoilt. And so he
> contemplated as the idea of his mission, not the propagation of the faith,
> nor the exposition of doctrine, nor the catechetical schools; whatever
> was exact and systematic pleased him not; he put from him monastic
> rule and authoritative speech, as David refused the armour of his king.
> No; he would be but an ordinary individual priest as others: and his
> weapons should be but unaffected humility and unpretending love.[49]

In attempting to breathe the Church's pure and unearthly spirit into the university, Newman suggests that the Church should imitate St. Philip in putting aside
the exposition of doctrine and authoritative speech. In the case of the university
this would seem to mean that the Church emphasize the extra-curricular, non-
doctrinal elements of faith, e.g., the administration of the sacraments, in its attempt to safeguard the identity of the Catholic university.[50]

[46] Ibid., p. 164.
[47] Ibid., p. 178.
[48] Ibid., p. 179.
[49] Ibid.
[50] It is perhaps not accidental that Newman's description of the Church's presence
within the university seems to roughly correspond to the modern day Newman Center.

Having outlined the positions of Newman and Augustine on the nature of Catholic education, space does not permit me to attempt a resolution of the tension between Newman and Augustine. Let me end, therefore, with a question. To what extent is the present crisis in Catholic higher education a result of the break with the organizing principle of Augustine's program of studies in *On Christian Doctrine*, viz., that the secular sciences should be pursued not for their own sake, but for the sake of theology? Or, to phrase the question another way, to what extent does Newman's *Idea of a University* represent the solution to the current crisis by placing the needed emphasis upon the extra-curricular influence of the Church, and to what extent is the idea of liberal learning it defends responsible for the current crisis by abandoning the model of Augustine? How one answers this question will depend upon how one answers a series of further questions of which I will mention just a few. It will depend, firstly, upon whether one concurs with Newman's rather dark assessment of the deep-seated hostility of science and literature to theology, an hostility that appears to stand in the way of a university curriculum ordered towards theology as queen of the sciences. If one does concur with Newman's opinion regarding the hostility of literature and science, other questions arise. Is the need to appear credible in the eyes of the world a compelling reason to study disciplines that may be hostile to sacred theology? Could Catholics, for example, be considered competent and respected critics of modern natural science if science was not numbered among the disciplines taken seriously at a Catholic university? And if science ought to be studied with some seriousness within the Catholic university, is it possible to study it adequately without pursuing it, at least in part, as an end in itself? I do not pretend to have answers to these questions, but whether we incline towards the model of Augustine or Newman, we ought not to take lightly the important differences between them regarding the aim and scope of a Catholic university.

Preserving the "Catholic Moment" by Inaugurating Catholic Studies at Non-Catholic Colleges and Universities

Frederick Erb III

This paper is intended to convey to educators and intellectuals who embrace (or at least respect) the Catholic intellectual tradition,[1] a simple but urgent message: Preserve the "Catholic moment"—which in this context means to make the study of Catholic philosophy, theology and history, accessible and available as an elective or optional course of study to every student enrolled in any American college or university. Its underlying thesis is that, in order to preserve and maintain the Catholic intellectual tradition, regardless of how one chooses to define it—to keep it alive and vibrant and a potential influence on America's cultural and religious future, or as an optional alternative worldview to the present normative values that regularly invoke criticism from the Catholic ecclesiastical hierarchy—Americans will have to be given access and opportunity to study the Catholic intellectual tradition as part of their higher education. Access to such courses and programs

[1] The term "Catholic intellectual tradition" is subject to a very broad range of interpretation, historically and in contemporary discourse, from neo-conservative to neo-liberal. Maritain sometimes referred to the "Aristotelian and Thomist" tradition. His description, if applied to Catholic studies in post-Vatican II American culture, would certainly elicit a mixture of reviews. Mary Ann Hinsdale recognizes a four-fold typology of Catholic studies programs, based on significantly different understandings of the "Catholic intellectual tradition," in an unpublished paper discussed in detail later in this article. Hinsdale's paper, entitled "Catholic Studies: Models and Motives," was read on November 22, 1999 at a conference of the American Academy of Religion, and as of this writing is available online at: sterling.holycross.edu/departments/religiousstudies/mhinsdal/Research99.html

is needed to reach Catholic Americans who do not attend Catholic institutions of higher learning. Put another way, without the availability of courses and programs in Catholic studies at the post-secondary level in schools that are non-Catholic,[2] the vast majority of Americans—including and especially Catholics—will lack the opportunity to become (re)formed as persons possessing unique vocations in the Church and in the world. Neglecting only one generation can break a long and venerable chain of tradition.

Regardless of the conservative or liberal stance Catholic intellectual leaders may be inclined to assume concerning their Church's place or position in the world, it would not hurt them to stop and think: If a large-scale (re)formation does not soon take place, and a new generation of Catholics abandon their faith because the tradition has become incomprehensible to them, then American Catholicism will have squandered its unique "moment."

A REASSESSMENT OF "CATHOLIC MOMENT"

Writing more than a decade ago, Richard John Neuhaus used the expression "Catholic moment"[3] to describe a particular confluence of events that could present a unique opportunity for Catholics in American cultural and religious history. Recent historical research by George M. Marsden,[4] Julie A.

---

[2] I am using the term "non-Catholic" both in the title and throughout this paper to avoid having to differentiate between those colleges and universities that are "secular" and those that claim to maintain some vestige of their original Protestant or other religious affiliations, since this paper is limited to the argument that exposure to Catholic studies should not be relegated exclusively to Catholic institutions. Such a differentiation would be difficult in any event. It would do well to keep in mind that secularist views pervade and in some instances dominate the academic cultures of most American colleges and universities, regardless of their charters. As Neuhaus cautions, "A secular university is not a university pure and simple; it is a secular university. Secular is not a synonym for neutral" ("The Christian University: Eleven Theses," *First Things* 59, [January 1996], p. 20).

[3] Richard Neuhaus used this term and the phenomenon he claimed it accurately describes in his controversial book, *The Catholic Moment* (New York: Harper and Row, 1987).

[4] George M. Marsden's influential historical treatment of the role of religion in American higher education is *The Soul of the American University: From Protestant Establishment to Established Unbelief* (New York: Oxford University Press, 1994). Except for a few hints in a "Concluding Unscientific Postscript," pp. 429–44, which suggests the extent of current discrimination by scholars and administrators who wish to keep religious viewpoints out of mainstream American higher education, Marsden offers no real solution. This comes later in *The Outrageous Idea of Christian Scholarship* (New York: Oxford University Press, 1997).

Reuben,[5] James Tunstead Burtchaell,[6] and others amply illustrates the rapid decline and collapse during the 1960s of the influence of a largely Protestant morality that once dominated mainstream American higher education,[7] a decline that was over a century in duration, so that by the early 1970s those Christian values were effectively marginal to the academic culture. This marginalization of morality is concomitant with the intellectual transformation of the academy into its present state. As a consequence, mainstream academia is dominated by faculty and administrators who have adopted a secular posture that is exclusivist in the sense that it systematically bars Catholic and evangelical Christian voices from participation through its hiring and tenure decisions, and is sometimes openly hostile toward Christian scholarship.

Thus, as we bravely enter postmodernity, the spiritual vacuum left by the absence of even the symbols of Christian stewardship in American intellectual life, is likely to be filled in one of two ways: The first is *complete* secularization. The emergent American culture is seen to be moving steadily along the path toward subjective moral relativism in response to religious diversity and the lure of a global economy. It is a confluence of ideologies that publicly attributes equal merit to all religious beliefs—whether traditional, eclectic, or syncretic. In practice, however, this new academic establishment permits a kind of "dabbling" into strange and novel spiritualities as if to demonstrate its open-mindedness, while relegating to the private domain those traditional faiths such as Catholicism and evangelical Protestantism

---

[5] Julie A. Reuben's *The Making of the Modern University: Intellectual Transformation and the Marginalization of Morality* (Chicago: The University of Chicago Press, 1996), paralleling Marsden, demonstrates how influential faculty and college presidents managed, over several generations and often unwittingly, to undermine the moral purpose of the American college and university that many of them were striving to protect and preserve.

[6] James Tunstead Burtchaell's *The Dying of the Light: The Disengagement of Colleges and Universities from their Christian Churches* (Grand Rapids, Michigan: Eerdmans, 1998) contains 17 case studies from Catholic to Congregationalist, Evangelical and Charismatic, to mainstream Protestant colleges and universities. While echoing many of Marsden's and Reuben's sentiments, Burtchaell raises other questions about the nature of secularization. Unlike Marsden's prognosis, which appears to be cautiously optimistic, and Reuben whose work is purely historical, Burtchaell seems utterly pessimistic about the chances of reversing the "slippery slope" of secularization in American higher learning.

[7] This applies not only to those colleges founded and once-controlled by the various religious denominations, but arguably to the Land Grant and subsequent public institutions as well—despite current popular misconceptions about the proper legal meaning of separation of church and state.

that are still perceived as posing a potential challenge to the *Zeitgeist* or dominant "spirit of the age."

An alternative future for American higher education, at least according to Neuhaus, could come about provided Catholic educators and intellectuals recognize their strength in number, conviction, and opportunity, and are able to set aside their internal differences and unite long enough to exert a potentially decisive influence on the course of American public life. Neuhaus envisioned Catholics seizing their unique "moment" which he understood as having been brought about by the vacuum in Protestant moral and political leadership. As Neuhaus seemed to suggest, Catholics alone were in a position to profoundly influence American life by virtue of their numbers and by their already entrenched structures of higher learning.

Neuhaus predicted that the majority of influential American Catholics would fail to recognize their "moment" until it had long passed. As evidence of a longstanding trend toward secularization among the majority of leaders of Catholic colleges and universities, Neuhaus cited the 1967 *Land O'Lakes* declaration which, in his view, constituted a failure of Catholic higher education to retain its uniquely "Catholic" identity in the face of external pressures. In other words, by declaring its independence from all forms of authority "external to the academic community" these institutions were *de facto* offering "a perfect invitation to follow in the footsteps of those who have gone the way so decisively traced by George Marsden."[8]

Setting aside the lively debates that arose from *Land O'Lakes*,[9] but assuming a reasonable accuracy in Neuhaus's assessment of the state of American intellectual life a decade ago, does it necessarily follow that the "Catholic moment" thus described was a mere snapshot in time—a fleeting opportunity which, once lost, can never be recaptured? Perhaps Shakespeare speaks to this situation through Brutus's words of caution: "There is a tide in the affairs of men which, taken at the flood, leads on to fortune; omitted, all the voyage of their life is bound in shallows and in miseries."[10] Equally plausible, however, is the possibility of extending that crucial "moment" by protecting and preserving the heritage until such time as Catholic intellectual life again becomes sufficiently robust and mature (and presumably more adequately prepared) to enable it to take its place in American public life and play a dominant role in the reshaping of the broader culture. In October 2000, an article in *The*

---

[8] *First Things* (January 1991), p. 7.

[9] An assessment of the ultimate impact of the *Land O'Lakes* declaration and its aftermath remains a matter of debate and lies beyond the scope of this paper.

[10] Words spoken by Marcus Brutus to Cassius in *Julius Caesar*, act 4, scene 2, *The Complete Oxford Shakespeare* (Oxford: Oxford University Press, 1987), pp. 1113–14.

Chronicle of Higher Education quoted Marsden as saying: "The general consensus is that there's no reason to have to continue along the slippery slope toward secularism. This is a moment of opportunity for religious colleges." Marsden's optimism could easily be extended to the prevailing climate at public and non-denominational private colleges and universities, where interest in "faith-based scholarship" appears to be coming into vogue. Fears of renewed cultural marginalization notwithstanding, Catholic scholars representing the left, right and center of Catholic thought, may indeed owe it to themselves and to their children to make *this* their "moment."[11]

If the foregoing appears naïve to some Catholic scholars, yet signals a "call to arms" for others, that is probably because there is not, and never really has been, a univocal or uniform understanding of the Catholic intellectual life in America. Catholic culture—which for the purposes of this paper has been construed broadly and loosely, is mind-bogglingly complex, diverse, dynamic, multiform and polythematic. Its dynamism has always been graced and plagued by the continual process of enculturation, despite well-known and oft-misrepresented efforts on the one hand (from the Nicene Fathers to the Inquisitors, to the campaign against Modernism[12] and—according to some voices—to the current advocates of the *mandatum*[13]) to ensure orthodoxy by curbing dissent, and by such diverse "agents of change" on the other hand, as Aquinas, Ignatius, Teresa of Avila, Maritain, Rahner, and Congar, to name but a few, to preserve what each considered to be the heart of the tradition while capturing and reinterpreting through their distinctively faith-filled lenses the best insights of the spirit of their respective ages. Indeed, at every time and place throughout its long history, some degree of tension has

[11] A somewhat different viewpoint on the effects of secularization on Catholic thought and the potential for a renewal of first tier Catholic scholarship in postmodern America is expressed by John D. Caputo in "Philosophy and Prophetic Postmodernism: Toward a Catholic Postmodernity," *American Catholic Philosophical Quarterly* 74, no. 4 (Autumn 2000), pp. 549–567).

[12] "Modernism" was not a single movement but more accurately a tendency among some Catholic intellectuals to make use of the methods and presuppositions of contemporary, mostly Protestant or agnostic, scholarship (much of which was perceived as hostile to traditional Catholic beliefs) over and against neo-scholastic norms. See James C. Livingston, *Modern Christian Thought*, vol. 1 (Upper Saddle River, New Jersey: Prentice Hall, 1997), p. 379.

[13] The proposed *mandatum* is a canonical "certification" to be issued by local bishops to Catholic theologians who teach in U.S. Catholic colleges and universities; it will constitute an acknowledgement by Church authority that a Catholic professor of a theological discipline is a teacher within the full communion of the Catholic Church. See *Application of Ex Corde Ecclesiae for the United States*, 4, 4, approved by NCCB on Nov. 17, 1999).

existed between those interests that would conserve and preserve the tradition precisely as it was received by them, and opposing interests within the same tradition that would attempt to reinterpret or reframe the Catholic intellectual heritage so that others in subsequent generations might again conserve and preserve the creative synthesis achieved by those creative contributions.

It is certainly plausible that more than one "Catholic moment" may appear and vanish relatively unnoticed, but the coming together of unique circumstances that presents a rare opportunity for Catholics to influence the public life of America is unmistakable. Yet few Catholic leaders today seem aware that this could be their "moment." Regardless of how one might argue, this opportunity can only be met effectively if the stage has already been properly set. In this case, the stage is the American college and university. Most Catholic analysts would agree that the preservation of any distinctively Catholic worldview is inextricably bound to the broad accessibility and widespread popularity of a genuinely Catholic higher education.

MODELS OF CATHOLIC STUDIES PROGRAMS

In 1997–98, the most recent statistics available, there were a total of 4,096 U.S. post-secondary institutions.[14] Of these, only 220 colleges and universities (or fewer than 5.5% of the total number of U.S. schools of higher learning) were denominational schools that identified themselves as Catholic. With roughly 3,876 non-Catholic colleges and universities in America, there is no lack of opportunity to establish Catholic studies initiatives at campuses that have no connection with the Roman Catholic Church or the Catholic tradition.

There has been growing interest in recent years in Catholic studies programs at several of the 220[15] American denominational colleges and universities that identify themselves as Catholic.[16] With few exceptions, however,

[14] This total included 615 public 4-year; 1,092 public 2-year; 1,536 private 4-year non-profit; 169 private 4-year for-profit; 184 private 2-year non-profit; and 500 private 2-year for-profit schools. See *The Chronicle of Higher Education Almanac* 47, no. 1, September 1, 2000, p. 9.

[15] Database of the Association of Catholic Colleges and Universities (ACCU), One Dupont Circle, Suite 650, Washington, DC 20036–1134, as of October 11, 2000. (The ACCU had 241 U.S. Catholic colleges and universities in its database on October 1, 1996.)

[16] See Hinsdale "Catholic Studies: Models and Motives," cites a number of specific programs of Catholic studies that have flourished in recent years *on Catholic campuses*. However, I am aware of little work that has been done as of this date, and certainly no serious studies have been released which examine the relative success of the dozen or so Catholic studies initiatives (typically an endowed faculty chair) at public and private non-Catholic colleges and universities, possibly comparing those results with Catholic studies outcomes at Catholic institutions.

Catholic studies at the post-secondary level has not been promoted apart from these Catholic colleges and universities—despite the fact that slightly fewer than 14%[17] of all traditional-age American Catholic college students are enrolled in colleges or universities identified as Catholic. The fact that nearly 87% of all baptized (or "cradle") Catholic college students in the United States today (i.e., roughly six out of seven Catholic college students, or somewhere in the neighborhood of four million) attend schools *not* identified as Catholic, raises the question: How and where will these Catholics (as well as some non-Catholic students who also may be interested in learning about Catholic beliefs, scholarship, and culture), ever become exposed to, much less afforded an opportunity to become appropriately "formed" in, that tradition? From these numbers it is apparent that if the Catholic intellectual tradition (broadly defined) is to be made readily accessible to the vast majority of American Catholic college students as part of their formal higher learning, then programs of Catholic studies of one type or another must be established at non-Catholic colleges and universities.[18]

As of this date no formal study has been published that focuses on an assessment of Catholic studies faculty chairs and programs at non-Catholic

[17] This percentage, admittedly approximate, was obtained by extrapolating and combining data from several sources; unfortunately, there was no simple and "painless" way to obtain reliable information. I wish to thank Professor Monika Hellwig, ACCU executive director, for her kind assistance. In a phone interview on October 13, 2000, Hellwig estimated that roughly twelve to thirteen percent of all Catholic American traditional college-age (18-to-23-year-old) students who attended college enrolled at Catholic colleges and universities. According to Hellwig, among the approximately 660,000 students who enrolled in the 220 U.S. Catholic colleges in fall 1999, between 60% and 70% were Catholic. Seventy percent of 660,000 is 429,000—the midpoint estimate of the number of Catholics that were enrolled at U.S. Catholic colleges in fall 1999. Approximately one-fourth of the U.S. population (estimated at 272,690,800 in fall 2000) was Catholic. *The Chronicle of Higher Education*, estimated U.S. undergraduate enrollment of 12,450,587, a conservative estimate of Catholics enrolled in all U.S. colleges and universities in fall 1999 was 3,112,500 (September 1, 2000, p. 7). Thus, a rough estimate of Catholic Americans attending non-Catholic colleges is 2,683,500 or 86.2%.

[18] Individual Catholic parishes, missions, and apostolates throughout the United States, as well as campus ministries and student organizations at Catholic and in some instances non-Catholic colleges (e.g., Newman Clubs), offer educational opportunities for teens and adults to learn about the Catholic faith and especially the catechism, e.g., RCIA (Rite of Christian Initiation of Adults), and CCD (Confraternity of Christian Doctrine). These programs, however, are almost exclusively apologetic in focus and content; and while some attempt to be "formational" they are generally too brief and necessarily superficial to significantly affect the way in which participants view themselves, their world and reality. More importantly, most lack the depth or breadth of intellectual inquiry that is possible by means of "Catholic studies" approached as a post-secondary academic discipline.

colleges and universities. However, a modest but informative body of (largely anecdotal) literature is developing with regard to Catholic studies initiatives at Catholic colleges and universities. Since there would be obvious substantial similarities in program content, subject matter orientation, curriculum, organization and the like, a fair portion of the literature dealing with Catholic studies at Catholic colleges can be useful as a starting-point for inquiry into Catholic studies opportunities for students at non-Catholic schools.

Even at Catholic colleges and universities, the very notion of Catholic studies is of recent vintage.[19] From the available literature, several variables are evident as to how Catholic studies initiatives have developed and fared at Catholic colleges. First, these programs have differed widely in terms of stated (and, in some instances, implied or covert) purpose, aim, goals, and mission. As a result, such programs are variously defined by subject matter content and by their relationship to the overall curriculum. Generally, however, such programs appear to have grown up as a consequence of the perception of at least some influential constituencies that a renewal of emphasis on "Catholic identity" is desirable on the part of the parent or sponsoring institutions (i.e., the Catholic colleges and universities to which the respective Catholic studies programs are affiliated or an integral part), and that a Catholic studies program is a practical means of accomplishing that aim. Second, Catholic studies programs have met with varying degrees of success.[20] And third, the "political" agendas of involved faculty, parent institutions, and funding sources have all shaped the development of these programs, giving them some of their more distinctive characteristics. Doubtless, the character,

[19] Interest in Catholic studies programs at Catholic colleges and universities has grown significantly during the 1990s. Doubtless several programs were the result, at least in part, to growing perceptions (especially in the light of *Ex Corde Ecclesiae*) that Catholic studies in the curriculum constituted a form of tangible evidence of the host college's Catholic identity. A few colleges have offered Catholic studies in one form or another for longer, e.g., the University of San Francisco's Saint Ignatius Institute recently celebrated its twenty-fifth anniversary.

[20] The University of San Francisco's Saint Ignatius Institute is a well-publicized instance of a Catholic (Jesuit) university that offers *both* a Catholic Studies Certificate Program as part of its mainstream curriculum, and a "separate" Saint Ignatius Institute that aims to provide a formational experience for 160 undergraduates who participate in its "Great Books" program. Until January 2001, the Institute by design stood apart from the rest of the campus, with participating students taking roughly half their classes at the Institute "where core faculty members view themselves as defenders of traditional Catholic teachings and values." On January 19, 2001, the conservative Institute's director was summarily dismissed and the Institute was placed under the same direction as the university's Catholic Studies Certificate Program, setting off a storm of controversy according to *The Chronicle of Higher Education* "Conservative Roman Catholics Criticize U. of San Francisco President," February 15, 2001).

purpose and mission of Catholic studies programs, as well as enrollments and relative importance within the parent institutions, can depend as much upon the motives and agendas of funding sources as upon the mission and self-identity of the parent institution and the involved faculty. (We shall return to this later.)

How can one characterize Catholic studies programs at Catholic colleges and universities? Mary Ann Hinsdale recently identified four models of Catholic studies at Catholic colleges based on each program's chief aim or purpose. Hinsdale refers to the first type as the "cultural studies" model. This approach is to study Catholicism as a multi-faceted "culture." Like "area studies" the "cultural studies" approach is heavily interdisciplinary, drawing not only from theology and religious studies but also from philosophy, history, the social sciences, literature and art faculties. Hinsdale argues that while Catholic "cultural studies" initiatives claim an unbiased stance, e.g., "Catholicism is simply a tradition with a long, influential history, and, therefore, worth studying," the very presence of Catholic "cultural studies" at Catholic colleges "suggests that this particular cultural identity has become marginalized, whether that be through some process of institutional secularization (through design or by default), or as a by-product of the assimilation of white, European immigrant Catholics into mainstream American culture."[21] Hinsdale cautions that this approach actually is far from neutral (i.e., that indeed it has an agenda, or is motivated by an "advocacy-orientation") to the extent that it prompts the "sense" that the Catholic intellectual heritage has been marginalized (or re-marginalized?) in American culture. Ironically, Hinsdale notes an irony in that the very claim of this approach to neutrality makes it a difficult model to serve as a formative means of passing on a Catholic culture.[22]

The second model Hinsdale identifies as "apologetic" because this approach unashamedly promotes "Catholic identity" which is often viewed as an antidote to the secularization of American culture. The "apologetic" Catholic studies program, Hinsdale says, seeks to "restore a unified Catholic worldview" by introducing students to the thought of Catholic "greats"[23] such as Newman, Dawson, Chesterton, Lewis, Maritain, Gilson, Pieper, etc. This approach draws mainly from the college's philosophy, theology and English departments, and often faculty and courses are widely solicited for inclusion in the overall program; however, faculty who are allowed to teach the "core course" in these programs are generally closely monitored, presumably to assure consonance with the program's educational objectives and

[21] Hinsdale, "Catholic Studies: Models and Motives," p. 7.
[22] Ibid., p. 8.
[23] Ibid., p. 9.

consonance on the part of participating faculty with the "Catholic character" of the program. According to Hinsdale, the true character of such programs is often "monocultural" in that they frequently promote a distinctively "Anglo-American" form of Catholicism.[24]

The third approach to Catholic studies Hinsdale identifies as the "Catholic intellectual tradition" model. Described as a hybrid of the two previously described approaches, this model like the "cultural studies" approach seeks to be interdisciplinary, but like the "apologetic" model it strives to preserve and expand a long tradition of Catholic intellectual life. Hinsdale describes this approach as tending toward a wider definition of Catholicism, thereby allowing greater inclusion of often-marginalized voices within Catholicism, e.g., women, African Americans, Native Americans, Latinos, working-class and poor Catholics. According to Hinsdale, this approach is strongly historical, including exposure to the tradition's "dark side" (e.g., the Crusades, witch burning, Inquisition, ties with colonialism, slavery, anti-Semitism). Hinsdale criticizes the "Catholic intellectual tradition" model as missing the sense of Catholicism as a world religion and how it has become inculturated into non-Western cultures.[25]

The final category of Hinsdale's four-fold typology is referred to as the "formative" or "formational"[26] model. In contrast with the other three models, this approach does not seem to exist as an entity in itself. Typically appearing as a service-learning component of programs that attempt to integrate campus intellectual life with the particular charism of its sponsors (Hinsdale uses the example of a Jesuit emphasis on "men and women for others") or through series of retreats. Hinsdale perceives this genre of Catholic studies as attempting to provide an intellectual structure that grounds some service approach such as social justice outreach or peace studies to help make these apostolates more comprehensible as vehicles for "handing on the tradition."[27]

While stopping short of endorsing one model over the others, Hinsdale does consider "unconscionable" any program of Catholic studies that she regards as "monocultural." Hinsdale argues emphatically for programs that meet today's challenges of multiculturalism and pluralism, on the basis that "[T]he experience of American Catholicism is too rich to neglect the contributions of different ethnicities and regions." Any approach to Catholic studies that meets these challenges would, in fact, provide a strong argument for its implementation at a non-Catholic college or university, since most secular

[24] Ibid.

[25] Ibid., p. 10.

[26] Both terms are used, apparently interchangeably, throughout Hinsdale's paper.

[27] Ibid., p. 11. Hinsdale notes that she could not find much evidence of successful "formative" programs. Perhaps further studies along these lines could be useful.

institutions of higher learning today pride themselves in meeting the challenges of multiculturalism and pluralism. Indeed, Hinsdale's concerns appear consonant in some important ways with Jacques Maritain's social and educational philosophy.

Identifying approaches to Catholic studies does not provide a complete picture of their diversity. Fortunately, Hinsdale also identifies the most common motives or agendas that lie behind Catholic studies initiatives at Catholic colleges and universities, which can be summarized as follows: 1) nostalgia (or, put another way, disillusionment and/or disenfranchisement with much of mainstream "postmodern" scholarship); 2) an antidote to loss of a culture, or "religious illiteracy"; 3) evangelization, or "handing on the faith"; 4) the pursuit of knowledge (i.e., Catholicism is viewed as a body of knowledge that is worth studying); and finally 5) the solution to "Catholic identity" concerns by parent institutions.[28] With the obvious exception of "Catholic identity," each of these could serve as contributory motives or agendas for Catholic studies at non-Catholic colleges. Hinsdale further notes that the most successful programs are those that are enriched by several different agendas, even if these are competing motives accompanied by different ideological stances. Among the ideological positions she identifies are: 1) conserving (a past culture, tradition, heritage or history); 2) dialogical (interacting with culture, moving toward a new synthesis); and 3) pluralist (toleration with little or no evaluation or analysis).[29]

Hinsdale's cautions about some of the motivations for Catholic studies notwithstanding, the fact remains that roughly six out of seven Catholic American college students are unlikely to receive any exposure to the Catholic intellectual tradition, unless and until some form of Catholic studies is made accessible to them at their non-Catholic campuses. This is not to minimize the important contributions made by Newman clubs and Catholic campus ministries in providing formational activities at secular colleges, such as retreats, speaker series and similar fare. However, a Catholic higher education which, in the days of the Jesuit *ratio studiorum* typically required exposure to ten philosophy and four theology courses, could scarcely be considered an adequately "received" formation on the basis of a few retreats, lectures and self-help gatherings. Without imparting to the student a clear vision of reality—which, in our day, constitutes to some extent *an alternative worldview*—there is little chance of inspiring the typical student to challenge her or his mainstream collegiate "postmodern" worldview, and even less

[28] Ibid., p. 12.
[29] Ibid.

chance of empowering future generations of Americans with a Catholic intellectual tradition that for so many was their natural birthright.

OBSTACLES TO CATHOLIC STUDIES AT NON-CATHOLIC CAMPUSES

Millions[30] of American college students currently lack the opportunity to take courses in Catholic studies because the college or university they have chosen to attend does not consider the subject matter of the Catholic intellectual tradition sufficiently useful, relevant or suitable to be included in the curriculum. Granted, many colleges that have Religious Studies offer courses in Biblical studies or the history of Christianity. But the similarity between such courses and Catholic studies is generally no greater than the proximity of modern analytic philosophy to neoscholastic metaphysics. Much of Catholic studies, as Hinsdale's typology suggests, involves students in a particular worldview that really is at odds with the prevailing *Zeitgeist* of American culture, which tends to be echoed in the ethos of the modern secular university. At its best Catholic studies initiates students into a very different mode of thinking about themselves and their world; it introduces students to an alternative perception of reality that, frankly, some academic leaders today mistakenly look upon as antithetical to or competitive with their personal visions of reality. Other academic leaders, including a few evangelical Protestants who recall ancient prejudices even in this post-Vatican II era, naïvely treat Catholicism as inherently superstitious and anti-intellectual. Still others, schooled in anti-Catholic biases associated with some non-Western or postmodern interpretations of history, privately stereotype the Catholic intellectual tradition as narrow-minded, bigoted, or imperialistic.

Doubtless there are many "covert" reasons that could cause academic leaders on secular campuses to shy away from Catholic studies. Few would publicly acknowledge their fears that Catholic studies might promote an ideology with which their non-Catholic faculty is uneasy, and therefore unwilling to support. The reasons they might offer publicly are likely to have a very different

---

[30] As of fall 1997, among the 12.45 million American college undergraduates estimated by the U.S. Dept. of Education (www.ed.gov), minus the 660,000 students who according to the ACCU attended Catholic colleges, close to 11.79 million students are in this category—a figure that will rise to approximately 16 million by 2010. (Non-Catholics as well as Catholics may wish to avail themselves of Catholic studies courses. More than one inquirer has discovered and adopted Catholicism as her faith in just such a way.) Although students attending non-Catholic colleges in some urban areas *could* gain access to Catholic studies courses with some effort, rarely do colleges make it convenient for these students to transfer credits in Catholic studies to non-Catholic schools except as "pure" electives, which are seldom useful toward graduation.

ring. Such arguments might include the objection that the existing curriculum already offers too many electives, or that Catholic studies would be too costly, or that it is not the proper time to expand, or too few students are Catholic, or those who are Catholic are less than enthusiastic about the proposed program, or the appearance of Catholic studies could strain an otherwise harmonious atmosphere of campus life. Other academic leaders might express concern over possible lawsuits from civil liberties activists if they were to permit the teaching of religion at a publicly supported college or university.[31] Another likely argument is that colleges are "market driven" and can only thrive in turbulent times following the trends, such as technology oriented programs, and a Catholic studies initative clearly does not fit this objective.

These lines of argumentation could be quite misleading and their (mis)use could become a serious deterrent for any proposed initiatives that would seek to draw Catholic scholarship into the public university. Of course, virtually every one of these objections and similar concerns should be anticipated and can be successfully countered. Unfortunately, objections often have a divisive effect upon groups that, once aired, can thwart or delay the inauguration of a new Catholic studies program even though proponents of the initiated were able to offer a reasonable response. While some of these objections are likely to be based on legitimate concerns, there is none that cannot be resolved where the desire exists. The greater difficulty seems to arise with hidden agendas or "covert" objections that are difficult to address because they are never acknowledged or brought into the open. Some hesitation is to be expected among certain segments of the faculty and administration, and perhaps a few trustees may be opposed to the idea of Catholic studies. Unfortunately, the opposition may not be forthright and direct about the true nature and scope of its objections. The culture of the American academy, much like that of big government and large corporations, is such that centers of resistance to innovations are difficult to address because they often shield themselves from view within their respective bureaucracies and rarely voice their objections openly and honestly within the

---

[31] Actually, matters pertaining to religion are found in Article 6 of the Constitution as well as the First and Fourteenth Amendments. However, since the matter of teaching religion in a public school was clarified by the U.S. Supreme Court in *Abington School District v. Schempp*, 374 U.S. 203 (1963), the legal "bottom line" for publicly supported colleges and universities is that the Catholic intellectual tradition can be taught in the classroom as a body of knowledge suitable for study, in the same way that evangelical Christian, Native American, Buddhist and Wiccan religious beliefs and practices can be taught. See Robert Booth Fowler and Allen D. Hertzke, *Religion and Politics in America: Faith, Culture, and Strategic Choices* (Boulder, Colorado: Westview Press, 1995), p. 1. See Marsden, *The Soul of the American University*, pp. 435–36.

wider university faculty and administrative communities. In other situations, of course, perfectly sincere and potentially valid arguments and concerns may be raised, most of which can be adequately addressed by knowledgeable advocates of Catholic studies.

One obstacle to the introduction of Catholic studies in non-Catholic colleges arises from a misperception commonly shared by students, faculty and parents that, although Catholics represent the largest religious denomination in the United States, any student who has any interest whatsoever in learning about the Catholic intellectual tradition can and will necessarily matriculate in a Catholic school.[32] This notion is easily refuted by UCLA's national annual poll of entering freshmen, which makes it clear that there are many different (and often more compelling) reasons for the selection of a college or university than its religious affiliation.[33] This is not to suggest that Catholic students are insufficiently curious about their heritage or so uninterested in their faith that they would not bother to enroll in Catholic studies courses, e.g., as general studies electives or for personal enrichment, assuming that

[32] Some "market driven" Catholic college leaders hesitate to discourage this misperception due to concern over preserving their Catholic "niche." They believe, unnecessarily in my opinion, that the perpetuation of this "myth" especially among Catholic parents is essential to keep Catholic higher education afloat by perpetuating its "corner" on the Catholic higher education market. In reality, their concern is overblown, since students choose colleges for a variety of reasons other than its religious affiliation. To use my *alma mater* as an example, among all undergraduate students at Penn State's main campus at University Park (State College, Pennsylvania) who in spring 2000 listed their religious preference drawing from a list of 36 possible selections including "other" and "unknown," the largest percentage by far identified themselves as Roman Catholic (35.7%). It is ironic that one of the largest public universities in the United States, with fully one-third of its diverse student population reporting themselves as Catholic, has yet to perceive sufficient student interest for a single course specifically designed to teach the Catholic intellectual tradition, despite the fact that its Religious Studies program supports an expansive Jewish Studies major which includes an endowed chair, and sponsors the peer-reviewed, award-winning online *Journal of Buddhist Ethics*. (To be fair, Penn State does offer several Religious Studies courses in various aspects of Christianity, which are taught from an ostensibly faith-neutral or "history of religions" perspective.)

[33] A mere 5.8% of the 261,217 incoming college freshmen surveyed in fall 1999 representing 462 American colleges and universities indicated the religious affiliation/orientation of the institution was very important in the college they selected. In contrast, far greater numbers of respondents gave other reasons for selecting their college as very important, e.g., academic reputation (47.6%), social reputation (23.1%), financial assistance (30.2%), special program offerings (19.5%), low tuition (27.7%), proximity to residence (20.5%), size of college (31.1%), and perceived ability to gain admission to a top graduate school (27.5%) and/or to get a good job upon graduation (44.6%). From "The American Freshman National Norms for Fall 1999," American Council on Education and University of California at Los Angeles Higher Education Research Institute. *The Chronicle of Higher Education Almanac*, February 15, 2001, p. 28.

more pressing economic and career-related reasons for attending a particular college or meeting specific curricular requirements have already been satisfied or are in the process of being fulfilled. Many future scholars claim to have taken their first course in philosophy, theology, or history merely out of curiosity or to satisfy a humanities requirement, only to become so inspired by the subject matter that it made all the difference in their lives.[34]

Typically the traditional college-age person (eighteen to twenty-four year old) stands at a crucial point in their spiritual and moral development. College is a time of tremendous change between the relative safety of family life during late adolescence and the great unknown of young adulthood.[35] Most adolescents in their pre-college years are dependent upon significant others for confirmation and clarity about their self-identity and meaning; they have not yet developed a transcendental perspective from which to evaluate self-other relations. The act of leaving home for the first time, in combination with the college experience itself with its seemingly inexhaustible diversity and competing values, often triggers a sort of crisis during which the entering student begins to critically examine her tacit system of values, beliefs and commitments. Simultaneously, the personality that had been previously formed and supported by its roles and relationships is forced to struggle with the question of identity and worth apart from its previously defined connections. At the heart of this double movement is the emergence of third-person perspective taking. By acquiring this transcendental capacity, the college student is able to more effectively adjudicate the diverse voices and conflicting expectations of external and internal authoritative voices.[36] James Fowler, an expert in stages of faith development, suggests that in order to sustain their reflective identities, persons in this stage

> Compose (or ratify) meaning frames that are conscious of their own boundaries and inner connections and aware of themselves as worldviews.

---

[34] Prof. Louis P. Pojman recounts (in a personal word to students prefacing one of his many college textbooks) the unexpected outcome of the first college course he took in philosophy, a course that led Pojman to read Søren Kierkegaard's *Fear and Trembling*: "Kierkegaard's book had a devastating effect on me, forcing me to become totally dissatisfied with the mediocre life I had been living in college and drove me to depths of intensity and seriousness that I have still not recovered from." *Philosophical Traditions* (Belmont, California: Wadsworth, 1998), p. xix. See Paul M. Anderson, *Professors Who Believe: The Spiritual Journeys of Christian Faculty* (Downers Grove, Illinois: InterVarsity Press, 1998).

[35] See Ernest T. Pascarella and Patrick T. Terenzini, *How College Affects Students: Findings and Insights from Twenty Years of Research* (San Francisco: Jossey-Bass, 1991).

[36] James W. Fowler, *Faithful Change: The Personal and Public Challenges of Postmodern Life* (Nashville, Tennessee: Abingdon Press, 1996), pp. 61–63.

Utilizing their capacities of procedural knowing and critical reflection, persons of [this] stage "demythologize" symbols, rituals, and myths, typically translating their meanings into conceptual formulations. Frequently overconfident in their conscious awareness, persons of this stage attend minimally to unconscious factors that influence their judgments and behavior. This excessive confidence in the conscious mind and in critical thought can lead to a kind of "cognitive narcissism" in which the now clearly bounded, reflective self over-assimilates "reality" and the perspectives of others into its worldview.[37]

College should be and often is a special time in the lives of most persons who are fortunate enough to attend. The search for identity and meaning in an apparently absurd world necessitates a rethinking of previously held values and often leads either to a recommitment to one's previous held beliefs or to the adoption of a new faith commitment. Developmentally, the traditional college years are an especially fitting period in which to introduce a person to her intellectual heritage, especially if that heritage constitutes the foundation for an emerging life-perspective or worldview prompted by the college experience. Moreover, the college or university is the appropriate *situs* for intellectual inquiry that constitutes spiritual formation or involves the content of faith.

Nor is it reasonable to assume that Catholics are equally "at home" on secular campuses. The largely anecdotal evidence I have accumulated over the last six years[38] suggests the contrary—that significant numbers of Catholic students, especially those who graduated from Catholic high schools, soon after they enter secular colleges and especially larger universities experience anxiety which arises from exposure to contrasting systems of moral values and an unfamiliar environment that is often hostile to an explicitly or implicitly Catholic worldview.[39] I do not wish to overstate my case. My perception is that the

[37] Ibid., p. 63.

[38] One of my ongoing research interests is to measure the impact of higher education's academic and environmental circumstances upon the moral and faith development of Catholic students. In this connection, I used in-depth interviews to compare and contrast experiences of first-year Catholic students attending a Catholic university (Fordham) with those of Catholic students at a secular university (Penn State). See Frederick Erb III, *Spiritual Development and the College Experience With Emphasis on First-Year Catholic Students* (unpublished paper presented Dec. 7, 1994, Penn State University's Higher Education Program).

[39] This appears consistent with the enrollment successes enjoyed at Catholic colleges which advance traditional, conservative, evangelical and/or classics ("Great Books") outlooks, such as the Franciscan University (Steubenville, Ohio), Christendom College, (Front Royal, Virginia), and Thomas Aquinas College, (Santa Paula, California). Critics accuse such formational approaches to higher education of sheltering young adults from the "real world" to their detriment, while proponents argue that a proper formative experience better equips a person to defend their chosen ideology against an obstructive or, at best, less than supportive world.

majority of Catholics studying at non-Catholic colleges, especially those who do not arrive directly from a Catholic high school background, tend to be much more comfortable with the student culture of the secular academy. Among the more religiously conservative Catholic first year students who initially feel "out of place" at secular colleges because their beliefs and lifestyles differ markedly from those of the majority of students, most tend increasingly to conform to pressures from peers and faculty as their college careers progress, while only a small percentage complete the college experience with their Catholic faith intact.[40]

What does this psychological snapshot of the traditional college-age student's spiritual development suggest to us about the popularity that Catholic studies courses or programs would likely enjoy on non-Catholic campuses? Although it is difficult to make a blanket generalization, it stands to reason that even if a modest percentage of Catholics at non-Catholic campuses were to choose to include individual courses in the Catholic intellectual tradition among their general education electives, and an even smaller number were to major, minor or earn a certificate in Catholic studies, the secular colleges and universities would be enriched and the Catholic intellectual tradition at its best would have the necessary means first to survive and then to thrive. The universities, most of which in the United States are non-Catholic, can provide both the fertile ground and the leading minds necessary for the Catholic tradition to flourish.

So, given these circumstances, why do academic leaders resist? Why are there so few Catholic studies at non-Catholic colleges? Framed in a more personal way, why is Catholic studies overlooked at major universities like my *alma mater* Penn State, despite the fact that there is no Catholic college within a fifty mile radius of its main campus at University Park, and Penn State enrolls about the same number of Catholic students at its main campus as the entire undergraduate student population of the University of Notre Dame? George Marsden hints at some likely underlying causes of the present

---

[40] Although *intact* is a "loaded" term, it conveys my point better than "unaffected" or "untouched" because virtually every traditional college-age student must struggle to some extent with the symbols and stories by which their lives were previously constructed. The issues involved are complex; however, Fowler suggests that a fair percentage of young people, especially males, experience a split between the emotional and cognitive functioning that can be directly attributed to unresolved relations and issues from early childhood. In such cases, emotional development fails to keep pace with cognitive functioning, resulting in overconfidence coupled with insensitivity toward others. Such persons are often drawn to more rigid forms of religion and authoritarian leaders because of seemingly unambiguous teachings. (Fowler, *Faithful Change*, pp. 62–63.)

paucity of Catholic studies programs on secular campuses. At the risk of oversimplification, Marsden argues convincingly that some of the most powerful interests within mainstream academia today, groups such as secularists, postmodernists, persons of Jewish descent,[41] ex-fundamentalists, Marxists, radical feminists, lesbians and gays, typically view traditional Christianity as one of those oppressive powers from which the world needs to be liberated.[42] Since virtually all of these groups have suffered at the hands of Christians when Christianity dominated the Western world, and since the differences between some of these groups and traditional Christians on fundamental issues of morality are quite incompatible, Marsden explains:

> Academic struggles over such issues take place in a cultural context of bitter contests over moral standards for public policy. So the issues cannot be resolved simply by tolerance and learning to get along better. The fact is that many contenders on the various sides of such debates are imperialistic in the sense of wanting to set the moral standards for all of society.
>
> Granting that there is some basis for concern [among academics from these dominant groups] about resurgent Christian imperialism, we should ask whether such concerns are sufficient to justify the effective silencing of traditional Christian voices in much of mainstream academic culture.[43]

Marsden answers in the negative. In his opinion, secular academic voices have far less to fear from Catholic and evangelical Christian voices than the reverse. He cautions that

> there is more danger [within the academy] of the imperialism of secularism excluding conservative Christian voices than of the reverse. . . . I do not want to imply that conservative Christian voices have been totally excluded from mainstream academia. They may be rare, but sometimes

---

[41] That Jews as a group have suffered terribly under Christian hegemony cannot be denied historically and should not be forgotten. This caveat notwithstanding, Marsden prudently clarifies the inclusion of Jews on his list of powerful academic lobby groups that are potentially if not actually opposed to the readmission of Christian scholarship at secular campuses: "Many Jewish scholars . . . are understandably wary of any suggestion of resurgent Christian influence. In the view of such scholars the issue is more a matter of politics and power than of abstract principle. Jewish scholars might readily support Jewish studies centers where scholars openly advocated Zionism and the preservation of Jewish practice. On the other hand, they might ardently defend separation of church and state in this country and oppose overt expressions of Christian perspectives. The difference in their minds is that Christians have been the oppressors and, as the majority in this country, are not to be trusted." See Marsden, *The Outrageous Idea of Christian Scholarship*, p. 32.

[42] Ibid., p. 34.

[43] Ibid., pp. 32–33.

they indeed do get a hearing. That granted, it remains true that some powerful lobbies would like to see those voices silenced. . . .[44]

According to Marsden, it is those forces that promote a more standardized and secularized academic culture that should not be underestimated.[45] As Marsden explains:

> The irony of the current situation is that much of the animus toward conservative religion comes in the name of multiculturalism and diversity. . . . When it comes to religion in public life, the impulse for integration and uniformity typically overcomes diversity, despite the rhetoric to the contrary. Certainly this is the case in mainstream universities. . . . The result is not diversity, but rather a dreary uniformity. Everyone is expected to accept the standard doctrine that religion has no intellectual relevance.[46]

The process of the secularization of American higher education leaves little room for Catholic and evangelical voices precisely because these are so often perceived by dominant groups especially within the larger secular universities as antithetical to the academic culture. Paradoxically—and this seems to be a main point of Marsden's book—if Christian scholarship at its best were allowed to enter the academic mainstream, then its inclusion would have the effect of intellectually enriching American higher education.

It is reasonable to assume that proponents of a successful new Catholic studies initiative at a non-Catholic college and university will have first "done their homework" by thoroughly researching the viability of such a program in that particular setting. They will have identified those academic interest groups that would be most likely to resist Catholic studies, and will have prepared appropriate responses to mollify any legitimate concerns, presumably prior to bringing their case before those academic leaders who make the ultimate decision.

STRATEGIES FOR INTRODUCING CATHOLIC STUDIES AT NON-CATHOLIC CAMPUSES

Apart from the rhetoric, the politics, the posturing and the neglect, the true motivations of academic leaders will remain a matter of speculation. In contrast, the dearth of Catholic studies in the curricula of non-Catholic colleges is an irrefutable fact. Only a small number of teaching faculty who specialize in Catholic studies at non-Catholic U.S. colleges and universities hold designated or endowed chairs in academic specializations that are even re-

---

[44] Ibid., p. 34.
[45] Ibid., p. 109.
[46] Ibid., pp. 34–35.

motely related to Catholic studies. Most of these chairs were instituted within the last decade. Although at least twelve schools currently (or intend to) offer individual courses in Catholic philosophy, theology, or history, into their curriculum, few (if any) currently offer their students a major, minor or certificate in Catholic Studies.

Several years ago I developed a typology of Catholic higher learning that included several creative strategies aimed at providing American undergraduate students not enrolled at a traditionally Catholic college or university the option of a higher education of a distinctively Catholic character.[47] Among the alternatives described were four approaches for structuring Catholic studies[48] at public and private non-Catholic colleges and universities. These structural models included: 1) individual courses or programs in Catholic history, philosophy, theology, etc., arising from the establishment or endowment of chairs in Catholic studies, modeled on the Harvard University chair once occupied by Christopher Dawson; 2) Catholic studies offered within a non-Catholic college, either as an independent department or program, or as part of the college's religious studies, theology, philosophy, history or similar department typically situated in liberal arts or humanities; 3) the "Catholic studies consortium" model, in which two or more separate institutions of higher learning, including at least one Catholic and one non-Catholic college or university, become involved in an effort to offer Catholic studies "for credit" to students enrolled at participating non-Catholic colleges; and 4) the development of initiatives made possible through more innovative organizational structures. I will refer to this as the "independent Catholic institute" approach, since it would aim to offer Catholic studies at a convenient off-campus location through an arrangement with any fully accredited Catholic college to guarantee participating students the necessary regional accreditation and to facilitate the transfer of course credits to the non-Catholic college or university where the participating students are enrolled.

Of the four approaches described above, the most common is the academic chair in Catholic studies (although only a dozen or so have been established at non-Catholic institutions). As professors who have held these chairs know only too well, the existence of an endowed chair does not necessarily

---

[47] See Frederick Erb III, *Profiles of Catholic Higher Education in America: Prognosis and Prescription* (unpublished M.A. thesis, Pennsylvania State University, January 1998), pp. 85–113.

[48] The term "Catholic studies," while broadly defined, is delimited here to postsecondary programs that offer degrees, majors, minors, certificates, or individual courses for undergraduate or graduate credit.

lead to a full-fledged Catholic studies program, complete with a major, minor and certificate in Catholic studies. It is possible to move in that direction, of course, beginning with a faculty chair. (The University of Illinois at Chicago appears to be moving in that general direction.) More needs to be researched and written on this model, which is developing slowly but is likely to emerge as the most commonly implemented model.

The "consortium" approach is somewhat more creative, and may only be feasible in urban communities or in highly unusual situations where a smaller non-Catholic college comes to recognize the need to add Catholic studies to its curriculum but lacks the resources to do so effectively. General consortia of colleges and universities exist today in large urban areas, and often both Catholic and non-Catholic institutions participate; however, no consortium of colleges and universities comes to mind that facilitates a program of Catholic studies as such.

Certainly the most innovative and arguably the approach best suited to the more challenging circumstances is that of an "independent Catholic in-stitute." An initiative of this type would be built on the design and develop-ment of an independently funded, fully accredited institute for Catholic studies, housed in an easily accessible off-campus location that ideally would include adequate classroom space, administrative offices, library, faculty and student lounge and reading areas, possibly a refectory to pro-mote faculty-student discourse outside the classroom, and an explicitly and exclusively Catholic chapel where services are offered daily to students. The ideal Catholic institute would retain its own faculty and staff, and would offer fully accredited courses (initially, at least) through a contrac-tual arrangement with a like-minded Catholic college or university as its sponsor. The accreditation might work as a variation on the distance educa-tion and web-based learning practices for which regional accreditation is becoming increasingly commonplace.[49] In all cases in which an off-campus institute or consortium model is utilized, appropriate articulation agree-ments would have been reached between the Catholic studies program (possibly through its sponsoring Catholic college) and the adjacent or nearby non-Catholic college or university, so that students enrolled at both places could easily transfer credits that can be counted toward requirements for graduation. Likewise, arrangements would have to be made concerning financial aid. The successful institute would ensure that the entire process

[49] As of this writing, repeated requests for clarification on some important points concerning the "independent Catholic institute" model have not yet received an ap-propriate response from a regional accrediting agency.

of taking courses in Catholic studies and receiving appropriate credit for them should be made as streamlined and seamless as possible. The total concept of an independent institute for Catholic studies would be to offer students from the adjacent non-Catholic college options ranging from a single course in Catholic studies, to a "second major" in Catholic studies, to a fully "formational" experience of living the religious and moral life associated with the best of the Catholic intellectual tradition.

Admittedly in some instances a means of last resort, this Catholic institute model ostensibly may be well suited for situations in which influential members of the faculty at the targeted non-Catholic college or university either have effectively resisted or rebuffed all initiatives to implement the first three approaches listed above, or appear likely to interfere with or sabotage the process of effectively growing an on-campus Catholic studies program.

The development of alternative models such as these would be greatly facilitated through proactive cooperation on the part of registrars, bursars, financial aid officers and academic administrators both at the involved Catholic "sponsoring" and non-Catholic "recipient" institutions. Although it may be possible in some situations to develop a successful off-campus program even in a quasi-hostile environment, provided sufficient student support is forthcoming, the importance of first "taking the high road" by making every effort to garner faculty and administrative support from the non-Catholic college or university cannot be overemphasized.

Returning briefly to Hinsdale's paper, three words of caution are offered to anyone interested in promoting Catholic studies at a Catholic college—and, again, these insights also apply to non-Catholic institutions: 1) There is no "cookie cutter" formula that fits all situations; in fact, each set of circumstances is unique. Every institution has its own academic culture and must be approached individually—there can be no McDonald's or Burger King of Catholic studies programs suitable for all student populations, campus sizes and geographical locations, and college traditions. 2) Student interest should be measured before time and expense is thrown into a program. 3) Multiple funding sources should be sought to avoid the potential danger of accepting support from a single donor who then seeks to impose on the program an inappropriate or untenable agenda.[50]

Next to the purpose and mission of the program, funding may be the most important concern, at least initially. Preliminary evidence suggests, however, that the current climate is favorable toward individuals and institutions that seek investment for Catholic studies. Thomas J. Donnelly, a Catholic

---

[50] Hinsdale, "Catholic Studies: Models and Motives," p. 15.

philanthropist and board member of FADICA,[51] recently called for increased Catholic diocesan support to programs aimed at Catholic students in state sponsored and secular universities and not just to Catholic institutions of higher learning. He urged local churches to "move beyond strictly institutional interests and to go where the majority of Catholic, college-age students can be found." Donnelly, echoing the sentiments of Harvard professor J. Bryan Hehir, said Catholic students need more than simply a substantial prayer life and a generous spirit—they also need to ground those virtues in an intellectual understanding of the faith.[52]

Another serious point of discussion that is likely to surface in the near future is what criteria and procedures will determine whether the character and content of particular Catholic studies initiatives are sufficiently "authentic" to be called "Catholic." Until now, debates concerning the "Catholicity" of particular American colleges, programs and faculty in the wake of *Ex Corde Ecclesiae* have been directed by the Vatican *only* at Catholic higher education institutions and theologians whom they employ. At present one of the more controversial aspects of the apostolic letter is the judgment that Catholic theologians on the faculty of American Catholic colleges and universities should possess a canonical *mandatum*. This "license" or certification, which beginning May 3, 2001, must be requested by all Catholics who teach theology at Catholic colleges and is to be either conferred or withheld by the local bishop, requires teachers to declare their role and responsibility "within the full communion of the [Catholic] Church," that they are "committed to teach authentic Catholic doctrine and to refrain from putting forth as Catholic teaching anything contrary to the Church's magisterium."[53]

A discussion of the relative merits of *Ex Corde Ecclesiae* and the *mandatum* are beyond the limits of this paper, insofar as these pertain only to Catholic colleges and universities. However, their impact on Catholic studies programs elsewhere has yet to be realized. The emergence of "Catholic consortium" and "independent Catholic institute" models of Catholic studies initiatives at non-Catholic colleges, regardless of their charters or missions,

---

[51] FADICA is an acronym for Foundations and Donors Interested in Catholic Activities, Inc., a non-profit organization located in Washington, D.C.

[52] A press release describing Donnelly's remarks to a group of more than one hundred Catholic campus ministers at Allenspark, Colorado, on June 14, 1999, was retrieved from the FADICA web site, www.fadica.org/direct.html on January 3, 2000.

[53] Excerpts from a sample "Attestation" included in the *Draft Guidelines concerning the Academic 'Mandatum' in Catholic Universities* (canon 812), presented by the ad hoc committee chaired by Archbishop Daniel Pilarczyk to the NCCB, November 2000.

will eventually trigger some degree of concern for Rome, the American bishops, Catholic educators, and other groups and individuals whose perceived interests may be affected in various ways. As the number and variety of Catholic studies initiatives at non-Catholic colleges increases, it is entirely possible that some conservative groups within the Catholic Church may attempt in some manner to extend the certification process to these faculty. Whether a Catholic scholar who teaches in a theological discipline for a Catholic studies program at a non-Catholic college could, or should, seek a canonical *mandatum*, poses very serious questions for the teacher, the program and the host college.

The notion of extending the reach of *Ex Corde* and the *mandatum* to "certify" Catholic studies programs or their faculty at non-Catholic colleges may seem preposterous, but it has already been suggested by at least one conservative Catholic priest.[54] Such a stance, if sanctioned either by the American bishops or the Vatican, could play into the hands of detractors by giving them additional grounds for resisting new Catholic studies initiatives and for refusing support to existing programs. They could be joined by regional accrediting agencies and faculty rights organizations such as the American Association of University Professors (AAUP) in denouncing Catholic studies initiatives that require a canonical *mandatum* on the grounds that such programs effectively deny the academic freedom of their faculty. Such circumstances could make it more difficult or impractical to inaugurate Catholic studies programs by exacerbating those centers of resistance that already exist toward the idea of Catholic studies among a substantial number of secular and other non-Catholic faculty and administrators and even among some Catholic scholars. Ideally some middle ground should be negotiated that would ensure fidelity to the Catholic tradition as well as the academic freedom of Catholic studies faculty situated in non-Catholic environments—not that this acceptable middle ground would be easy to achieve. Avery Cardinal Dulles, noting that theologians of the

[54] Monsignor John J. Strynkowski asks, "An authentically Catholic theologian teaching at a secular institution . . . why can't s/he get an ecclesiastical certification equivalent to the *mandatum*?" (Fr. Strynkowski, *www.mandata.org*, February 20, 2001). This site *ranks* Catholic colleges, seminaries and universities in the U.S. from zero to five stars according to their "MQ" or "*mandatum* quotient"—calculated as a percentage of theologians employed by a particular Catholic college or university who have received a canonical *mandatum*. It is entirely conceivable that significant numbers of Catholics, prospective students and their parents, will use such means to select schools based on their MQ which, in the popular mind, may be perceived as a valid indicator of "Catholicity."

stature of Rahner and Lonergan regularly taught with a canonical mission or its equivalent, suggests that it is possible to have both ecclesiastical control and a high level of theological research, and offers some useful clues as to how a balanced approach might be achieved that is fair and just toward Catholic higher education in the United States:

> [T]he prevailing secular model of academic freedom, as described by standard authorities, requires some modification before being applied to Catholic or other church-related institutions. The model shows signs of having been constructed as a laudable but one-sided purpose of protecting university professors from incompetent outside authorities, who might unjustly seek to impose their own ideas. This model overlooks the responsibility of theology to the community of faith and the mandate of the ecclesiastical magisterium to assure the doctrinal soundness of theology.
>
> The secular model, moreover, is somewhat narrowly based on a theory of knowledge more suited to the empirical sciences than to theology, which rests primarily on divine revelation. The dogmas of faith do not have the same status in theology as currently accepted theories have for secular science. Those who practice theology with the conviction that revealed truth exists and is reliably translated by authoritative sources will see the need to work out a properly theological concept of academic freedom. Such an adapted version will protect authentic theology but will not separate theologians from the body of the Church; it will not set them in opposition to the community of faith or its pastoral leadership. Theologians and bishops, in spite of their different roles in the Church, are fundamentally allies because they are alike committed to maintain and explore the unfathomable riches of Christ, in whom alone is given the truth that makes us free.[55]

There is no simple solution. However, it is fair to caution scholars who may be contemplating Catholic studies initiatives at non-Catholic colleges to avoid the tendency of some Catholics and evangelical Christians who absolutize the culturally relative, even in the name of Christ.[56] Highly charged polemics are not only historically suspect and often promote less than the best scholarship, they also contribute unnecessarily to the natural tension that already exists between Christian scholarship and other voices within the academic community. It is also incumbent upon Catholic Church officials to be careful not to stifle the Catholic intellectual tradition by placing excessive oversight and controls on initiatives, which, by their very nature, should be

---

[55] Avery Dulles, S.J., *The Craft of Theology: From Symbol to System* (New York: Crossroad, 1995), pp. 176–77.

[56] Marsden, *The Outrageous Idea of Christian Scholarship*, p. 100.

vibrant, dynamic, and in some sense evolutionary.[57] It is equally essential, however, that Catholic studies programs continually seek to maintain and preserve that middle ground which seeks to avoid the sort of collegial breakdown and programmatic atrophy that one often associates with extreme forms of conservatism, radical liberalism, or confusing agendas that attempt to incorporate a wide spectrum of views under one faculty umbrella. While such formulas may succeed in the selection of faculty for other disciplines, the nature of Catholic studies requires a faculty that at least shares a faith commitment to the tradition they teach, research and serve.[58]

Although the shape of Catholic studies at non-Catholic colleges and universities already seems to conjure up an inexhaustible variety of possible approaches, there are several strategies for its study and implementation that appear especially promising:

1) Organizations such as FADICA that promote or support Catholic eleemosynary activities are already urging foundations and individuals to invest in endowed chairs in Catholic studies (presumably at non-Catholic as well as Catholic colleges), and are looking closely at Catholic students who attend non-Catholic colleges as an under-served population. According to Marsden, endowing chairs is a proactive way to counter the prevailing trend in the academic culture today, in which faculty tend to hire people like themselves, a practice that could eventually obliterate loyalties to any distinctive religious heritage. "Instead of encouraging pious donors to finance a new steeple for the chapel, administrators might encourage the endowment of such a chair." Judging by the dozen or so endowed chairs in Catholic studies at non-Catholic institutions, this seems an appropriate means in some instance of "testing the waters" to estimate student interest prior to making a major investment in a full-bodied Catholic studies program or institute.[59]

---

[57] Consider how Catholic philosophy and theology might have been diminished, perhaps irreparably, if Bishop of Paris Étienne Tempier's Condemnation of 1277 had not been overturned, since it directly though posthumously affected the work of Thomas Aquinas (who drew heavily upon Averröes' commentaries on Aristotle). Bishops and their curial assistants, especially since *Ex Corde Ecclesiae* gives the Church more "muscle" over the Catholic sector of American higher education, would do well to resist the urge to move in haste against any Catholic theologian on the basis of technical matters in which they may not be fully competent. See Dulles, *The Craft of Theology: From Symbol to System*, pp. 174–75.

[58] In addition to teaching and research functions, Catholic studies faculty serve as role models and mentors to students. There is also debate about whether a theologian must be a believer—an important question since nearly every aspect of Catholic studies involves theology to some extent. See Marsden, *The Outrageous Idea of Christian Scholarship*, p. 168.

[59] Marsden, *The Outrageous Idea of Christian Scholarship*, p. 106.

2) Existing scholarly institutes that support the concept of Catholic studies, e.g., *Collegium* at Fairfield University, Fairfield, Connecticut,[60] and the Institute of Catholic Studies at John Carroll University, Cleveland, Ohio,[61] which until now understandably have been mainly concerned with the creation and development of Catholic Studies programs of various models for students enrolled at Catholic colleges and universities, may enlarge their vision to proactively encourage Catholic studies initiatives at non-Catholic schools, and especially to share with potential leaders of such initiatives the practical wisdom resulting from their experiences with Catholic studies at Catholic colleges.

3) New academic organizations such as the recently proposed Institute for Advanced Catholic Studies[62] may assist Catholic intellectuals in sorting out their differences and helping to clarify the need for Catholic studies initiatives at non-Catholic colleges and universities.

4) Scholarly studies are needed that focus on recent and current initiatives to endow chairs and promote programs in Catholic studies at non-Catholic colleges and universities. Especially useful would be studies that provide insights into successful efforts to develop a suitable philosophy of education and mission statement, setting goals, recognizing the true sources of support and resistance, and finding successful ways of breaking down barriers to Catholic studies, organizational development, and curriculum concerns. To engage in research along these and similar lines would be an appropriate activity for communities of scholars such as faculty associated with the Higher Education Program at Boston College, or with secular institutes such as Penn State University's Center for the Study of Higher Education.

5) Another area where research could produce useful findings is to explore successful approaches to higher education organization outside the United States, especially in cases where Catholic studies are pursued within larger institutional contexts that are state supported. One example that comes to mind as a stellar example of successful symbiosis between explicitly Catholic

---

[60] The *Collegium* program, located at Fairfield University, Fairfield, Connecticut includes an annual colloquy and is self-described as "a joint effort by over 50 Catholic colleges and universities to recruit and develop faculty who can articulate and enrich the spiritual and intellectual life of their institutions" (www.fairfield.edu/collegiu).

[61] Directed by Francesco C. Cesareo, the Institute of Catholic Studies hosted a national conference on Catholic studies in March 2000. In its magazine, *Prism*, the Institute describes its mission, in part, as follows: " . . . to promote serious reflection on the Catholic intellectual tradition and its place within the academic mission of the university. . . ." (*Prism*, no. 5 [Summer 2000], p. 33).

[62] The Institute for Advanced Catholic Studies is temporarily located in Greensburg, Pennsylvania (www.ifacs.com).

and public higher education is the combination of St. Michael's College, St. Augustine's Seminary, the Pontifical Institute of Mediaeval Studies, and the Christianity and Culture Programme, each of which is a component of (or has close ties with) the University of Toronto, Canada's premier public research university. As Avery Dulles notes, "[I]n many other religiously pluralistic countries, such as Germany, Holland, Australia, and Canada, there seems to be no difficulty about teaching Catholic and Protestant theology in publicly funded state universities."[63]

6) Research from a legal perspective could be useful in exposing the facts and the best legal opinions concerning church-state relations and the implications, if any, of various types of charters and organizational structures upon the successful implementation of Catholic studies in American higher education situated within larger private or public non-Catholic environments.

7) Finally, definitive statements from regional accrediting authorities would go far toward clarifying the processes necessary for various organizational models of Catholic studies initiatives to acquire full accreditation. Sample curricula and articulation agreements would also be helpful to administrators who are attempting to piece together Catholic studies initiatives in unusual or unique circumstances.

SUMMARY AND CONCLUSION

According to Neuhaus and others, American Catholics have reached a moment in history that may determine whether the future of the Catholic intellectual tradition will be to play a vital and effective role in mainstream American political and intellectual life, or whether its influence will fade as has the Protestant leadership of America's past. The single most crucial factor in determining the outcome of the "Catholic moment" will be the health of Catholic scholarship (i.e., higher education research, teaching and service). As Marsden suggests, Christian scholarship will only realize its potential if it can establish a strong institutional base.[64] Without in any way denigrating or compromising the outstanding contribution made by Catholic colleges and universities and by theological, philosophical, and historical studies at those schools, it is absolutely essential that Catholic scholarship build a broader base—if only to reach the vast majority of college-age Catholic Americans. And while one can only speculate about

[63] Dulles, *The Craft of Theology*, p. 162.
[64] Marsden, *The Outrageous Idea of Christian Scholarship*, p. 101.

the longevity of the crucial "moment" it can be stated without hesitation that the need is urgent.[65]

Regardless of how Catholic intellectuals may construe the "Catholic moment," a compelling argument can be made for inaugurating Catholic studies in American non-Catholic colleges and universities. In brief, the argument can be stated as follows:

Assuming Catholics can agree that American Catholicism has something to say to American individual and political life, and/or to the perception of reality (or formation) of the next generation of Americans;

And further assuming the centrality of higher learning as the focal point of any effort to inform the consciences of young people and lead them to the virtuous life, however it may be defined or understood;

Then, some form of Catholic studies is needed to carry out the task;

And since more than 86% of all traditional-age college students who identify themselves as Catholics nevertheless attend state-supported or private non-Catholic colleges or universities;

Therefore, the best opportunity to seize the "Catholic moment" is for Catholic leaders to provide opportunity and access for all young Catholics and lifelong learners to study their intellectual heritage—even as Catholic intellectuals may among themselves continue to debate the context and meaning of "Catholic" studies.

The vast majority of America's 220 Catholic colleges and universities were founded to provide access to a distinctively "Catholic" education for effectively marginalized Catholics. Today Catholic life, insofar as it stands in contrast with the dominant American culture, must be made accessible through additional means. Certainly there is a place for Catholic colleges and universities. But there needs to be something more. And this "more" is to inaugurate Catholic studies at non-Catholic colleges and universities, thereby preserving and sustaining the "Catholic moment"—the potential for Catholics *as* Catholics, through greater and more effective participation in American higher learning, to profoundly influence the future course of America's intellectual and cultural life.

---

[65] A shortage of excellent teachers would alone be sufficient to bring to a rapid stop any movement for Catholic studies in public universities, yet this may occur within a decade unless the current trend is reversed. Notably, a fall 1998 survey of philosophy department heads at U.S. Catholic colleges and universities warns of a near-term shortage of Catholic scholars in this core discipline for Catholic studies programs. See Paul J. Weithman, "Philosophy at Catholic Colleges and Universities in the United States: The Results of the ACPA-Notre Dame Survey," *Proceedings of the American Catholic Philosophical Association* 73 (2000), p. 312.

PART IV

SOCIETY AND CULTURE

The Natural Restoration of Fallen Angels in the Depths of Evil: Concerning the Obscure Origins of Absolute Human Autonomy in Political Philosophy

James V. Schall, S.J.

The sin of the Angel does not presuppose either ignorance or error in the functioning of the intellect as such. His sin thereby reveals to us the frightening and, as it were, infinite power proper to free will. That will can choose evil in full light, by a purely voluntary act, and without the intellect's being victim of any previous error.[1]

—Jacques Maritain

Lucifer, without doubt, will be the last one changed. For a time, he will be alone in the abyss, and he will believe that he is the only one condemned to endless torment. But for him one will also pray and cry out. And in the end, he too will be restored in the natural order alone; he will be restored despite himself to the natural love of God, carried by a miracle into Limbo where the night sparkles with stars. There he will take up again his office of prince—forever reproved, in regard to glory; loved again, in regard to nature.[2]

—Jacques Maritain

[1] Jacques Maritain, *The Sin of the Angel*, trans. William L. Rossner, S. J. (Westminster, Maryland: The Newman Press, 1959), p. 9.

[2] "Lucifer sans doute sera le dernier changé. Pendant un temps il sera seul dans l'abîme, et se croira le seul condamné aux tourments sans fin, et son orgueil sera sans bornes. Mais pour lui aussi on priera, on criera. Et à la fin lui aussi sera restitué au bien, dans l'ordre de la seule nature, rendu malgré lui à l'amour naturel de Dieu, porté par miracle dans ces Limbes dont la nuit brille d'étoiles. Il y reprendra son office de prince—reprouvé toujours, au regard de la gloire; aimé de nouveau, au regard de la nature" (Jacques Maritain, *Approches sans Entraves* [Paris: Fayard, 1973], p. 28).

[The Angels] knew that God Himself and God alone is the primary object of this happiness and that the vision is in no way interrupted by the existence of any neighbour nor by any number of them. Yet they [the fallen angels] prefer that lower good which is possessed as a privilege of their angelic nature or as wholly personal, to a good common to many and dispensed according to the free choice of God Himself Who can make the last first and the first last.[3]

—Charles De Koninck

I

A t first sight, social and political philosophy would seem to have little interest in or appreciation of presumably baffling theological and philosophical discussions about the inner lives of what Aristotle called "separated substances" or of what revelation called angels. Yet, St. Thomas was not called "the angelic doctor" for nothing. He understood that the relations among divine, angelic, and human things were delicate, and that, to recall Aristotle, a slight error in the beginning of such matters could, in some unexpected place, lead to a huge error in the end. That is to say, what we believe or argue about the ultimate destiny of angels might well, on examination, indicate something of what we maintain about the destiny and nature of human society and the rational, finite beings who make it up.

G. K. Chesterton, likewise, was particularly struck by Aquinas's speculative endeavors concerning the being, mind, and final fate of the angels. "St. Thomas was rather specially interested in the nature of Angels, for the same reason that made him even more interested in the nature of Men," Chesterton pointed out in his *St. Thomas Aquinas*. "It was a part of that strong personal interest in things subordinate and semi-dependent, which runs through his whole system: a hierarchy of higher and lower liberties. He was interested in the problem of the Angel, as he was interested in the problem of the Man, because it was a problem; and especially because it was a problem of an intermediate creature."[4] The two principal intermediate creatures, no doubt, *pace* animal and vegetable rights folks, are angels and men, the finite, rational beings. How can they stand outside of nothingness? How can they be free? Finally, as Maritain put it, what are the consequences, if any, of this "frightening and infinite power proper to free will?" Why "frightening?" Why

---

[3] Charles De Koninck, "In Defense of Saint Thomas," *The Aquinas Review* 4, no. 1 (1997), p. 341. This volume also contains De Koninck's "On the Primacy of the Common Good" and "The Philosophy of the New Order," along with I. Th. Eschmann, O.P.'s "In Defense of Jacques Maritain."

[4] G. K. Chesterton, *St. Thomas Aquinas* (1933; rpt. Garden City, N. Y.: Doubleday Image, 1956), p. 165.

"infinite?" St. Thomas's interest in the "hierarchy of higher and lower liberties" itself suggests some connection in the line of principles of being running through what is common to angels and men. We are, in fact, concerned here with precisely "the higher liberties" and their consequences, consequences that necessarily lead to questions of beatitude and, indeed, to questions of evil.

My immediate concern with this problem of angels comes from corresponding with and reading the many but too-little known writings of E. B. F. Midgley, in Aberdeen, in Scotland.[5] Midgley has long been puzzled by certain obscurities in Maritain. He has not yet written a final study on his position, but he has indicated the basic problem he sees in Maritain as it is occasioned, in particular, by his explanations of the fate of the fallen angels. Much as Midgley appreciates many of Maritain's insights, he holds that it was in part at least through Maritain's social philosophy that there came into Christian social teachings an unwelcome undercurrent of autonomous liberalism or relativism. In turn, this modernity undermined any permanent order of secondary causes with their relation to the truths of reason and revelation.[6] The problem centers around one meaning of the word "personalism" that, as

[5] Professor Midgley has been for some time at work on his *magnum opus*, a long awaited multi-volume history of political philosophy from the point of view of St. Thomas. The following are among Midgley's principal published works: *The Natural Law Tradition and the Theory of International Relations* (London: Elek, 1975); *The Ideology of Max Weber: A Thomist Critique* (Totowa, New Jersey: Barnes & Noble Books, 1983); *Hobbes: Leviathan* (Alcalá: Crítica Filosófica, 1988); "Natural Law and Fundamental Rights," *American Journal of Jurisprudence* 21 (1976), pp. 144–65; "Concerning the Modernist Subversion of Political Philosophy," *New Scholasticism* 53 (Spring 1979), pp. 168–90; "On 'Substitute Intelligences' in the Formation of Atheist Ideology," *Laval théologique et philosophique* 36 (October 1980), pp. 239–53; "The Crisis of Modernity in the Theory of International Relations," *Year Book of World Affairs* 36 (1981), pp. 235–47; "Man's Knowledge of Truth vis-à-vis the History of Ideology: Some Reflections on Thomistic Anthropology," *Anthropología Tomista*, in vol. 3 *Atti del IX Congresso Tomistico Internazionale* (Vatican City, 1991), pp. 416–24.

[6] On this point, Midgley recommends the reading of Hamish Fraser, "Jacques Maritain and Saul Alinsky: Fathers of the 'Christian' Revolution," Supplement to *Approaches*, no. 71 (Saltcote, Scotland, 1980). This essay contains an English translation of R. Th. Calmel, O.P.'s review of *Approches sans Entraves*, from *Itinéraires*, no. 181, March 1974. Calmel writes, "The book is composed, in equal parts, of teaching which is faithful to classical Thomism and of his own creation which can be called Maritainism; and more than once the two are inextricably mixed. So on the one hand we have excellent summaries of the great genuine Thomism . . . and also general explanations which probe Thomism in its proper direction. . . . Side by side with the great professor of Thomism . . . is the Maritain that must be called Maritainism: the Maritain of theories, '*approches*' or *essays* which aim at directing Thomist doctrine along the deviating lines of the moderns" (p. 57).

De Koninck intimated, subordinated all common goods, including the divine one, to human personality. It also deals with a certain independent autonomy in the natural being of angels that would exaggerate the power of reason to direct us to or deflect us from the good, the proper object of the will. Included in this problem also is the degree to which Maritain was successful in relating modern natural rights, with their origins in Hobbes, to classic natural law.

Midgley's problem, however, arises most graphically from Maritain's treatment of the sin of the angels together with the final fate of Lucifer. Midgley's apprehension, if I understand him at all correctly, concerns Maritain's later reflections on eschatological subjects found in *Approches sans Entraves* (1973). However curiously presented as mere musings of an old philosopher to the Brothers in Toulouse, in no way intended to contradict any position of revelation, these philosophical speculations were in fact indicative of a deeper problem.[7] Maritain was said to have left the uncorrected galleys of these passages on the angels on his desk just before he died as a very old man in his 90s.

These "essays" on eschatology, it is said, help explain those tendencies in Maritain's social philosophy that made it, unexpectedly, an opening to the left, as it is called. By the "left" in this context, I mean any view that derives its understanding of the world from autonomous will, itself not dependent on reality.[8] Hence, this view uses essentially ungrounded ideology to refashion the world in its own image of order. This endeavor is unrestricted by *what is* or by lessons of experience. Maritain, of course, considered himself to be and in general was a realist. The problem was whether these angelic reflections did not in fact undermine at certain points the very grounds of his realism. This is the issue about which I shall attempt to make some sense.

If we look at Maritain's whole career, no doubt, he is usually understood early on to have begun rather as a man of the right with *Action Française.*

---

[7] See *Approches sans Entraves: "Avant-Propos*," pp. 3–5 and "*Imagerie*," pp. 7–8.

[8] "[T]wo senses of the words 'right' and 'left,' a physiological sense and a political sense. In the first sense one is of the 'right' or of the 'left' by a disposition of temperament. . . . The pure man of the left detests being, always preferring, in principle, in the words of Rousseau, *what is not* to *what is*. The pure man of the right detests justice and charity, always preferring, in principle, in the words of Goethe . . . *injustice* to *disorder*. Nietzsche is a noble and a beautiful example of the man of the right, and Tolstoy, of the man of the left. In the second sense, the political sense, left and right designate ideals, energies, and historic formations into which the men of these two opposing temperaments are normally drawn to group themselves. . . . There are no more dreadful revolutions than revolutions of the left carried out by men of the rightist temperament (Lenin). There are no weaker governments than governments of the right run by leftist temperaments (Louis XVI)" (Jacques Maritain, *The Peasant of the Garonne: An Old Layman Questions Himself about the Present Time*, trans. Michael Cuddihy and Elizabeth Hughes [New York: Hold, Rinehart and Winston, 1968], pp. 21–22).

Subsequently, he became, with *Integral Humanism,* more of a man of the left, verged back to a man of the center with his wartime and post-wartime writings such as *Christianity and Democracy, The Rights of Man and Natural Law,* or *Man and the State,* and was even a conservative with his book, *Reflections on America.* Finally, in the minds of many on the left, he was seen as a candidate for a man of the right again with his *Peasant of the Garonne,* in which he was critical of Teilhard de Chardin and many post-Vatican II movements in the Church. Midgley does not like this pat schema. He finds a rather contrary philosophic undercurrent in Maritain that exists in parallel with his admittedly correct interpretations of Aquinas. This "secondary" current would place Maritain more in conformity with certain strands of modern ideology at variance with natural law than would at first sight seem possible because of his Thomist positions.

Indeed, in a similar concern, even *Man and the State* is seen by the Hungarian philosopher, Aurel Kolnai, in a recently republished 1951 review, to indicate the problem that bothers Midgley. "My quarrel with Maritain is not, then, that he is too partial to 'Caesar,' be it a Christian or even a pagan 'Caesar,'" Kolnai wrote, "but that he would abolish Caesar altogether and *therefore* conjure up the spectre of an infinitely worse Caesar who, as it were, has expropriated the transcendent God and swallowed up the spiritual substance of Christ."[9] Theology and *sapientia* thus become anthropology. Again such concerns, on their first hearing, are surprising since Maritain's whole philosophic work seems ordered to rejecting such a Hegelian, Feuerbachian, and totalitarian alternative. Let me see if I can get to the bottom of this disquiet of Midgley and Kolnai.

II

The idea of the eventual salvation of the devil has a long history. Its classic source appears to be Origen (185–254 A.D.), who seems first to have broached the topic of the eventual salvation of Satan and all the damned, angelic and human.[10] It is a heady game, one that regularly recurs in the history

[9] Aurel Kolnai, "Between Christ and the Idols of Modernity: A Review of Jacques Maritain's *Man and the State*," in *Privilege and Liberty and Other Essays in Political Philosophy*, ed. Daniel J. Mahoney (Lanham, Maryland: Lexington Books, 1999), p. 179.

[10] "Si quis dicit aut sentit, Dominum Christum in futuro saeculo crucifixum iri pro daemonibus, sicuti pro hominibus, A. S." Virgilius, 537, "*Canones adversus Origenem*," Denziger, 209. "Si quis dicit aut sentit, ad tempus esse daemonum et impiorum hominum supplicium, eiusque finem aliquando futurum, sive restitutionem et redintegrationem (αποκατάστασιν) fore daemonum aut impiorum hominum, A. S" (Denziger, 211).

of philosophy and religion. It is not unknown, indeed it is quite popular, in some form or other in contemporary theology, though the nuances of the arguments need to be attended to. What seems ultimately to be at stake here is the significance of free acts of finite and free creatures, of whether it makes any real difference in some transcendent sense what we think or do. The link between act and consequences seems jeopardized by making less significant an objective order in which human or angelic acts take place.

Nor is this concern unrelated to classical Pelagianism which seems to propose a self-salvation that elevates human nature to a power that it does not possess by itself, the power to achieve one's own salvation by oneself. At bottom, I think, these are among the issues that worry Midgley about Maritain's position on the sin and subsequent curious restoration of the fallen angels to their previous natural state, as if they had never been offered a higher end. Nor did they seem to suffer as a result of their rejection of it except, perhaps, for their awareness of their loss.

Maritain's own particular hypothesis, that again he presents as a "would it not be nice if" sort of argument, presupposes certain doctrines in classical theology that are seldom heard of since Vatican II, most noticeably, the doctrine of Limbo. But this doctrine, whatever we might think of it, had a perfectly intelligible origin and, in that form, suited Maritain's later arguments about "the end of Satan." If we suppose that the doctrine of Limbo has no speculative grounding whatever, then, no doubt, Maritain's solution will not hold. Yet, how Maritain dealt with this issue can still provide great insight into his own philosophy.

Limbo specifically meant that certain innocent un-baptized infants, in particular, those who do not perform any formally rational acts in their lives and who die before possibly doing anything, would not receive the beatific vision promised to all the faithful baptized. Rather, they would spend eternity in that natural place reserved for mankind had it not fallen and been elevated by grace to the supernatural vision of God. The point at issue here is simply that a form of natural happiness could be envisioned that would be due to a given creature, even though in fact such a natural creation was never put into effect by God from the beginning. In this hypothesis, there could be no complaint if this creature did not receive something gratuitous beyond its natural due. Hence worry about the "pains of Hell" would be ultimately mitigated. God would, as it were, be exonerated from having to punish anyone for anything he did since everyone would simply follow his own nature.

With this teaching in mind, let us see how Maritain proposed to use it. An ancient accusation against God implied that He somehow was a failure if He could not in fact save or redeem all creatures that were, by His original intention in creation, promised eternal life if they obeyed Him. Maritain is careful throughout his discussion of evil to make angelic or human choice, not God, to be responsible for any de facto rejection of God. Thus the failure, if there be a failure, is not on the side of God. This attainment of God's original purpose in creation, to associate other rational beings in His own inner life, thus had to face the problem of free will, angelic and human. Any gift could be rejected by an authentically free being. Of course, without such free-willed creature, no high drama would exist in the universe. Everything would be determined by non-free agents, assuming such a universe without free will is conceivable. Thus, we must be careful to keep clear what is at stake here. On this point, Maritain at times proposes a God so all-powerful that He can, if He chose, bring any free creature to His desired end. But normally, he thought, God did not act in this way but left free creatures in their own environment. However, Maritain, particularly in the case of Satan, does not propose that he be transported to the same destiny granted to the angels who did not fall.

Rather, what Maritain proposes is Limbo as a fit place for the fallen angels and men. Limbo has the psychological advantage of implying no real, continued, or eternal punishment. He maintains, with classic teaching, that the all-powerful God loves all that He has created, including the "being," but not the sin, of the damned angels and men. However, God, in consequence of His power and love, can nevertheless restore or elevate fallen creatures, even those who positively and definitively rejected Him. God could, without contradiction, it is argued, transport damned beings from Hell to Limbo. If God can perform this feat, why should He not do it? Therefore, He would do it. This is the impression with which we are left in reading Maritain's reflections on the "end of Satan." That Satan still would have a sense of missing out on something greater, Maritain does not deny. But something drastic has evidently changed in the universe. On the basis of this thesis, granted it is only a "musing," the ultimate worry of real damnation, of real seriousness about our responsible acts, is mitigated or eliminated.

At this point, it is also worth noticing that, in the chapter of *Notebooks* entitled, "Apropos of the Church in Heaven," dated 1963, Maritain has a related reflection concerning the proportionate number of the damned and the saved. It would seem that his further reflections about Lucifer are a logical outcome of his efforts to save most, if not all, people no matter how forceful the counter-argument from Scripture or tradition might appear against his position. Maritain points out that for Augustine, based on his reading of human nature, few could be expected to be saved. He adds that Aquinas agreed with this argument: "Because the vision of God exceeds the common state of human nature—which moreover and above all bears the wounds of original sin—*pauciores sunt qui salvantur*, the chosen are fewer in number than the damned."[11] This conclusion has seldom been greeted as a happy one. Though it may in fact be the truth, it leaves us with the impression of either a harsh or impotent God, an impression Maritain wants to mitigate or efface.

Arguing on the basis of the Cross, of the fact that in principle mercy is higher than justice, Maritain suggests that there were more saved than damned. "I am persuaded that the idea of the *greater number of the chosen* imposes itself and will impose itself more and more on the Christian conscience."[12] Maritain did not argue at this point that his new thesis necessarily excluded "a great number in Hell," but they were outnumbered by an even more vast array of saved. However, he did suggest that the teaching that a greater number were in Hell caused most people to lose hope, surely not the intention of a revelation of love. It also tended to break the link between the Church Militant and the Church Triumphant.

III

In retrospect, it seems clear, whatever be its truth, that Maritain's feeling about what most Christians have come to hold on this issue seems largely correct. Hell itself and the greater number of damned in it are seldom mentioned today. That anyone at all might be damned is, in fact, embarrassing for most people and is presented as contrary to God's love. But the point I am making here is simply that Maritain's thought did direct him both in philosophy and theology towards a view of the world in which, whatever they did, most, if not all rational beings, would be saved, or at least exempted from real and lasting punishment on the basis of their acts. This position would seem to lessen the grandeur of human choice. In spite of his consistent teaching that God is never the cause of evil, Maritain makes God to appear rather heartless *if* He does not follow this theory about subsequently mitigating the punishment of the damned.

Some flavor of the background of Maritain's thinking can be gathered from this rather poignant passage from *God and the Permission of Evil*:

> In proportion as the conscience of men, under the very influence of Christianity, became more sensible of the dignity of the human person and of the outrages which are inflicted on him by evil, while on the other hand the dimensions of evil, of injustice, of cruelty, of all the kinds of

[11] Jacques Maritain, *Notebooks,* trans. Joseph Evans (Albany, New York: Magi Books, 1984), p. 270.
[12] Ibid., p. 271.

crimes at work in history were made more and more revealed in it in depth as well as in extension . . . — in proportion, consequently, as such a process developed, the problem of evil has taken on a more tragic importance for the human conscience. It is this problem which is at the origin of many forms of atheism, at the origin also of what one could call in many the bewildered Christian's conscience.[13]

Through his theory of Limbo, Maritain evidently wishes to "un-bewilder" the Christian conscience by explaining how the finite creature can choose evil and at the same time have any consequences for doing so mitigated.

Behind all of this reflection on Satan's ultimate status lies Maritain's understanding of the sin of the angel. He proposes what seems like a unique theory, namely, that even in a state of pure nature, the autonomy of the angel could reject God even though God in creation had given this creature everything it could rightly expect to achieve its natural end. Maritain points out that the Thomist school in general did not think that angels in a purely natural order, "because of the perfection of their intelligence and wills," would have been able to sin. They were "potentially peccable" but only "in relation to a purely possible supernatural order."[14] However, for Maritain, neither in theory or practice is there any natural impeccability. This position seems, at first sight, logical enough, namely, that all finite beings can and therefore some or many probably will fail at times.

However, this position runs into difficulty with another account of the nature of the fall. This view would argue that, in their original state, angels were offered something higher than their own natural end, that is, the contemplation of God by their own powers. Had this higher end not been offered, none would have sinned, not even Satan. But they were offered the beatific vision. Had they not been offered something that they could reject, they would not have fallen in any sense. That is, they would have naturally, in practice, been "impeccable" because they would have had no reason to choose something else other than the natural happiness for which they were ordained by nature and in which they rejoiced. "From the moment that created persons are naturally peccable, there will be some who will in fact sin. . . . Hence, we must conclude that in fact God would not have created nature if He had not ordained it to grace and to that charity by which man becomes, under grace, freely the friend of God, and that sin is the ransom of glory."[15] The apparent denial of this possibility of a practical impeccability is one of the main points

[13] Maritain, *God and the Permission of Evil,* trans. Joseph W. Evans (Milwaukee, Wisconsin: Bruce Publishing Company, 1966), p. 3.

[14] Maritain, *The Sin of the Angel,* p. 39.

[15] Ibid., pp. 37–38.

at issue here. Paradoxically, this denial serves not to lessen but to elevate the autonomy of angelic nature even beyond its initial powers. This same elevation seems to lessen both the power and providence of God with regard to His actual creation and its initial purposes. This is what concerns Midgley.

It is often held that the reason why the angels, Lucifer in particular, fell was because they inordinately loved their own good, a genuine good, no doubt, in preference to the beatific vision, a gift, a gift not "due" to them, but capable of being freely received by them in grace should it so be offered by God. It was also held that the angels, by their own natural knowledge, could not *not* know that they were not God. This issue is often cast in the form of their rejecting, as something beneath them, the idea of an Incarnation whereby God became man, on the whole, a rather vile creature. They saw God's offering of His inner life as a gift to angels and men to be contrary to their own peculiar but real glory. They denied a good common to all, a good not exclusively theirs. The fall, thus, would not have happened, that is, there would have been no angels who did not reach their natural end had they not been offered something higher that they must, in the act of its being offered to them, either accept or reject. It is to be noted, in this sense, that God might be blamed for offering natural creatures something more than themselves. There is a kind of incipient philosophic individualism present here.

This account of the fall is, no doubt, the ultimate origin of the City of God and the City of Man in Augustine's sense. Paradoxically, it differs from Maritain's account by rejecting one part of his notion of the expected fall of angels in the natural order. It does not think this natural fall would in fact have happened. And here lies the root of the concern that Maritain, in this discussion, reveals an autonomy of natural creatures over against the power and omniscience of God, an autonomy that would, in fact, have no serious consequences if even Satan ended up in Limbo and not Hell.

IV

What are we to make of these considerations? We might simply say that they are the reflections of an old man that never should have been published as they are contrary to his normal teachings. However, such thoughts of Maritain are apparently not just thoughts of his old age. Moreover, it seems to be quite true that in his normal presentation of how evil is freely chosen by finite creatures, he gives a standard Thomist explanation.[16] For example in *God and the Permission of Evil*, Maritain assigns the following explanation of

---

[16] Jacques Maritain, *St. Thomas and the Problem of Evil* (Milwaukee, Wisconsin: Marquette University Press, 1942).

why free creatures find themselves in Hell. In this account, we find no hint that this final condition is likely to be changed by a subsequent act of God reducing the sentence, as it were, of the fallen creature. "It is through their (the condemned's) fault and by reason of their demerits that they will have been less loved," Maritain wrote:

> I have already noted that St. Thomas takes great care to call them the fore-known (and not the "negatively-condemned"!). God knows from all eternity that they will be, that they are condemned—but not because He would have condemned them in advance, even negatively; on the contrary it is they who have refused God. It is *post praevisa demerita*, "after" their "fore"-seen demerits that they are condemned, because they have withdrawn from divine grace by their free initiative of nihilating the first cause. In short, it is they themselves who have "discerned" or discriminated themselves for evil and for Hell, when at the end of their life they have irrevocably shattered the last grace offered. At that time they have forever preferred their own grandeur—to be to themselves their last end—to the supernatural beatitude which presupposes the love of God over and above all. They prefer Hell even while cursing it. They have that which they willed, that which they have themselves chosen as the supreme good; they have put their beatitude in themselves and they will hold fast to it, they are fixed in aversion to God.[17]

In this passage, as far as I can ascertain, we find little hint that at least some of the creatures who are in Hell because of their own acts will be "restored" in some fashion. It seems that this is their permanent location because of the nature of these acts. That is, they are where they ought to be, granted the nature of what they chose, that is, basically themselves over the gift offered to them.

Maritain's presentation of the "end of Satan," then, does make perplexing reading. If we can take him seriously, which is indeed a question, his "musings" would appear to provide a theory whereby there would, in fact, be no eternal punishment in the normal sense of that term as it has been understood in tradition.[18] Technically speaking, Maritain's position is not "heretical." We often hear stated the paradox that we must believe there is a Hell, but we do not have to believe anyone is in it. Assuming that the evidence of revelation does not in fact suggest that at least some, if not many, are in fact in Hell due

---

[17] Maritain, *God and the Permission of Evil*, p. 109.

[18] The following short passage from James Boswell indicates the view that a lack of transcendent punishment might have civil and social effects: "He (Samuel Johnson) strenuously opposed an argument by Sir Joshua Reynolds, that virtue was preferable to vice, considering this life only; and that a man would be virtuous were it only to preserve his character" (*Boswell's Life of Johnson* [London: Oxford, 1931], II, p. 259).

to their own choices of themselves, we might let Maritain's position go at that, a position with which he himself seems to disagree in his more direct teachings on evil and its consequences. At bottom, in Maritain, we see a very nuanced theory about the outcome of evil. His thesis about the end of Satan does, when spelled out, tend to separate, in the name of the divine goodness and mercy, free acts from their ultimate and expected effects in a manner that does not imply acknowledgment and forgiveness. Logically, knowledge of this happier ending would apparently lessen any solemnity or seriousness about the objective order of natural laws and commandments. Their deliberate violations would have no overly worrisome effect, granted that the loss of beatific vision itself, as a gift, could be something distressing.

V

What remains to be examined about this position concerning the possible restoration of even the damned is the social or political implications such a view might have. Again, this might seem like an odd intellectual endeavor. There is a passage in Robert Browning that reads, "Infinite mercy, but, I wish, Infinite mercy, but, I wish, as infinite a justice too."[19] Justice, of course, is the political virtue, mercy a theological one. They do not blot each other out. Thomism, no doubt, strives to keep the distinction between mercy and justice in such a way as to preserve the essential meaning of both in a coherent view of the whole. Maritain's studies in social and political philosophy were intended to take what was good in modernity and relate it systematically with St. Thomas and the general Catholic tradition of social thought. Maritain thought this reconciliation could be smoothly accomplished on a principled basis.

At first sight, Maritain's social philosophy is quite tough-minded. His well-known critique of Machiavelli, the first and perhaps still the most disruptive of the modern political thinkers, sought to blend intelligence, strength, and morality.[20] Maritain seems to have to have had no delusions about the evil depths to which bad leaders and corrupt morals can lead a society, however sympathetic he was to the people involved. At the end of his

---

[19] Robert Browning, "The Heretic's Tragedy" in *The Poems and Plays by Robert Browning,* 1844–64, vol. 2 (New York: E. P. Dutton & Co., Inc., 1928), i, 4, p. 433.

[20] Jacques Maritain, "The End of Machiavellianism," in *Social and Political Philosophy of Jacques Maritain,* eds. Joseph Evans and Leo R. Ward (Notre Dame, Indiana: University of Notre Dame Press, 1976), pp. 292–325. See James V. Schall, "Justice, Brains, and Strength," in *Jacques Maritain: The Philosopher in Society* (Lanham, Maryland: Rowman & Littlefield, 1998), pp. 1–20.

Marquette Lecture, Maritain rather graphically and with some attention to the history of philosophy touched on the importance of considering evil:

> The French socialist, Georges Sorel, who was a friend of Charles Péguy, and whose books were carefully read by Mussolini and by Lenin, and who was fond of theology said one day that the crucial work of the philosophers, in the new age into which we are entering, would consist in recasting and penetrating more deeply into the problem of evil. As a matter of fact, we are surely called upon to build up a theory of evil if we are to interpret philosophically our time.[21]

A "theory" of evil is needed to interpret "philosophically" a given time, "our" time. Maritain added that the theory of St. Thomas on evil provided "the basic principles" for this worthy enterprise.

The notion of "recasting and penetrating more deeply into the problem of evil" must, in retrospect, be seen both in light of Maritain's "essay" on the "end of Satan" and in the light in which public life in modernity has deviated from the good, especially since the time of Maritain's own death, though he was aware of its direction. Does this "recasting" so change the very meaning of evil, however accurately its coming to be may be explained, such that what we normally worry about when doing evil, namely, its consequences, is no longer operative or operative with the same intensity? A theory of the forgiveness of evil, of course, presupposes that something seriously wrong has taken place. Forgiveness is not a mitigation of evil itself, but an acknowledgment of it.

In *Integral Humanism,* in 1936, Maritain wrote, with some evident exasperation: "It is high time for Christians to bring things back to truth, reintegrating in the fullness of their original source those hopes for justice and those nostalgias for communion on which the world's sorrow feeds and which are themselves misdirected, thus awakening a cultural and temporal force of Christian inspiration able to act on history and to be a support to men."[22] Obviously, supporting men and acting in history do relate to justice and communion. Maritain shows a certain impatience here. Earlier Christian thought and action are held to be somehow at fault for "not bringing things back to truth."

Midgley is wont to pose, in this regard, the question of whether Christianity, as a revelation of truth, would be any less true somehow if its basic

---

[21] Maritain, *St. Thomas and the Problem of Evil,* p. 39.

[22] Jacques Maritain, *Integral Humanism: Temporal and Spiritual Problems of a New Christendom,* trans. Joseph W. Evans (Notre Dame, Indiana: University of Notre Dame Press, 1973), p. 6.

principles were never in fact incorporated into some or many cultural histories? If the answer to this question is, in fact, "no," it casts the problem of the success or un-success of culturalization in a different light. Christianity, perhaps, its truth, may not depend on popular or wide-spread acceptance, however nice that might be and however much this seems to be at least an indirect purpose of evangelization. If Christ was rejected in His own time, we cannot think Him a failure if He is rejected in any time. The failure may be due to the rejectors.

This position is not the same as saying that Christianity ought not to be incorporated into a culture if possible, however imperfectly. But it does allow us to keep a certain distance from the criticism of Christianity for failing because it did not in modernity also accomplish a proper cultural and political incarnation. The reason for such a failure might, after all, following Maritain's Thomist explanation of evil, be a free and abiding rejection by actual people of the basic elements of reason and grace that Christianity put into the world. No reader of Augustine would be surprised by this possibility.[23]

The rise of current theologies that propose to save everyone whether baptized or not, whether he holds or practices anything of Christianity or not—the world of interchangeable religious pluralisms—appears to be the result of the un-likelihood of successful Christian evangelization in the contemporary world.[24] If our culture is indeed a "culture of death," however, perhaps it is the last thing into which Christianity ought to be incorporated. The moral decline of our public standards and life, however prosperous, does seem to follow a "logic" by which progressively the rational and moral standards of human worth are overturned in the name of philosophical principles such as "human rights," which have come to mean any arbitrary rule that is proposed and enforced by legislature and courts. Our "humanism" is more secularist or even atheist than what Maritain called "integral." Is it possible that Maritain's underlying optimism that is revealed by the end of even Lucifer made him overly confident about the institutions and principles of modernity which seem, in retrospect, to have been working themselves out inexorably in a direction opposite to that which he might have envisaged following St. Thomas on the primary and secondary principles of natural law and their order?[25]

[23] Robert Kraynak's forthcoming book, *Christian Faith and Modern Democracy: God and Politics in the Fallen World* (Notre Dame, Indiana: The University of Notre Dame Press) re-proposes an Augustinian correction to these trends in Christianity that have been overly open to the theoretical positions of modern democratic theory.

[24] See Jacques Dupuis, *Jesus Christ and the Encounter with World Religions*, trans. Robert Barr (Maryknoll, New York: Orbis, 1991).

[25] See *ST* I-II, q. 94.

Aidan Nichols recalled, however, that Maritain, in a famous chapter, rejected the modern notion of sovereignty as a concept to be applied to the head of state or to society. Sovereignty was originally a theological idea that referred to God. Thus, if we attribute such an idea to the state, as modern political theory often did, we have, implicitly, given the modern state quasi-divine powers, which in fact it often implicitly, at least, claims.[26] Maritain is aware of and often elaborates the dangers of theoretical explications of the state that provide no limits for its scope. Yet, his theory on the end of Satan would seem equally applicable to the end of the most famous of the modern tyrants and their lesser minions. With no effective eternal punishment or deterrent, the distinction between virtue and vice, good and evil, is made less graphic. Once this distinction is in practice diminished, it is difficult to find grounds to reject what was classically called vice and evil.

The question arises, moreover, about whether the democratic state itself had any boundaries so that Maritain's efforts to limit the state through establishment of modern democratic institutions might have had the opposite result.[27] Nichols puts the matter this way:

> Secularism can scarcely be acknowledged by Christians as a good *per se* since the good of the creation (which Christian secularists claim to uphold) is only available to us within the resurrection order which is found restored and then (not a chronological but an ontological "then") transfigured. Secularism . . . was never *voted in* at all. It is simply what happened when traditional societies entered a liberal thought-world. Liberalism is the imposition on the person of the priorities of secularity and prosperity over against deeper needs, and why should that be supinely accepted? To a duty functioning Christian sensibility it can only be an impossible project, for it results from the extreme separation of the supernatural from the natural when in fact these realms interpenetrate utterly.[28]

No doubt, Maritain sought to preserve "the primacy of the spiritual." He did not want such an "extreme separation" of the supernatural and the natural. But if God in His power can blot out the consequences of the acts that are not forgiven by the normal processes in this world, it would seem that Kolnai is right, that there is danger of an absorption of everything into God in such a

---

[26] Aidan Nichols, O. P., *Christendom Awake!* (Grand Rapids, Michigan: Eerdmans, 1999), p. 79. See Jacques Maritain, *Man and the State* (Chicago: The University of Chicago Press, 1951), pp. 28–53.

[27] See James V. Schall, "A Reflection on the Classical Tractate on Tyranny: The Problem of Democratic Tyranny," *American Journal of Jurisprudence* 41 (1996), pp. 1–19.

[28] Nichols, *Christendom Awake!*, p. 80.

way that the distinction between intermediate creatures and God is diminished. Finite freedom, in the end, has little to fear or worry about if its results are of little ultimate consequence.

VI

In his *The Peasant of the Garonne*, Maritain noted that "the history of the world progresses *at the same time* in the line of evil and in the line of good."[29] What is the end of the "line of evil"? In this book, written later in his life (1966), but still a few years before his death (1973), Maritain discussed the question of the temporal end of man on this earth. He thought it a legitimate issue, though not the same as man's ultimate destiny. He was concerned that there be a Christian contribution to this temporal end. Indeed, he held that there must be such a contribution if it were to be achieved at all. However, he did not think that we could produce any perfect society in this world. "The Christian can, and must, ask for the coming of the kingdom of God in glory, but is not entitled to ask for—nor to propose as the end of his temporal activity—a definite advent of justice and peace, and of human happiness, as the term of the progress of temporal history: this progress is not capable of any final term."[30] Maritain thus appears to hold that the world can be improved and indeed is improving with the advent of certain modern democratic institutions. Whatever might happen, this improvement itself is not the Kingdom of God where, presumably, the end of Satan is to be accomplished.

Indeed, Maritain shows himself in *The Peasant of the Garonne* to be rather exasperated by Christians, especially clerics, who after Vatican II, seemed to have been suddenly converted to an inner-worldly project as the essence of Christianity.[31] Parodying ideas that he observed prevalent in the 60s, Maritain wrote:

---

[29] Maritain, *The Peasant of the Garonne*, p. 4.

[30] Ibid., p. 202. "But will the non-Christian (or even the non-Catholic) also understand the meaning and the reason for this distinction, and not be scandalized because in certain instances, the Christian (or the Catholic) must maintain at all costs the autonomy of the spiritual in regard to the temporal, and refuse to transform Christianity into a kind of theocratic agency charged with assuring the well-being of the world, universal peace, pay raises, and free room and board for all?" (ibid., p. 82).

[31] "No one, however, has to look very far to marvel at the resources of human foolishness, and to understand that foolishness and theological faith can certainly keep house in the same brain, and hold a dialogue there—as everybody is doing now with everybody else—even though such contact is likely to prove unhealthy for the latter. I will have to come back to this, although it scarcely amuses me, in order to say something about the neo-modernism that flourishes today" (ibid., p. 2).

The objective content of which the faith of our forefathers clung, all *that* is myth, like original sin for example (isn't our big job today to get rid of the horrendous guilt complex?), and like the Gospel of the Infancy of Christ, the resurrection of the body, and the creation. And the Christ of history, of course. The phenomenological method and form criticism have changed everything. The distinction between human nature and grace is a scholastic invention like transubstantiation. As for hell, why take the trouble to deny it, it is simpler to forget it, and that's probably what we had also better do with the Incarnation and the Trinity. Frankly, do the mass of Christians ever think of these things, or of the immortal soul and the future life?"[32]

I cite this rather acid passage because it does suggest that the basic Christian doctrines were quite operative in Maritain's soul at this time. In particular, he seems to have no problem with hell, but with those who would deny or ignore it. The devil is still an actor—"the world is the domain *at once* of man, of God, and of the devil."[33] Lucifer still seems to be a lost being.

With such observations in mind, what are we to make of the original question, namely, was Maritain's position on the sin of the angel in fact corruptive of his more straight-forward efforts to explain evil and to provide a valid Christian political philosophy? In part, the answer to this question will depend on whether we hold that Maritain's position on the sin of the angel, particularly the end of Satan, was something of an aberration, something so dubious that it need not be taken for the "real" Maritain. Perhaps we can take Maritain's word for it that these were merely tentative "musings" offered as a sort of "play" to see where ideas might lead but with no intention of undermining any basic position in philosophy or theology.[34]

We might also want simply to reject any notion of Limbo so that Maritain's proposed solution simply would not work.[35] Either God's salvific will

---

[32] Ibid., p. 6.

[33] Ibid., p. 35.

[34] Maritain's "Foreword" to *God and the Permission of Evil* (1963) is of some interest in this regard: "This book has grown out of three seminars which I gave in May, 1963, to the Little Brothers of Jesus who take their studies in Toulouse. Their teachers are the theologians of the Dominican House of Studies in Toulouse. My job as a teacher is completely ended; what remains to me to do here on earth is of another order. The seminars in question were simply friendly conversations, altogether personal, by way of play, if I might put it, and by way of goodbye" (p. vii).

[35] "St. Thomas added that children who died un-baptized—before being able, in the act of freedom, to accept (or refuse) the grace of Christ offered to all—were doubtless deprived of beatitude and the vision of God, but would enter into a state of natural felicity exempt from all pain and sorrow. This doctrine of Limbo, scorned by so many of today's theologians who don't know what they are doing, should be recognized as a precious treasure of every intelligent Christian" (Maritain, *The Peasant of the Garonne*, p. 155, n. 21).

and power saved absolutely everyone or there were some free beings in hell. There could be no third alternative. Yet, Maritain himself did hold this position about Limbo throughout his life so it is not easy to remove its effects from his overall position. In practice, the doctrine served to provide the basis of a curious theological optimism that would mitigate or eliminate the seriousness of the moral and political structures of the actual world and the acts that take place within them. In a sense, Maritain's endeavor to enhance the importance within time of inner-worldly affairs as a part of the Christian position seems, with this position on the "end of Satan," to end up making us wonder whether any worldly event made any ultimate difference. The fact that the drift of modernity, within modern institutions, has continued in a radically anti-Christian direction can lead us to suspect some problem with this entire endeavor to "save" Lucifer, an endeavor the potential dangers of which Maritain himself seemed aware in much of his more formal writing.

Evil and Providence:
Toward a New Moral Order

Alice Ramos

T here is no doubt that the problem of evil in the twentieth century has
been a stumbling block for many in their belief in God, and yet despite
the atrocities recorded of man against man during this century—one has
only to think of the horrors of the Holocaust, the extermination of six million
Jews, and the deaths of over ninety million people due to the wars of this century—Pope John Paul II in 1995 at the United Nations exhorted us to believe
that from the destruction and ashes of the twentieth century would come a
"new springtime of the human spirit." And now, on the threshold of the new
millennium, when wars and injustices of one human being to another are still
very much part and parcel of every day news, one wonders if the words of the
Pope are merely an instance of wishful thinking or if indeed they do contain
truth. The Christian is not exempt from doubts, but in his more lucid moments
when he might ponder on the *felix culpa* or on the life and glory that result from
death on a cross or on the very paradoxical nature of the Christian life—the one
who loses his life will gain it—he will realize that the tears of the twentieth
century may in effect contain the seeds for a new flowering of humanity.[1]

[1] See Pope John Paul II, *Tertio Millennio Adveniente* (Boston: Pauline Books and
Media, 1994), no. 18, pp. 24–25. The preparation for the Great Jubilee of the year
2000 was meant to contribute to the eventual "springtime of the human spirit," provided that there be docility to the workings of the Holy Spirit. The Pope notes that the
tragic events of the twentieth century "demonstrate most vividly that the world needs
purification; it needs to be converted," p. 24. See also the Pope's address to the United
Nations General Assembly (October 5, 1995), in *Catholic Dossier*, 2, no. 4 (July-Au-
gust 1996), pp. 38–44: "I come before you as a witness: a witness to human dignity, a
witness to hope, a witness to the conviction that the destiny of all nations lies in the
hands of a merciful Providence. . . . We must not be afraid of the future. We must not
be afraid of man. It is no accident that we are here. Each and every human person has
been created in the 'image and likeness' of the One who is the origin of all that is.

The purpose of this paper will be first to explore briefly the problem of evil in selected texts of Aquinas, along with his treatment of providence, for in a world created by a loving and good God evil will not obviously have the last word. St. Thomas's solution to the problem of evil consists in two basic points, namely, that God permits evil and that He orders it to the good.[2] To the evil which God wills to permit there corresponds a prevailing good: for example, the existence of defectible natures is necessary for the integrity of the universe. God rules things according to their natures, which is a greater good than the elimination of individual defects; and in some cases the good of one thing cannot be achieved without evil occurring to something else. Examples of this abound in Aquinas: without persecution by the unjust there would be no patience of the just. God's goodness and omnipotence can therefore draw good from evil. Aquinas makes it clear that although evil is disorder with respect to its proximate cause, it is reduced to order by the superior cause. Moreover, the evil which God orders to the good is not always ordered to the good of the one in whom the evil occurs, but sometimes to another's good or to the good of the whole universe. All evil then contributes in the end to the good of the universe: not of itself, but by reason of the good joined to it. St. Thomas even sees a certain beauty in the presence of good and evil in the universe.[3]

Secondly, in this paper I wish to consider the close link between human suffering and evil: man suffers because of evil, which is a lack or a distortion

---

We have within us the capacities for wisdom and virtue. With these gifts, and with the help of God's grace, we can build in the next century and the next millennium a civilization worthy of the human person, a true culture of freedom. We can and must do so! And in doing so, we shall see that the tears of this century have prepared the ground for a new springtime of the human spirit," p. 44.

[2] "Even though evil inasmuch as it issues from its own cause is without order and, for this reason, is defined as a privation of order, there is nothing that keeps a higher cause from ordering it. In this way evil comes under providence," *De Veritate*, q. 5, a. 4, ad 3. I am making use of Robert W. Mulligan's translation of *The Disputated Questions on Truth*, vol. 1 (Chicago: Henry Regnery Co., 1952).

[3] In a number of texts, Aquinas compares God's care of the universe to the prudence of a man who allows a small evil so that a greater good may occur. In *De Veritate*, q. 5, a. 4, ad 4, Aquinas says: "Any prudent man will endure a small evil in order that a great good will not be prevented. Any particular good, moreover, is trifling in comparison with the good of a universal nature. Again, evil cannot be kept from certain things without taking away their nature, which is such that it may or may not fail; and, while this nature may harm something in particular, it nevertheless gives some added beauty to the universe. Consequently, since God is most prudent, His providence does not prevent evil, but allows each thing to act as its nature requires it to act. For, as Dionysius says, the role of providence is to save, not to destroy, nature."

of the good. One could say that man suffers because of a good in which he does not participate, from which he is excluded or of which he has deprived himself. Although suffering has been explained in terms of punishment for sin, it is also possible to consider the educative and creative value of suffering and to see in it the possibility of reconstructing the good in the subject who suffers, of consolidating the good not only in oneself but also in relation to God and to others. Suffering should therefore serve for conversion, for man's return to God and the return of the entire universe to God. For this part of the paper I intend to draw from some of the writings of Pope John Paul II on suffering, evil, reconciliation, and the renewal of world order.

Let us begin with St. Thomas's admission that divine providence does not entirely exclude evil from things. Given the nature and activity of God, Aquinas's discussion of divine providence as governing things and yet not preventing corruption, defects, and evil from being in the world, does not argue primarily from the presence of evil, but rather from the existence of goodness, beauty, and order in the world (since evil could not subsist without the good). God, in creating, communicates His goodness to things such that there is a diversity of creatures and thus grades of goodness, which are to manifest His perfection and glory: some things are better than others and some creatures are found to be more like God than others. According to Aquinas, if the order resulting from the distinction and disparity among things were abolished, then the chief beauty in things would also be eliminated.[4] God did not simply create diverse beings, but a community or order of beings: beings adapted or suited to one another, helped by one another, and harmoniously arranged. This order of the universe constitutes "the ultimate and noblest perfection in things."[5] St. Thomas also adds that the diversity and gradation among beings is a more perfect imitation or reflection of God than if God had created all things of one degree only.[6]

For the perfection of the universe both higher and lower degrees of goodness are thus required: "[T]he higher degree of goodness is that a thing be good and unable to fail from goodness; and the lower degree is of that which can fail from goodness."[7] Since it belongs to divine providence to preserve perfection in the things governed, God's providence does not entirely exclude

[4] *Summa Contra Gentiles* III, chap. 71. Hereafter cited as *SCG*.

[5] Fran O'Rourke, *Pseudo-Dionysius and the Metaphysics of Aquinas* (Leiden: Brill, 1992), p. 270. See also my article, "Beauty and the Perfection of Being," in the *Proceedings of the American Catholic Philosophical Association*, 71, (1997), pp. 255–68.

[6] See *SCG* II, chap. 45.

[7] Ibid.

from things the possibility of failing from goodness, and it is precisely from this possibility that evil occurs, since what can fail, occasionally does fail.[8] And this deficiency of the good is evil. In addition, God not only preserves perfection in things, He also provides for things according to their degree of perfection. Because creatures receive being, perfection, goodness from God according to a certain mode or measure, which is their nature, God also governs, provides for, creatures according to their mode or nature. It would be contrary to God's providence and government were creatures not allowed to act in accordance with their nature. And when creatures act thus, corruption and evil result in things: one thing may be corruptive of another because of the contrariety and incompatibility which exist in things.[9] Besides, in intending some good, an evil can sometimes be produced; knowing this, God who is the cause of all goodness, in His providence does not exclude from creatures all intention of particular goods; for if this were the case, much good would be eliminated from the universe. To this effect, Aquinas gives the following example: "[I]f fire were deprived of the intention of producing its like, a consequence of which is this evil, namely the burning of combustible things, the good consisting in fire being generated and preserved in its species would be done away [with]."[10] In fact, Aquinas argues that many good things would have no place in the universe were it not for evils: "[T]here would be no patience of the righteous, if there were no ill-will of the persecutors; nor would there be any place for vindictive justice, were there no crimes; even in the physical order there would be no generation of one thing, unless there were corruption of another."[11] God's omnipotence and His goodness therefore permit evil for a greater good, unlike the particular provider who sees only the part of which he has care and wants perfection for his part to the exclusion of all defects.[12]

---

[8] *Summa Theologiae* I, q. 48, a. 2, resp. Hereafter cited as *ST.*

[9] *SCG* III, chap. 71.

[10] Ibid. See also *ST* I, q. 22, a. 2, ad 10: "Since God, then, provides universally for all being, it belongs to His providence to permit certain defects in particular effects, that the perfect good of the universe may not be hindered, for if all evil were prevented much good would be absent from the universe. A lion would cease to live if there were no slaying of animals, and there would be no patience of martyrs if there were no tyrannical persecution. Thus Augustine says (*Enchir.* ii): 'Almighty God would in no way permit evil to exist in His works, unless He were so almighty and so good as to produce good even from evil.'"

[11] Ibid.

[12] *ST* I, q. 22, a. 2, ad 2: "[A] particular provider excludes all defects from what is subject to his care as far as he can, whereas one who provides universally allows some defect to remain, lest the good of the whole should be hindered."

Thus, while there may be a deficiency of the good in a part of the universe, God looks to the good of the whole.[13] As Aquinas puts it:

> [I]t belongs to a prudent governor to overlook a lack of goodness in a part, that there may be an increase of goodness in the whole. . . . Now if evil were taken away from certain parts of the universe, the perfection of the universe would be much diminished; since its beauty results from the ordered unity of good and evil things, seeing that evil arises from the lack of good, and yet certain goods are occasioned from those very evils through the providence of the governor. . . .[14]

It would appear then, as Aquinas argues, that man's good would be lessened were there no evils in the world: "For [man's] knowledge of the good is increased by comparison with evil, and through suffering evil his desire of doing good is kindled,"[15] just as the sick appreciate the good of health and are more desirous of its recovery than those who are in possession of it. Thus, from what has been said, the presence of evil in the world should not lead to the denial of God, for without the order of good, whose cause is God, there would be no evil. To those, therefore, who argue that there is no God because of the obvious evil in the world, Aquinas counters: "If there is evil, there is a God."[16]

Moreover, while it is true that God is the cause of all effects and actions, of being and perfection, and that agents act by the power of God, evil and defect themselves, as well as evil deeds, are not due to God but rather result from the condition of the secondary causes, which are or may be defective; thus, the motion in the act of limping is caused by the motive power, whereas what is defective in it does not come from the motive power, but from the crookedness of the leg.[17] "And, likewise, whatever there is of being and action in a bad action is reduced to God as the cause, whereas whatever defect is in it is not caused by God, but by the deficient secondary cause."[18] From the preceding, it is evident that God's providence of permission, that is, His permission of evil in the things governed by Him is not inconsistent with His goodness: for to completely eliminate evil from things would be tantamount to governing them according to a mode which does not correspond to them and thus would be a greater defect than the particular defects eradicated; also, as was seen above, the exclusion of evil renders impossible much good in the

---

[13] *ST* I, q. 48, a. 2, ad 3.
[14] *SCG* III, chap. 71. See also note 3.
[15] *SCG* III, chap. 71.
[16] Ibid.
[17] Ibid. See also *ST* I, q. 49, a. 2, ad 2.
[18] *ST* I, q. 49, a. 2, ad 2.

universe; evil is thus ordained to some good; and the good is, according to Aquinas, rendered more estimable when compared with particular evils.

Now the only real evil, as Aquinas puts it, is the evil of fault, since man's will, whose object is the good, can withdraw itself from the order of good. Thus, although Aquinas does speak of evil as being twofold, either as a taking away of the form or of any part required for the integrity of a thing, such as blindness, which evil has a non-moral nature, or as a withdrawal of a due operation in voluntary beings, which has the nature of fault, since he who has mastery of his acts through his will is responsible for his disordered act of the will, it is clear that the gravity of the evil of fault consists in man's becoming evil, in his frustrating his perfection or actualization, by opposing himself to the uncreated good, that is, by opposing the fulfillment of the divine will and refusing divine love. (Man's original refusal of love must then be countered by a show of love.)[19] Through fault man becomes, as Aquinas puts it, worthy of punishment, and thus he makes it necessary that the evil of penalty be dealt out to him, since the order of justice belongs to the order of good, to the order of the universe.[20] Men who do not respect the order of their nature, who act in discordance with their dignity as rational creatures, will suffer the evil of punishment. Aquinas tells us that if men act contrary to their rank in nature, that is, as brute animals,

> then God's providence will dispose of them according to the order that belongs to brutes, so that their good and evil acts will not be directed to their own profit but to the profit of others. . . . [Therefore], God's providence governs the good in a higher way than it governs the evil. For, when the evil leave one order of providence, that is, by not doing the will of God, they fall into another order, an order in which the will of God is done to them.[21]

Man's rebellion from God's will through the evil of fault or sin thus incurs God's just punishment.

However, while we generally accept the fittingness of punishment for sin, it becomes more difficult to accept why those who do not sin, those whom we may call just, are punished, as it were, or subjected to trials. What appears in Aquinas's answer to the tribulations of the just or innocent is that the evil befalling the just can be or will be ordered to their good: "Justice or mercy," Aquinas says, "appear in the punishment of the just in this world, since by afflictions lesser faults are cleansed in them, and they are the more raised up from earthly affections to God. As to this Gregory says: 'The evils that press

[19] *ST* I, q. 48, a. 6, resp.
[20] *ST* I, q. 49, a. 2, resp.
[21] *De Veritate*, q. 5, a. 7, resp.

on us in this world force us to go to God.'"[22] It would seem then that the evils afflicting the just serve not only to purify them but to attach them, to convert them, to the One who alone is Good. Through suffering, through the endurance of trials, the just are, so to speak, spiritualized (to live spiritually is to remain in communion with God); they are able to recognize the value of material goods, whatever these may be: health, riches, physical beauty, honor, in contrast with the One True Good.

Given what we have said regarding evil and providence in Aquinas, I wish to turn now to a brief consideration of evil and suffering in a few of the writings of Pope John Paul II. Conversant as he is with Thomistic thought, the Pope's analysis of the evil of fault is reminiscent of Aquinas; for both of them, evil of fault is contrary to man's dignity, to his order or rank in the universe, and constitutes a refusal to submit to order and to God's will. In his encyclical letter *Reconciliation and Penance*, the Pope describes sin as being disruptive of the original order of good which God meant there to be: sin wounds man in himself by severing or weakening his relationship to God and to his fellowmen. In speaking of the *mysterium iniquitatis*, mystery of sin or evil, the Pope cites as prime examples the first sin in Eden and the story of Babel, and says that by sinning the creature not only disobeys God but implicitly rejects the one who gives him being and conserves him in life. Besides, "[Man's] internal balance is also destroyed and it is precisely within himself that contradictions and conflicts arise. Wounded in this way, man almost inevitably causes damage to the fabric of his relationship with others and with the created world."[23]

The rupture of man's relationship with God is poignantly recounted in the parable of the prodigal son, which is given a prominent place in the encyclical *The Mercy of God*. There this severed relationship gives rise to the drama of man's lost dignity, his dignity not only as a rational being, but more importantly, his dignity as a son. After the prodigal son has squandered his inheritance, he suffers from hunger and the loss of material goods, he suffers due to a good from which he has deprived himself. He measures himself against the hired men in his father's house who have bread in abundance, whereas he is dying of hunger. Hidden in his reference to the loss of material

---

[22] *ST* I, q. 21, a. 4, ad 3. Aquinas also speaks of the "excellent" way in which God provides for the just in *ST* I, q. 22, a. 2, ad 4: "God . . . extends His providence over the just in a certain more excellent way than over the wicked, since, He prevents anything happening which would impede their final salvation. For *to them that love God, all things work together unto good* (Rom. 8:28)."

[23] *Reconciliation and Penance* (Boston: Pauline Books, 1984), no. 15, p. 35. Hereafter cited as *RP*.

goods is the drama of his lost dignity, the consciousness of being responsible for his lost filiation. Thus, when he decides to return to the father's house, he knows that his sin has made him unworthy of being called a son, and so wants nothing more than to occupy the place of a hired man. Through his situation and because of sin, the prodigal son has been able to mature and to realize the meaning of his lost dignity. The suffering that he undergoes effects an internal change in him. In wishing to be treated as no more than a hired man in his own father's house, he accepts the humiliation and shame which the rejection of his father and of his place rightfully deserve. Such reasoning on the part of the prodigal son demonstrates that he has finally become aware of that dignity which he lost in severing his relationship to the father.[24] And so the recognition of that relationship and of his worth due to his relational being allows for the return to the truth of himself, a being known and loved for himself. He has finally been able to grasp the meaning and value of spiritual goods over material goods; the evil which he has experienced has thus brought him to the recognition of the true good.

It is evident here that the mystery of sin does not have the last word. As the Pope puts it:

> [I]n [the economy of salvation] sin is not the main principle, still less the victor. Sin fights against another active principle which—to use a beautiful and evocative expression of St. Paul—we can call the *mysterium* or *sacramentum pietatis*. Man's sin would be the winner and in the end destructive, God's salvific plan would remain incomplete or even totally defeated, if this *mysterium pietatis* were not made part of the dynamism of history in order to conquer man's sin.[25]

Without entering into a whole explanation of what is meant by the *mysterium pietatis* which makes reference to the mystery of Christ, let us say briefly that the iniquity of sin, man's rebellion from God's will, is countered by the mystery of Christ's passion and death, by His loving submission to the Father's will, and by His resurrection and glorification. The *mysterium pietatis* revealed in the excellence of Christ's submission to the Father makes possible the reconciliation of man with God. The mercy and love of God, as well as His omnipotence, become manifest in the mystery or sacrament of *pietas*. John Paul II says: "[The] mystery of God's infinite loving kindness toward us is capable of penetrating to the hidden roots of our iniquity, in order to evoke in the soul a moment of conversion, in order to redeem it and set it on course

---

[24] *The Mercy of God* (*Dives in Misericordia*) (Boston: Pauline Books, 1980), no. 5, pars. 4–5, pp. 19–20. Hereafter cited as *DM*.

[25] *RP*, no. 19, p. 49.

toward reconciliation."[26] The task of reconciliation is to harmonize man internally, to harmonize him with God and with neighbor, and with the whole of creation.[27]

The mystery of divine love, revealed in the person and redemptive mission of Christ, as well as in the creation and sanctification of man in His Son attests to the overabundance of goodness bestowed upon man; God always gives more than is due to us. The parable of the prodigal son exemplifies the mercy and love of God through the figure of the father. The faithfulness of the father to his paternity, to the love for his son, is totally centered on the humanity of his lost son, on his dignity. Upon his return the son, who is the object of the father's love and mercy, does not feel humiliated and ashamed—even though he recognizes that he deserves this—but rather as the recipient of the father's loving kindness he is found again and revalued, since the father's sole concern is that the good of his son's humanity be saved.[28] The suffering which the prodigal son experiences prior to his return to the paternal home—a suffering which is both physical and moral, the privation of both material and spiritual goods—opens the way to the grace which transforms his soul and serves for his conversion. The suffering which he undergoes is transformative: it is a call to virtue, to hope and trust in someone other than himself, a call to an interior maturity, to a recreation of the self, a reconstruction of the good in him.[29] The prodigal son's recognition of his lost dignity, of his sonship, and the father's loving kindness, which calls out to the son, even in his misery away from home, make possible the son's return to the paternal house; good has triumphed over evil, and we might say that the painful experience of his alienation from the true good enables him in a sense to become worthy once again of the paternal home, of being welcomed into it. Interestingly, when Pope John Paul II writes on the Christian meaning of suffering he makes it clear that through suffering we make ourselves worthy of the kingdom of God.[30] Although the objective redemption was accomplished once and for all through Christ's passion and death, the subjective

[26] *RP*, no. 20, p. 51.

[27] *RP*, no. 8, pp. 21–23.

[28] *DM*, no. 6, pp. 20–23.

[29] *On the Christian Meaning of Suffering* (*Salvifici Doloris*) (Boston: Pauline Books, 1984), no. 12, p. 17. Hereafter cited as *SD*.

[30] *SD*, no. 21, p. 33. See also no. 22, where Pope John Paul II says: "To the prospect of the kingdom of God is linked hope in that glory which has its beginning in the cross of Christ. The resurrection revealed this glory—eschatological glory—which in the cross of Christ was completely obscured by the immensity of suffering. Those who share in the sufferings of Christ are also called, through their own sufferings, to share *in glory*."

redemption will continue until the end of time: each one of us, through physical and/or moral suffering have the opportunity to prepare ourselves, to mature, and thus become worthy of the kingdom, of glorification. In suffering,
contrary to what many think, God's providence is manifest, for He is calling
us to the higher goods, to the One who alone is good, to that which will truly
make us happy.

But not only can suffering and evil effect an interior transformation in the
one who experiences it, by making the person aware of his spiritual worth
and of God's merciful love; there is also an interpersonal dimension of suffering: the one who suffers should be assisted by others. Suffering should
evoke in those who observe it compassion and an effective desire to help. In
his reflections on the parable of the good Samaritan, John Paul II says:

> [S]uffering, which is present under so many different forms in our
> human world, is also present in order to unleash love in the human per-
> son, that unselfish gift of one's "I" on behalf of other people, especially
> those who suffer. The world of human suffering unceasingly calls for, so
> to speak, another world: the world of human love; and in a certain sense
> man owes to suffering that unselfish love which stirs in his heart and ac-
> tions. The person who is a "neighbor" cannot indifferently pass by the
> suffering of another: this in the name of fundamental human solidarity,
> still more in the name of love of neighbor.[31]

So human suffering can give rise to both individual and institutional forms of
activity to relieve suffering, to do good to those who suffer. Through the sufferings of others, God makes us participants in a special way of His providence, so as to provide for others, help them, love them, and so cause goodness, as God Himself does.[32] Again, John Paul II says: "[S]uffering is present
in the world to release love, in order to give birth to works of love towards
neighbor, in order to transform the whole of human civilization into a 'civilization of love.'"[33]

Certainly, the twentieth century has seen suffering and evil as perhaps
never before; now at the beginning of this twenty-first century, it is possible
that we are also at the threshold of a new civilization which each person
through an interior conversion such as that of the prodigal son can help to

[31] *SD*, no. 29, p. 50.

[32] St. Thomas also refers to the participation of God's providence in creatures,
which participation is another manifestation of His goodness: "[T]here are certain in-
termediaries of God's providence, for He governs things inferior by superior, not on
account of any defect in His power, but by reason of the abundance of His goodness,
so that the dignity of causality is imparted even to creatures," *ST* I, q. 22, a. 3, resp.

[33] *SD*, no. 30, p. 54.

bring about,[34] a civilization of interconnected persons being a moral support for one another and thus reflecting the understanding and love of the supreme communion of persons that exists in God, and in this way corresponding to God's creative and salvific love. Just as the physical and moral suffering of the prodigal son was a call to hope and trust, to a reconstruction of the good in him, so also the sorrows of the end of the twentieth century are a call to the construction of a new moral order. The "new springtime of the human spirit," of which Pope John Paul II speaks, will be possible if we never forget man's dignity, his transcendent dimension, his aspiration to the true good, and that his destiny lies in the hands of a merciful Providence.[35] The recreation of civilization into a "civilization of love" may seem a utopian dream, so I end with the words of T. S. Eliot: "For us there is only the trying, the rest is not our business."[36]

[34] Perhaps we are now at a moment in history, in which the conversion of individual persons will bring about a reconstruction of social and political structures for the transformation of civilization into a "civilization of love." It may also be the moment of which St. Paul speaks in Rom. 8:19–20: "For the eager longing of creation awaits the revelation of the sons of God."

[35] In his address to the UN General Assembly in October of 1995 (see n. 1), Pope John Paul II says that in order to ensure "a new flourishing of the human spirit" in the new millennium, "we must rediscover a spirit of hope and a spirit of trust" and thus conquer our fear of the future. The Pope's description of hope is grounded in the merciful love of God and in man's aspiration to goodness: "Now is the time for new hope, which calls us to expel the paralyzing burden of cynicism from the future of politics and of human life. . . . Inspired by the example of all those who have taken the risk of freedom, can we not recommit ourselves also to taking the risk of solidarity—and thus the risk of peace? . . . Hope and trust are the premise of responsible activity and are nurtured in that inner sanctuary of conscience where 'man is alone with God' (*Gaudium et Spes*, no. 16) and he thus perceives that he is not alone amid the enigmas of existence, for he is surrounded by the love of the Creator! . . . The answer to the fear which darkens human existence at the end of the twentieth century is the common effort to build the civilization of love, founded on the universal values of peace, solidarity, justice, and liberty. And the 'soul' of the civilization of love is the culture of freedom: the freedom of individuals and the freedom of nations, lived in self-giving solidarity and responsibility," pp. 43–44.

[36] "East Coker," in *Four Quartets* (New York: Harcourt, Brace & Co., 1943), p. 17.

Culture:
Blessing or Misfortune for
the Jewish Religious Commitment?

Leon Klenicki

I'm grateful to have been invited to address the American Maritain Association for several reasons. For one, because of my spiritual debt to Jacques Maritain. In my native Argentina, I started reading his work in high school. In those days, the political liaison between General Juan Domingo Perón, president of the country, and the hierarchy of the Catholic Argentinean Church resulted in the fact, among other things, that Catholic religion was being taught in high schools. Jewish and Protestant children, or children of parents who didn't have any religious commitment, or children whose parents were left-wing politically oriented, had to take a course on "Morality." The course on morality was, naturally, closely related or indirectly inspired by Catholic moral standards—standards that belonged to the days of Vatican Council I or were inspired by the spirit of *L'Action Française*, an ideology still dear in certain Argentinean circles. I had to take the course during my last two years of high school. My school followed the model of a French Lycée, an educational experience that didn't last long because General Perón, with his populist policies and neo-fascist ideology, degraded the entire system to a standard mediocrity and expelled the good teachers, replacing them with mediocre ones or nationalists.

My first teacher was a nice middle-class Catholic girl, who was saving for her dowry and was clearly terrified by the class. It was evident that she was told that her Jewish students were part of the people who, according to medieval and contemporary reactionary Catholic thought, "killed Jesus," that socialists or communists and other dangerous representatives were in her class, and that she should be very careful of her spiritual integrity. She was so terrified that she gave all of us "A's" on the final exam and we devoted each class to reading our favorite literature: Marxist books for the left-wingers or the latest French novels, as some of us read. I read Camus and Sartre, and tried not to fall asleep while exploring Marcel Proust. The teacher for the second year, however, was a young Catholic man who, from the very first day, said that we shouldn't waste time with the official high school text and gave us a bibliography to read. Among the writers that we read with great interest were: Jacques Maritain, Emmanuel Mounier, Léon Bloy, Gabriel Marcel, Martin Buber and other writers of the twentieth century. We were enchanted with this teacher and we had long, passionate discussions presenting different points of view, from a traditional, committed-Yiddish background that I came from, to people who were "illuminated" by contemporary culture, or left-wing ideology. The teacher, naturally, lasted but one year and was replaced by a sweet soul, who tried to convert the students to Catholicism. She failed, but some of us felt that after reading the new trends of Catholic thought recommended by the previous teacher and represented by intelligent philosophers, Maritain among them, we had been introduced to new thinking dimensions of Catholicism.[1]

And here I am, in the United States, at the University of Notre Dame, in a program honoring Jacques Maritain. I feel like the Marcel Proust character, though nobody has invited me yet to eat a Madeleine. But, at the same time, I feel that by rereading some of Maritain's books, after so many different experiences in Argentina and in the United States, that I would like to propose to you some thoughts on the question of culture as it relates to my Jewish religious commitment and Maritain's thought. I reread Jacques Maritain's *Religion and Culture*[2] and much of my thinking before preparing this paper was reflected in this little book, but there also was my uneasiness about some of Maritain's ideas about the meaning of God's Covenant with Israel, religious Judaism, and our presence in the world—a presence that will continue despite the historical horrors of Nazism and Communism or the ongoing, ever-present teaching of spiritual and political contempt, vis-à-vis my religious commitment, and my people.

---

[1] Leon Klenicki, "Jacques Maritain's Vision of Judaism and Anti-Semitism," in *Jacques Maritain and the Jews*, ed. Robert Royal (Notre Dame, Indiana: University of Notre Dame Press, 1994).

[2] Jacques Maritain, *Religion and Culture* (London: Sheed & Ward, 1931).

CULTURE: BLESSING OR MISFORTUNE?

The subject of my paper will be "Culture: Blessing or Misfortune for the Jewish Religious Commitment?"

Jews as a community of faith have a long history since Abraham's call by God and the Sinai covenantal relationship. Jewish spirituality is a meeting, an encounter entailing two dimensions. One is the covenantal relationship God-Israel, the other is its implementation in a daily actualization of the experience of God, His Call and Presence, in individual and community existence.

There is no precise theological expression for spirituality in Hebrew, though two terms could be considered: *Halahah* and *Emunah*. *Halahah*, wrongly translated as law, *nomos*, by the Christian biblical translators, is a way of being and doing, a means of implementing the covenantal relationship in ritual. *Emunah*, faith, is the experience of reliving daily the covenantal relationship in prayer. *Emunah* is an attitude of the spirit, of hope and realization. It is the spiritual acceptance of God followed by the implementation of God's Call in and through the ritual commitment. It is to say continually yes to God. *Emunah* and *Halahah* convey the whole range of Jewish spirituality.

The halahic experience requires an explanation. Its meaning has been misunderstood since Paul's days and this theological misapprehension is evident in Maritain's discourse.

The Roman destruction of the Jerusalem Temple resulted in the exile of the Jewish community from the city, but not from the Land. It marked the end of the sacrificial ritual, its atoning and salvific symbolism, and the ecclesiastical bureaucracy of the Sadducees. The end of the sacrificial offering yields to the exercise of inner life and the service of the heart, prayer. Study and the sanctification of daily existence, the halahic exercise, become a substitute for sacrifice and the splendor of the Temple. The destruction of the Jerusalem Temple started the rabbinic rebuilding that no power or political upheaval could destroy; the Temple became an interior construct in the heart of Judaism both at the individual and community levels.

Rabbinic spirituality was rooted in the Ezra-Nehemiah exploration of the biblical text and the need to actualize the covenantal relationship after the destruction of the Temple. The rabbi's task was to enlarge the Oral Torah, *Torah She ba'Al Peh*, oral halahic tradition, by expounding the Written Torah, *Torah She-bikhtav*, the tradition received at Mount Sinai. The expounding, commentary and explication unfolded *Halahah* as a normative criterion that guided the life of the community as a whole and each member's personal commitment.

Biblical ordinances are presented in an outline and require an explanation.

For example, Exodus 20:8–11 and Deuteronomy 5:12–18 do not detail the prohibition of working on the Sabbath. Rabbinic expounding of the text itemized what was permitted and what was not. While the *Mishnah* devotes one book, twenty-four chapters to the subject, the *Talmudim* present a phenomenology of Sabbath-spirituality in a dense volume of commentaries and explanations. The observance of dietary laws, the synagogue service of the Sabbath, and family purity are directed to lift up everyday existence toward God, so that all of life becomes holy.

Several theological and halahic compilations resulted from the rabbinic expounding of the biblical text. The *Siddur*, prayerbook, the *Mishnah*, halahic interpretation of biblical law, the *Midrash*, literary interpretation of the Bible, and the two *Talmudim*, the *Jerusalem Talmud* and the *Babylonian Talmud* are examples of the rabbinic search for implementation of the Word of God in daily life.

THE MEANING OF CULTURE IN
JEWISH COMMUNITY EXISTENCE

God's Call and religious life have been with us from the very beginning of our history. This is not so with culture. Culture was present in the surroundings of the covenantal experience, as well as throughout history, but it was not part of the Jewish commitment. We have been consumers of culture, in general, though we are producing culture now, both in Israel as well as outside Israel, especially in the United States. But we can ask honestly if it is "Jewish" culture.

Culture was a luxury for those who lived in medieval Europe and the ghettos, and even after the French Revolution and Modernism. Culture was the enterprise of "the others," not necessarily ours. But ironically, culture in its philosophical dimension was influential in some of our most important thinkers. Greek thought was present in medieval philosophy, as well as in the whole Cultural Revolution started by the *Haskalah* cultural experience in Eastern Europe. *Haskalah* is the Hebrew term for the Enlightenment movement and ideology which began within Jewish society in the eighteenth century. The movement helped Jews, in many ways, to enter into European society, but it did not help Jews to be accepted by European society. European culture, even civilization, tolerated Jews rather than accepted them as part of their societies. The encounter with European civilization, at times was a dialogue, and at times a confrontation between general culture, the wisdom of the nations, and the Torah tradition, which was not a phenomenon of modern times.

One of the first challenges of rabbinic theology was the encounter with Greek thought. A good example of that was Philo of Alexandria, who wrote biblical commentaries under the influence of Greek philosophy, a cultural experience that ended in the confrontation between Jerusalem and Athens in the centuries preceding the Common Era and continuing for centuries. Elias Bickerman says in his book, *The Jews in the Greek Age*:

> We have often contrasted Hebrew and Greek thought . . . but we have rarely pointed to Greek influences. In the first place, Jerusalem was no more unchanging than Athens. Many unexpected trades that appeared to be un-Jewish . . . may result from . . . the existence of an unknown force of the first magnitude that disturbs any calculation of influences . . . a common Levantine civilization stubbornly persisted under Macedonian rulers . . . on the other hand, Greek ideas did percolate down to the Jews in Judea, even to those who lacked the advantages of a Greek education. Although, in isolated and fragmentary manner . . . the Jews drew upon new insights, adopting those elements of Greek culture that appeared to them useful or stimulating, and neglecting the rest . . . discoveries of borrowing and influences have only a modest heuristic value unless we can learn why and to what purpose the new motive was woven into the traditional design. . . . As Vico observed more than two centuries ago, people accept only the ideas for which their previous development has prepared their minds, and which, let us add, appear to be useful to them.[3]

Bernard Jackson, in his *Essays in Jewish and Comparative Legal History*, says very intelligently that, "The effect of Greece was also that of a catalyst—a fertility drug rather than a parent."[4]

Culture was a tool rather than an end in itself. This was the reality in the experience of Philo or Maimonides, but it was a serious problem when Jews had to decide between their religious heritage and a society that was demanding of Jewish citizens to be like the other citizens in the country, putting aside a tradition of millennia for a culture that was essentially deeply influenced by Christianity. Culture became a source of danger, and even a tool of destruction for Jewish spirituality. The study of Goethe, good spoken German, or the influence of French literature, became more important than the study of Torah. The wisdom of the world took over the wisdom of God's Covenant. This is a problem that we faced in the past, but it is still present in our lives, though it has been reinterpreted in a more creative way, as we shall see later on.

[3] Elias Bickerman, *The Jews in Greek Age* (Cambridge, Massachusetts: Harvard University Press, 1988), p. 298.

[4] Bernard Jackson, *Essays in Jewish and Comparative Legal History* (Leiden: Brill, 1975), pp. 1–24.

TORAH UMADDA AND *TORAH IM DEREH ERETZ*

The relationship of culture and Torah, understood as religious study and the religious exercise of God's Revelation, is a problem still open for consideration in Jewish religious life. It was a question in rabbinic days in the discussions of the writers of the *Mishnah* and the *Talmud*, as well as in medieval philosophical thought. In general, the rabbis and teachers wished to demonstrate to both private individuals and to those in rabbinic seminaries the permissibility, even the desirability, following *Halahic* criteria, of involving oneself in the study of the various disciplines that are part of general culture. General culture was to be incorporated, but not to become an end in itself, replacing the religious way of living.

The beauty and meaning of learning, and religious study, was brilliantly described by Simon Rawidowicz in his book, *State of Israel, Diaspora, and Jewish Continuity*:

> What learning meant to traditional Judaism can probably be best inferred from the fact that the rabbis linked it up with the supreme Jewish idea, the *idea of God*. Christendom, speaking in the name of a God of love and mercy, has always castigated Israel for its God of law, legality, revenge, and so on. Neither Christianity, Islam, nor any other of the creeds has ever noticed the fact that with the establishment of learning as a national ideal, *the* national ideal in Israel, the God of Israel became a *learning God.*
>
> *A learning God!* Learning, of course, indicates a want, a need to fill a gap, a desire to improve one's mind, to widen one's understanding, to make up for deficiencies, to free oneself from ignorance and all imperfection involved in it. It is, therefore, of the greatest interest that midrashic-talmudic Judaism, though considering God the symbol of highest perfection possible, created at the same time the concept of a God who studies, a learning God. . . . God has not only studied His Torah more than a hundred times before He gave it to Moses for Israel. God is in midrashic Judaism the *eternal student.* He learns *with* Israel, learns always and everywhere. . . . Rav, the leading *amora* of the second century, went even so far as to describe exactly the daily agenda of God Almighty: The first three hours of his twelve-hour day of work, God learns Torah; the second three hours, He judges all the world; the third three hours, He feeds all the world; the last three hours, He plays with the Leviathan. God learns three periods daily. I wish some of our "non-professional" Jewish brothers and sisters would believe in *imitatio Dei*—or in the commandment "*Ve-halakhta biderakhav,*" "You shall go in His Ways"—and would have at least one period of Torah a day.[5]

---

[5] Simon Rawidowicz, *State of Israel, Diaspora, and Jewish Community* (Hanover, Massachusetts: Brandeis University Press, 1998), pp. 135–36.

Two Hebrew phrases translate the word culture: *Torah Im Dereh Eretz* and *Torah Umadda*. The word *Dereh Eretz* has several meanings. One is "labor" as it appears in *Pirkei Avot*, the *Ethics of the Fathers*, when it says that the study of Torah should be accompanied by labor. A second meaning is "proper norms of conduct." The Midrash, *Genesis Rabbah* 76:3, declares that *Dereh Eretz* preceded the teaching of the Torah by twenty-six generations. The German-Jewish nineteenth century theologian, Samson R. Hirsch, interpreted the words *Dereh Eretz* to be identical with the concept of culture as understood in the Western world. This is the way we will interpret it, including in this concept: literature, philosophy, the arts and science.

Hirsch wrote about the relationship of *Dereh Eretz* and Torah, saying that "twenty-six generations did *Dereh Eretz* precede Torah . . . the way is culture, and only then can one reach to the Tree of Life, to the Torah. Culture starts the work of educating the generations of mankind, and the Torah completes it." In this way, culture might be a prerequisite to acquire the total knowledge of religious teaching, the Torah.[6] As Sol Roth elaborates in *The Jewish Idea of Culture*:

> Primarily the followers of Hirsch adopt the positive view of human experience in general; they maintain openness to the achievements of the human mind and to cultural progress. They are willing to take the risk that science and philosophy might be perceived, though erroneously, as antagonistic to religion, and erode Jewish commitment. They believe, however, that the risk is minimal; that given the open society in which we live, the risk is, in any case, ever-present; and that integration of culture into Torah is a better expression of Torah's attitude toward human life and experience than the bifurcation that results from its exclusion.[7]

Torah Umadda is a concept shared by religious people who feel that there should be a synthesis between two universes, the covenantal religious life and the world of culture, though culture is devoid at times of any religious value. The religious mind has to integrate those two dimensions, Torah and culture, into a significant, useful unity. The attitude of the followers of *Torah Umadda* would say that the two, Torah and culture, can be harmonized and that this is a creative manner to live a truly religious life.

Such a view is followed by the great Jewish theologian, Joseph B. Soloveitchik, who explains these ideas in his classic, *The Lonely Man of*

[6] Samson R. Hirsch, *The Nineteen Letters of Ben Uziel* (New York: Feldheim, 1960), Letter 16, and Samson R. Hirsch, *Judaism Eternal* (London: Soncino Press, 1956), pp. 174–78.

[7] Sol Roth, *The Jewish Idea of Culture* (Hoboken, New Jersey: Ktav Publishing House, Inc., 1997), pp. 4–5.

Faith.[8] He points out that the two Genesis accounts of the Creation of Man correspond to two human attitudes that are part of the human experience in the world.

Genesis I says: "So God created man in His own image, in the image of God He created him, male and female created them. And God blessed them and God said unto them: 'Be fruitful and multiply, and fill the earth and subdue it, and have dominion over the fish of the sea, over the fowl of the heaven, and over the beast, and all over the earth.'" This narrative corresponds to the description of what Soloveitchik calls "Adam the First." Adam the First receives the mandate from God to fill the earth and subdue it. Both male and female were created concurrently. Adam the First describes the man of culture who is creative in the domain of nature. The aim and task of his life is to exercise control over nature and have the world serve him. He takes initiatives, he faces the complicated world, solving problems and finding ways that will improve, in general, the quality of life. Adam the First is a man of action, whose task it is to change himself, change the world and make of it a better place for humanity.

The second narrative of the creation of the human being differs greatly from the one I have just read. It says: "And the Eternal God formed the man of the dust of the ground and breathed into his nostrils the breath of life and man became a living soul . . . and Eternal God planted the Garden eastward in Eden . . . and Eternal God took the man and placed him in the Garden of Eden to serve it and to keep it." Adam the Second was fashioned from the dust of the ground and God breathed into his nostrils the breath of life. While Adam the First was created in the image of God, nothing is said about his body. Adam the Second is charged with the duty of cultivating a garden and to keep it, and he emerged alone, while Eve appears later on as his helpmate and complement. Adam the Second is the man of the Torah, concerned with his acceptance of God's Will through obedience to Torah and classical teaching precepts, and involving himself in a direct relationship with God through prayer.

Soloveitchik, in his rabbinic interpretation of the two stories, attempts to harmonize the two versions projecting an understanding of the possibilities of Torah and culture being blended creatively. One creation of man explains the work of culture, and the other the religious covenantal creativity of the God-person relationship. Still, is not religion tempted to submerge itself in culture

[8] Joseph B. Soloveitchik, *The Lonely Man of Faith* (New York: Doubleday, 1992), chaps. 1 and 2.

and lose its own vocation? Following Soloveitchik's idea of confrontation, is not the relationship religion-culture essentially a confrontation between two points of view?

Mordecai Kaplan (1881–1983), an American Jewish thinker, added a special dimension to the question of culture and religious commitment. He started a new religious movement called Reconstructionism, rooted in Jewish theological tradition but aimed towards a new concept of God and its implementation in daily, individual, and community existence. In 1935 Kaplan published *Judaism as a Civilization*, where he defined Judaism as an evolving religious civilization where the covenant God-Israel is expressed in stages of spiritual development, of understanding the religious experience in prayer and ritual. Culture should be incorporated, according to Kaplan, to help shape the new religiosity that makes meaningful God and its translation in word and community action in this century. Kaplan contributed as no other Jewish theologian to bridge culture and religion in a meaningful experience as an example of a response to the world and its challenges.

RELIGION AND CULTURE:
JACQUES MARITAIN'S VIEW

Jacques Maritain devoted a book on the question of religion and culture, expressing his Catholic, essentially Thomist view, of this matter. At the very beginning of the book, he pointed out the attitude of the prophets vis-à-vis culture and their critical approach. The prophets denounced the culture of nations surrounding Israel as well as the culture infiltrated in the King's palaces, influencing behavior in society. The prophets were critical of culture in its pagan manifestations when it tried to replace the covenantal relationship God-Israel, its duties and commitment. The problem is ever present and Maritain read the Hebrew biblical text *in situ*.

Maritain points out that, "[E]verywhere in the ancient world, nationalism sponged upon and corrupted religions; it absorbed religion in culture, made it an element of a civilization, of a culture." He would also add:

> I mean to say that the ancient world, while riveted in social life too, and occasionally crushing it, and while honoring religion with a terrifying power of veneration, while enslaving man to the gods, nevertheless enfeoffed religion to civilization—not in the least after the manner of the modern profane world, which makes religion the mere servant of civilization considered as something superior, but on the contrary, by making religion the governing principle of the state, yet individuated by the state, living with the same unique and indistinct life, ruling like a despot over the state, but inconceivable without the state, and bound substantially to it, enclosed within the state, determined and circumscribed by

the state and, finally in an absolutely metaphysical sense, existing for the state, as the soul of a plant exists for that plant.[9]

He would emphasize:

> True religion, however, is supernatural, come down from Heaven with Him who is the author of grace and truth. It is not of man, or of the world, or a civilization, or a culture, it is God. It transcends every civilization and every culture. It is the supreme beneficent and animating principle of all civilizations and cultures, while in itself independent of them all, free, universal, strictly universal, Catholic."[10]

I agree totally with Maritain, though as a religious Jew I feel uncomfortable with his reference to "Catholic." I would ask if "Catholic" is a synonym for "universal," as he stresses previously, or a reference to the Catholic Church?

Later on in his book, Maritain will emphasize the need for Catholicism to penetrate culture and give it its essential meaning. He says: "It is of fundamental necessity to the life of the world that Catholicism penetrate to the very depths of, and vivify, culture and that Catholics form sound cultural, philosophical, historical, social, political, economic and artistic conceptions, and endeavor to transmit them into the reality of history."[11] He would later add:

> That the religion of Christ should penetrate culture to its very depths is not required merely from the point of view of the salvation of souls and in relation to their last end: in this respect, a Christian civilization appears as something truly maternal and sanctified, procuring the terrestrial good and the development of the various natural activities by sedulous attention to the imperishable interest and most profound aspirations of the human heart. It ought, from the point of view also of the specific ends of civilizations itself, to be Christian. For human reason, considered without any relation whatever to God, is insufficient by its unaided natural resources to procure the good of men and nations. As a matter of fact, and in the conditions governing life at present, it is not possible for man to expand his nature in a fundamentally and permanently upright manner unless under the sky of grace.[12]

Would Jews and non-Christian religious people, or indifferent people, be able to act or live in a culture that is totally foreign to their religious or spiritual commitments? This is a problem that we Jews have faced for millennia, and it has been a serious problem in our so-called integration into Western European culture. A difference should be made, however, between

[9] Maritain, *Religion and Culture*, p. 11.
[10] Ibid., p. 12.
[11] Ibid., pp. 29–30.
[12] Ibid., p. 31.

the "integration by toleration" of European societies, societies that were essentially intolerant and prepared an atmosphere that made the Holocaust possible. Quite different is the Jewish experience in pluralistic societies where Jews are either accepted or not, but not tolerated only as second-class citizens, which is the case in many countries in Europe and Latin America.

Maritain exemplifies what we said about "toleration" and "acceptance":

> I have already observed that it is proper to insist upon it: "All religions other than the Catholic religions are in more or less narrow and servile fashion, according, as their metaphysical level is more or less elevated, integral parts of certain definite cultures, particularized to certain ethnic climates and certain historical formations. The Catholic religion alone is absolutely and strictly transcendental, super-cultural, super-racial and super-national, because it is supernatural."[13]

Maritain will express a thought that pictures for us post-Holocaust Jews the essence of Western "toleration" of its Jewish citizens, both culturally and religiously:

> What I mean (to speak in general and of the inner attitude of the average Christian) is that for a long time we loved non-Christians—truly and sincerely—although they were not Christians (it was this visible fact which took precedence). In other words, we loved non-Christians primarily inasmuch as having the misfortune not to be Christians, they were called to become so; we loved them primarily not as men or for what they were, but as Christians to be or for what they are called to become. . . .
> But now, by virtue of the great inner reversal I am stressing, we love non-Christians above all because they are, at least potentially, of this incarnate Truth whom they do not know and whom the errors professed by them deny. In short, we love them first of all in their own unfathomable mystery, for what they are, and as men in regard to whom the first duty of charity is simply love. And so, we love them first and foremost the way they are, and in seeking their own good, toward which, in actual existence, they have to advance within a religious universe and a system of spiritual and cultural values where great errors may abound, but where truths worthy of respect and of love are likewise certainly present. Through these truths, it is possible for the One who made them, for the Truth who is Christ, to touch their hearts in secret, without themselves or anyone in the world being aware of it.[14]

Maritain, however, aware of a Jewish concern over Catholic triumphalism, will be careful in separating Catholics, as individuals, from Catholicism. He would also point out that certain religious attitudes might transform

---

[13] Ibid., p. 34.

[14] Jacques Maritain, *The Peasant of the Garonne: An Old Layman Questions Himself About the Present Time* (New York: Holt, Rinehart and Winston, 1968), p. 71.

"Catholicism in the minds of those affected by it into a party and Catholics into partisans." He would also add: "Such a transformation appears with most manifest characteristics in the state of mind of anti-Semites, who proclaim the gospel by a series of pogroms, and people who attribute all the wars of life to a permanent world-wide conspiracy of the wicked against the good."[15]

Maritain would stress, to the surprise of many in Eastern Europe or in Latin America today, that "Catholicism is not a religious party; it is religion, the only true religion, and it rejoices, without envy, in every good, even though it may be achieved outside its boundaries—for that good is only apparently outside the boundaries of Catholicism, in reality it belongs to it invisibly."[16] Maritain's words reminded me sadly of a new Holy See document, which the Holy See Congregation for the Doctrine of the Faith has issued called "Declaration *Dominus Iesus*" on "The Unicity and Salvific Universality of Jesus Christ and The Church."

The document issued by the Congregation for the Doctrine of the Faith deals with the centrality of Jesus in the message and mission of the Church. It is not directed to Jews but rather to other Christians who do not belong to the Catholic Church. The first reactions to the document came from the World Council of Churches, as well as the Church of England, and many other Christian voices. The document, by stressing that Jesus is the way of salvation and its instrument is the Church, reflects a fundamentalist overtone that reminds Jews of the teaching of contempt of centuries gone by. The document recalls the old expression, "Outside the Church there is no salvation," a theological concept that hurt the Jewish people for centuries and justified the Crusades and the contempt for the Jewish people. By emphasizing the uniqueness of Rome, the other Christian denominations appear as being not totally Christian and require, for their return to Jesus, the acceptance of Rome as the central voice of Christianity. The document is in clear contrast to what the Talmudic sources say about the righteous of all nations of the world who have a stake in the world to come.

The document also follows a line that was common many years ago, which pointed out that non-Christian people are "secret Christians" and that their faith is essentially a way of Jesus to manifest his message. The document says, "Therefore, the sacred books of other religions which in actual fact direct and nourish the existence of their followers, receive from the mystery of Christ the element of goodness and grace which they contain."

[15] Maritain, *Religion and Culture*, p. 42.
[16] Ibid.

Paragraph twenty-two of the Holy See document is a text that concerns
Jews and especially the Catholic-Jewish relationship. It says: "With the coming of the Savior Jesus Christ, God has willed that the Church founded by
Him be the instrument for the salvation of all humanity (cf. Acts 17:13–31).
This truth of faith does not lessen the sincere respect which the Church has
for the religions of the world, but, at the same time, it rules out, in a radical
way, the mentality and indifferentism, characterized by a religious relativism
which leads to the belief that one religion is as good as another." The document also stresses that "If it is true that the followers of other religions can receive divine grace, it is also certain that objectively speaking they are in a
gravely deficient situation in comparison with those who, in the Church, have
the fullness of the means of salvation."

This language is of great concern to us Jews because of past experiences.
It reflects concepts used by medieval theologians, as well as theologians up
to the Vatican Council II statements on Jews and Judaism. We seem to be
back to triumphalism and contempt. This triumphalism is reflected in Maritain's theological consideration of Judaism.

MARITAIN AND TRIUMPHALISM

I admire Maritain for his religious life and his thought. As I mentioned
earlier, it inspired my spiritual development in Argentina while I was in high
school. I feel, however, that he also expressed a teaching of contempt for Judaism, one that reflects much of Christian thought through the centuries. It
has been expressed in some of his books, indirectly in *Religion and Culture*,
but clearly in his commentary on St. Paul. This is not to our total surprise because the teaching of contempt is part of the Western culture and Jews have
faced and experienced it for centuries. I would even say that it is part of the
Western collective unconscious.

Maritain's reflections on Israel represent "a Christian perspective" that is
"metaphysical and religious." His interpretation is a Catholic examination
that reflects in many ways tendencies that are difficult to accept or understand after Vatican Council II. This is evident in a 1938 text where he pointed
out that:

> If there are Jews among the readers of this essay, they will understand, I
> am sure, that as a Christian I try to understand something of the history
> of their people from a Christian viewpoint. They know that according to
> Saint Paul, we Gentile Christians have been grafted onto the predestined
> olive tree of Israel in place of the branches which did not recognize the
> Messiah foretold by the prophets. Thus we are converts to the God of Is-
> rael who is the true God, to the father whom Israel recognized, to the son

whom it rejected. Christianity, then, is the overflowing fullness and the supernatural realization of Judaism.[17]

This is indeed triumphalism at its best!

There is a paradox in his approach, an ambiguity of the heart. This text seems to contradict another text in his book, *On the Philosophy of History*:

> [Israel] is not only a people, but a people endowed with a mission which pertained to the very order of the redemption of mankind. And Israel's mission continues in a certain manner—no longer as an "ecclesial mission"—after its lapse, because it cannot help being the chosen people, for the gifts of God are without repentance, and the Jews are still beloved because of their fathers. So we might say that whereas the Church is assigned the task of the supernatural and supratemporal saving of the world, to Israel is assigned, in the order of temporal history and its own finalities, the work of the *earthly leavening* of the world. Israel is here . . . to irritate the world, to prod it, to move it. It teaches the world to be dissatisfied and restless so long as it has not God, as long as it has not justice on earth. Its indestructible hope stimulates the life forces of history.[18]

Maritain defended the Jew as a citizen, his rights and equality in society, and denounced anti-Semitism passionately. His theology, however, and especially his reading of St. Paul, projected a sense of contempt for Judaism, for the Sinai God-Israel commitment and its development through the centuries. He fought for the civil rights of Jews, but denied meaning to Jews in their spirituality and covenantal vocation. In many respects, and I tremble in pointing this out, he was a metaphysical anti-Semite, as Martin Buber classified some Christian theologians in Germany before Nazism, especially Adolf Von Harnack.

FAITH AND LAW

A theological confrontation originated with the Church Fathers, which has become part of Western culture in the alternative "Law" and "Faith." Maritain's reference to the limitations and death of the law reminds the Jewish reader of the theological teaching of contempt towards Judaism, which denied Israel a place in God's design after Jesus:

> The Law is holy because it is the created expression of the wisdom of God. But while the Law makes us know evil, it does not give us the

[17] Jacques Maritain, *A Christian Looks at the Jewish Question* (New York: Arno Press, 1973), pp. 23–24.

[18] Jacques Maritain, *On the Philosophy of History* (New York: Charles Scribner's Sons, 1957), p. 92.

strength to avoid evil. And by making evil known, the Law is, for evil (Romans 2:3). Thus the Law bears death with it. If there were no law, there would be no transgression, and hence there would be no death. . . . Paul's line of reasoning supposes this fact, that the Jews are set apart, in view of the world's salvation, for a purity and holiness of life—highly superior, even though principally external, to the moral ideals of all the gentiles—which were required by the Law and for whose fulfillment not the Law, but the grace of the Christ to come (and now come) alone is efficacious. A people elect, and a people victim—they are bound up in their Law as though in God's trap—so long as they withhold faith in Him Whose death, wrought by their priesthood in the name of the Law, now brings them their deliverance. But this deliverance, which implies their salvation comes to all by the Cross, not by the Law, requires also that the Jews recognize that the regimen of the Law has come to an end, and that at the same time they renounce the keeping to themselves alone of the privileges which that regimen conferred to them.[19]

Maritain's Pauline critique of law shares some characteristics with other Christian thinkers who are not at all in theological harmony. Calvin, in his *Institutes of the Christian Religion*, commenting on Romans 10:5–8, points out that "righteousness which is given through the Gospel has been freed of all conditions of the law. . . . The Gospel promises are free and dependent solely upon God's mercy, while the promises of the law depend on works."[20] Law is criticized here as an end in itself, while Jews would experience and live *Halahah* as a means, a way to make actual God's Covenant and command.

Maritain turns his attention to Paul's concept of justification:

And now all the moral precepts of the Law, far from being destroyed, are confirmed, because Faith makes it possible to fulfill them in a lasting and complete fashion, and because from thenceforth they represent only that behavior which is fitting to a being already made just and free of sin in his root powers, to the extent that he clings to Christ and receives his life from Him. The meaning of those precepts has thus been transfigured: They no longer command bad men to be good and to grow into something which they are not; rather do they command good men not to be bad, and not to fail in that which they already are, not to fall back into the state of slavery from whence they have been freed. Justification is received through faith, quite apart from works. But once justified, man is more than ever held to good works (be it only, as it was in the case of the good thief, as far as the disposition of the soul is concerned). And this is not because the works of man would have power to save man by themselves, but because good works proceed from the charity which has been

---

[19] Jacques Maritain, *The Living Thought of Saint Paul* (New York: Longmans, Green and Co., 1941), p. 70.

[20] Jean Calvin, *Institutes of the Christian Religion*, trans. Ford Battles, ed. John McNeill (Philadelphia: The Westminster Press, 1960), vol. 1, p. 751.

given to man and which is his life—his new and eternal life—and which is joined to faith when faith is living: "faith working through charity" (Galatians 6). And also because the works of charity, which is a fruitful and effective life, themselves are deserving of life, to the extent that man, acting freely under the inflowing of grace, receives from God's mercy the dignity of being a cause—secondary and instrumental—in the matter of his salvation. "God is not unjust so as to forget your works. . . ." (Hebrews 6:10). "The crown of righteousness which the Lord, the just judge, shall award to me on that day" (2 Timothy 4:8).[21]

Grace and faith are not foreign to Jewish spirituality as Maritain seems to imply. Both concepts are present in the core of the biblical account and guide Jewish life. Grace is loving kindness (Psalms 89:3), and according to rabbinic theology one of the three elements by which the world is sustained (*Mishnah Avot* 1:2). Grace and faith (*emunah* in Hebrew, an amen to God's Call) are part of the *imitatio dei* exercised by the *halahic* discipline.

A FINAL REFLECTION

I have dealt in my presentation with two aspects. One is what culture means in our Jewish involvement, with culture as part of the Jewish integration into Western society. The other aspect is Maritain's view of culture and religion, and his understanding of Judaism, or in his words, "the mystery of Israel."

Culture was our goal in the nineteenth century when the social changes in Europe opened partially their doors for Jews to enter a society that essentially disliked them. Culture was our way to return to social normalcy. Our acceptance of culture brought about in general an abandonment of religious tradition and God's Covenant. Culture became our obsession up to our own days when we reflect on a past full of illusions. Auschwitz shattered that hope and obligated us to return to a more realistic view of tradition and general culture. We do not deny the importance of culture where we play a special role as consumers and producers—to a certain degree. *Torah Umadda* is our goal, God's Covenant and culture as enriching the religious life. This is still a challenge and especially after the Holocaust.

Jacques Maritain is still my teacher despite his ambiguities vis-à-vis Judaism and the witnessing of Israel. His ambiguities remind us of the ambiguities of culture, specifically, Western culture, vis-à-vis Judaism. This culture allowed us to enter its realm as semi-equal citizens. It did not accept us as persons of God. Maritain reflected this attitude in his thoughts on Judaism.

As a Catholic thinker, Maritain was sincerely concerned about the human

---

[21] Ibid., p. 62.

situation of the Jewish people in the days of Nazi and Communist totalitarianism. He denounced and condemned anti-Semitism at times of ecclesiastical silence or indifference to the Jewish situation. Yet ironically his understanding of Judaism and the God-Israel covenant was negative and he did not recognize the ongoing meaning and validity of the Jewish religious commitment. He accepted the Jewish citizens and their social rights. Yet, he denied the Jewish person the privilege of continued covenantal partnership with God. This duality requires all who are members of the contemporary joint Christian-Jewish reflection to make efforts to fathom the full meaning of God's Calls to all of us.

The matter of our presentation, "Culture: Blessing or Misfortune," is still a question for us. The response depends on how we exercise our religious commitment. I am inclined to accept culture—philosophy, science or art—in the measure that it strengthens my faith commitment, the faith commitment to Israel, and advances the understanding of God's Word and world. That was done by Philo, Maimonides or Soloveitchik in our days. It can be done again and very especially in the pluralistic reality of American democracy, but we should be aware of the constant danger of making the cultural exercise an end in itself. Our basic concern is God and the ongoing relationship with God: our religious duty.

Religious Belief, Political Culture, and Community

William Sweet

There is a widely-shared view in many Western countries that religious faith should have no place in debates on matters of public policy. And it is a view often defended by philosophical liberals who—whether libertarian or quasi-social democratic—hold that appeals to principles based explicitly on religious faith, ideology, or some other kind of fundamental commitment, are inconsistent with fruitful discussions in a culturally pluralistic environment. And religion, more than ideologies or other commitments, is often singled out.

Such a view, however, is not universal. We find thinkers, such as Jacques Maritain, who hold that religion has an important role in building a democratic and liberal state. On this account, Christianly-inspired religious principles are necessary for a political society that is personalist, pluralist, and just. (Maritain outlines this view in such works as *Integral Humanism*, *Principles of a Political Humanism*, and *Man and the State*, although he does not discuss in any detail how his model "Christian" polity might be realized.)

In this paper I want to argue that at a time in which society is marked by not only diversity, but increasing divisiveness and antagonism, religious belief—particularly Christian religious belief—and religious believers have an important role in the building of community. Believers note that they are called by their faith to act to build community—"the kingdom of God"—which is not just a community of believers, but one which is both open to, *and proposed to*, others. To show how religious belief has such a role, I want to touch on some of the values and principles that underlie the idea of community, and note that, while they are recognized and supported by Christianity, they should not be considered as simply *private* religious values. Indeed, it is because of this that a number of Christians, such as Maritain, hold that such principles and values can serve as a basis for a broad national, or even international, community. Religious belief, therefore, has a role in building community and in contributing to political culture, even in a pluralistic world.

I

A canon of Enlightenment and post-enlightenment thought—and one that comes to us almost intact today—is that religion must not go beyond the private sphere. More specifically, liberals such as John Rawls[1] and Richard Rorty insist that in a world that is increasingly culturally diverse a viable political culture and the building of community require the "privatization" of religious faith. As Rorty puts it in his 1994 paper, "Religion as Conversation-Stopper,"[2] we cannot "keep a democratic political community going unless religious believers remain willing to trade privatization for a guarantee of religious liberty."[3] He concludes that "dropping reference to the source of the premises of . . . arguments"—i.e., that they are one's *religious* convictions— "seems a reasonable price to pay for religious liberty."[4]

What are the arguments here? There seem to be two kinds. First, many contemporary liberals hold that arguments concerning matters of public policy that employ principles or premises derived from religious faith work from assumptions that are not shared by all, and that any such "foundationalist" view in a pluralist world is doomed to failure. Thus, religion and religious faith are "non-starters." But there is a second, more critical, point made. Many liberals argue that reference to religious faith or religious belief, in the public forum, is divisive—that religions are intolerant of difference, demand a unity or similarity in belief that shows little respect for the equally legitimate basic commitments of others—or are, at the very least "conversation stoppers"; they bring discussion and the possibility of dialogue and cooperation to a halt.

I should add that some religious believers are sympathetic to the separation of religion and politics, though for different reasons. For some, religious faith should not be brought to bear on public policy because public policy deals with the corrupt "City of Man" which is entirely separate from the

[1] See John Rawls, *Political Liberalism* (New York: Columbia University Press, 1993).

[2] Richard Rorty, "Religion as a Conversation-Stopper," *Common Knowledge* 3, no. 1 (Spring 1994), pp. 1–6.

[3] Ibid., p. 3.

[4] Ibid., p. 5.

"City of God." Others argue that drawing on faith in discussing public policy can only endanger or bring disrepute to faith, in the same way in which attempts to defend certain religious beliefs by appeal to scientific "evidence" has enabled some to challenge these beliefs, because of what this move presupposes concerning the epistemic character of religious belief.

But if we say that religious belief and religious believers as such have no place in the public sphere, then what would Rawls, Rorty, and others have believers do? Presumably the answer here is that they should focus on being good citizens, engage in dialogue, seek consensus and social well-being and harmony, and promote a community based on these principles and particularly the principle of toleration. So, even though there can be no appeal to a common good (transcendent or otherwise), or to a universal standard of truth and falsity, and no way of *demonstrating* that one view or commitment is better than any other, many of those who are influential in contemporary liberal political culture hold that we can build community—a community that is both tolerant and consistent with the demands of many people's faith or ideological or religious commitments.

It is difficult to see how this option would appeal to many religious believers, and particularly to Christians, however. To begin with, it proposes a view of social life and of moral action that has met with a good deal of criticism: one where the private is to be separated from the public. As some have argued, our beliefs and actions are not easily compartmentalized into "public" and "private"—nor should they be. Moreover, for the believer to try to "compartmentalize" her or his beliefs in such a way, would do violence to the content of those beliefs themselves. Again, some would note that believers have an obligation to promote the kingdom of God, and that this cannot be accomplished except by entering into the public sphere. But there are other reasons to reject the "liberal" approach as well. Some would argue that this post-Enlightenment liberal ideal has excluded some of the potential that might be used to address the conflicts in modern society. In insisting that religion and other deep commitments are just part of the "private sphere" so that individuals are reluctant to (or simply cannot) draw on their personal "commitments" in engaging in action in the public sphere, resources for building community are left unused. And, finally, one might object that we have the example of thinkers like Maritain, who hold that Christian religious principles are in fact necessary if we are to defend human freedom and democracy. On this view, the result of introducing religion into conversation need not be one of stopping conversation, or of insulting individuals or groups who do not share it, but offering options and alternatives that discussion might otherwise overlook.

So what, then, *could* the role of religious belief be in contemporary political culture? What I want to do now is to sketch out a response to the concerns of those, like Rorty and Rawls, about the place of religious belief—and of religious believers—in maintaining or building community. To do so I will draw on some features of Maritain's "traditional" view—an account of human nature, of human ends, and the identification of a common good—but approach the issue in a way very different from that of Maritain.

II

First, what do I mean by "community" when I refer to maintaining or building community? A community is (in a broad sense) a group of individuals whose members show certain affinities with one another, who may share history, language, and culture (and perhaps religious faith) and, hence, who have common interests and a common good. These individuals are, then, socially interdependent, "share certain practices . . . that both define the community and are nurtured by it,"[5] and are, as a group "capable of establishing and legitimizing institutions."[6] These institutions are sets of human practices (e.g., they may be legal, religious, political, and/or economic institutions), and it is through them that the members of that group express themselves, both as individuals and as a collectivity.[7] But there is at least one other feature that should be added; community importantly involves loyalty—which suggests an allegiance of its members to these institutions that goes *beyond* casual choice.[8]

Now, how might Christian religious believers participate in the building and development of a political community? A detailed answer to this latter question is not possible here because a precise response would depend on a number of *empirical* issues, particular to the situation believers might find themselves in. Nevertheless, it is possible to sketch out a proposal that is consistent with a pluralistic account of community, and which is compatible with Christian belief. It is, I would argue, a model in keeping with the way in which many Christians see their religious commitment.

First, let me say something about religious belief or faith. I would claim that although faith or religious belief involves assent to a series of beliefs,

[5] See Robert N. Bellah et al., *Habits of the Heart: Individualism and Commitment in American Life*, (Berkeley, California: University of California Press, 1985), p. 333.

[6] See Leslie Armour, *The Idea of Canada and the Crisis of Community* (Ottawa: Steel Rail, 1981), p. 150.

[7] Ibid., p. 156.

[8] Thus, I would distinguish "communities" from "associations."

these beliefs are both descriptive (i.e., have a relation to *this* world and not just to a reality which is beyond the empirical, observable, and material), *and* have an expressive role or function in a person's life. Specifically, they indicate one's disposition (or intention) to act in a way that is consistent with, or is a part of, a certain set of social practices. Moreover, religious belief itself is a practice (or set of practices) through which one makes sense of, or understands, and acts *in the world*. And so the "dominant ideas" and beliefs that are part of religious belief involve not only the transcendental, but the temporal commitments, needs and interests of human beings. For the Christian, these "dominant ideas" include "God," "Christ and Christ's mission," "faith," the "divine," and "spirit," but also "health," "knowledge," "love" and "justice" (which include friendship, cooperation, forgiveness, compassion, the promotion of peace), "moderation in one's life," "joy," and so on. And these dominant ideas, and the related beliefs to which the believer appeals, are reflected in institutions—both distinctive ecclesiastical institutions and various other social institutions that are part of the environment in which believers live.

The above-mentioned ideas of the Christian believer are principles fundamental to the Christian community, but many of them are also fundamental to life in *any* community. They are ideas which respond to (and reciprocally determine) human needs, reflect interests and goods that are shared with others, and include among them a conception of a certain general or common good. And, further, at least some of them are principles that are basic to the believer's noetic structure itself. A believer's religious belief is a fundamental part of his or her identity, and it is no surprise that the object of that belief (since religious beliefs are not just dispositions of "trust" but "trust-in" something or someone) inspires—but also requires—a certain loyalty. It indicates a willingness to go beyond what has been justified by demonstrative proof and argument—"through thick and thin." It has such a hold over believers that, if one gave it up, one would no longer be who he or she was. One's religious belief is not, then, just a choice, an "option," or an "attitude."

For individual believers, and for believing communities as well, belief involves *acting on* one's belief and *acting out of* that belief; this has consequences for building and extending community. If we see religious belief as a practice that involves a disposition to act, and if we recognize that the "dominant ideas," which are present in religious beliefs, involve commitment and must be instantiated in practice, religious belief clearly involves acting towards the building of a community. This is explicitly reflected in the Gospel message in Christianity, which calls on believers, individually and collectively, to "go out to all nations,"[9] to act in solidarity with others, and to work towards the realization of "the kingdom of God."[10] To *fail* to act on one's belief is at the very least inconsistent with one's belief, if not to show that one does not actually believe what one says one believes at all. The dominant ideas that are part of religious belief serve as guidelines or principles in order to make such activity possible and to ensure it lasts. Thus, religious belief epistemically "underpins" believers and the believing community, but it also indicates where an individual or the community is (or should be) going, and what is necessary to sustain it. (In fact, some, such as Robert Bellah, have argued that religion—both in the institutional sense and in the sense of providing a way of understanding the world and a "second language" for grounding basic commitments—is *necessary* in order to build community.[11])

Now, it is a fundamental feature of Christian religious belief that not only are believers called on to build community, but that this community is one that is both open to, and proposed to, others. It is, moreover, a community that is not necessarily just a community of Christians. Nor does it require that those who are to be part of it must become Christian (though, admittedly, this seems to be preferred), for believers hold that many of the values, principles, and dominant ideas that underlie this community, while recognized by Christianity, are not uniquely Christian values. These dominant ideas and principles reflect generally the needs and ends of human beings, and the values essential to leading a fully human life. It is for this reason that a number of Christians (e.g., Jacques Maritain) hold that such ideas and values could serve as a basis for a broad national, or even international, community.

The dominant ideas present in this Christian conception of community, then, by no means make it a *closed* system. Besides, the Christian call to building community involves a set of practices that are bound up with other (e.g., ethical and empirical) discourses and practices that themselves change or develop over time, and so the conception of community must to some ex-

---

[9] See, for example, Matthew 28:19: "Therefore go and make disciples of all nations, baptizing them in the name of the Father and of the Son and of the Holy Spirit" (*New International Version*).

[10] See Colossians 4:11: "[T]hese are the only Jews among my fellow workers for the kingdom of God, and they have proved a comfort to me." The notion of the "kingdom of God on earth" has been understood in Catholicism as the "Church of Christ." See *Dei Verbum*, no. 17; "St. Peter, Prince of the Apostles" in *The Catholic Encyclopedia*; see James V. Schall, "From Catholic 'Social Doctrine' to the 'Kingdom of God on Earth,'" *Communio* 3 (Winter, 1976), pp. 284–300; reprinted in *Readings in Moral Theology, no. 5: Official Catholic Social Teaching*, eds. Charles E. Curran and Richard A. McCormick (New York: Paulist Press, 1986), pp. 313–30.

[11] See Bellah et al., *Habits of the Heart*, e.g., pp. 247–48.

tent reflect them. (We might think here of the discourse or language of human rights that has come to be an integral part of Christian social teaching.) Moreover, the ideas and the interests found within Christian institutions are themselves not all absolute and unchanging. In fact, in living in the world and with others who do not share the same religious views, believers may find themselves being called out of their present views to reflect on (and, as appropriate, "invent" new) "structures of meaning" so that they can better take account of, and more fully grasp, both the changing environment in which they live and the infinite reality that is God. Finally, given the "infinity" that is part of the Christian conception of the divine, and given the physical, environmental, and social diversity in the world, it is clear that no finite community can instantiate all possible legitimate social and cultural practices. Thus, there is no problem in imagining a Christian model of community that can be open to diversity. And this openness is consistent with the recognition that community and solidarity do not just follow from belief; they must be built in cooperation with others.

The view of life and of the community that a Christian believer might propose does not, then, entail uniformity; it not only allows but expects diversity.[12] Indeed, this model of community, more than many non-religious models of common life, is broad. It allows for dominant ideas and a conception of the good that include *spiritual* values. Still, the openness that is characteristic of this community does not entail that, to build it, one must "give up" or move away from one's faith. Building community, like believing itself, is not done in a vacuum. The religious believer engages in the building of community "out" of his or her dominant ideas or, broadly speaking, out of the system that constitutes his or her belief. At the same time, this community is not a mere extrapolation from one's beliefs. Like all practices, building community and promoting solidarity take place in a world that is *external* to one's own beliefs and practices.

Of course, as noted above, for the Christian there are certain dominant ideas and fundamental principles, which recognize human character and human needs and wants, that allow for and give rise to a *unified* community. But this need not lead to conflict with non-Christians. It is attaining such an equilibrium of unity and diversity that, no doubt, Jacques Maritain had in mind in describing his vision of a pluralistic yet Christian political community (see his *Man and the State* (1951) and *Integral Humanism* (1936))—a community where a leadership role would be played by a multiplicity of "civic fraternities," founded on freedom and inspired by the virtues of Christianity, but

---

[12] See Armour, *The Idea of Canada*, pp. 141–42.

where such groups would not necessarily exercise political power and where there would be a recognition of, for example, cultural diversity and difference of religious conscience. Thus, although pluralistic, this account of the place of Christian religious belief in building community remains compatible with Christian orthodoxy. And one model of how those having a religious commitment can cooperate and build community with others who do not share the same "final vocabulary" is, I would suggest, reflected in the dialogue that has taken place, particularly in the latter part of the twentieth century, under the name of "ecumenism," and in the reflection on religious truth that has taken place in the process called "inculturation."

The ecumenical movement—and those who more generally promote inter-Christian, inter-religious (e.g., Christian-Buddhist, Hindu-Christian, and, to a lesser degree, Muslim-Christian, and religious-atheist, e.g., Christian-Marxist) dialogue—aims at "promoting cooperation and better understanding among different religious denominations." But the aim is not (as some instances of ecumenism may seem to propose) *simply* to understand one another or even just to find a way for individuals to come to a consensus about what is important and what is not. It is to promote cooperation—and for this to be effective, individuals must, at least in principle, be able to come to recognize, despite the diversity of expressions and elaboration of belief in different cultures and communities, that their respective elaboration of belief reflect shared insights and concerns about what is fundamental to the human condition. This is particularly evident in the process of "inculturation" in which those outside of a tradition or set of practices recognize its positive values—those that enrich human life and culture—as objective values which are open to further articulation, which "lay bare the seeds of the Word,"[13] but which also provide an occasion for one to rethink and to come to better understand one's own faith and values. It is in becoming aware of what they share and in cooperating, ecumenism holds, that they will be able to live more fully.[14] The aim of ecumenism, then, is ultimately unity, though a unity that is consistent with diversity and difference. And, to date, people of sometimes quite diverse backgrounds and traditions have met and have, in varying degrees, found common ground on which they have been able to build. Still, it is important to note, this does not imply or entail relativism or subjectivism, or taking one's

[13] *Decree on the Mission Activity of the Church (Ad Gentes)*, (promulgated by Pope Paul VI on December 7, 1965), no. 11; see also *Redemptoris Missio*, John Paul II, December 7, 1990, nos. 28, 56.

[14] I develop these ideas in more detail in my *Philosophy, Community, and the Model of Ecumenism* (forthcoming).

religious (or non-religious) commitments any less seriously. Thus, the way in which many Christians see their faith and what is expected of them is quite compatible with the existence of, and with an obligation to build, a pluralist community.

Therefore, on this "ecumenical" model of discourse, the Christian believer can envisage—and can have an obligation to participate in the building of—a community that is both pluralistic and reflects Christian values. What precise form such a community would take depends largely on the concrete circumstances in which individuals find themselves and from which they would begin. Nevertheless, it is important to recognize that the obligation to build a pluralist community is not only a feature of post-Enlightenment liberalism, but also a consequence of Christian religious belief.

III

What beliefs and ideas can or could Christian believers appeal to in order to build community with other believers and with non-believers?

It has been claimed above that, when religious believers are called on to build community—to help in the construction of "the kingdom of God on earth"—they draw on the dominant ideas and notion of a common good that are part of their faith. And these are, as noted earlier, such principles as love, compassion, justice, and peace, but also ideals of "a truly human life," "flourishing," "fairness," "justice," "cooperation," and so on. Moreover, to build community, the believer is called on, where necessary, to find or to construct a discourse through which people can communicate with one another. This too entails finding the principles or dominant ideas shared by the interlocutors.

What might this discourse and these principles be? At the most elementary level, certain objective and material conditions must be assured, e.g., the presence of resources for subsistence, shelter and security, as well as the possibility of satisfying not only other physical, but certain intellectual, moral and spiritual, needs. At an equally elementary level, the people present have to share or be capable of sharing a discourse and sets of practices, and they must recognize that they have at least some interests, needs and goals in common with, and that require or involve the participation of, others. They must also recognize individually the superiority of some values to others, though they can (at least, to begin with) disagree with other persons about which things are needs, about the importance of certain interests and goals, and about *which* values are superior to others.

But there are other material or quasi-material sets of conditions that must exist, and that are necessary for many of these elementary conditions to exist.

First, the individuals concerned must "recognize" one another as beings with whom they can live and act and, second (though this is not actually independent of the first), they must—or must be able to—share a number of beliefs, attitudes, and opinions about the character of physical reality (nature), what constitutes a basic human need, how one might or must satisfy these needs, and so on. This is what I have meant when I have referred to "dominant ideas."[15]

It is important to note that the "dominant ideas" and the kinds of beliefs that are necessary for the existence of a community are not *casual* beliefs. These ideas are about the world (e.g., how it operates, its regularities and irregularities) and about what human persons require as persons (e.g., how to live in the world, how to acquire certain material and non-material goods, and so on). Though conditioned by context and history, they are not purely contingent or arbitrary, and they are not the kinds of things that people can lightly, or perhaps even explicitly, choose to adopt, or not adopt, or abandon. They are the kinds of ideas which not only allow conscious and purposeful action, but which also constitute part of one's sense of identity and which, if we gave them up, we would (as one might in conversation say) no longer be who we were before. These ideas also include, then, ideas of value, of right and wrong, of how one can expect reality to function, and so on, and their dominance is shown in how one (regularly) responds in new situations.

As I have suggested above, these "dominant ideas" make community possible, i.e., they provide a set of background ideas or context through which collective action and a life in common can occur; they also provide, as it were, guidelines or principles in order for action to be possible and persist. Indeed, it is also only through sharing (at least some of) them, that there can be conversation or discussion among individuals. Unless there were some such ideas, unless there is the recognition of others as other persons, and unless one knows or has assurance that these ideas are shared, community cannot exist. Still, it is obvious that all the ideas that are dominant in a culture are not given *ab initio*, and at no time is the set of dominant ideas exhaustive. Certain ideas come to be dominant over time—think of the "ideas" of human rights and human dignity which, even if not always respected, are characteristic of most

---

[15] For a more complete discussion of the "psychological" character of this view, see Bernard Bosanquet, *The Philosophical Theory of the State* (1923), eds. Gerald F. Gaus and William Sweet (South Bend, Indiana: St. Augustine's Press, 2000), pp. xxvii, 164, 166–67, 249ff, 301–02 and *Bosanquet's Psychology of the Moral Self* (1897), in *The Collected Works of Bernard Bosanquet*, ed. William Sweet (Bristol, UK: Thoemmes Press, 1999), vol. 8, pp. 34–46. See also *Essays on Aspects of the Social Problem and Essays on Social Policy* in *The Collected Works of Bernard Bosanquet*, vol. 14, pp. 58–59, 121ff.

contemporary ethical and political discourse. But from the fact that certain ideas come to be dominant and recognized to be so, it does not follow that these are arbitrary, or are simply to be arrived at or settled by consensus. For some of these ideas and beliefs hinge on certain facts about reality (e.g., material conditions necessary for life and growth, the nature and value of various characteristics of the human mind, the human desire for knowledge and understanding, and more), about rationality, and about the nature and value of others. In short, then, these ideas reflect "objective" (or, at least, "inter-subjective") conditions about society, political and economic reality, the level of technology, etc., and show that they are rooted in a reality that is external to one's beliefs, ideas, and practices.

Of course, given that any person's dominant ideas and beliefs are not exclusively religious, there may be other "points of access" to building community that one may share with others, e.g., moral ideas and beliefs. And the believer could look here, too, to find shared ground. Finally, since believers hold that the basis for their actions and their commitment is something right and objectively true—that they are based on certain fundamental truths and objective principles which cannot be compromised—they can assure themselves and others that the model of community that they propose is not just the product of consensus or of determining what to do in light of a Rawlsian "wide reflective equilibrium." The community is *not*, in other words, simply based on agreement or consensus, because this would leave the door open to all sorts of things—including shared vicious principles.

The preceding remarks provide an outline of how individual believers can participate in the building of community. It involves constructing opportunities or occasions for dialogue and finding (or making possible) shared ideas—but it also involves the development of a measure of humility and a willingness to learn.

More concretely, though, and as Jacques Maritain would argue, the preceding accounts of religious belief and community involve acting in solidarity, for economic justice, and for the acknowledgment and respect of basic human rights—by which I mean something like the set of rights elaborated in the United Nations Declaration of 1948, and in the subsequent covenants arising out of it.[16] Human rights at least are necessary not only for community, but also for discourse and discussion of basic values to be possible.

---

[16] Maritain's own list of rights, which antedate and are reflected in those of the UN Declaration, are to be found in *The Rights of Man and Natural Law*, trans. Doris C. Anson (New York: Charles Scribner's Sons, 1943); see chap. 4 of *Natural Law: Reflections on Theory and Practice by Jacques Maritain*, ed. William Sweet (South Bend, Indiana: St. Augustine's Press, 2000).

This view is compatible with the existence of cultural diversity, i.e., with the fact that different groups of people can have different attitudes, values, and views of the world, and that many of the attitudes and views that now exist have changed (and will continue to change) over time. It is also compatible with respect for diversity so far as it recognizes that we build community out of our dominant ideas, basic commitments, and beliefs about ourselves *and* about the world. (This is, perhaps, obvious, since we *always* act out of our beliefs, and cannot help but do so.) Furthermore, it is consistent with pluralism, since any group reflecting different cultural, ethnic, or religious traditions would be able to maintain much of this diversity within a single political community. Finally, since it is clear that no single set of ideas, beliefs, commitments, and practices can exhaust all human possibilities, and taking account of the fact that individuals do live and develop in different geographical, economic, social, and political circumstances, it would be inconceivable that there is exactly one ultimate and universal set of practices that ideally constitute community. Each person, then, must be open to the possibility—or even likelihood—that there is a, or some, "truth" in the views of those having other basic commitments. My point here is not simply that it is possible that one can see "one's" truth in "another's" view. It is, rather, that there are truths that appear in a number of discourses.

Nevertheless, while the account I propose suggests that each person must be open to this diversity and to the possibility that there is a "truth" in the views of others, this does not mean that one cannot reasonably prefer one view to another, or that there is no objective truth. Nor is being open to others simply a way of saying that what one believes is not true, or need not be taken seriously. There can be, then, certain core ideas or beliefs which are true or authoritative. For example, given the features and conditions noted above, the extent to which these material and non-material needs can be satisfied is a criterion for having a rational preference for one community over another. This is not, of course, to say that one may be able to "prove" the preferability of one kind of community over others, starting with an abstract set of first principles, as implied by a classical foundationalism, but one could plausibly do so in a way, where the standard for rational belief is that which would suffice in a courtroom, following the principles of the common law. Claims to the superiority of some beliefs over others need not appeal to a "neutral" ground of justification, but they do suppose that there are some fundamental principles or common ground which individuals from diverse backgrounds share which can justify such claims.

Again, this account could appropriately be said to be an "objectivist" (i.e., non-subjectivist) view, as it provides, in general outline, features necessary to life in society that are not determined merely by the will of the subject. To begin with, it starts from what would seem to be scarcely disputable claims about the world, supposing that communities are composed of human persons, and that communities must respond to certain objective features about persons, such as their material needs (e.g., for food and shelter), emotional needs (e.g., for friendship and other kinds of affection) and intellectual and spiritual needs, and their desires for personal growth and self-development. Moreover, it also claims that such things as environment, the kind of political association and the kind of economic and technological development that exist, influence how one understands oneself and others, and that lead to and color the kind of community one can build. (The level of technology in a society, for example, can influence basic attitudes and beliefs and, in turn, the extent to which one can be "in community" with even those with whom one is not in daily contact.) And even though the recognition of others as members, or potential members, of a community is something that, again, takes place over time, this account suggests that this is not an arbitrary or random activity (even if it is something that is not explicit and of which we may not be fully conscious). And, finally, it is important to note that the dominant ideas and beliefs from which individuals start are not just an individual's or a group of individuals' ideas or beliefs, but a community's beliefs, and that our communities of origin provide the epistemological and moral environment in which our basic beliefs and our dominant ideas exist. One can say, then, that in some measure, this account of the conditions for community reflects a theory of "human nature," i.e., it recognizes that there are others "like us," who have the needs and desires that we have, and who have the capacity for flourishing and developing as we do, and with whom we can be called into action. And so the traditional view of the basis of solidarity and of building community may in some measure be sustainable. Thus, individuals can be "called out" of themselves by their own tradition to construct a more comprehensive community, and can come to have a commitment or loyalty to that.

There is, no doubt, more to community, and to what must exist for a believer to respond to a call to build community, than is covered in the preceding remarks. Still, I would claim that the above account is at least largely descriptive *and* that it has, for those with certain basic commitments and trusts, a normative force. The believer, then, is called to build a community that would be an "open society," built around certain principles and values based on what it is to be human and on the character of the world in which we live. It is a community that is related to not just narrowly sectarian, but also to general religious, ethical, and empirical concerns. And even though the preceding comments do not require believers to support a particular kind of political structure, these principles and values would suggest that the community to be built be a democratic one that recognizes human rights and human dignity.

IV

I have argued in this paper that it is possible (and, arguably, obligatory) for the Christian religious believer to work towards the realization of a moderately pluralistic community together with other believers and with non-believers. In saying this, I take issue with those believers who hold that their faith requires them to stay "above" matters of public policy, and I also disagree with those who claim that religion should have no place in the public sphere because it is divisive or a "conversation stopper."

One's basic commitments, beliefs, and dominant ideas cannot be separated from praxis—for the believer, faith cannot be separated from works. Moreover, the "dominant ideas" and the common good which generally (and, in the case of Christianity, typically) constitute part of religious belief and to which the religious believer must respond are, in large part, features that involve an openness to others and to diversity within the political community. A model of this way of building community is ecumenism. Here, one can see how individuals and groups of people might come to work with others in a way that recognizes the values in other perspectives and is open to change, but is not arbitrary, and is also consistent with Christian religious belief.

Those who favor a political society that is respectful of human dignity and open to the moral, social, intellectual, and spiritual life of individuals—that is, a society that is just, pluralistic, and democratic, without being subjectivistic—have no good reason to object, then, to the presence of religious faith in debates concerning public policy. One need not resort to the claim of liberals like Rawls and Rorty who insist that religion and religious belief be excluded from discussion of matters of public interest.

Obviously, building community is not an easy task, and it is all the more difficult in a world where the beliefs concerning principles and values, and even concerning empirical matters, are frequently considered to be simply matters of interpretation. And strategies concerning the ways in which one might go about building community may legitimately vary. Sometimes "sentimental education," sometimes appeals to self-interest or consistency, and sometimes argument may be fruitful. Yet, despite the "divided state of humanity, the alienation across ideological abysses, and the bitterness between moral or political camps,"[17] there need be no cause for despair. For believers

---

[17] See Hendrik Hart and Kai Nielsen, *Search for Community in a Withering Tradition*, (Lanham, Maryland: University Press of America, 1990), p. xi.

and non-believers alike do or can share ideas, commitments, and beliefs that will serve to bridge these divisions. And to deny religious faith a place in building such a bridge, is to exclude a force that can make a truly human community a possibility.

The Philosophy
and Politics of Freedom:
Classical Solutions to Modern Problems

Jeanne M. Heffernan

The concept of freedom or liberty has had a central place in the American republic since its inception, as our great founding documents attest. The creedal section of the *Declaration* counts liberty as an unalienable right, divine in origin, whose protection is the very object of government. And, as the *Declaration* has been called the animating soul of the *Constitution*, we are not surprised to find the concept of liberty permeating this document too, from the preamble to the Bill of Rights. It is at the heart of our fundamental law. Yet, while freedom is the core principle of the American republic—championed by left and right alike—it is also the most contested concept in our public life. In classrooms and courtrooms, Americans debate such foundational matters as the nature of freedom and the purpose of politics, and the power to define these concepts in public law is perhaps the most coveted of spoils in the culture war.

DEMOCRACY'S DISCONTENT

As Michael Sandel observes in *Democracy's Discontent*, freedom does not have and has never had a univocal meaning for Americans. Indeed, rival political theories that have competed for primacy as America's public philosophy have invested the concept with vastly different meanings and have in consequence envisioned the role of government in the lives of its citizens in vastly different terms. Sandel notes that procedural liberalism is *the* dominant political theory of our day. Yet, while it enjoys the status of America's public philosophy, and has for the past century, its adequacy is doubtful. Our democracy, according to Sandel, is in a "winter of discontent," not likely to

312

be turned "glorious summer"[1] by the sun of liberalism, for it cannot remedy the ills that afflict us; specifically, liberalism cannot on its own terms repair the loss of our self-government or the erosion of our communities.[2] Why not? In Sandel's reckoning, liberalism's deficiency stems from the fact that it has an impoverished anthropology and political vision. One best perceives the character of American liberalism and its deficiency, according to Sandel, in contrast to its main rival throughout our history: civic republicanism.

To envision this rival tradition requires of us, who have been schooled in the terms of liberalism, some imagination, for at the center of the conceptual scheme of civic republicanism lies the community of citizens, not the isolated rights-bearing individual. Civic republicans speak in terms of membership in a political community with its corresponding roles, identities, and obligations. In Sandel's words, the individual in civic republicanism is an "encumbered self,"[3] rooted in a web of connections many of which it did not choose.

Freedom and politics follow from this primary anthropology. The tradition of civic republicanism considers freedom as essentially connected to the capacity for self-government and economic self-sufficiency, and it views the cultivation of the virtues necessary for such rule as one of the principal ends of government. Thus politics, whatever else it includes, entails positive action on the part of the state to foster certain ways of life and discourage others.

By contrast, civic republicanism's challenger and successor, procedural liberalism, weakened, if not severed, both of these connections. In Sandel's estimation, this change reflects a fundamentally different anthropology. Liberalism works with a "voluntarist"[4] conception of the self, the self as an individual agent independent of and prior to his ends. It places primacy upon the individual as a bearer of rights and seeks to protect these rights against the encroachments of other individuals or of the state. Freedom is no longer conceived in terms of self-government and economic self-sufficiency, but rather more broadly as the ability to select one's life goals using the means of one's choosing so long as those means are not deemed harmful to another.[5] Relat-

---

[1] William Shakespeare, *Richard III*, ed. David Bevington (New York: Bantam, 1988), p. 5.

[2] Michael J. Sandel, *Democracy's Discontent: America in Search of a Public Philosophy* (Cambridge, Massachusetts: Belknap Press, 1996), p. 3.

[3] In contrast to the "unencumbered self" embraced by liberalism; see Sandel, *Democracy's Discontent*, pp. 119, 322.

[4] Ibid., p. 92.

[5] American liberalism effectively adopted J. S. Mill's harm principle: "[T]he sole end for which mankind is warranted, individually or collectively, in interfering with the liberty of action of any of their number, is self-protection. That the only purpose for which power can be rightfully exercised over any member of a civilized community, against his will, is to prevent harm to others. His own good, either physical or moral, is not a sufficient warrant"(*On Liberty and Other Essays*, ed. John Gray [Oxford: Oxford University Press, 1991], p. 14).

edly, government in the procedural liberal scheme adopts a stance of neutrality with respect to the life plans of its citizens and largely forsakes its educative, character-building function, in favor of a regulatory one. Reminiscent of Aristotle's description of a mere alliance versus a true polis found in the *Politics*, a liberal state concerns itself with curbing injustice between its citizens, not with habituating them in virtue. Appealing to John Rawls's work, Sandel summarizes the point this way: "The liberal state . . . does not discriminate; none of its policies or laws may presuppose that any person or way of life is intrinsically more virtuous than any other. It respects persons as persons, and secures their equal right to live the lives they choose."[6]

In Sandel's catalogue of the most salient conflicts that have shaped the republic, the disparate character of these theories is strikingly apparent. In the weightiest matters of political economy and social policy, procedural liberalism and civic republicanism have diverged, each relying upon an opposing view of man and the state.

In the first half of the nineteenth century, American statesmen were preoccupied with the economic design of the new republic. In short, they wrestled with the question of whether to remain largely agrarian with small, contained industry or to follow the path of our rapidly industrializing cousins across the pond. Civic republican and liberal alternatives claimed center stage. For the civic republicans, what was at stake was much more than a narrow economic issue. The choice of economic design was laden with political and social consequences. Why did the civic republicans burden this decision with such gravity? Because they perceived that the manner of economic production shapes character and that the character of a people affects its vision of freedom and politics.

Thomas Jefferson, perhaps the most eloquent exponent among the civic republicans, vigorously opposed large-scale manufactures as breeding grounds of vice. As Sandel explains, wage laborers were not free men in Jefferson's eyes; their economic dependence rendered them servile and the drudgery of their work rendered them susceptible to all manner of vices. The owning class itself would be consumed with avarice, softened by luxury and would encourage a petty acquisitiveness among the citizenry. All of which would corrode the institutions of self-government upon which liberty depended. Hence Jefferson's plea for the state to discourage domestic manufactures and promote instead agrarianism and skilled craftsmanship as modes of production conducive to independence of mind, thrift, industry, and the pride of ownership—traits of democratic citizens.

[6] Sandel, *Democracy's Discontent*, p, 13.

In contrast to this vision of political economy, the liberal account, so ably defended by Alexander Hamilton, held that the development of large-scale domestic manufactures should proceed apace. The government should aid its development and allow the natural dynamism of industrial capitalism to unfold. It is not for the government to determine which modes of production are worthier than others. Rather, what is paramount is prosperity and fairness.[7] Liberalism won. Hence the now familiar path of industrialization, wage labor, and the corporate economy—ultimately with protections in place for the worker as contract maker and for the consumer as buyer, but with remarkably little attention to the political and civic effects of the economic process.

While the conflict between civic republicanism and liberalism in the economic arena reveals a striking shift in public philosophies, nowhere is the change more remarkable than in the area of social policy, especially in the jurisprudence of privacy. According to Sandel, one finds in the Supreme Court's reflections on the "right of privacy" a marriage of liberalism's fundamental tenets: state neutrality and individual autonomy.[8] The story of privacy jurisprudence evinces a dramatic shift from an older, civic republican defense of privacy to a novel, liberal defense. Traces of the older view remain as late as 1965 with the famous contraception case, *Griswold v. CT* in which we find the Court's first explicitly constitutional recognition to the right of privacy. Yet this right is defended upon traditional grounds. The Court does not deny Connecticut's right to adopt a view of the good, or to legislate in such a way as to foster a certain conception of virtue. It does have the right to regulate the distribution of contraceptives, though it does not have the right to regulate their use. But this restriction on state power is not justified on the basis of a "right to use contraceptives"[9] but rather on the grounds that the social institution of marriage is a privileged sphere that commands a degree of privacy the Connecticut law would violate. Less than ten years later, however, the Court abandons this view and strikes down a law restricting the distribution of contraceptives to unmarried persons. *Eisenstadt v. Baird* now adopts a liberal defense of privacy and "re-describe[s] the bearers of privacy rights from persons *qua* participants in the social institution of marriage to persons *qua* individuals, independent of their roles or attachments."[10] The decision also expands the concept of liberty from the more restricted notion of freedom

---

[7] Ibid., p. 124.
[8] Ibid., p. 91.
[9] Ibid., p. 95.
[10] Ibid., p. 97.

from surveillance to the much larger notion of freedom to engage in certain activities without government restrictions. "The Court," Sandel writes, "protected privacy . . . not for the social practices it promotes but for the individual choice it secures."[11]

The most controversial application of the right of privacy occurred one year later in the famous 1973 case of *Roe v. Wade*. Here we see the triumph of the procedural liberal view of individual autonomy and the neutral state. In its decision, the Court affirms the right of privacy to mean the right to make certain sorts of choices free from interference by the state (or husbands or parents). And it uses the language of autonomy to describe the privacy interest at stake. Privacy rights do not depend upon the virtue of the practice engaged in, but rather on the principle that the individual exercises free choice in intimate matters.[12]

In these contests between these rival political philosophies, procedural liberalism won. Its view of liberty and the proper role of government increasingly defines the nature of the American political process. Nowhere is this more evident, according to Sandel, than in contemporary jurisprudence in the areas of family, church-state, and privacy law. For Sandel, this turn of events marks a decline; the retreat of civic republicanism represents the loss of a rich vision of the polity that liberalism cannot supply. Indeed, as Sandel sees it, the American republic is in a crisis. As the subtitle of his book suggests, America is in need of a new public philosophy. Having exposed the weaknesses of procedural liberalism, Sandel concludes that we must refashion a public philosophy more adequate to the complex task of governing a modern polity, and he appeals to the older tradition of civic republicanism to do so.

CLASSICAL SOLUTIONS TO MODERN PROBLEMS

There is another source, as yet regrettably little known, to which Sandel might turn in this task. That is the work of Yves Simon. It holds promise, I think, for offering classical solutions to the modern problems identified by Sandel. I refer to Simon's work as classical in two senses: it not only draws upon the rich heritage of classical learning through the Aristotelian-Thomistic tradition, but it also represents a living engagement in the perennial philosophy. As such, I will argue that Simon's careful analysis of freedom, autonomy,

---

[11] Ibid., p. 97.
[12] Ibid., pp. 99–100.

and authority constitutes a vital resource for thinking about the philosophy and politics of freedom in this new century.

As noted above, Sandel spots the hegemony of liberalism in many places, but especially in contemporary jurisprudence and particularly in the area of privacy law. In this vein, I would like to address a recent Supreme Court case that evinces the strength of that liberal hegemony, that is, the hold it has on the legal imagination, as well as its intrinsic philosophical weakness.

The 1992 decision in *Planned Parenthood v. Casey* is a test case of the topic of this paper, namely, the philosophy and politics of freedom. In it, one sees the logical conclusion of the anthropology behind political liberalism both with respect to its vision of human autonomy and the proper role of political authority. By way of a brief summary, the majority decision in Casey, supported by five of the justices, sustained the fundamental right of abortion, first elaborated in *Roe v. Wade*, as a matter of substantive due process. Accordingly, the Court struck down several provisions of a Pennsylvania law that placed certain constraints, such as spousal notification, on the abortion process. What is striking in this case is not simply the fact that the justices admit the fallibility of *Roe*, or that they offer a crudely utilitarian defense of the availability of abortion, though these are striking enough. What is especially noteworthy, as various commentators have pointed out, is the Court's anthropology operative in the now famous, or infamous, "mystery passage."

At the beginning of their decision, the majority solemnly warns that "Liberty finds no refuge in a jurisprudence of doubt." To which Yves Simon would say, "Amen." Then the justices note that although the right to an abortion has been nationally protected for nearly twenty years—recall this is a 1992 decision—"that definition of liberty is still questioned." The Court dutifully supplies us one. Enter the "mystery passage." According to the justices, the Fourteenth Amendment's due process clause protects the freedom to make choices "central to personal dignity and autonomy." Indeed, the Court continues, "[a]t the heart of liberty is the right to define one's own concept of existence, of meaning, of the universe, and of the mystery of human life. Beliefs about these matters could not define the attributes of personhood were they formed under compulsion of the State."[13]

Time does not permit an extensive analysis of this puzzling passage. Suffice it to say that the passage, and the larger holding of the Court, is problematic on three counts, namely, in its conception of liberty, autonomy, and authority. It is precisely in light of these concepts that Yves Simon's work is so

---

[13] *Planned Parenthood v. Casey*, 112 S. Ct. 2791 (1992).

illuminating and provides a helpful framework for assessing the claims of the Court in this case.

First, from a Simonian perspective, the Court's view of liberty fails because it is tied to an untenable, radically subjective epistemology. For Simon, the Court has failed to grasp the essential connection between freedom and truth. Simon would affirm what the Court does not consistently affirm, namely, "Liberty finds no refuge in a jurisprudence of doubt." Instead, liberty finds a sure footing only in a jurisprudence of belief, belief in the power of the mind to perceive truth. (Incidentally, this seems to have been the assumption behind the celebrated progressive decisions of the Warren Court.) This is so because liberty is intrinsically connected to truth.

But this connection, Simon laments, was ill-perceived by liberalism, the basic philosophical foundation behind the *Casey* decision, because it adopted a faulty view of liberty as a whole. In general, according to Simon, liberalism has misunderstood freedom as indeterminate choice. Man is free because he can choose x, y, or z, irrespective of the character of the objects chosen.[14]

But, as Simon notes, "[T]he charms of indetermination are often mistaken for those of freedom."[15] Freedom conceived as indeterminate choice constitutes only a pale reflection of full freedom. It constitutes, what Maritain would call, initial freedom, that is, freedom in its primitive stage, as opposed to terminal or developed freedom.

A brief remark about Simon's anthropology is in order here. Essential to Simon's view of man is the notion that human beings have a nature and that it is in our nature to be oriented toward an end, namely, happiness. Corre-

---

[14] Yves Simon supplies a rather humorous and perhaps exaggerated example of this view drawn from the youthfully romantic travel diary of René de Chateaubriand who relates: "Many boast of loving liberty, yet almost no one has a proper understanding of it. When, in my travels among the Indian nations of Canada, I left the European settlements and found myself, for the first time, alone in the middle of a sea of forest, a strange revolution took place in my soul. In the kind of delirium which got hold of me, I was not following any track; I was going from tree to tree, to the right and to the left indifferently, and I was saying to myself: here, there are no more ways to be followed, no more cities, no more narrow homes, no more presidents, republics or kings, above all, no more laws, and no more men. Men here? Yes, a few good savages who do not bother about me anymore than I do about them; who—again like me—wander freely where thought drives them, eat when they want to, and sleep where and when they please. And to test whether I was at last reinstated in my original rights, I elicited a thousand acts of will which infuriated the tall Dutchman who served as my guide and who, in his soul, believed that I was crazy." To which Simon wryly adds, "Who would disagree with the Dutch guide?"(Yves R. Simon, *Freedom of Choice* [New York: Fordham University Press, 1992], pp. 2–3).

[15] Simon, *Freedom of Choice*, p. 121.

spondingly, our will is by nature oriented toward the good, the absolute good, and finds itself attracted to partial or limited goods insofar as they instantiate some degree of the *bonum in communi* or comprehensive good.[16] Now initial freedom includes the possibility of choosing rightly or wrongly. Herein lies its deficiency. Freedom is the power to make a choice between the means offered to our action. But there are authentic means, means that lead to our end and inauthentic means, illusory means that lead us away from our end. But, "[f]reedom to choose illusory means is itself only an illusion of freedom, for a means which does not lead to the end is not a means."[17] Here is where truth comes in. The will cannot be protected from choosing illusory means, of making wrong choices, if the intellect is clouded by error. Thus, Simon insists, "All of our real freedom is contained within the limits of our knowledge of truth."[18] The High Court notwithstanding, liberty does not flourish, but rather founders on the shoals of skepticism and subjectivism.

The second count on which the *Casey* decision fails is in its view of autonomy. Behind the Court's reaffirmation of *Roe* lies a conception of autonomy tinged with the individualism that informs the Court's understanding of liberty. The individual agent's reasoning and decision is paramount. As the justices put it: "The destiny of the woman must be shaped to a large extent on her own conception of her spiritual imperatives and her place in society."[19] Yves Simon also places a primacy on autonomy, but he defines it in a very different way. Autonomy, for Simon, is not the state of initial freedom, as the Court supposes it to be. It is not the ability to choose x, y, or z in conformity with what we subjectively prefer. Rather, it is the state of fullest freedom whereby the moral law has been interiorized and definitively guides our decision-making. Simon regards such autonomy as "a vocation and a conquest."[20] It is what our nature calls us to, but its achievement is arduous. In this condition, one that we only fitfully and gradually approach, our intellect makes sound judgments as to what is to be done, and our will virtuously adheres to those judgments. The spontaneous inclinations of the agent coincide with the demands of the moral law. Far from eliminating freedom of choice, as some might suspect, this adherence of the mind and will to the good in the state of terminal liberty, opens up the field of action, for within the limits of the good, there are many possibilities for choice. Simon appeals to St.

---

[16] Ibid., p. 23.
[17] Yves R. Simon, *Freedom and Community*, ed. Charles P. O'Donnell (New York: Fordham University Press, 2001), p. 4.
[18] Ibid., p. 4.
[19] *Planned Parenthood v. Casey.*
[20] Simon, *Freedom and Community*, p. 18.

Thomas in explaining this phenomenon. The will, according to Thomas, is not naturally determined with respect to particular goods. And this is a perfection. "The more a being is elevated in the ontological hierarchy, the more it is self-sufficient, and independent of the particular means in the achievement of its perfection."[21] Thus, for Simon, the more perfectly man conforms to his ontological status as a free, creative agent, the greater the plurality of means open to him. Enlightenment, he contends, increases our amplitude of choice. It rules out illusory means and multiplies genuine ones. Hence, the glory of the autonomous individual is precisely his ability to reflectively evaluate in freedom a whole range of means to achieve his end.

But this deliberation is not carried on in isolation. For Simon the quest for autonomy is pursued in community, and the moral law with which autonomy accords concerns not the isolated individual, but the person in community. Thus, autonomy is essentially related to the common welfare. To achieve the common welfare, Simon observes, requires authority. In a community of a certain type and size, it requires *political* authority. It is important to note that in Simon's view political authority and personal autonomy do not in principle conflict but rather complement one another.[22] Each is necessary for a healthy polis. According to Simon, the principle of authority entails that some organ of the community must choose the means to the common good when those means are plural; it must, in short, will both formally and materially, the conditions of the common welfare. The principle of autonomy or subsidiarity entails that whenever a task or decision can be satisfactorily achieved by the initiative of the individual or small social units, it should be, in order that the capacities of intellect and will in such persons or groups be developed most fully. Political authority, then, in its most basic function does not substitute for the judgment and decision of its citizens in areas within their competence.[23]

This leads us to the third count on which the *Casey* decision would fail for Simon. The decision offers an inadequate picture of the role of political authority. (Indeed, in light of its radically subjective view of freedom and knowing, the Court undermines the legitimacy of law and its own legitimacy as a definitive interpreter of law.) In stark contrast to the picture of the state

[21] Yves R. Simon, "Beyond the Crisis of Liberalism," in *Essays in Thomism*, ed. Robert Brennan (New York: Sheed and Ward, 1942), p. 412, n. 9.

[22] Yves R. Simon, *Philosophy of Democratic Government* (Notre Dame, Indiana: University of Notre Dame Press, 1993), p. 71.

[23] Yves R. Simon, *A General Theory of Authority* (Notre Dame, Indiana: University of Notre Dame Press, 1980), p. 57.

outlined in *Casey*, Simon invests the state with genuine authority to determine the conditions of the common good. Pursuant to its essential function, political authority will proscribe by law certain actions as inimical to the general welfare. A law restrictive of abortion, like the Pennsylvania law in question, arguably fits this description. But this need not, in principle, impinge upon personal autonomy; rather, assuming it is just, the law works to remove certain bad choices as possible courses of action and in so doing, in Simon's words, actually delivers human freedom from "its heaviest burden."[24] It removes illusory means to the end, thereby freeing the will from its possible irresolution and from the dangers of choosing wrongly.[25] Good law thus assists the individual and the community; it encourages the cultivation of virtue requisite to autonomy and in so doing fosters the development of a community of free men—the great desideratum of social life.

In summary, then, Simon's understanding of liberty, autonomy, and authority serves as a vital resource for assessing the deficiencies of liberalism as evidenced in contemporary jurisprudence. But the value of Simon's work is not merely critical. Indeed, it has much to contribute positively to the task to which Michael Sandel and others have urged us, the refashioning of a public philosophy to guide the American republic in this new century. A public philosophy grounded in Simon's Thomistic anthropology and political vision would reinvigorate the crowning values of the republic—life, liberty, and happiness—immortalized in Jefferson's *Declaration*. It would, I think, in the first place, protect life in its every stage; it would also safeguard liberty as the capacity to realize the good, and, finally, it would enshrine happiness as the *telos* of personal and social life and confirm its place as the polestar of democratic politics.

---

[24] Simon, *Freedom and Community*, p. 43.
[25] Ibid., p. 55.

Contributors

David Arias, Jr. is at present a graduate student at the Center for Thomistic Studies at the University of St. Thomas in Houston, Texas. He has an M.A. in Theology from Loyola Marymount University, and has recently worked as a full-time intern for *New Oxford Review*. His philosophical interests are mainly concentrated in the areas of medieval philosophy, Thomism, and philosophy of God.

Mariano Artigas is presently Professor of Philosophy of Science and Philosophy of Nature at the University of Navarra in Pamplona, Spain, where he is also Vice-Dean of the Ecclesiastical Faculty of Philosophy. He has been an Ordinary Member of the Pontifical Academy of St. Thomas (Vatican) since 1999. He holds three doctorates: one in Philosophy from the Pontifical Lateran University, another in Philosophy from the University of Barcelona, and a third in Physics from the University of Barcelona. His main publications include fourteen books and over one hundred articles. Among his most recent publications are: *The Ethical Nature of Karl Popper's Theory of Knowledge* (Peter Lang, 1999) and *The Mind of the Universe* (Templeton Foundation Press, 2000). He is presently working on a new book on Galileo, in collaboration with William Shea, a renowned authority on Galileo.

Gavin T. Colvert is Assistant Professor of Philosophy at Assumption College in Worcester, Massachusetts. Holding a Ph.D. from the University of Toronto, his research interests include: medieval philosophy, moral and political philosophy, and the philosophy of religion. Recently he has published articles on William of Ockham's theory of signification and Thomas Aquinas's ethics and moral psychology.

Frederick Erb III is Senior Lecturer in Religious Studies at Penn State University where he has taught since 1996. He is also adjunct faculty at Saint Francis University, Loretto, Pennsylvania, and at Mount Aloysius College,

322

Cresson, Pennsylvania. He holds advanced degrees in religious education and higher education from LaSalle University, Philadelphia, and Penn State, respectively; and he is a doctoral candidate in contemporary systematic theology at Fordham University, where he was a Teaching Fellow. His current research interests include the transmission of the Catholic intellectual tradition through higher education, effects of religion and culture on institutions of higher learning, and patterns of spirituality and faith development during the college years.

Heather McAdam Erb is presently Visiting Assistant Professor of Philosophy at Saint Francis University, Loretto, Pennsylvania, and has been a Senior Lecturer in Religious Studies at Penn State University since 1996. Prior to that, she taught for several years in the Department of Philosophy at Fordham University. Her doctoral dissertation in philosophy at the University of Toronto dealt with natural priority in Aquinas's metaphysics, and her current research involves the nexus between metaphysics and mysticism.

Alfred J. Freddoso is Professor of Philosophy at the University of Notre Dame. His main interests are metaphysics and ethics in the Catholic intellectual tradition, and he has published articles on and translations of the work of William of Ockham, Luis de Molina, and Francisco Suarez, along with several recent papers on faith and reason. He is currently working on a translation of St. Thomas's *Summa Theologiae*.

Marie I. George received her Ph.D. in philosophy from Laval University in 1987. Her dissertation was on the notion of *paideia* in Aristotle. She is currently an Associate Professor at St. John's University, New York. An Aristotelian-Thomist, her interests are chiefly in natural philosophy, philosophy of science, especially philosophy of biology, bioethics, and philosophy of education. She has published articles on Aquinas on reincarnation, Paley's argument from design, and the anthropic cosmological principle.

John Goyette is Associate Professor of Philosophy at Sacred Heart Major Seminary in Detroit where he has taught since 1994. He received his Ph.D. in 1998 from The Catholic University of America. He serves as the Chair of the Philosophy Department at Sacred Heart and, during his tenure at the seminary, initiated and brought about a comprehensive revision of the philosophy curriculum resulting in the establishment of a Great Books program in philosophy. He is presently co-editing a volume of essays on "St. Thomas and the Natural Law Tradition."

Jeanne M. Heffernan received her Ph.D. from the University of Notre Dame in 2000. She is currently Assistant Professor of Political Science at Pepperdine University in Malibu, California. She has published essays on the political thought of Yves R. Simon and Reinhold Niebuhr and on Maritain's aesthetics in two American Maritain Association volumes. She has also written book reviews on Thomism for *The Review of Politics*.

Leon Klenicki was the director of the Department of Interfaith Affairs of the Anti-Defamation League for twenty-eight years and also served as ADL's Co-Liaison to the Vatican. He is currently ADL's Interfaith Consultant. He has been named the first Hugo Gryn Fellow at the Centre for Jewish-Christian Relations at Cambridge University. His recent publications are: "On the Death of Jesus: Jewish and Christian Interpretations," co-edited with Eugene J. Fisher; "Matthew 23:13–33. A Commentary by Prof. Dennis McManus and Rabbi Leon Klenicki"; *The Holocaust Never to Be Forgotten: Reflections on the Holy See's Document 'We Remember,'* with commentaries by Avery Cardinal Dulles and Rabbi Leon Klenicki, and an address by Edward Idris Cardinal Cassidy.

Ralph McInerny has taught at the University of Notre Dame since 1955, where he is the Michael P. Grace Professor of Medieval Studies and Professor of Philosophy. A fellow of the Pontifical Academy of Saint Thomas Aquinas, he is a lifelong member of the American Catholic Philosophical Association, the American Philosophical Association, the Metaphysical Society of America, and the Fellowship of Catholic Scholars. He has written extensively on Thomas Aquinas, most recently the Penguin Classic, *Selected Writings of Thomas Aquinas* (1999). He gave the Gifford Lectures in Glasgow in October 1999 and February 2000, published by the University of Notre Dame Press as *Characters in Search of Their Author*.

John F. Morris is Assistant Professor of Philosophy at Rockhurst University in Kansas City, Missouri. His areas of specialization are ethics and medical ethics, with a background in medieval philosophy and St. Thomas Aquinas. His publications include: "Is Medicine Today Still An Art? Maritain and Managed Care," in *Beauty, Art, and the Polis* (CUA Press, 2000) and "The Contribution of Francisco de Vitoria to the Scholastic Understanding of the Principle of the Common Good" (*The Modern Schoolman*). He is currently editing a volume entitled: *Medicine, Healthcare, & Ethics: New Essays from the Christian Tradition*. He is a member of the Ethics and Human Values Committee at St. Joseph's Health Center in Kansas City, and a public member of the American Occupational Therapy Association's Commission on Standards and Ethics.

Warren Murray is Professor of Philosophy of Science and of Ancient Philosophy, Laval University, Quebec. He has been an invited professor in France, Argentina, and the United States. He is President of the Society for Aristotelian Studies. His research interests are in the areas of ancient Greek philosophy, Thomas Aquinas, philosophy of science, and ethics. His publications include: "The Nature and the Rights of the Foetus" (*The American Journal of Jurisprudence*), "Value Theory in the Measure of the Good" (*Philosophia Perennis*), and "Les Langages scientifiques" (*Peripatetikos*).

Peter A. Pagan-Aguiar received his Ph.D. in philosophy from Fordham University in 1998. He is Assistant Professor of Philosophy at Wheeling Jesuit University. A former IMPACT fellow of the Association of Jesuit Colleges and Universities, he is currently a member of the Fellowship of Catholic Scholars, the American Philosophical Association, and University Faculty for Life. His research interests include Thomistic studies, natural law theory, philosophical anthropology, and, more recently, the interface between science and theology. His publications include "St. Thomas Aquinas and Human Finality: Paradox or Mysterium Fidei?," *The Thomist*. He is presently working on a paper addressing contemporary debates on the nexus between modern science and natural theology.

Alice Ramos is Associate Professor of Philosophy at St. John's University in New York. She holds a Ph.D. in French literature from New York University and a second Ph.D. in Philosophy from the University of Navarra in Pamplona, Spain. She is the recipient of fellowships and grants both here and abroad. She has published a book in Spanish on contemporary semiotics and a metaphysics of the sign, and articles in areas such as Thomistic metaphysics, Kantian ethical theology, MacIntyre's ethical inquiry, and Karol Wojtyla-John Paul II's Christian anthropology. She edited the AMA 2000 volume entitled *Beauty, Art, and the Polis*, and is the newly elected President of the AMA. Her present research projects deal with the foundations of ethics and the transcendentals in Aquinas.

Teresa I. Reed received her Ph.D. from the University of Notre Dame. She is Associate Dean of the College of Arts & Sciences and Associate Professor of Philosophy at Rockhurst University in Kansas City, Missouri. She teaches phenomenology, existentialism, modern philosophy, philosophy of time, and philosophy of mathematics. Her publications and papers focus on Husserl, Marcel, and epistemology, and include "Husserl's Presuppositionless Philosophy" (*Research in Phenomenology, XX*) and a book on Husserl forthcoming from Ohio University Press. She is secretary-treasurer of the Gabriel Marcel Society.

Robert Royal is president of the Faith & Reason Institute in Washington, D.C. He writes and lectures frequently on questions of ethics, culture, religion, and politics, and has appeared on television and radio stations around the United States. His books include: *1492 And All That: Political Manipulations of History* (1992), *Reinventing the American People: Unity and Diversity Today* (1995), *The Virgin and the Dynamo: The Use and Abuse of Religion in the Environment Debate* (1999), *Dante Alighieri in the Spiritual Legacy Series* (1999), and *The Catholic Martyrs of the Twentieth Century: A Comprehensive Global History* (2000).

James V. Schall, S.J. is Professor of Government at Georgetown University. He has taught in the Gregorian University in Rome and at the University of San Francisco. He has written over sixteen books, among which are: *Another Sort of Learning*; *Reason, Revelation and the Foundations of Political Philosophy*; and *Redeeming the Time*.

William Sweet is Secretary-General of the World Union of Catholic Philosophical Societies, President of the Canadian Jacques Maritain Association, and Professor of Philosophy at St. Francis Xavier University (Nova Scotia, Canada). He is the author of *Idealism and Rights* (1997) and *Anti-foundationalism, Faith, and Community* (2001). He has edited several collections of scholarly essays, including *The Bases of Ethics* (Marquette, 2000), *Idealism, Metaphysics, and Community* (Ashgate, 2001), *and God and Argument* (Ottawa, 1999). He has co-edited *The Philosophical Theory of the State and Related Essays by Bernard Bosanquet* (with Gerald F. Gaus, St. Augustine's Press, 2001), and edited *Natural Law: Reflections on Theory and Practice by Jacques Maritain* (St. Augustine's Press, 2001). He is Editor of the journals *Maritain Studies* and *Philosophy, Culture and Traditions*.

Dallas Willard is Professor in the School of Philosophy at the University of Southern California in Los Angeles. His philosophical publications are mainly in the areas of epistemology, the philosophy of mind and of logic, and on the philosophy of Edmund Husserl, including extensive translations of Husserl's early writings from German into English. His *Logic and the Objectivity of Knowledge*, a study of Husserl's early philosophy appeared in 1984. He also lectures and publishes in religion. His books in this area include: *The Divine Conspiracy, The Spirit of the Disciplines*, and *Hearing God*.

Index

Faith,
Scholarship,
and Culture in
the 21st Century

American Maritain Association Publications
General Editor: Anthony O. Simon

Jacques Maritain: The Man and His Metaphysics
Edited by John F.X. Knasas, 1988
★ ISBN 0-268-01205-9 (out of print)

Freedom in the Modern World: Jacques Maritain, Yves R. Simon, Mortimer J. Adler
Edited by Michael D. Torre, 1989, Second Printing 1990
★ ISBN 0-268-00978-3

From Twilight to Dawn: The Cultural Vision of Jacques Maritain
Edited by Peter A. Redpath, 1990
★ ISBN 0-268-00979-1

The Future of Thomism
Edited by Deal W. Hudson and Dennis Wm. Moran, 1992
★ ISBN 0-268-00986-4

Jacques Maritain and the Jews
Edited by Robert Royal, 1994
★ ISBN 0-268-01193-1

Freedom, Virtue, and the Common Good
Edited by Curtis L. Hancock and Anthony O. Simon, 1995
★ ISBN 0-268-00991-0

Postmodernism and Christian Philosophy
Edited by Roman T. Ciapolo, 1997
◆ ISBN 0-8132-0881-5

The Common Things: Essays on Thomism and Education
Edited by Daniel McInerny, 1999
◆ ISBN 0-9669226-0-3

The Failure of Modernism: The Cartesian Legacy and Contemporary Pluralism
Edited by Brendan Sweetman, 1999
◆ ISBN 0-9669226-1-1

Beauty, Art, and the Polis
Edited by Alice Ramos, 2000
◆ ISBN 0-9669226-2-X

Reassessing the Liberal State: Reading Maritain's Man and the State
Edited by Timothy Fuller and John P. Hittinger, 2001
◆ ISBN 0-9669226-3-8

Faith, Scholarship, and Culture in the 21st Century
Edited by Alice Ramos and Marie I. George, 2002
◆ ISBN 0-9669226-5-4

★ Distributed by the University of Notre Dame Press
◆ Distributed by The Catholic University of America Press